CITY
of
GANGS

Also by Andrew Davies

The Gangs of Manchester

About the Author

Andrew Davies is a Senior Lecturer in Modern British History at the University of Liverpool. He specialises in the history of crime in modern Britain and has published and broadcast widely on gangs, crime and policing. His previous book *The Gangs of Manchester* was published in 2008.

For more information and background on this book,
visit www.glasgowgangs.com.

CITY

of

GANGS

ANDREW DAVIES

HODDER

First published in Great Britain in 2013 by Hodder & Stoughton
An Hachette UK company

First published in paperback in 2014

1

Copyright © Andrew Davies 2013

Maps © Suzanne Yee and Sandra Mather

A CIP catalogue record for this title is available from the British Library

ISBN 978 1 444 73979 4

Printed and bound by Clays Ltd, St Ives plc

Hodder & Stoughton policy is to use papers that are natural, renewable
and recyclable products and made from wood grown in sustainable forests.
The logging and manufacturing processes are expected to conform to the
environmental regulations of the country of origin.

Hodder & Stoughton Ltd
338 Euston Road
London NW1 3BH

www.hodder.co.uk

For Selina Todd

Contents

Contents

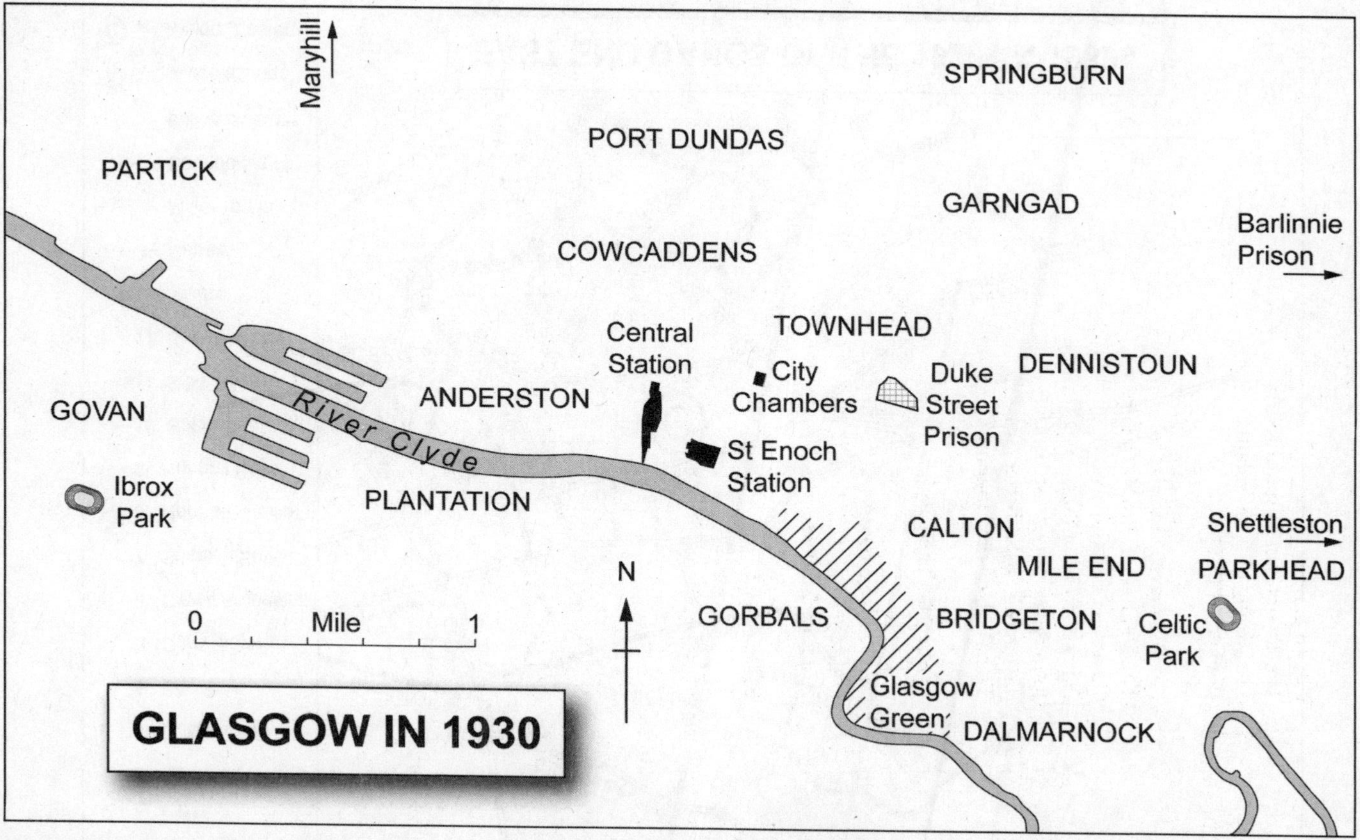

Maryhill
SPRINGBURN
PORT DUNDAS
PARTICK
GARNGAD
Barlinnie Prison
COWCADDENS
TOWNHEAD
Central Station
City Chambers
DENNISTOUN
Duke Street Prison
ANDERSTON
GOVAN
River Clyde
St Enoch Station
Ibrox Park
PLANTATION
CALTON
Shettleston
MILE END
PARKHEAD
N
0
Mile
1
GORBALS
BRIDGETON
Celtic Park
Glasgow Green
DALMARNOCK
GLASGOW IN 1930

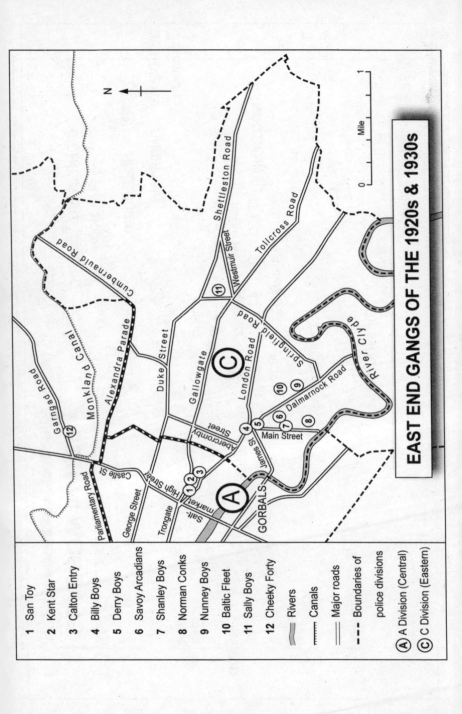

EAST END GANGS OF THE 1920s & 1930s

1 San Toy
2 Kent Star
3 Calton Entry
4 Billy Boys
5 Derry Boys
6 Savoy Arcadians
7 Shanley Boys
8 Norman Conks
9 Nunney Boys
10 Baltic Fleet
11 Sally Boys
12 Cheeky Forty

~~~ Rivers
...... Canals
=== Major roads
--- Boundaries of
      police divisions

Ⓐ A Division (Central)
Ⓒ C Division (Eastern)

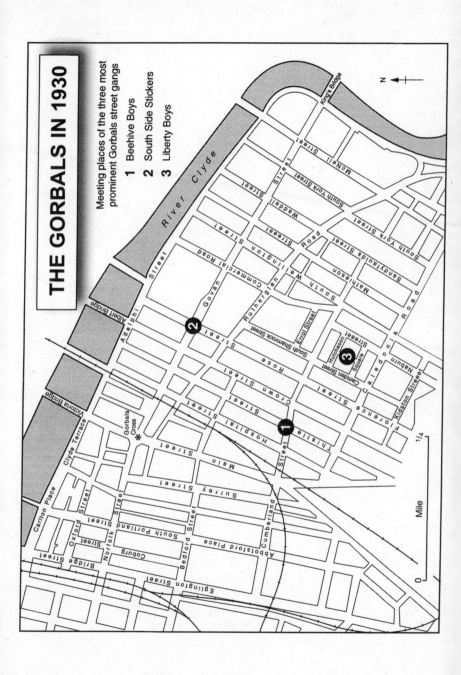

THE GORBALS IN 1930

Meeting places of the three most prominent Gorbals street gangs

1 Beehive Boys
2 South Side Stickers
3 Liberty Boys

Introduction

In the summer of 1930, Glasgow's *Evening Citizen* lamented the damage done to the city's reputation by the growing notoriety of its gangsters. Glasgow, the *Citizen* declared, was becoming known throughout the world as a 'city of gangs'. Dozens of gangs, with a combined membership – by one police estimate – of between 5,000 and 7,000, were said to exercise a reign of terror in the city's poorer districts.

While alarmist in tone, press reports on Glasgow's gang menace were not without foundation. Territorial conflicts, frequently laced with religious sectarianism, were being fought out in pitched battles on the city's main thoroughfares, in fights in cinemas and dance halls, and in highly targeted raids on the homes of the leading belligerents. Some of the larger gangs operated protection rackets in the districts to which they laid claim, leading to widespread allegations in the national as well as local press that Glasgow's gangsters had adopted 'American' crime methods.

Glasgow was not the only British city to be blighted by gangs during the early decades of the twentieth century. The 1920s witnessed a violent struggle for control of protection rackets at race meetings in south-east England. Gangs from London and Birmingham fought with razors, knives and guns in what became known as the 'Racecourse Wars', even though most of the violence took place on the streets of the capital. In August 1925, twenty men fought with razors in Shaftesbury Avenue, prompting the Conservative Home Secretary, Sir William Joynson-Hicks, to declare war on the 'race gangs' in an interview with the *Daily Express*. Nor was violence confined to London: in Sheffield, a

..nning dispute between two gangs vying for control of a ..uge open-air gambling ring on the city's outskirts was only curtailed when a police flying squad met force with force. Glasgow's gangs were not unique, but they were more numerous, more entrenched and harder to police than those found elsewhere in Britain.

Why was Glasgow different? Part of the answer lies in the density of the city's population. Glasgow was the most congested place in Britain, its homes the most overcrowded, its streets more boisterous than those of London, Birmingham, Manchester or even Liverpool. The bulk of Glasgow's population lived in four-story tenements, their grey stone blackened by decades of smoke. When young men gathered in groups on the street corners, the sheer density of population in the tenement districts meant that they did so in much greater numbers than their counterparts in England. Another factor that made Glasgow more combustible than the major English conurbations was the persistence of a virulent strain of religious sectarianism. While bigotry was by no means unique to Glasgow – Liverpool, too, saw communal skirmishes between Protestants and Catholics on key days in the festive calendar – sectarian violence was a bigger part of everyday life in Glasgow's poorer districts than elsewhere in Britain. Here, even football allegiances were laced with 'religious' antagonisms.

Glasgow acquired its unenviable and enduring reputation as the most violent place in Britain during the 1920s and 1930s as gang conflicts intensified in this age of mass, long-term unemployment. Glasgow's two staple industries, shipbuilding and heavy engineering, fell into steep decline after the First World War, never to fully recover. During the 1920s, thousands of young men were denied the opportunity to follow their fathers into the Clydeside shipyards and engineering works. After the Wall Street Crash of 1929, Glasgow's plight worsened. By 1931, a third of the city's workforce was unemployed. Along with poverty and overcrowding, unemployment was more widespread in Glasgow than in most other British cities, and it persisted further into the 1930s: while those cities closer to London bene-fited from a slow recovery spurred by the expansion of light manufacturing industries, Glasgow – 'Second City of the Empire' and shipbuilding capital of the world as recently as 1913 – stagnated. In 1936, 90,000 of the city's registered workers were unemployed compared to just 21,000 in Birmingham.

Within Glasgow, unemployment was keenly felt among working-class Protestants, who had traditionally enjoyed a near monopoly of skilled industrial occupations and the relatively high and secure wages that these offered. Catholics, too, felt a profound sense of grievance, complaining that many Protestant employers discriminated against them when hiring workers. Regardless of their religion, young men found unemployment frustrating as well as dispiriting. Unemployment benefit (dole) was enough to ward off destitution, but not enough to participate fully in the new world of leisure symbolised by the glitzy *palais de danse* that had sprung up in Glasgow, as elsewhere in Britain, fuelled by the national euphoria that greeted the end of the Great War. The construction of these palatial places of entertainment against the backdrop of dole queues and widespread poverty fuelled anger and a widespread resort to crime.

For young men from Glasgow's poorer districts, gang membership offered a source of kudos that was difficult to find in the world of work. The ability to instil fear – and intimidate more prosperous passers-by – was no little compensation for those who routinely endured the indignities of low-paid, low-status employment, or the interminable queuing and petty humiliations of the labour exchange. As a gang member, a youth might enjoy a degree of prestige along with the prospect of making some money on the side.

On the street, the Glasgow gangster was instantly recognisable by his swagger. Albert Mackie, who worked in the city as a journalist during the late 1920s and 1930s, described how:

When he walked abroad, he made the most of himself. His gait . . . had something in it of the strut of the pouter pigeon. The head wove defiantly, the hands swung palms downwards and open, like a cowboy's ready to be quick on the draw.

Like his walk, the gangster's clothes were designed to attract attention. He wore a short jacket, a waistcoat with fancy lapels, flared trousers and patent leather shoes with pointed toes. On his head he sported a tweed cap, known as a 'bunnet'. 'When one met a youth so attired,' Mackie recalled, 'one treated him with respect and kept one's distance, particularly if he came in strength.' In a city of stark social divisions, this tacit acknowledgement of the toughness of the denizens of the slums meant a great deal.

To make sense of the growing menace posed by the gangs during the 1920s and 1930s, police officers and members of the judiciary as well as journalists looked to America. Hollywood, it appeared, had Britain in its thrall. As the *Evening Citizen* put it in 1926:

> The cinema is the biggest propaganda-agent that the world has ever seen; and it is daily and nightly, in every British town and village, propagating American ideas, American manners, American language, and American methods. The cinema is helping to destroy British character. It is doing its best to make us American.

Young people in the city's poorer districts showed few such misgivings. To them, America represented the Modern Age. The growth of the cinema helped to usher in new styles of music, dance and dress: Hollywood spelled glamour and romance. During the early 1930s, the popularity of gangster films such as *Little Caesar* (1930), *The Public Enemy* (1931) and *Scarface* (1932) prompted fears of an unparalleled wave of 'copycat' crime.

On the surface, Glasgow's gangsters confirmed the worst of these fears. They modelled their appearances, gestures and vocabulary on those of Hollywood tough guys like George Raft and Paul Muni, while their rackets were said to draw inspiration from the exploits of Al Capone. Against this backdrop, Glasgow was widely labelled the 'Scottish Chicago'. This was pure hyperbole: in stark contrast to Chicago, where 500 gangland slayings had been reported during the 1920s, Glasgow's gangsters seldom killed each other or anyone else. However, the novelty of cinema and the prevailing fear of 'Americanisation' fostered shallow explanations of gang conflict. In reality – as more acute commentators in the local and national press sometimes acknowledged – Glasgow's gangs were deeply rooted in the everyday life of the city. Their members, on closer inspection, were surprisingly ordinary.

Delving into the ganglands of the 1920s and 1930s requires sustained historical detective work. Then, as now, gang members craved notoriety, but only on their own terms: they took great care to screen their activities from the police and they were deeply wary of strangers. The vast bulk of the surviving information on the gangs and their activities was compiled by outsiders, most of them socially remote from, and hostile to, the people whose actions they were describing. Feature articles in the local and national press were frequently based on briefings by senior police officers, who provided insights into the nature of the gangs, the size of their respective followings and the basis of their feuds. This information was divulged with a clear purpose: to show the City of Glasgow Police as a model force. The ability of the police to deal with the gangs is frequently over-stated as a result.

The most extensive records to survive from the first half of the twentieth century are press reports on the trials of gang members in Glasgow's courts. The three local evening newspapers – the *Evening Citizen*, *Evening News* and *Evening Times* – all carried reports on selected court cases, as did the *Glasgow Herald*, the newspaper of choice of the city's middle class. Gang cases loom large in these reports. The local press therefore provides historians with a vast amount of information on those gang members brought before the magistrates, often including the defendants' ages, addresses and occupations, as well as descriptions of their alleged offences and details of the sentences imposed on those found guilty. Additional snippets, including statements made in court by gangsters and their alleged victims, offer vital clues to the pretexts for outbreaks of violence.

Pieced together, trial reports provide a compelling, if partial, account of Glasgow's gang conflicts and those who took part in them. Cross-checked against the registers of Glasgow's prisons, they underpin both detailed profiles of individual offenders and collective portraits of the gangs to which they belonged. Surviving police files document the relationships between gang members as they collectively planned and carried out crimes ranging from safe-blowing to smash-and-grab raids, while background reports on prisoners from murder trials held at the city's High Court provide insights into their family lives and employment histories.

A second batch of newspapers provides a quite different perspective on the same people and events. Coverage in popular Scottish weeklies, such as *Thomson's Weekly News* – published on Saturdays – and the *Sunday Mail*, inevitably lacked the immediacy of reports in the daily newspapers. Forced to seek new angles on events that had already been extensively publicised, their editors demanded fresh, human-interest stories. These were obtained in interviews with the family and friends of both victims and perpetrators of gang violence, and the resulting feature articles cast gang members in a different light: young men desperate for work, dutiful sons or loving husbands and fathers. Stories of gang members in their family settings give glimpses of their lives in the round. Of course, accounts by friends and relatives were partial, too, while information gleaned from poor relief case-files sometimes shows gangsters in a harsher light: not as the 'family men' they claimed to be, but as neglectful providers for their wives and children.

One gang above all came to symbolise Glasgow's reign of terror during the 1920s and 1930s: the Brigton Billy Boys. The 'Billies' took their name from William of Orange – 'King Billy' – whose victory at the Battle of the Boyne in 1690 had secured Protestant rule in England and Scotland as well as Ireland. They recruited Protestant youths from Bridgeton – known locally as 'Brigton' – and adjacent districts in Glasgow's East End, such as the Calton – an impoverished district wedged between Bridgeton and the city centre – and Mile End. With around 500 members during the 1930s, the Billy Boys formed the largest and most powerful of the city's gangs. They engaged in bitter, long-running feuds with half-a-dozen Catholic gangs across the East End, their principal adversaries being the Kent Star, the San Toy and the Calton Entry Boys, three well-established gangs from the Calton. The Kent Star and the San Toy could raise as many followers between them as the Billy Boys. The Billies' other notable opponents were the Shanley Boys from Bridgeton, the Cheeky Forty from the Garngad and the Norman Conks (Conquerors) from Norman Street in Dalmarnock.

In contrast to their counterparts in the East End, the leading gangs in the Gorbals district on Glasgow's South Side contained Catholic, Protestant and Jewish members, in keeping with the cosmopolitan character of the local population. The South Side Stickers and the Liberty Boys were at war for more than a decade from the early 1920s, while members of the Beehive Boys – the other major Gorbals outfit – saw themselves as 'clever' gangsters, motivated by profit rather than by fighting for its own sake. Some of the smaller gangs in the district did proclaim sectarian allegiances – notably the Naburn Street Billy Boys – but the Orange Order was less entrenched in the Gorbals than in Bridgeton and, for the most part, South Side gangs focused their energies on territorial skirmishing, either within the Gorbals or between the Gorbals and the Calton. The South Side gangs, however, were by no means confined to the Gorbals: the adjacent district of Plantation was riddled with them. So, too, was Govan, further to the west.

The names adopted by gangs denoted their collective identity as 'boys' bonded by territory, religion, or both, and celebrated their toughness. The Kent Star gathered on the corner of Kent Street in the Calton; their allies the Calton Entry Boys congregated on the nearby street of that name. The Derry Boys – named after the apprentices who barred the gates of Derry against the Catholic forces of James II in 1689 – were immediately recognisable as Protestants, as were the gangs of Billy Boys found in districts from Bridgeton and Anderston to the Gorbals. Catholic gangs of the East End included the Calton Emmet, named after the legendary Irish nationalist Robert Emmet. Other gangs adopted names that signalled their fighting prowess: the

Blackburn Street Diehards, from Plantation, and Gorbals gangs like the Kidston Street Bruisers and the South Side Stickers.

Gangs were hierarchical organisations. Larger gangs such as the Billy Boys, San Toy and Kent Star were run by committees, with secretaries and treasurers to administer subscriptions and arrange payments for lawyers, as well as recognised leaders. Some operated 'senior' and 'junior' sections, mirroring the apprenticeship system in local industries. New recruits joined the junior ranks, transferring to the senior gang only after they had 'served their time' – and proved their mettle. In this way, gangs reproduced themselves across generations and maintained their numbers in the face of clampdowns by the police. As an unnamed police officer complained to the *Weekly Record*: 'If a senior is arrested or "sent away", a junior takes his place, and the gang is kept at full strength.' The Billy Boys' junior section – the Derry Boys – was comprised of lads aged between fourteen and twenty-one. According to a detective from the Eastern Division, speaking in 1936, the Derry Boys formed a 'school' for aspiring Billy Boys. By his reckoning, 90 per cent of the 'Derries' were unemployed – to them, membership of the senior gang must have appeared a more realistic prospect than finding legitimate employment in the Clydeside shipyards – the traditional ambition of Protestant youths in Glasgow's East End.

If gangs were rooted in inequality and religious bigotry rather than in Hollywood, it is no surprise that traces of gang activity can be found stretching back into the nineteenth century. Glasgow's 'gang menace' may have made national and international news during the 1930s, but the clues were already there in the 1870s and 1880s.

Part I

The Rise of the Gangs

I

'The Terrorists of Glasgow'

At the height of Glasgow's gang menace, during the 1930s, police officials were at pains to point out that the city's problems were not new. As one unnamed officer insisted to the *Evening Citizen* in 1930: 'The gangs have always been with us.' Memories stretched back across five decades to the Penny Mob of the early 1880s, whose members reputedly paid a penny a week into a fund for the payment of fines. According to police lore, the gangs of the 1880s were motivated not by criminal gain but by sectarian antagonism, exacerbated by pure love of mischief and fighting.

Gangs were an enduring presence on the streets of Glasgow, but the depth of the anxieties they provoked varied over time. Reports in the local press suggest that concern intensified in the early 1880s, peaked in the mid-1900s and recurred, fleetingly, during the First World War when the city's hooligans 'came out in force and made the lives of peaceful citizens a terror'.

Party Bands and Fighting Mobs

Recollections of the gangs of the 1880s were entwined with memories of parades by sectarian 'party' bands. The Penny Mob, based in Townhead on the northern edge of Glasgow city centre, were Protestants. In later decades, they were remembered as vandals as well as street fighters: much of their notoriety had been earned by smashing the windows of Catholic chapels. They were recalled by Daniel Harvey, born in 1871, in a memoir published in 1930:

> Religious feeling ran very high in those days. Every district in the city had its mobs, and these were all known by different names.

The mob I knew best boasted the name of the Muldoons; at Infirmary Square there was another mob known as the Penny Mob. These two were often at loggerheads, and the police offices were always full as a result.

These factions were rampant all over Glasgow. Every district had its flute band, and these bands used to march through the streets followed by great crowds of people all looking for the scalps of those whose religious principles were adverse to their own.

To Harvey's readers in 1930, such tales of gang feuds and sectarian riots were only too familiar.

Harvey's recollection that religious feeling 'ran very high in those days' is borne out by newspaper reports of widespread sectarian disturbances in Glasgow during the 1870s and 1880s. In the wake of mass Irish immigration, religious divisions had become inextricably bound up with, and inflamed by, the Ulster conflict. A substantial minority of Irish migrants to Glasgow were Protestants, and they brought with them the Orange Order with its aggressive assertion of Protestant ascendancy and its annual Twelfth of July parades to commemorate King Billy's triumph at the Battle of the Boyne. These 'Orange Walks' were prohibited in the county of Lanarkshire (of which Glasgow was a part) from 1857, following repeated outbreaks of violence. The ban was lifted in 1872. Membership of the Orange Order increased significantly in Glasgow thereafter, especially in the East End, where Bridgeton became a notable Orange stronghold during the 1870s.

Growing support for the Orange Order was in part a defensive response, both to the restoration of the hierarchy of the Catholic church in Scotland in 1878 and to the increasingly vocal – and visible – support among Glasgow's Irish-Catholic community for Irish Home Rule.

In August 1880, a pro-Home Rule demonstration was marred by outbreaks of violence both in the city centre, where furious Orangemen had gathered en masse, and in many of the major routes into the centre, where the processionists were greeted with shouts of 'To hell with Dan!' – 'Dan' stood for the legendary Irish Nationalist, Daniel O'Connell, and served as a moniker for Catholics of Irish descent in Glasgow in much the same way that 'Billy' stood for a Protestant with Orange sympathies.

Glasgow's Irish Nationalists responded to the resumption of the annual Orange Walk in 1872 by investing St Patrick's Day with a parallel political symbolism: henceforth, the 17 March celebrations incorporated vigorous expressions of support for Home Rule. In 1879, the festivities were marred by a week of disturbances as Orange flute bands took to the streets of the city centre and the East End. Hostilities culminated on the evening of Saturday 22 March when a number of bands paraded between the Saltmarket and Townhead. Their appearance drew large crowds of youths – 'bulking lads and hoydenish girls' according to the *Glasgow Herald* – who packed High Street and Infirmary Square to cheer the bands and 'execrate' the Pope. Police attempts to disperse the bands were fruitless: constables were showered with stones, while the flautists, who were not wearing uniforms, simply hid their instruments up their sleeves and melted into the throng, only to reassemble at a different spot where the inflammatory melody of 'Boyne Water' was resumed. (The song's 'unofficial' version depicted King Billy's 'wee bulldog' paddling 'up to his knees in Fenian blood'.)

A police report from the day detailed how one band – said to be from Bridgeton – paraded from High Street to the Garngad accompanied by 'a large and disorderly mob'. Rioting broke out as soon as the band reached Garngad Road, and it took the police fifteen minutes to restore order. They made seventeen arrests, but at some cost: two officers suffered severe head injuries. As the band made its way back to Bridgeton, its followers smashed the windows of two Catholic chapels: St Mary's in the Calton and Sacred Heart in Bridgeton. Rival bands paraded the Calton later that night, as the police struggled to maintain order across the East End.

The *Glasgow Herald* firmly blamed the Orange bands for the disturbances, but Protestants were quick to issue counter-allegations: one angry reader complained that the rioting had been caused by a Catholic band from the Garngad, whose supporters had smashed the windows of a mission hall in the Calton.

Riots sparked by parades by Orange bands increased in both scale and severity during the months that followed. In November 1879, newspapers alleged that a state of terror prevailed in some quarters of Glasgow following disturbances across the city centre, the East End and South Side. Most of those arrested during party riots were young men, and witnesses highlighted the role of organised gangs, or mobs, in orchestrating the violence.

On Saturday 8 November, hostilities commenced with a bout of stone throwing after the Apprentice Boys' band appeared in the Saltmarket. The band marched along Trongate with a thousand followers, one of whom was arrested after yelling: 'To hell with the Pope!' and 'Five pounds for a kick at the Pope!' Rival mobs roamed the streets off High Street for the rest of the night; dozens of arrests were made as violence spilled over into the Garngad and the Gorbals. At half past eleven, between 200 and 300 Catholic youths were spotted in Brunswick Street shouting: 'To hell with Billy!'

Six youths were jailed for their part in disturbances in the Garngad. Two Protestants got thirty days each for assaulting a Catholic in Garngad Road, while four Catholic boys – said to be members of the Little Muldoon Mob – were convicted of breaching the peace and malicious mischief. They had paraded along Garngad Road, Cobden Street and Tharsis Street shouting about 'Dan' and 'Billy' and had smashed the windows of nine houses before launching a hail of stones at the windows of the United Presbyterian Church in Tharsis Street. Their leader, William Brown, got sixty days.

More serious cases were tried at Glasgow Sheriff Court. (This was an intermediate court: sheriffs tried cases that were deemed too serious to be dealt with by a magistrate at one of the city's police courts, but not serious enough to be tried before a judge at the High Court.) John Graham, who had paraded with the

Apprentice Boys' band, was charged with assaulting a man on Albert Bridge. A series of witnesses was called, and the counsel for the defence repeatedly quizzed them about the (Catholic) Muldoons. Asked whether he was aware of the rules of the 'Muldoon Society', one replied: 'Yes – to watch for and half kill Protestants. They have a reserve fund for paying the fines of members taken up for party [sectarian] fighting.' Another witness told the court that the Muldoons held weekly meetings on Wednesdays, adding that their members contributed three-pence a week for the payment of fines.

The attempt to deflect attention onto Catholic brawlers was in vain, however: Graham was jailed for sixty days with hard labour.

As Graham languished in prison, another follower of the Apprentice Boys' band lay in the Royal Infirmary. Samuel Woods, an apprentice fitter from Bridgeton, had suffered a badly frac-tured skull when he was kicked on the head in King Street in the city centre: doctors feared for his life for several weeks. Three of his alleged assailants stood trial at Glasgow Sheriff Court on 14 January 1880. David Warden, John Muldoon – probably a member of the family from whom the gang took its name – and Michael McDermid were charged with assaulting Woods resulting in his severe injury.

Woods told the court that he had joined up with the band in High Street. They had paraded to the South Side district of Kinning Park and back to the city centre. As they were passing through King Street, four lads had suddenly rushed out of a passageway shouting: 'Are these the Sons of William?' ('William' referred to William of Orange, or King Billy.) The lads knocked him down, and he was kicked as he lay on the ground. Thirteen-year-old John Dewar testified to the prisoners' part in the assault. Asked whether he knew what tune the band had been playing, he replied: 'To Hell With The Pope.' Warden, Muldoon and McDermid were all jailed for fifteen months with hard labour.

In the wake of these disturbances, tit-for-tat raids by rival gangs of youths became an established feature of life in Glasgow's central and eastern districts. On the night of 27

September 1880, a young Protestant named William Kerr was stabbed in Cathedral Square, the knife penetrating his lung. No arrests were made that night, but detectives subsequently rounded up four youths, three of whom were identified by Kerr as having taken part in the assault. The prisoners stood trial at the sheriff court on 8 December. Kerr claimed that he had been playing a game called 'Smugglers' with some friends in Cathedral Square when some other boys suddenly attacked them. Witnesses identified two of the prisoners – James McMahon and John McAulay – as prominent Muldoons. One witness, sixteen-year-old Charles Sweeney, admitted to the court that he 'sometimes kept company with a number of lads calling themselves Muldoons'. He described how, on the night of 27 September, around twenty Muldoons headed for Cathedral Square, looking for 'the boys who call themselves the True Blues' (the 'Blue Banner of the Covenant' was one of the most powerful symbols of the Protestant Reformation in Scotland). Asked whether they had gone looking for a fight, Sweeney replied: 'Yes, we meant to fight them if we could get at them.' They had got more than they bargained for: around forty True Blues intercepted them and chased them into Drygate. The Muldoons entered Cathedral Square at the second attempt. James McMahon confronted Kerr, demanding to know 'what he was' [Catholic or Protestant]. Kerr was attacked before he could reply. Three other Muldoons testified that McMahon subsequently boasted that he had carried out the stabbing.

McMahon and McAulay were jailed for three months, having already spent ten weeks in prison awaiting trial. McMahon was seventeen, McAulay a year older. They both lived in the Havannah – a 'narrow, evil-smelling, tumble-down thorough-fare' off High Street, whose occupants were legendary for their drunken violence and readiness to fight the police. Despite the poverty of their surroundings, both lads were fashionably dressed. On the night that William Kerr was stabbed, McMahon was wearing a silk cap, white scarf and light jacket, while McAulay sported a black jacket and a Balmoral bonnet – during the 1880s, as later, gang members were as much concerned with their appearance as with their fighting cachet. Youths in the East End adopted the London costermonger's bell-bottomed trousers, adorned with silver buttons. 'You were not reckoned to be of any account in the Gallowgate unless you wore these clothes,' Daniel Harvey recalled.

The reports of gang feuds and larger-scale sectarian skirmishes during the 1870s and 1880s offer revealing parallels with events in Glasgow during the 1930s. Gang conflicts were frequently laced with sectarianism, especially in the East End – home to a large swathe of the city's Irish-Catholic population, but also the Glasgow stronghold of the Orange Order. Party bands from East End districts such as Bridgeton regularly paraded to the city centre and beyond, frequently venturing into the South Side, where their musical homages to King Billy and anti-papal spleen were sure to provoke the ire of local Catholics. And thus the rival causes of 'Billy' and 'Dan' were taken up by successive generations of children, who roamed the streets issuing the challenge: 'Wha' are yese? Billy or a Dan?'

The wrong answer was grounds for a fight, as was a refusal to respond.

Glasgow's Hooligans

Over time, Glasgow-based journalists would note that the city's gang conflicts appeared to come in waves. As the *Eastern Standard* observed in 1926:

> The 'gang' feeling seems to take concrete expression in well-defined cycles, which end only when public and police attentions become so hot as to be uncomfortable. A period of immunity follows and again the old trouble breaks out.

As the *Standard* recalled, an unprecedented recurrence had been reported twenty years earlier, when Glasgow witnessed its first full-blown panic over gangs. In 1906, the level of anxiety was such that Glasgow's disorderly youths were relabelled 'hooligans' – a term coined in London and popularised after a spate of disturbances, led to an unusually large number of arrests for disorderly conduct, drunkenness, assaults on the police and fighting, over an August bank holiday weekend in 1898.

The reported upsurge in hooliganism in Glasgow was debated at a series of meetings of the Corporation (city council) from March 1906 onwards, and two special conferences of the city's magistrates were convened to discuss the judicial response. That summer, the letters page of the *Glasgow Herald* would be dominated by a furious debate on the potential deterrent value of flogging. (Under the Scottish legal code, the 'lash' could only be inflicted on men convicted of living on the immoral earnings of women.)

Many of the early reported outbreaks of hooliganism featured a gang known as the Hi Hi from the Cowcaddens, a notorious slum on the northern fringe of the city centre. In March 1906, Superintendent Mennie of the City of Glasgow Police told the *Glasgow News* that the gangs of the northern district were not new. They were, however, increasingly prone to coming into conflict with the wider public. The gang 'system', the superintendent added, was operated by lads aged around fifteen to eighteen, many of whom had no regular employment. Asked how the gang got their name, he replied: 'They got their name through their leaders shouting "Hi, Hi" wherever the company assembled.'

The Hi Hi were relentlessly targeted by the police. On the night of Saturday 24 March, John Macpherson was arrested following a disturbance in the gallery of the Pavilion theatre. He was brought before the Northern Police Court where officers variously described him a member of the Hi Hi, and one of its leaders. Questioned about Macpherson's gang allegiance, one constable was adamant: 'I know him well. He frequently carries a nicely polished hammer, and I have chased him often.' The magistrate then quizzed Macpherson directly: 'Are you a member of the Hi Hi gang?' Macpherson replied: 'I dinna exactly ken [don't exactly know]. I go about Hope Street, and everyone that goes about that district is supposed to be a member of the Hi Hi gang.' Macpherson's implication was clear: any youth frequenting the district associated with the Hi Hi was liable to be deemed a hooligan and harassed by the police. His protest was in vain: he was jailed for sixty days.

The ranks of the Hi Hi included girls as well as boys or young men. Three days after Macpherson's appearance, four girls aged between fourteen and sixteen were brought before the same court. Sarah Patrick, Maggie Collins, Emma Anderson and Nellie Miller were charged with disorderly conduct for jostling passers-by in West Russell Street – police officers told the court that the girls had ignored repeated cautions. They kept company with young lads 'of the hooligan type', while one of the four was known as the 'Queen' of the Hi Hi. Press reports did not identify the 'Queen' by name, but Sarah Patrick and Maggie Collins were fined 10 shillings, with the alternative of seven days' imprisonment in default of payment.

The hooligan 'outrages' were first raised at the meeting of Glasgow Corporation on 22 March. Bailie Gibson alleged that law-abiding citizens were enduring a 'reign of terror' at the hands of dangerous gangs. (Bailies were elected councillors, some of whom also served as magistrates at the various district police courts, while a full-time, stipendiary magistrate presided at the city's Central Police Court.) Gibson alleged that the gangs were stabbing and robbing their victims, and that respectable people were left with no choice but to carry firearms to protect themselves. Bailie Watson replied that a special meeting of the magistrates had already been convened to consider the recent spate of articles in the press, but he sounded a note of caution: newspaper reports were not always to be relied upon. Pressed for a comment by the *Glasgow News*, the city's chief constable, James Stevenson, insisted that the situation was less serious than was generally supposed. 'It was no new thing for Glasgow to be troubled with street roughs,' he declared, and 'there was no necessity for people carrying firearms because of what was alleged to have taken place in the city of late.'

The magistrates met again at the City Chambers on 26 March. They were addressed by the chief constable, who again insisted that reports of hooliganism had been exaggerated. Chief

Constable Stevenson admitted that a number of gangs of youths had posed problems of disorder, but he claimed that these had been broken up – hence there was no cause for panic. The magistrates were instructed to deal with each case that came before them on its merits, and were reminded of their power to impose sentences of sixty days for disorderly conduct. They were further requested to consider prohibiting parades by party bands, which many people in Glasgow viewed as the root cause of the city's hooligan problem. The *Glasgow Herald* welcomed the decision to focus attention on these 'perambulating patriots – Orange and Green', commenting that it was absurd that the civic authorities had not acted sooner to abolish 'the silly ritual of an ancient feud'.

The magistrates took action on 10 April 1906 when they issued a proclamation banning all unlicensed parades by bands: processing with instruments and flags without a licence would henceforth constitute a breach of the peace. The chief constable provided further justification for the ban when he reported that in the year to 1 March 1906, police officers had been withdrawn from their ordinary duties on nearly 400 occasions to accompany bands as they paraded the streets – and disorder had still broken out on numerous occasions. From mid-June to early September, the chief constable stated, a reserve of two sergeants and fourteen constables was kept at the Central Police Office every evening in anticipation of disorder provoked by the bands and 'certain street preachers', who encouraged or engaged them.

The chief constable's earlier assurance that Glasgow's gangs had been broken up soon rang hollow, however. Within a week of the proclamation banning unlicensed parades, two lads were stabbed in a clash between members of the Tim Malloys and the Village Boys in the Gorbals, and the Hi Hi wreaked havoc on a steamer bound for the popular tourist resort of Rothesay. Hooliganism continued to make headline news throughout the summer of 1906: in June, the *Glasgow Herald* reported that there were around a dozen organised gangs in the city: the San Toy had between 400 and 500 members, the Tim Malloys 400, the Hi Hi 300 and the Coliseum Boys 250.

In this period, the San Toy from the Calton was a 'mixed' gang, with both Catholic and Protestant members – a rarity in the East End. Taking their name from rhyming slang ('san toys' stood for boys), they specialised in blackmailing English bookmakers at race meetings at Ayr, Paisley and Hamilton Park. They also fought a long-running feud with the Tim Malloys from the South Side, and their fearsome reputation prompted some of their adversaries within Glasgow to carry revolvers. John Wilson and Alf Francis were bound over to keep the peace for six months after they threatened to shoot James Stewart of the San Toy during a fight in Trongate. One witness told Glasgow Sheriff Court how Stewart led fifty members of his gang into the fray: 'They all came round the corner like bees.' The witness, who claimed to have been threatened and assaulted in the days leading up to the trial, told the court that he had recognised some of Stewart's followers as 'street paper boys'. Stewart, he insisted, 'belongs to the San Toy gang, and is considered the captain'.

The Tim Malloys were as notorious as the San Toy, while their bravado in court incensed the magistrates. In May 1906, Peter Lindsay was convicted at the Southern Police Court of assaulting a police constable with an iron bolt during a row in Cumberland Street, in the Gorbals. According to the police, Lindsay was:

> the leader of the gang known as the Tim Malloys, which infested the Southern district, causing a great deal of annoyance to the public, who had to keep clear of the pavements if the Tim Malloys were near.

Sentenced to sixty days' imprisonment, Lindsay exclaimed: 'I could do that standing on my head.' When the magistrate suggested that sixty lashes might make him think about his actions, Lindsay replied: 'I'll take the lashes with you any day.' In later decades, the Tim Malloys were remembered for terrorising shopkeepers. The *Evening Citizen* recalled how the gang's members would calmly walk into a shop, help themselves to whatever they wanted and distribute the booty among themselves.

The Tim Malloys were not alone in wreaking terror on the city's South Side. In July 1906, the self-styled leader of the Village Boys, twenty-four-year-old John McAndrew, was shot and killed by Joseph Ventura, the Italian owner of an ice-cream parlour in the Gorbals. McAndrew had previously been jailed for breaking into Ventura's premises, so when McAndrew entered the parlour at eleven o'clock on the night of Saturday 14 July, Ventura picked up a rifle to defend himself.

Ventura stood trial for murder at the High Court in Glasgow, where he claimed to have lived in terror of the gang, and insisted that the shooting was accidental. He was unanimously acquitted.

The Village Boys relished their reputation – none more so than John Johnstone, who gleefully adopted the label bestowed upon him in damning reports in the local press: 'He styles himself "the notorious John Johnstone" when taken to the police station, and he has come to be known by the title, which he evidently enjoys,' noted the *Glasgow News*.

The debate on how to tackle hooliganism came to a head at a meeting of Glasgow Corporation on 2 August. Bailie Scott called for the city magistrates to petition Parliament for the powers to impose longer prison sentences and to order hooligans to be flogged. The demand for corporal punishment was criticised by the *Glasgow Herald*, which viewed the practice as a threat to 'the dignity and humanity of the community' and questioned its effectiveness as a deterrent. The dozens of letters to the editor published over the remainder of the month told a different story, however: two-thirds of the correspondents were vehemently in favour of the lash, with some citing biblical justifications, while others claimed that flogging had effectively suppressed nineteenth-century outbreaks of street robbery.

Glasgow magistrates held a second meeting to consider how to deal with hooliganism on 25 September. The chief constable presented a report which purported to detail all of the cases that 'might be characterised as hooliganism' brought before the city's police courts between 1 January and 13 August. The report listed ninety-six cases, which was fewer than had been covered in newspaper reports of hearings at the city's various police courts – a deliberate ploy, as it turned out. Of those, thirty-eight charged were aged between fifteen and nineteen; another forty-four were in their twenties. Half of the cases had been heard at the Southern Police Court and just seven at the Northern, where magistrates had been struggling to deal with the Hi Hi. Some divisional superintendents had clearly rigged their statistics, but the tactic worked: anxieties among both the Corporation and the local press faded during the autumn of 1906. After six months, Glasgow's first hooligan panic had effectively burned itself out.

Hooligans in Wartime

Concern with the city's gangs was reignited during the spring of 1916. A new generation of disorderly youths appeared to have seized the opportunity presented by the Great War – not least a depleted police force and darkened streets – to establish their own reign of terror: in March that year, the Home Office warned of a wave of juvenile crime sweeping across Britain's major cities.

In Glasgow, newspapers such as the *Bulletin* immediately identified the perpetrators as the successors of the Hi Hi. Condemnation of the new generation of hooligans was especially fierce following the introduction of conscription in May 1916. Many of the youths charged following outbreaks of violence and vandalism were munitions workers, enjoying exemption from military service and better-than-usual wages. To one furious commentator in the local press, they were 'cowardly Huns . . . in our own city'.

The *Bulletin* first highlighted the resurgence of hooliganism on 23 March 1916. The city's new hooligan menace was more formidable than ever, the *Bulletin* claimed, since youths from many different parts of the city had combined forces to form 'one large and more or less organised' gang.

The Redskins' operations reportedly extended from Bridgeton in the East End, to the western dockland district of Anderston.

One estimate put the gang's membership at close to a thousand. Armed with 'heavily leaded batons of wood and rubber' in preference to the knuckle-dusters said to have been favoured by the Hi Hi, their conduct could hardly have been more discreditable to the Second City of the Empire:

> Cowardly in their tactics, the 'Redskins' have conscientious objections to fighting man to man, and when they have inveigled an unsuspecting victim into a brawl, a gang of them set upon him – and then clear off at the very first warning of the approach of the police.

The targets of their rackets included the patrons of East End dance halls:

> Most people will hardly credit that a band of youths, even in the days of wartime, should swoop down on a 'jigging' and that one of their members should go around with a cap in one hand and a bottle in another and demand contributions on the pain of being felled. Yet this was done!

The police response – as in March 1906 – was to downplay the hooligan threat. And, once again, the attempt to dismiss a hooligan scare in its early stages was in vain.

A spate of cases at the police courts over the following weeks revealed that the Redskins held no monopoly on hooliganism in Glasgow. Members of East End gangs such as the Hazel Bells and the Waverley Boys were jailed for shopbreaking as well as assaults and breaches of the peace. At Glasgow Sheriff Court, it was alleged that the Hazel Bells were holding Bridgeton and the adjacent district of Mile End to ransom following a series of raids on shops and public houses.

On 16 May 1916, the *Bulletin* published an angry account of Glasgow's **'REIGN OF TERROR'**, lambasting the police for their failure to heed warnings of 'the growing menace of organised hooliganism'. Had the police acted decisively in March, the *Bulletin* alleged, the gangs could have been suppressed. Now they had extended their operations to burglary and the blackmail of shopkeepers, and anyone who dared to appear in court to give evidence against them was 'marked for revenge of the most persistent and cowardly kind'. It was little wonder, the *Bulletin* concluded, that the police now found themselves unable to persuade victims, as well as witnesses, to come forward.

Stung by the renewed criticism, police officials briefed the *Bulletin* on the difficulties posed by wartime conditions. Two days after its exposure of the city's gang terror, the *Bulletin* published 'A Defence of the Police', acknowledging both the depletion of police ranks – one division alone had lost sixty men to the armed services – and the additional burdens imposed by the requirement to round up absentees and deserters under the Military Service Act. 'Never in our communal history,' the *Bulletin* conceded, 'was the Glasgow Police Force labouring under such grave difficulties.' However, this was followed by the startling admission that, so far as the police were concerned: 'There are not in Glasgow at the present time sufficient police to effectively maintain law and order.' To make matters worse, the British national press seized on Glasgow's difficulties: the *Sunday Chronicle* recycled the *Bulletin*'s coverage in an apocalyptic account of 'THE "TERRORISTS" OF GLASGOW':

> Ladies are held up and robbed; policemen are clubbed or cut with bottles when trying to take some of the ruffians to prison; and old men are beaten and left lying after their pockets have been gone through.

If the *Chronicle* was to be believed, entire swathes of the city were gripped by fear: 'even men have often to run for their lives'.

Within Glasgow, attention turned to the causes of the new wave of hooliganism. The *Glasgow News* identified both the failings of the city's schools and the ignorance and slackness of the hooligan's parents: 'We are half inclined to think that the hooligan's father and mother ought to be put in the dock with him.' The remedy, according to the *News*, lay with the police and magistrates: telephones and motor cars should be used to mobilise flying squads of constables to make mass arrests and, if Chief Constable Stevenson was short of uniformed men, special constables should be recruited to bolster their ranks. For their part, the magistrates should recognise that fines of £2 or £3 were no deterrent – stiff jail sentences were the only appropriate punishment.

The police responded to the *Bulletin*'s allegations with a clampdown on breaches of the peace. At the Southern Police Court, young people appeared in droves on charges of disorderly conduct and malicious mischief. Among them were Mary Kennedy, Jeannie Reid and William Harkness, who were convicted of smashing more than twenty windows in houses and shops as they made their way home from a party at five o'clock in the morning on Sunday 21 May. Kennedy and Reid were fined 21 shillings, and Harkness 10 shillings. On Friday 26 May, more than a dozen youths and girls aged between fifteen and seventeen were charged with breaching the peace by 'shouting and making an unseemly noise' in the street late at night in Tradeston. The magistrate fined them all 5 shillings, commenting that they appeared 'respectable', but were 'beginning life very badly'.

Despite heightened police vigilance, clashes between rival gangs were reported throughout the summer. The Waverley Boys ventured from Bridgeton into the South Side to fight the Bloodhound Flying Corps: two youths were fined 30 shillings each after they admitted fighting in Govan Street, and police constables told the Southern Police Court they had had a rough time quelling the disturbance. Three Kelly Boys from Govan told the same court that they were 'in opposition to the gang known as the Red Skins'. They were more reticent when asked why their fellow Kelly Boy David Crosbie, aged twenty, had arrived at a dance hall armed with an iron bludgeon, while seventeen-year-old John Rooney carried a revolver.

The Redskins traded on their reputation for brutality. In July 1916, a bookmaker named Arthur Green was approached by a dozen men at Glasgow's Carntyne racecourse. He recognised them as members of the Redskins. One of the men held out his hands and demanded: 'Drop us a dollar (five shillings)!' Green refused. The men returned shortly afterwards, led by James Martin, who quizzed the bookmaker: 'You are the man who refused to give the boys a dollar?' Martin then punched Green, knocking him to the ground, but a crowd of race-goers stepped in to prevent a more severe beating. Two days later another bookmaker, Frank Gilmour, was attacked by the same group of men in Bell Street in the Calton. Gilmour later claimed that a shot was fired at him as he fled. That night, the two bookmakers were walking through Main Street in Bridgeton together when they were set upon. Police arrested two men at the scene: James Martin and John Evans.

The prisoners were tried at Glasgow Sheriff Court, where they pleaded guilty to the assault on Arthur Green at Carntyne racecourse after witnesses described how a crowd of men had 'gone round all the bookmakers extorting money'. They were both jailed for six months. John Evans was no youthful hooligan: he was twenty-eight years old and married with four children. His criminal record, which stretched back to 1905, included five convictions for assault and one for theft by housebreaking; he had also repeatedly been arrested for drunkenness, while in 1913 he had been jailed for thirty days for assaulting his wife, Elizabeth. Following Evans's conviction for the assault on Arthur Green, Elizabeth was forced to apply for outdoor poor relief – meagre subsistence payments issued by the local parish in lieu of admission to a poorhouse, subject to household inspections, intrusive questioning and moral scrutiny by relieving officers. A parish official noted that the couple's house – a one-roomed apartment – was in fair condition and 'seems clean enough'. The official's profile of John Evans was more revealing:

> Police describe Evans as one of the ringleaders of the 'Redskins', a loafer, was in army and deserted. Police attempted to arrest him for desertion but he jumped the window and broke both his legs, afterwards discharged from army.

John Evans had enlisted in March 1915, only to go absent without leave four months later.

Concern intensified again in September after a Bridgeton resident wrote to the magistrates' committee of Glasgow Corporation complaining of continued harassment by gangs of hooligans. The letter was discussed by the Corporation on 7 September, and a special police night patrol was established to target the city's gangs.

Yet again, however, police officials tried to downplay the problem, insisting that little serious crime was committed by 'organised gangs'. According to the police, groups of young people loitering at street corners were a permanent feature of the city's landscape, and while they annoyed and sometimes molested passers-by, most of their violence was directed at local people who aroused their hostility. Random assaults and robberies, the officials claimed, were no more numerous than in previous years and, in any case, were generally carried about by known thieves acting alone or in twos or threes. Most criminal cases involving bands of youths involved little more than minor mischief or petty theft. In the same meeting, the Lord Provost refused to discuss rumours that a number of hooligans had been deemed unfit for military service on account of their criminal records.

The following weekend, eight Redskins were arrested in Bridgeton during a clash with the Bell-On Boys. They were tried before Sheriff Lyell at Glasgow Sheriff Court, where one of the prisoners appeared in his soldier's uniform and the other seven sported munitions workers' badges – confirming their exemption from military service – as did three of their opponents. The Bell-On Boys claimed that they had been beaten with bottles and iron bolts during the fight.

Sheriff Lyell was livid. Pointing out that the Minister of Munitions had the power to de-badge men as well as badge them, Lyell declared:

It was high time these disturbers of the peace were de-badged and sent to do their bit at the front, and that decent men who had already done their bit in France were released from the colours to take the places at home of these hooligans, who would probably make very good soldiers. These were times for much more Cromwellian methods than courts of law could exercise . . .

Lyell fined three of the Redskins – Bernard Kelly, Thomas Kilcullen and William Convery – £10 each with the alternative of sixty days' imprisonment.

Like the Hi Hi of the 1900s, the Redskins reportedly boasted a 'queen'. In November 1916, Annie Rennie – a 'well-dressed young woman' according to reporters – stood trial at Glasgow Sheriff Court, where she was charged with assaulting Mary Glen by stabbing her. Glen, who confirmed to the court that she was married to a soldier on active service, described how she and Rennie had an argument at a dance hall on the night of 23 October. Blows were exchanged, and they agreed to meet at a different dance hall the following night to 'fight it out'. Rennie did not turn up. The two women, however, met later that night in Argyle Street, where – according to Mary Glen – Rennie was 'accompanied by a lot of her gang, known as the "Redskins", both young men and girls.' As soon as the crowd spotted Glen, the shout went up: 'Off [with] your shawl, Annie, and into her!' Rennie had thrown her shawl to a young man, and launched herself at Glen.

In court, Glen described how 'in the middle of the fight, she felt herself stabbed'. A doctor confirmed that he had found fourteen small puncture wounds on Glen's body, although none was serious – in the doctor's opinion, the wounds had probably been caused by a pen-knife. Annie Rennie told the court that Glen was the aggressor in the original quarrel and denied that she was 'known as the "Queen of the Redskin Gang", or had anything to do with them.'

Sheriff Lyell was appalled:

The fact that so-called men stood around aiding and abetting the fight was utterly brutal and degrading, and a more intolerable invasion of public safety and liberty could not be conceived.

He saved the worst of his ire not for Annie Rennie, but for Mary Glen ('Greatly to blame,' in the sheriff's view). Glen's status as a married woman, who frequented dance halls while her husband risked his life at the front, appears to have offended the sheriff almost as much as the unseemly descriptions of the two women brawling in the street. Rennie was ordered to 'find £10 caution to be of good behaviour for twelve months, or go to prison for 30 days.'

The *People's Journal* took stock of Glasgow's hooligan problem in November 1916. The *Journal*'s 'special commissioner' interviewed a police inspector who was keen to stress that hooliganism in Glasgow was nothing new, relaying a series of tales of the 'penny mob' era of the 1880s. He also explained that the Redskins had taken their name from the Apaches – the hooligans of Paris – whose exploits in the years before the war had been widely reported in the British press. As the *Scotsman* had observed, following the killing of a police officer in Paris in 1912, the Apache '[did] not shrink from incendiarism and murder'. According to the inspector, in Glasgow the term 'Redskin' had captured the public imagination to the extent that even young boys who got into fights were prone to claim that they had been 'fighting Redskins', while the Redskins themselves were becoming fed up with the name because so many cases of theft and assault were wrongly attributed to them. In reality, they were just one of the many gangs whose members gathered on street corners and in dance halls, music halls and cinemas.

Other prominent Glaswegians preferred to emphasise the unique difficulties presented by the war. An unnamed – but 'well-known' – Glasgow gentleman told the *Journal* that the city's hooligans had been stirred by stories from the Western Front: with 'a little drink' inside them, they imagined themselves to be mighty soldiers too, and the sight of a rival gang 'sets aflame the fighting spirit'. Yet the *Journal*'s investigation ended on a surprisingly sober note: fights between rival gangs could be tolerated, it suggested:

> As long as the gangs keep within bounds and let off steam among themselves, one almost feels that such a safety valve has its uses.

It is where we find that apache spirit . . . that any captures should be dealt with severely.

This conclusion, however, revealed a great deal about the depth of social divisions in Glasgow: slum youths, the *Journal* implied, might be permitted to fight among themselves so long as 'respectable' citizens were left unharmed. It also glossed over evidence of extortion as practised both by hardened criminals like John Evans and more youthful gang members. Their victims no doubt found it harder to forget than the journalists.

2

From Hooligans to Gangsters

The term 'hooligan' was still being used to describe gang members in Glasgow during the 1920s and 1930s. However, from the mid-1920s onwards, it was increasingly displaced by a new American term – 'gangster' – which implied both a heightened degree of menace and a greater level of organisation.

Accounts of crime in the United States were a staple item in both the national and local press in Britain. Glasgow's three evening papers, the *Citizen, News* and *Times*, all carried regular news reports from New York and Chicago, augmented by feature articles and editorial commentaries on the careers of leading gangsters such as Jack Diamond and Al Capone. Glaswegians, therefore, were constantly reminded of the wave of violent crime spawned by Prohibition – especially in Chicago, where rival gangs from the city's North and South Sides wrestled for control of the illicit liquor trade. In Chicago, however, the use of firearms was customary and murder was commonplace; Glasgow's murder rate was minuscule by comparison, even though the city's gangs seemed to be more prolific and more dangerous than those elsewhere in Britain.

The Eclipse of the Gangs

Glasgow's wartime hooligan panic subsided in 1917. In any event, by the latter stages of the Great War, concern with youthful depravity had been overshadowed by a more profound threat to the established order: the growing militancy of the city's industrial workers which led to the epithet 'Red Clydeside'. This reputation had been forged during the war years following a rent strike in protest at profiteering by private landlords, and a series of disputes among munitions and shipyard workers, which had led to accusations that Glaswegians were jeopardising the war effort.

Now, in the aftermath of war – January 1919 – Glasgow's hooligans were thoroughly eclipsed by a local general strike among the city's engineering and shipyard workers. The strikers' demand for a forty-hour working week found little favour with the London-based British national press, which fiercely condemned both the revolutionary fervour of the strike's leaders and the alleged lawlessness of their followers. The *Daily Mirror* told how bottles, rivets and stones were thrown at the police during a mass demonstration in front of the City Chambers in George Square on 31 January, and only police baton charges had dispersed the crowd. The break-up of the demonstration was followed by outbreaks of looting in the city centre and beyond: stock worth £2,000 was stolen from a jeweller's in Paisley Road West in Govan. Ten thousand troops were posted in the city the following day; tanks and machine-guns were positioned in George Square. The *Mirror* devoted its entire front page to **'GLASGOW'S ARMY OF OCCUPATION'** – a series of photographs showed squads of soldiers, many in steel helmets, carrying rifles with fixed bayonets as they guarded railway stations, bridges and tramcar and lorry depots.

The events of 1919 cemented an image of Glasgow as the most turbulent of Britain's cities. The aim of the 'irreconcilable revolutionaries' on the Clyde was nothing less than 'the overthrow of government and capitalism', reported the *Daily Express*.

With attention squarely fixed on 'Bolshevik' agitation, the more parochial vendettas among the city's street gangs effectively disappeared from view. In January 1920, the *Evening Times* proclaimed that, 'Organised hooliganism has practically ceased to exist in Glasgow.' The police, whose violent dispersal of demonstrators had polarised opinion within the city the previous year, were keen to take credit for the new 'sense of security', but reports of the demise of the gangs during the early 1920s would prove to be greatly exaggerated.

In October 1920, the *Sunday Mail* ran an isolated report on

Glasgow's 'terrorist' gangs: 'Pitched street battles between rival gangs are becoming frequent,' it warned, 'and unless peaceful pedestrians take shelter, they run the risk of being injured by flying missiles.' The *Mail* insisted that the clashes were neither spontaneous nor random. 'In most cases, they are the outcome of bitter feuds between rival gangs.' No gangs were named in the *Mail*'s report, however, and Glasgow's daily newspapers appeared reluctant to follow up the claims.

As fear of the gangs temporarily diminished, Glasgow's judicial authorities shared in a wider anxiety – felt across Britain – that crimes of violence had greatly increased since 1918 due to the brutalising effects of the First World War: both ex-servicemen and the civilian population, it was feared, had become dangerously accustomed to violence. Jailing a young man named William Lamont for eighteen months in May 1920 following two assaults on 'respectable shop girls', Sheriff Lyell complained that: 'There seemed to be an orgy of brutal violence in the streets of Glasgow at present.'

The Irish War of Independence inflamed the city's enduring sectarian antagonisms yet further. The conflict reached the streets of Glasgow in May 1921, when Detective Inspector Robert Johnstone was shot and killed during a botched attempt to free Frank Carty – believed to be a commandant in the Sligo Brigade of the IRA – from a police van as it approached Duke Street Prison. Police raided a series of addresses in the Calton that afternoon, culminating in the arrest of a group of men – including the parish priest, Father Patrick McRory – in the chapel house of St Mary's in Abercromby Street. Thousands of Father McRory's parishioners gathered outside the chapel that night amidst 'wild rumours'. The arrival of police reinforcements further incensed the crowd, some of whom hurled bottles and stones at the constables before running amok in the Gallowgate, smashing the windows of public houses, restaurants and banks, and attacking tramcars.

More than thirty people were arrested on suspicion of involvement in Detective Inspector Johnstone's murder. Threatening letters were sent to Chief Constable James Stevenson, warning that if any more Catholic clergymen were arrested: 'We will put you and your colleagues up in the air . . . Make no bones about it.' Eighteen of the prisoners – including Father McRory – were freed on 22 July. Their release was met with rejoicing in the Calton, where 'almost every window in Father McRory's parish flaunted the Sinn Fein flag and banners of welcome were stretched across the roads.' Thirteen men stood trial for murder and conspiracy at the High Court in Edinburgh the following month: they were all acquitted.

In August 1922, a flurry of communal assaults on the police reignited fears of an epidemic of violence. Outbreaks were reported in the Gorbals, the Garngad and Govan, while in Anderston, where six men were arrested following a raid on an illicit bookmaker, officers were stoned by a hundred-strong crowd. One of the constables told the Western Police Court: 'It was a bad habit of the children in this district to gather together stones when the police were being assaulted.'

The *Glasgow Herald* reflected at length on the prevailing 'spirit of violence'. It identified a cluster of underlying causes – slum housing, unemployment, poverty, drunkenness and the declining influence of the churches – but warned that these long-standing social problems had been aggravated by the volatility of the city's Irish population: 'Ireland has been responsible for more of our social trouble in Glasgow than the war and Bolshevist propaganda combined.'

The city's notoriety was exacerbated during the early 1920s by a spate of razor-slashings. The appearance of this apparently new breed of offender shocked members of the Scottish judiciary, who quickly identified the razor as a distinctively Glaswegian weapon. Henry Smithyman, an eighteen-year-old newspaper seller from Parkhead, was jailed for twelve months with hard labour at Glasgow Sheriff Court in October 1922 for slashing Thomas Connor's throat in a row over a bet. Sheriff Macdiarmid told the court that such cases had become exceedingly numerous in the city, with most being attributed to young men aged in their teens or twenties.

Four slashings were reported in a single night on New Year's

Eve in 1923. At the High Court, two days later, the judge – Lord Anderson – railed against the fondness for the weapon among 'Glasgow toughs'. Jailing Neil McAllister for twelve months for the attempted murder of John McKay by cutting his throat, the judge declared: 'It was a most outrageous thing that young men in Glasgow should go about with razors in their pockets for the purpose of drawing them across the throats of the citizens.' Prior to dealing with such cases in Glasgow, the judge subsequently remarked, he had thought the razor to be 'a weapon used only by Negroes' – the judge was clearly familiar with American racial stereotypes, whereby black men were routinely depicted as violent as well as untrustworthy and libidinous.

In any event, Lord Anderson asserted: 'It was un-British to use steel.'

The Killing of Noor Mohammed

The racist murder of an Indian pedlar in Port Dundas brought Glasgow's gangs abruptly back into the limelight in May 1925. An industrial district a mile north of the city centre, Port Dundas had seldom been noted for its gangs. Now, it was alleged at the High Court in Glasgow, street traders were required to pay a 'fee' to local gang members to ensure that they could sell their wares in the district unmolested.

At around half past ten on the night of Saturday 16 May, three young men had called at the tenement house of a pedlar named Nathoo Mohammed in Clyde Street. They announced that they wanted to buy jumpers and scarves. Mohammed asked them to return the following day, but the men refused to leave. They offered various items – including a pistol and dagger – in exchange for a jumper, but their bartering quickly turned to threats, with twenty-two-year-old John Keen warning: 'Give me a jumper or I'll kill you.' Mohammed fled, dressed only in a sheet. He ran to nearby Water Street to seek refuge in a house occupied by six of his compatriots. His tormentors followed, their numbers swelling en route, and gathered on the landing outside the house. They hammered at the door, and Noor Mohammed – a twenty-seven-year-old pedlar – opened it. He had armed himself with a broom, but was quickly overpowered: Robert Fletcher seized him, and John Keen stabbed him in the chest. Fletcher shouted that he would 'kill all the Indian men', but the raiders contented themselves with ransacking the house. They hurled cups and crockery at the terrified occupants, helped themselves to three suitcases of merchandise and then scattered before the police arrived.

Noor Mohammed was taken to the Royal Infirmary, where he died shortly after midnight. A post-mortem showed that the knife had penetrated a lung. Detectives from the Northern Division of the Glasgow police made nine arrests within twenty-four hours. A tenth suspect – John Keen – gave himself up after his wife was taken into custody.

The victims of the onslaught were identified as natives of the Punjab, who had been living in the room-and-kitchen house in Water Street for just two months. A reporter on the *Evening Citizen* found the house to be sparsely furnished: there was no covering on the floor, and five single beds were crammed into the room, with an additional 'set-in' bed in the kitchen. The occupants all worked as pedlars, hawking clothes such as silk scarves and jumpers door-to-door throughout Glasgow. Neighbours described them as gentle 'creatures' who gave no cause for offence: 'They come and go and trouble no one,' one woman remarked. Numerous local women were among their customers.

Three young men – John Keen, Robert Fletcher and John McCormack – were eventually charged with Noor Mohammed's murder, and faced additional charges of intimidation, assault and theft. They stood trial at Glasgow High Court from 31 August 1925.

The first witness, Nathoo Mohammed, gave a detailed account of the events that culminated in the fatal stabbing. McCormack's counsel then launched a counter-allegation, accusing Nathoo Mohammed of drug trafficking – the 'alien' dope-pedlar, and sexual predator, was a familiar menace in the public mind following the conviction the previous year of the 'Dope King', Brilliant Chang, at the Old Bailey in London. Restaurant proprietor Chang had been jailed for fourteen months for possession of cocaine; the *Daily Express* heralded the sentence as a triumph for British justice. Nathoo Mohammed denied that he had ever dealt in cocaine or been charged with trafficking. He admitted that he had been fined £2 in 1922 for possession of opium, but insisted that he had required the drug for medicinal purposes – his brother sent it by parcel from India to Edinburgh. He further denied that he had been in the habit of purchasing daggers with hollow handles for the purpose of concealing opium or other drugs.

Nathoo Mohammed's wife, Louie ('a white girl of Spanish extraction', according to the *Scotsman*), was cross-examined the following day. She told the court that she and Nathoo had been married for eight months, and denied that she was aware of any ill-feeling in the district over her marriage to a 'coloured' man. John Keen's counsel then suggested that her husband was both cruel and violent:

Was it not the case that Nathoo Mohammed was starving you?
– No.
Did he not make you go out peddling his wares in the street, and not give you enough money to keep you?
– No. He has always been kind to me.
Did he not strike you on occasions?
– Yes, and I struck him back.

Only with some reluctance did she admit to having complained to the police that her husband beat her.

John McCormack's counsel then put it to Louie Mohammed that her husband had gone to Water Street on the night of 16 May to rally his fellow-countrymen for a fight. She refuted the suggestion: 'The coloured men do not fight,' she insisted.

James Stirling, a seventeen-year-old neighbour, told the court that Keen had challenged the occupants of the house in Water Street to: 'Send down that countryman of yours.' When Noor

Mohammed came out of the house armed with a brush, Keen stabbed him on the chest. Mohammed was then dragged down the stairs into the tenement close (the common entrance to the building). Stirling was questioned about the relationship between Nathoo and Louie Mohammed. He described how, two weeks earlier, Mrs Mohammed had asked him to 'see if John Keen would fight her man'. When asked whether this was because Nathoo Mohammed had mistreated her, Stirling did not answer.

In his closing speech, Keen's counsel stressed to the jury that a large crowd was gathered on the landing when Noor Mohammed was pulled out of the house. Everyone knew, he told the jury, 'what Glasgow gangs – in fact the gangs of any city – were, and there might have been several in the crowd who wanted to vent their spleen on the dead Indian and who delivered the blow.' The judge, Lord Ormidale, told the jury that he was confident they would give 'the same consideration to the case as they would . . . if the victim of the murderous assault had been a native of Scotland or England.' The jury took ninety minutes to find John Keen guilty of murder. Their verdict was unanimous, but they tempered it with a strong recommendation for mercy. They found Robert Fletcher guilty of culpable homicide (the equivalent of manslaughter in the Scottish legal code). Keen and John McCormack were also found guilty of intimidation.

As Lord Ormidale pointed out, by law only one sentence could be passed upon a prisoner convicted of murder: he sentenced John Keen to death. Robert Fletcher was sentenced to seven years' penal servitude; John McCormack was jailed for nine months.

Keen, who broke down and wept as the trial drew to a close, protested: 'I am not getting justice in this case at all, my Lord. If I had got into the witness box, I could have cleared myself.' He was only too aware that newspaper reporting of the case as a gang murder had counted against him. In desperation, he pleaded: 'I have been called a hooligan and a gangster, but this I never was.'

Keen's family launched a petition calling for his reprieve with the support of James Stewart, Independent Labour MP for St Rollox. More than 50,000 signatures were collected in three days – many of them on the terraces at a match between Partick Thistle and Celtic. That number had doubled by the time the petition was forwarded to Sir John Gilmour, Secretary for Scotland in the Conservative government led by Stanley Baldwin.

Gilmour, however, was unmoved. John Keen was hanged in Duke Street Prison, Glasgow, on 24 September. Keen's father wrote to the *Evening News* to thank those who had campaigned on his son's behalf. He concluded: 'Our only consolation is the knowledge that our poor boy is innocent.'

The killing of Noor Mohammed prompted renewed investigations into the nature of Glasgow's gangs. On 20 May, the *Evening Citizen* ran a front-page 'Special' on '**THE HOOLIGAN PROBLEM IN GLASGOW**'. The accompanying illustration showed a fearsome weapon – a combined dagger and knuckle-duster – and the report dwelt on the city's 'somewhat unenviable reputation with regard to the crime of razor-slashing'. The *Citizen* offered a social explanation for gang violence: the root cause – unemployment – was linked to the fighting culture that prevailed in Glasgow's working-class neighbourhoods:

> For the most part the members of these gangs are young hooligans, who, having no work to do, loiter at street corners and form themselves into a gang. In some districts there are two or more gangs, and anxious for a fight on the least pretext, it is not long before they get at loggerheads and a feud ensues.

The writer had clearly been well briefed by the police, as readers were then assured that they had little to fear, despite the hooligans' formidable armoury. For the most part, the gangs fought only among themselves and, in any case, the police kept them under 'a very watchful eye' so that at the first sign of a disturbance, the offenders were hauled before the courts for salutary punishment. In effect, this was little other than police propaganda.

The Rise of the Gangster

The hanging of John Keen might have been expected to serve as a warning to Glasgow's hooligans, yet the city's gang conflicts intensified significantly over the remainder of the decade. The upsurge of gang warfare had, in fact, been foreshadowed two months before Keen went to the gallows, when the annual Orange Walk was marred by unusually severe outbreaks of communal violence.

On Saturday, 11 July 1925, around 40,000 men, women and children assembled at the Grand Lodge headquarters in Cathedral Street in Glasgow city centre before processing to Springboig on the outskirts of the East End. The outward procession passed off quietly with only one minor skirmish en route, and around 70,000 people attended the ensuing demonstration. Resolutions were passed unanimously declaring devotion to the Crown and the principles of the Reformation, and determination to 'combat every attempt of the Romish Church to regain supremacy to the land'.

The walk back to the city centre was more eventful: fighting broke out in Shettleston, and again at nearby Parkhead Cross. As the procession reached the Calton, a section of the parade then veered off the official route and entered Abercromby Street – 'a locality which gained notoriety at the time of the Sinn Fein outrage [the shooting of Detective Inspector Robert Johnstone] in Glasgow some years ago,' as the *Scotsman* recalled. Here, many of the tenement windows had been decorated with Sinn Fein flags, and hand-to-hand fighting erupted after some of the processionists began to hurl stones and bottles at the flags, with members of one Orange band using their instruments as weapons. Fifty arrests were made before the police managed to restore order.

Elsewhere in the city, however, disturbances raged beyond midnight. The most serious outbreaks of violence took place in the Garngad, where 200 youths rampaged through Cobden Street – known locally as an 'Orange' street – 'singing something about John Knox [the leader of the Protestant Reformation in

Scotland], and shouting something about King Billy'. The crowd began to stone the windows of pubs, shops and houses, whose occupants flung pieces of coal and other missiles in reply. A revolver was fired as fighting spilled over into Turner Street and Garngad Road: one young man was wounded. Sixteen youths were arrested.

Four of the prisoners appeared at Glasgow Sheriff Court on 23 July, when a resident of Cobden Street described how his wife was hit on the shoulder by a stone thrown through the window of their house. One of his neighbours described hearing cries of 'Kill the Orangemen!' Only one of the defendants was convicted: Arthur Bates was jailed for three months for breaching the peace and throwing stones.

Rumours of a resurgence of sectarian gang fighting swept through the East End the following year, with one gang repeatedly named in the Eastern Police Court: the Brigton Billy Boys. It did not take much to attract their wrath. On the afternoon of Saturday, 21 March 1926, a Catholic youth was making his way to Dalbeth Cemetery to visit his sister's grave when he was spotted by a group of Billy Boys in London Road. They told him to remove a green handkerchief from the top of his jacket pocket. He ignored them and walked on, only to find himself pursued and felled by punches and kicks. One of his attackers, twenty-year-old Clarence Jackson, was arrested. A search at the Eastern Police Office revealed that Jackson was carrying a razor: Jackson insisted that the weapon was essential for self-defence. His solicitor told Glasgow Sheriff Court that: 'Unfortunately, in this locality, there were young men who had narrow-minded views on religion. There was a Fenian gang, and another gang known as the Billy Boys. The latter were Orangemen.' According to Jackson's solicitor, the victim of the assault was a member of the Fenian gang, and had provoked the Billy Boys by flaunting the handkerchief. Sheriff Harvey was unimpressed; he jailed Jackson for sixty days with hard labour.

Catholic gangs in the East End launched regular forays of their own. On Tuesday 27 April, John Brogan led a gang of around thirty Norman Conks in a late-night raid on the Billy

Boys' regular gathering spot at Bridgeton Cross – those Billy Boys present quickly scattered. Robert McLaggan Kelly was caught, however, and he suffered a fractured skull when he was hit with a hammer: doctors at the Royal Infirmary removed five pieces of bone from his head. Two members of the raiding party were arrested.

At their trial at Glasgow Sheriff Court, John Brogan and William Murray were identified as 'members of an extensive gang known as the Norman Conks, having its headquarters in Norman Street, Bridgeton.' (Locals knew the district as Dalmarnock.) One of the defence witnesses – himself a prominent member of the Conks – admitted that he carried a bayonet down the leg of his trousers, but assured the court that: 'he never meant to use it, except to scare off anybody who attacked him.' The need was real, he insisted, since 'the Billy Boys had already come after him several times.' Brogan was jailed for six months, Murray for four.

The *Eastern Standard* was adamant that sectarian gang warfare threatened more than just the safety of passers-by and the police:

> Perfectly legitimate organisations like the Orange Order and the Ancient Order of Hibernians are blamed for the sins of this element which they do not condone, but cannot prevent; the 'religious' aspect of the gangs is an insult to every decent human being.

The *Standard*'s tirade echoed commentaries on the feuding between the Catholic Muldoons and Protestant gangs such as the True Blues and the Penny Mob during the early 1880s.

In May 1926, Glasgow's gang feuds were once again overshadowed by industrial conflict. Transport workers, railwaymen, dockers, printers, ironworkers and steelworkers across Britain came out in a General Strike in support of the nation's coalminers, who were faced with savage pay cuts. Glasgow was the epicentre of the strike in Scotland: support among the city's workers was widespread, but so was opposition – 7,000 volunteers enrolled for strike-breaking duties. Shops and public houses were looted in the East End, where police made repeated baton charges to clear the streets. The *Scotsman* warned of 'marked Communist sentiment in most of the working-class districts', noting that threats had been chalked on the doors of the houses of tramway workers who had refused to join the strike.

The dispute polarised the East End gangs. Members of the Billy Boys offered their services as strike-breakers, in keeping with their pledge 'to uphold King, Country and Constitution'. In contrast, members of one of the principal East End Catholic gangs set a trap for the police on the night of Saturday 8 May. A request was relayed to the Eastern Police for officers to investigate a theft in Norman Street in Dalmarnock. Ordinarily, two or three officers would have attended the scene, but the request was treated with some suspicion, and a much larger body of men was sent. When they arrived at Norman Street, they found that all the street lamps and other lights had been extinguished, a rope had been stretched across the roadway to create an obstruction and crowds had gathered in the tenement closes. The police sent for reinforcements, who arrived in a lorry that screeched down the street with its headlights on full beam. Twenty officers jumped out and 'dispersed the crowds', using their batons to mete out punishment on the spot. They made only three arrests: James Murphy, aged twenty; Francis Corrigan, eighteen; and Thomas Kelly, seventeen.

The prisoners appeared at the Eastern Police Court on the Monday morning, when they pleaded guilty to breaching the peace. Police witnesses identified the trio as members of the Norman Conks. Murphy, Corrigan and Kelly were each fined £5 and 5 shillings, with the option of sixty days' imprisonment. They got off relatively lightly: by 10 May, more than 200 people charged with strike-related disturbances at Glasgow's Eastern Police Court had been remitted for trial at the city's sheriff court. Most were jailed for between one and three months. The General Strike was called off after nine days in an overwhelming defeat for the trade unions. The miners stayed out on strike until Christmas when their union's funds ran out and they too were defeated.

In the wake of the General Strike, social commentators reflected on the city's stark social divisions. As a journalist on the *Eastern Standard* remarked in August 1926: 'There are two Glasgows, but when a visitor comes amongst us we show him only one.' The Second City of the Empire, as Glasgow still liked to style itself, boasted grand buildings, lavish shops and fine parks. In this Glasgow, luxury was everywhere on display: in Great Western Road, with its ornate lawns and motor cars; on the 'yacht pond' in Queen's Park; and in the windows of the department stores of Sauchiehall Street – as enticing as any in Bond Street in London. This Glasgow was a modern city, with 'flashy' cinemas as well as sumptuous theatres; its prosperous neighbourhoods peopled by 'well-built men and women with sunburnt faces and grammatical tongues'.

The 'other Glasgow' was revealed before the magistrates at the daily sittings of the city's ten police courts. As the *Standard*'s reporter put it:

> There you learn all about our unemployment, slums, dirt, drink, hooliganism, disease, and immorality. The play is acted every morning at 9 o'clock. The players are nearly all drawn from our C3 population. Many of them are habitual offenders, who know by name and head-mark every policeman in the division. They are all victims – of something.

'C3' – a hangover from the military classifications used to assess British men's fitness for combat during the First World War – denoted 'substandard': physically or mentally unfit. H. V. Morton, the leading English travel writer of the 1920s, endorsed this vision of Glasgow as a city of extremes: 'The splendour of riches and the abjectness of poverty, seen so close together, appear sharper than in most great cities. East and west ends run into one another in the most grotesque way.' Gangs were the unmistakeable product of the 'other Glasgow', but they also owed something to this startling proximity of plenty and want.

Stories of gang warfare in Bridgeton proliferated over the

summer of 1926. Many of the cases detailed in the local press still involved the use of razors: hardly a week passed without such an offence being reported, complained the *Evening Citizen* on 20 August 1926. At Glasgow Sheriff Court the following day, Patrick Kelly was jailed for three months for assaulting a man by slashing him across the face. Prior to passing sentence, Sheriff Robertson claimed that razor-slashing had been unknown in Britain until recent years:

> The only example of it [that] he had heard of before it arose in this country, and particularly in Glasgow, was among the half-demented Negro slaves of Brazil, and he regretted to think that any section of our population could equal itself with those degraded creatures.

Robertson was echoing comments made by Lord Anderson at the High Court two years earlier – these startling judicial pronouncements suggesting that Glaswegians, with their alarming propensity for violence, were themselves almost a race apart. Further cases of razor-slashing were reported that weekend: in Bridgeton, a cinema attendant was cut on the wrist after a group of gang members were denied entry, while forty-five-year-old James Foley was attacked by half-a-dozen youths and slashed on the face and neck as he walked through Bridgeton Cross at half past two on Sunday morning.

As a police officer explained to the *Scotsman*, Glasgow's razor-slashers had become quite calculating in their use of their weapons:

> they do not strike at their victim with the razor blade fully opened. That would be too dangerous, because they might inflict a deep wound with fatal consequences, or in the event of the razor slipping while in the act of striking, they might seriously injure themselves. The blade is pushed through the open bottom of the sheath, and the sharp protruding part does all the damage. Undoubtedly, the wounds are intended to disfigure the victims for life, and in this respect they succeed. Invariably the face is aimed at.

Of course, this 'restraint' also greatly minimised the punishments that razor-slashers were likely to face should they be brought before the courts.

The gangster and the razor-slasher were by now increasingly synonymous in reports in the local press. Glasgow's *Eastern Standard* made the connection more explicitly than most in an editorial on Saturday, 28 August 1926, which offered an unusually bold statement of the social roots of the city's gang problem:

> The youths who make up the gangs of razor-slashers come from the poorest quarters of the city. They are badly housed. They are badly educated. Often they are badly fed and badly clothed. Invariably they are not surrounded by good character-forming influences.

The *Standard* called for more wholesome outlets for the gangs' youthful energies, while the *Evening Citizen*, in hawkish mode, called for the flogging of all those convicted of fighting with razors or knives.

The following Thursday, 2 September, four Billy Boys were attacked by a large group of Norman Conks in Dale Street in Bridgeton. The Billy Boys were themselves armed, but they stood little chance against superior numbers. By the time police arrived at the scene, James McIntosh, aged thirty, had been knocked unconscious by a blow to the head with a hatchet and slashed twice on the neck with a razor, while a second Billy Boy, twenty-four-year-old Eli Webb, had been hit on the head with an iron bar. Both men were taken to the Royal Infirmary. A bystander told the *Evening Citizen* that 'something very serious would have happened if the police had not come on the scene'.

In the wake of the killing of Noor Mohammed the previous year, the *Citizen* had published a front-page 'Special' reassuring readers that the police had the city's gangs under control. Now the *Citizen* ran another 'Special' under the banner headline: **'THE METHODS OF GLASGOW GANGSTERS'**. Its tone was less confident, although it still insisted that: 'The greatest danger from this warfare is to the gangsters themselves.' In addition to listing the most prominent gangs, it described their organisational structures, profiled their members by age and marital status, and highlighted the difficulties encountered by the police in their attempts to suppress the violence. The Billy Boys and the Norman Conks were named as the most troublesome of the city's gangs, but the *Citizen* added a list of gangs from Bridgeton and the Calton, thus firmly identifying the East End as the heart of Glasgow's gangland.

The *Citizen*'s investigator had interviewed gang members as well as police officers before compiling his report. He found some of the gangs to be highly organised: 'They have captains and lieutenants and other officers, with rules and regulations for the conduct of their members and a complete system of signalling' – reinforcements were summoned by a 'particular kind of whistle'. The larger gangs had federal structures with subdivisions owing loyalty to the 'main body'. Most of their members, according to the *Citizen*'s inquiries, were aged between seventeen and twenty-one: it was hard to find a gangster aged above thirty, and some gangs routinely expelled those who married.

The *Citizen* identified the grounds for hostility between rival gangs as both 'party feeling' and quarrels between individuals. Full-scale 'battles' were often pre-arranged, with formal challenges issued: 'Just come up to such-and-such a street tomorrow night and see what you are worth.' However, as feuds escalated, it was common for individual gangsters to be ambushed by opposing factions with no regard for the customary notion of the 'square-go' (fair fight). Weapons were carried as a matter of routine. One youthful gangster, asked about the armouries deployed, replied simply: 'Nothing is barred.'

Police officers told the *Citizen*'s investigator that the gangs were not formed for 'criminal' purposes: their primary concerns were not theft from the person, or burglary, but reputation. Notoriety brought tangible rewards – not least the adulation of young women attracted by the excitement of gang life – and both individual and collective reputations were built through acts of desperate bravado. Very few gang fights resulted in criminal charges, however, often because the neighbourhoods colonised by the gangs were so terrorised that the police frequently found it impossible to persuade witnesses to testify against gang members in court. Officers interviewed by the *Citizen* were also adamant that heavier prison sentences ought to be augmented by flogging.

Those gang members who testified against their adversaries were frequently singled out for reprisal. On 21 September, William Carr and Samuel Marshall of the Norman Conks appeared at Glasgow Sheriff Court charged with assaulting Robert McLaggan Kelly. Two months previously, Kelly had appeared at the same court with his head swathed in bandages to testify against John Brogan and William Murray of the Conks following a fight at Bridgeton Cross. On that occasion, Kelly's skull had been fractured. He now described how, on the night of 26 August, he had been walking along Dalmarnock Road with two girls when he was 'rushed' by three men. He did not dare to fight back as he had been warned that another blow to his head would prove fatal. The girls tried to shield him, but he was punched to the ground and kicked.

Carr and Marshall told a very different story: they had been chased by a crowd fifty or sixty strong, and Kelly had been among their pursuers, yet Kelly insisted that he had left the Billy Boys on account of the injury he had suffered earlier in the year.

Having listened to the conflicting versions of events, Sheriff Macdiarmid asked: 'What is this that is happening in Bridgeton?'

The depute fiscal (public prosecutor) replied:

Bridgeton is simply seething with idle, unemployed young men, who band themselves together and attack each other by day and by night with hammers, hatchets, razors, batons of iron and wood, and, indeed, anything they can lay their hands on. The situation is serious indeed.

The sheriff accepted Kelly's story. Carr and Marshall were both jailed for three months.

Newspaper coverage of the gangs largely focused on the East

End – and Bridgeton, in particular – ov
months, and the Billy Boys and Norman
capture most of the headlines. One of the h
Boys, Billy Fullerton, was jailed in Octobe
Turnbull, one of Fullerton's closest associates, foll
prison the following month after he was convicted o
a member of the Conks on the head with a hatchet.

While Bridgeton was regarded as the epicentre of sectarian
conflict, reports began to emerge of skirmishes between rival
gangs across the city. Gangs named in trials at the various police
courts included the Kent Star from the Calton; the Dirty Dozen
from the Gorbals; and the Tripe Supper Boys from Govan. Two
Catholic gangs – the Romeo Boys from the Garngad and the
Kent Star – maintained long-running feuds with a gang of youths
from Townhead, variously referred to in court as the Lollipops
or the Lilypops (the latter name invoking one of the symbols
of the Orange Order). Sheriff Macdiarmid did not see the funny
side. 'It was like the Middle Ages,' he protested, jailing one of
the Romeos for six months in November 1926.

Editorial commentaries in the local press tended to be more
sanguine. The *Evening Citizen* was a staunch advocate of flogging for razor-slashers, but still recognised that the roots of the
gang problem lay in the conditions of life in Glasgow's slums.
'The gang spirit is universal among young men of all classes,'
it acknowledged in May 1927, going on to comment how, among
the rich, 'gangs' took the form of clubs, and the 'superfluous
energies' of youth had legitimate outlets on the rugby, cricket
or hockey fields. Among the poor, companionship was to be
found only on the streets, and gang fights were the inevitable
outlet for 'high spirits'. In these circumstances, the *Citizen*
concluded, gangs held an undeniable appeal: 'There is a spice
of danger, of adventure, and of romance in being a Billy Boy
and waging war upon some other society with an equally
romantic name.'

3
The Sad Tale of Jimmy Tait

The rising anxieties surrounding Glasgow's gangs gained both significant momentum and sharper definition in May 1928, following a fight between the Young Calton Entry and a junior section of the South Side Stickers (in Glaswegian patter, a 'sticker' was a game fighter). Both sets of youths were aged in their mid teens.

Members of the two gangs, and their female associates, had previously been on good terms: they went to the cinema together, frequenting both the Queen's in Watson Street close to Glasgow Cross – the regular haunt of the Calton boys – and the Paragon in the Gorbals. This latter cinema was one of Glasgow's least glamorous cinemas: housed in a converted Free Church building, its owners retained the pews, which they saturated with carbolic disinfectant on account of their patrons – 'a tough and dirty lot'. The gangs fell out after George Stokes of the Stickers struck Mary Dempsey from the Calton in the face with a handkerchief during a rowdy night in the Queen's. The altercation sparked a fight between the two groups, in which James McCluskey of the Stickers was wounded in the eye, and half-a-dozen clashes between the two gangs would take place over the following fortnight as the Stickers repeatedly crossed the River Clyde to confront the Calton lads in the Saltmarket.

'I've put that in one of them'

As the sudden enmity between the two gangs grew, the leader of the Young Calton Entry, Frank Kearney, challenged Joe Deehan of the Stickers to 'fight it out' on Glasgow Green. At around five o'clock on the afternoon of Sunday 6 May, Kearney asked a group of girls to go to the South Side to tell Deehan that he wanted to fight him that night. Kearney now proposed that the fight should take place on Albert Bridge – the principal crossing between the Calton and the Gorbals. The girls crossed over to the South Side, where they met Abraham Zemmil and James Walker of the Stickers in Rose Street. Zemmil told them that Deehan had not been seen that afternoon and that, in any event, Deehan was 'not fit' to fight Kearney. Zemmil told the girls to tell Kearney that nobody on the South Side wanted to fight him, adding if Kearney was determined to fight someone, then he – Zemmil – would take him on.

In the hours that followed, the fight was common talk around the street corners on both sides of the river. Zemmil arrived at Albert Bridge at around nine o'clock. He told Jessie Crawford and Martha Law to relay another message to Kearney. As Crawford later recounted:

> [Zemmil] again said that he did not want any fighting but told us to ask Kearney if he wanted a fight and if he did, then to say that Zemmil would fight him on the centre of the bridge single-handed. He said he wanted it to be a fair fight. The two gangs were to take up position at the opposite ends of the bridge and were not to interfere.

The two girls passed the message on to Kearney, who was waiting with members of his gang at the other side of the bridge. Kearney told them to tell Zemmil that it was Deehan he wanted to fight. The girls complied then, judging their work as emissaries done, went to join a group of their friends in Clyde Street on the north side of the river for a 'clabber-jigging' (open-air dance).

While Crawford and Law had been taking their messages back and forth across the bridge, Alex McCaughey, James McCluskey and David Vance of the Stickers had gone back to Rose Street to collect weapons. They had spotted their friend Andrew McCarthy at the corner of Rutherglen Road and McCaughey had told him: 'The Calton are over the other side of the bridge.' McCarthy accompanied them to McCaughey's house in Rose Street, and waited as he went up to his house. McCaughey came downstairs with a dagger and two swords. He gave one of the swords to McCarthy, keeping the other for himself, and gave the dagger to McCluskey. Thus armed, the four lads rushed to Albert Bridge to join the rest of the Stickers.

At around half past nine, between twenty and thirty of the Stickers crossed the bridge and entered Jail Square from the Saltmarket. Moments later, the Young Calton Entry filed into the square to meet them. In the shadow of the High Court, the two gangs stood about twenty yards apart, hurling bottles and stones and geeing themselves up with shouts of: 'Come on, the Stickers!' and: 'Come on, the Calton Entry!' Brandishing a sword above his head, Alex McCaughey of the Stickers shouted: 'Get Kearney!'

The Calton lads backed off at first, but then a group of them moved forward. Now the Stickers retreated: most scurried back across the bridge to the South Side, but ten stood their ground. These two smaller groups stood five or six yards apart, screaming at each other to: 'Come on!' The Stickers retreated onto the bridge, turning to make a stand half-way across.

Seventeen-year-old Jimmy Tait was standing watching the gangs square up from the corner of Clyde Street. Tait was not a fully fledged member of the Young Calton Entry, but his friend Jimmy Cunningham was – and the Stickers knew both lads by sight. James McCluskey of the Stickers slipped away from the mêlée as the two gangs spilled onto the bridge and, running up behind Tait, he plunged the dagger into his back. As Tait slumped to the ground, McCluskey shouted: 'I've got my revenge!' – he was still smarting from the eye-wound he had suffered in the fight in Queen's cinema two weeks earlier – and then ran onto the bridge. As he reached the Stickers, he waved the dagger in the air and boasted: 'I've put that in one of them!' The dagger was covered in blood.

As the Calton lads rushed to the stricken Tait, the remaining Stickers turned and fled.

Tait was carried first to the Central Police Office, then from there he was taken to the Royal Infirmary. Detective Lieutenant

John Montgomery took charge of the case. He visited Tait in the Infirmary at 11.15 p.m. Tait told him that he had been stabbed in the back by a man from the South Side, adding that his friend, James Cunningham, would be able to identify the perpetrator. Cunningham told Montgomery about the fight that had taken place between the South Side Stickers and the Young Calton Entry.

At quarter to one in the morning, Montgomery called at the house of James McCluskey in Cleland Street in the Gorbals. McCluskey was in bed. The detective questioned him and then charged him with assaulting James Tait by stabbing him in the back. McCluskey replied: 'I did it in self-defence.' McCluskey, who was aged sixteen, was taken to the Central Police Office, where he maintained: 'I had to do it. The crowd was round me and I had to stab into some of them. I got hit with a bottle on the shoulder.'

McCluskey named his companions as Alex McCaughey, Abraham Zemmil, Archie Gaughan and Pat Davitt. They were rounded up between two and three o'clock in the morning: when cautioned, they said nothing to incriminate McCluskey.

By four o'clock, James Walker and George Stokes had also been brought in. Walker claimed that he only learned of the incident after midnight, while Stokes was more forthcoming, telling detectives: 'I was standing in Rose Street with Zemmil. McCluskey came over and he was going over to get someone on the "sleekit" (sly). About half an hour later he came back and told me he had stabbed someone.'

The seven prisoners were taken to Tait's hospital bedside at noon. Tait identified McCluskey as the man who had stabbed him.

Jimmy Tait died at around 4.15 a.m. on the morning of Tuesday 8 May. The knife had punctured one of his lungs – post-mortem examination revealed that the wound had become septic, and death was attributed to the collapse of the lung, loss of blood and the onset of septic peritonitis. James McCluskey was charged with murder later that day, and the other prisoners were subsequently charged with acting in concert with him.

Zemmil, Gaughan and McCaughey all now confirmed Stokes's claim that McCluskey had boasted of carrying out the stabbing, McCaughey telling Detective Lieutenant Montgomery that he had thrown three weapons over a wall into a yard at 'Dixon's Blazes' – a vast ironworks whose open-topped furnaces lit up the night sky on the city's South Side. Montgomery took McCaughey to the yard, where two swords and a knife were retrieved. Dried blood was found on the knife.

The prisoners appeared at the Central Police Court on Wednesday 9 May. A large crowd gathered outside, but only police officials and reporters were admitted to hear the seven youths charged with murder. On Saturday 12 May, Patrick Davitt was liberated on the instruction of the procurator fiscal (public prosecutor). The remaining prisoners were again remanded.

The local press was quick to label Tait's death as a gangland killing: '**GANG-FIGHT TRAGEDY**' proclaimed the *Evening Times*'s front-page headline on 9 May. His death prompted a flurry of feature articles in the Scottish national press. On Saturday 12 May, the *Weekly Record* claimed to shed '**NEW LIGHT ON GLASGOW GANG FEUD**'. It announced that 'the gangster in Glasgow is a real menace' – so much so, that the city's police were frequently called out to investigate gang-related murders. Taking its cue from commentaries in the Glasgow press, the *Record* depicted the typical gangster as a razor-slasher: 'It is no uncommon thing to see a bunch of lads going about in the East-End looking for trouble with razors sticking out prominently from their breast pocket.' And while the gangs of the East End enjoyed the greatest notoriety, they held no monopoly on terror: 'Nearly all of the poorer class districts of the city have their gang, and in some cases there exist rival crowds who are contin-ually clashing and causing serious injury to one another.'

The *Record* depicted the clash between the Young Calton Entry and the South Side Stickers as the culmination of a month-long guerrilla war. In this account, the leaders of the two gangs had decided to settle their feud with a 'pitched battle'. The fight, it claimed, was to take place in the Saltmarket and sched-uled for a Sunday night since the thoroughfare would be clear of traffic. The 'sheer impudence' of the plan, commented the *Record*, 'makes one gasp with amazement'. The gangs assembled in opposing groups of fifty, armed with knives, razors, hatchets and hammers. Yet when they confronted each other in Jail Square, a sudden 'council of war' among the 'chiefs' led many of those present to decide not to fight. Some, however, were less easily assuaged:

> The hot-heads among them would not listen to anything that suggested peace, and without any more ado they go to grips. Tait, it is alleged, was in the vanguard of his mob, and almost at the outset he was felled with a knife-wound in the back.

The severity of the injury to Tait brought the fight to an abrupt halt. According to the *Record*, this alone prevented carnage: 'but for the fall of Tait, there would have been many serious casualties among the contestants.'

This detailed sketch of the fight was misleading in many of its key aspects – the degree of planning, the array of weapons and the gangs' intent to use them were all grossly exaggerated, as was Tait's part in the fighting – but no doubt made sense to readers primed over the preceding two years by stories of violent and highly organised gang 'wars'.

A very different portrait of Jimmy Tait emerged on the same day in *Thomson's Weekly News*. It was based on an interview with Tait's stepfather, William Thompson, who was interviewed at the family's home in Charlotte Street in the Calton within hours of Jimmy's death. Mr Thompson told how he heard of the fight when a boy ran up to him in the street, saying: 'Jimmy's dead, better get to the Central (Police Office).' He had arrived at the police office to discover that Jimmy was still alive, although his condition was critical. He accompanied his stepson to the Royal Infirmary, where he maintained a thirty-hour vigil at Jimmy's bedside. Jimmy refused to explain how he came to be stabbed. Mr Thompson told the reporter:

> How he came to meet his death in such a way I cannot understand. He was always very quiet and reserved. He did not keep

late hours, and he was usually in the house at the back of ten o'clock, or by eleven at the latest, if he happened to be going to the pictures.

This portrait of a quiet seventeen year old, unemployed for two years, was utterly at odds with the *Weekly Record*'s account of Tait as a gang leader 'in the vanguard of his mob' when he was wounded.

An eyewitness to the mêlée in Jail Square told the *Weekly News* that the fight between the Young Calton Entry and the South Side Stickers looked more like a skirmish between boys than a gang battle: 'Some of the lads who were struggling together were mere youngsters in short trousers. Thinking it was just an ordinary street scrap I walked on, but when I turned round I saw Tait falling to the ground.'

Had it not been for James McCluskey's determination to 'get someone on the sleekit', the incident would have been altogether unremarkable.

The Trial of the Sticker Boys

James McCluskey, Abraham Zemmil, Alex McCaughey, Archie Gaughan, James Walker and George Stokes stood trial before Lord Hunter at the High Court in Glasgow on 28 June. The trial attracted huge interest: the public benches were crowded – 'principally with youths and young girls' noted the *Evening Times*. The six youths were charged with murder and riot. McCluskey pleaded self-defence, while Walker put forward an alibi. The four remaining prisoners pleaded not guilty.

At the outset of the trial, Sheriff Macdiarmid read a deposition that he had taken from Jimmy Tait in the Royal Infirmary. It began:

> I am James Tait, 30 Charlotte Street, Glasgow. I am seventeen. I got stabbed . . . A chap Tuskey stabbed me. I don't know his real name. James Cunningham was with me. Stokes and Flynn were also in the mob. We did not attack them in any way. The gang that attacked us are the Sticker boys.

Tait's companion, James Cunningham, gave a vivid account of how he watched the two gangs fight their way from Jail Square onto the bridge. Cunningham, aged fifteen, admitted that he belonged to the Young Calton Entry, but insisted that Tait had not been a member of the gang. Cunningham claimed that, like Tait, he had only watched the clash between the two gangs on the night of 6 May. Asked who won the fight, he replied: 'Nobody won.' He was adamant, however, that it was McCluskey who stabbed Tait in the back.

A second member of the Young Calton Entry, fifteen-year-old Joe Adams, followed Cunningham into the witness box. Adams denied that he was associated with either of the gangs that had fought on the bridge, but his testimony implied that he recognised the opposing factions: 'the Calton Boys seemed to get the best of it'. Asked about his relationship with the deceased, Adams replied that he knew Tait by sight, 'but did not know whether he was a gangster or not'. Adams confirmed that the fight had been watched by a sizeable group of girls, a 'good many' of whom, he assented under cross-examination, followed the gangs and sometimes 'incited' them.

Two more members of the Young Calton Entry testified on the first day of the trial – their accounts were wildly contradictory. Seventeen-year-old James Burns told the court that he had brandished a bottle and a sword during the fight, and he admitted to having struck McCluskey with a bottle, but denied that it was full of paraffin. 'He did not,' he insisted, 'threaten to throw paraffin over anyone and set them alight.' Like James Cunningham, Burns was quite clear about who had inflicted the fatal blow: 'McCluskey stuck a knife in the back of Tait, who was standing quite harmless.' Frank Kearney, an unemployed labourer aged sixteen, gave a wholly different version of events. Kearney admitted that he belonged to the Young Calton Entry, but denied that he was the gang's leader. He told the court that he was fighting alongside Jimmy Tait when the fatal blow was struck. They had both lunged at McCluskey – Kearney with a sword, Tait with a razor – and McCluskey 'just saved himself'. Kearney claimed that he threw Tait's razor into the River Clyde before the injured youth was taken to the police office.

McCluskey's plea of self-defence was severely undermined when one of his fellow Stickers, Andrew McCarthy, appeared as a witness for the prosecution. McCarthy testified that McCluskey had run to the other Stickers gathered on the bridge, waving a blood-soaked dagger, before issuing his chilling boast: 'I've put that into one of them.'

McCarthy's breach of the Stickers' code of non-cooperation with the police and courts would be long remembered.

Police and medical witnesses were called on the second day of the trial. A constable explained that gang fights were usually timed to coincide with the change of police shifts: 'The shifts change at ten o'clock, and it is generally 10.20 or 10.30 before the constables reach Clyde Street as they have to "try" the beat [check locked premises] on the way down.' This gave the gangs the opportunity to fight without interference within 400 yards of the Central Police Office. Medical testimony was provided by Professor John Glaister, who confirmed that Tait's right lung had been punctured by a sharp, pointed instrument, used with 'considerable force'. Detective Lieutenant John Montgomery then detailed the statements made by the prisoners when Tait succumbed to his injury. The statements by Zemmil and Gaughan were especially damning: both told how McCluskey had boasted of carrying out the stabbing.

At this point in the trial, McCluskey's counsel asked for the court to be adjourned so that he and his colleagues might consider their position. When the proceedings resumed fifteen minutes later, fresh pleas were intimated: guilty of mobbing and rioting, and guilty of culpable homicide, on behalf of McCluskey; guilty of mobbing and rioting only on behalf of Zemmil, McCaughey, Gaughan and Stokes; not guilty on behalf of Walker. The jury returned formal verdicts in accordance with the revised pleas.

Addressing Lord Hunter, the Advocate Depute (senior public prosecutor) explained that he had reluctantly accepted the revised pleas on account of the prisoners' ages – as 'young boys' they were unlikely to suffer the death penalty even if a conviction for murder was secured. McCluskey's counsel, James Keith KC, likewise stressed the prisoners' childlike naivety: 'It was very much a case of misdirected energy, and children playing with weapons, and not realising the dangers of those and the risk they were running. There was never intention to kill.'

In his closing statement, Mr J. B. Paton KC, counsel for McCluskey, invoked a curious mixture of the exotic and the mundane. He claimed that his client had been:

> led astray by the example of older boys and by frequenting picture houses, where he saw lurid dramas and examples of violence which he could not understand could not be repeated in the city streets. These boys were brought up where the streets were their playground, where they settled their disputes with their fists. In many of these cases, the police left them to fight out matters themselves.

By Paton's account Hollywood had lent a dangerously unreal quality to the customary willingness among working-class boys to resolve their disputes by fighting.

Lord Hunter sentenced James McCluskey to five years' penal servitude, commenting that only the prisoner's age – sixteen – had spared him a longer sentence. Alex McCaughey, who had supplied the fatal weapon, was jailed for eighteen months. Archie Gaughan and George Stokes were jailed for twelve months, while fifteen-year-old Abraham Zemmil was sentenced to a year's detention. James Walker was discharged. The judge declared that the sentences were 'a warning to all the gangsters in Glasgow'.

The Stickers presented a sorry sight as the sentences were pronounced: 'All the accused sobbed bitterly,' noted the court reporter for the *Glasgow Herald*, 'and many people in the public benches were visibly affected.'

The conclusion of the trial prompted a fresh round of feature articles in the Scottish national press; in fact, reports on the killing of Jimmy Tait were to provide a template for subsequent press coverage of Glasgow's 'gang warfare': the vital elements in the clash between the Calton boys and the Stickers – territorial rivalry, the resort to lethal weapons and the role of girls and young women in 'inciting' the conflicts – would all surface repeatedly in reports of the 'gang menace' in the years that followed.

A 'special investigator' employed by the *Sunday Mail* latched on to the allegations at the High Court that girls incited feuds between rival gangs. His exposé of the '**GIRLS BEHIND GANG MENACE**' was prefaced by a historical account of the Glasgow gangs, in which the (unnamed) former 'Queen of the Redskins' loomed large. His report traced the resurgence of the city's gangs to 1925 – the year that John Keen was hanged for the murder of Noor Mohammed – before divulging the 'almost incredible' state of affairs in the city at present:

> I discovered young men and women who never venture into the street unless they are armed with some sort of instruments, a knife, a razor, or a revolver, and others who live in almost daily dread of being attacked and left in a quiet lane bleeding or dying.
>
> In different districts of Glasgow, particularly in the east end, there are in existence a number of gangs of young men who exist for no other purpose than to cause or make trouble.
>
> They are, for the most part, composed of youths who have never done a day's work and whose present intentions are that they will never bend their shoulders in labour.

Here the *Mail* grotesquely exaggerated the level of lethal violence in Glasgow's gang conflicts, while simultaneously reversing the claim – consistently advanced by more liberal commentators in Glasgow's local newspapers – that unemployment was one of the principal causes of gang formation.

The investigator's most lurid prose was reserved not for the 'city gangster' however, but for his female followers: 'Each gang has its entourage of young women and girls, who would appear to be the devoted slaves of rowdy.' They were not without feminine charm, he conceded. Quite the reverse – if 'properly groomed', the prettier among them 'would in appearance challenge comparison with any of their sex in higher walks of

Society.' They had apparently rejected all parental constraint, and their fathers – fearful of the gangsters' retribution – did not dare to object.

The girls themselves were delighted to be the cause of a battle:

> It is quite a common thing for one of these girls to give her affections to the man who possesses the most strength and can wield the quickest razor. There are many instances where a girl has actually promised herself to the youth who can come triumphant out of a fight with a rival.

No examples were provided in the *Mail*'s report, although its investigator speculated that the fight that led to the death of Jimmy Tait 'may well have been' planned at the instigation of the watching girls.

The *Mail*'s investigation was laced with a warning to prospective molls. Gangsters did not abide by a moral code:

> They do not marry. The girl goes on her unthinking way until a baby is born. Sometimes she is fortunate to find that the father of the child has a sense of responsibility, but more often she discovers herself a laughing-stock.

The *Mail*'s investigation was a triumph of sensationalism – its portrait of the gangster as sexual predator was hard to square with the figures of the South Side Stickers sobbing in the dock at the High Court two days earlier.

Ordinary Lives

Background reports on the six prisoners had been prepared by Robert Walkinshaw, the governor of Duke Street Prison. Walkinshaw had interviewed each of the prisoners in person, and augmented his own observations with information on their family circumstances, which had been gathered by officers from the Southern Division of the City of Glasgow Police.

The reports showed the youths to be remarkably ordinary. They came from impoverished and, in most cases, overcrowded, homes, but in each case police inquiries showed their families to be ordinary, too: none of the prisoners was immersed in a life of crime. They were not 'of criminal habits or tendencies' Walkinshaw dutifully noted in five of the six cases, in terms laid down under the 1908 Prevention of Crime Act.

Four of the six were Catholics; McCaughey was a Protestant and Zemmil was Jewish. Stokes and Walker were unemployed at the time of their arrest, while the others were in work, albeit low status and poorly paid. Nothing in Walkinshaw's reports suggested that the prisoners' previous conduct marked them out from many other youths growing up around Rose Street in the Gorbals.

James McCluskey was one of seven children. His mother died when he was five years old, and at the time of his arrest following the stabbing of Jimmy Tait he was living with his father, two brothers and four sisters in a three-roomed tenement house in Cleland Street. His father, Michael McCluskey, an iron moulder, was unemployed and in receipt of poor relief. One of his sisters stayed at home to 'look after the house'. James had left school at fourteen, although he still attended the Boys' Guild at St Luke's in the Gorbals. At the age of sixteen, he was earning just 12 shillings a week as a messenger boy. He had four previous convictions: three for playing football in the street and one for gambling. He told the governor that he attended chapel every week with his brothers and sisters, but admitted that he was a member of 'the Stickers' – by his own account, he spent most of his spare time with them. Police inquiries revealed nothing detrimental to the 'moral character and integrity' of his relatives, but confirmed that 'the character of his associates is bad'.

The police officer composing this report had probably had George Stokes in mind when he described McCluskey's associates. Stokes's father was in 'fairly regular' employment as a roofer, yet the family lived in a single-roomed house in Crown Street, which suggests that his father spent a substantial portion of his wages on himself. Nonetheless, so far as the police could ascertain, the family was 'respectable'. George's mother died in February 1928 – two months before his fateful altercation with

Mary Dempsey. George's own employment history was patchy. After leaving school at fourteen he worked for six months as a messenger boy. He then secured a better-paid job as a rivet-heater, which he held for eleven months before he was dismissed for 'inattention to duty'. He subsequently worked as a plumber's boy for eight weeks, but had been unemployed for four months prior to the clash between the Stickers and the Young Calton Entry on Albert Bridge.

Stokes's criminal record was more chequered than McCluskey's. He had appeared at Glasgow Sheriff Court twice at the age of thirteen on charges of housebreaking; on the second occasion, he was sentenced to six stripes with the birch rod. Two years later, in April 1926, he was again convicted of theft by housebreaking and was placed on probation for twelve months. No further property offences were recorded against him, and Walkinshaw concluded that Stokes was 'not of criminal habits or tendencies'. However, neither the rod nor penal supervision had cowed him, and he was fined 20 shillings for breach of the peace by cursing, swearing, shouting and throwing stones in October 1927. Stokes told the governor that he spent his spare time 'in billiard rooms, cinemas, and playing football'. He denied that he was a member of the Stickers, but admitted that he had occasionally been 'in their company'.

Like James McCluskey, Archie Gaughan admitted to Walkinshaw that he spent most of his spare time with the Stickers. Gaughan lived with his parents in a room-and-kitchen house in South Shamrock Street. His father, who was unemployed, kept the house while his mother worked as a hawker (street seller) – one of the most common sidelines among the Glasgow poor. Gaughan had also left school at fourteen. He earned 13 shillings a week and had three previous convictions: for playing cards in the street, playing football and breaching the peace. He, too, claimed to be a regular at chapel, while police inquiries suggested that: 'His parents appear to be respectable people.'

James Walker, like George Stokes, had enjoyed spells of relatively well-paid work: a year as a rivet-heater on 21 shillings a week after leaving school at fourteen, followed by eight weeks as a plumber's helper at John Brown's shipyard at Clydebank on 15 shillings a week. However, he had been unemployed for four weeks at the time he was taken into custody on suspicion of involvement in Tait's murder. Walker was one of nine children. His father was also unemployed, although James confided in the governor that his parents 'occasionally went out hawking'. Police nonetheless described his parents as 'respectable, working-class people', with whom James claimed to attend chapel every Sunday. He had just two convictions: for playing football and loitering in the street. He denied that he was a member of the Stickers, but admitted to Walkinshaw that he 'occasionally went to the pictures with one or two boys who were members of the gang'. By his own account, James spent more time at the Boys' Guild at St Luke's, where he was a member of the football team.

Alexander McCaughey was the sole Protestant among the prisoners. He made much of his religion in conversations with the governor, who noted: 'He stoutly denied being a member of a gang known as "The Stickers". He pointed out that all the members of the gang are Roman Catholics while he was a Protestant.' The confusion was understandable, McCaughey explained, since he both lived and worked close to the Stickers' adopted corner of Rose Street. Alex McCaughey was one of nine children. His father, an unemployed wireworker, was 'on the parish' (in receipt of poor relief), but his family – like those of Stokes, Gaughan and Walker – was deemed 'respectable' by the police. Alex had begun an apprenticeship in his father's trade upon leaving school, but had been laid off after fourteen months owing to bad trade. At the time of his arrest in May 1928, he had been employed as an apprentice baker on a wage of 10 shillings a week. He had two convictions for loitering, but had also been admonished at Glasgow Sheriff Court on two occasions after appearing on charges of housebreaking. He told the governor that prior to leaving school at fourteen, he had been a member of the Boys' Brigade and had attended the bible class at the United Free Church in Rose Street.

The only prisoner to trouble the governor was Abraham Zemmil, and it is hard to avoid the suspicion that anti-Semitism tainted Walkinshaw's otherwise liberal outlook. Zemmil's parents were Russian Jews, who had settled in Glasgow around the time Abraham was born in August 1912. They had four children. Police spoke highly of Zemmil's parents, noting that his father – sporadically employed as a capmaker – had been wounded while serving with British forces during the Great War. They were less enamoured of Abraham: 'He associated with irresponsible youths who were members of a gang and he was apparently one of the most aggressive of its numbers.' Zemmil had been apprenticed to a tailor for four months at the age of fourteen, but was working as a messenger boy at the time of his arrest. He had just started a new job on a wage of 10 shillings a week. Zemmil's criminal record was more extensive than those of the other prisoners, but was largely comprised of petty convictions. At the age of twelve, he had been convicted of theft and placed on probation for twelve months. He had eleven subsequent convictions: four for playing football in the street, three for breaching the peace, two for loitering in the street and one apiece for gambling and using obscene language. The frequency of his appearances at the Southern Police Court – ten in nine months, prior to his arrest following the death of James Tait – suggests that beat constables had singled him out for attention.

The governor read a great deal into Zemmil's repeated offending: it showed, Walkinshaw insisted, that the prisoner had no respect for the law. Most youths learned from their first minor conviction, but in Zemmil's case: 'Defiance and indifference have taken the place of fear'. No such inference was drawn from the repeated convictions recorded against Zemmil's associates. Walkinshaw was particularly offended by Zemmil's demeanour after his conviction for mobbing and rioting at the High Court: 'He is the only one of the gang who has, since conviction, shown little or no contrition.' The governor's portrait of both Zemmil and his parents was damning:

> He is in my view deceitful and cunning with no great desire to
> do good if by doing evil he can escape its consequences. His

parents are given a good character by the Police but apparently they are not free from moral guilt and their son's previous history does not speak highly of their control and discipline.

Walkinshaw was drawing here on a powerful anti-Semitic stereotype. As George Orwell observed, Jews were widely viewed in Britain as being 'superior in intelligence, [but] slightly deficient in "character".'

'You want to say something like that'

In the wake of the trial of the South Side Stickers from 27–28 June, Frank Kearney – known to the police as the leader of the Young Calton Entry – was charged with perjury and attempting to suborn two witnesses: Joe Adams and Hugh Martin.

Kearney, who had testified at the High Court that Jimmy Tait had attacked James McCluskey of the Stickers with a razor, stood trial at the High Court in Glasgow on 27 August. Adams, who also belonged to the Young Calton Entry, testified that Kearney had approached him in the witness room at the High Court during the trial of Jimmy Tait's assailants. According to Adams: 'Kearney said that he was going to try to help some of the "boys", and intended to say that Tait had a razor and was fighting about the middle of the bridge.' Kearney had advised Adams to follow suit: 'You want to say something like that and help the boys.' Adams, however, had reported the conversation to a detective.

Kearney's motivation in seeking to shield the Stickers in court is not difficult to discern. Glasgow's underworld was notoriously difficult for the police to penetrate – in British criminal circles, it was said to be the one city where the axiom of 'honour amongst thieves' largely prevailed. As an aspiring gangster and 'fighting man', Kearney appears to have subscribed to a parallel code whereby, whatever their differences on the streets, the Stickers and the Young Calton Entry were all 'boys' together once they reached the High Court.

Kearney's fellow gangsters, however, breached this code all too readily: no fewer than four of the Stickers had confirmed to detectives that their fellow gang-member, James McCluskey, had boasted of stabbing Jimmy Tait; and now Joe Adams testified to Kearney's machinations in the witness room.

Kearney's attempt to thwart the prosecution of Jimmy Tait's killers had been carefully crafted, not least in drawing on the powerful symbolism attached to the razor – by then widely recognised as the weapon of choice among Glasgow's more hardened gangsters. However, it was far from compelling: too many of his companions had been willing to testify that Tait had taken no active part in the fight on Albert Bridge. The Advocate Depute was sufficiently irked by Kearney's testimony to instigate criminal proceedings, and the jury at the High Court on 28 August found Kearney guilty of perjury. Jailing him for twelve months, Lord Fleming declared: 'It was essential that any interference with the course of justice should be suppressed.'

Reports on the killing of Jimmy Tait provided a template for subsequent press coverage of Glasgow's 'gang warfare'. The vital elements in the clash between the Calton boys and the Stickers – territorial rivalry, the resort to lethal weapons and the role of girls and young women in 'inciting' the conflicts – all surfaced repeatedly in reports of the 'gang menace' in the years that followed.

Part II

The 'Scottish Chicago'
1929–1932

4

The Drygate Tragedy

In the eighteen months that followed the trial of the South Side Stickers at the High Court in June 1928, police officers and journalists discovered a host of street gangs in Glasgow's poorer districts. From the Gorbals to the Garngad, and from Bridgeton to Anderston and Govan, large swathes of the city appeared to have been divided into a patchwork of gang territories. More than a dozen gangs vied for supremacy on the South Side alone. In the Gorbals, feuds raged between the Stickers, the Liberty Boys, the Beehive Boys, the Coburg Erin, the Kidston Street Bruisers, the Naburn Street Billy Boys, the Lime Street Lads and the Nudie Boys. In the adjacent district of Plantation, the Diehards from Blackburn Street held sway. Govan, like the Gorbals, was riddled with gangs: the Peril Boys, the Death Valley Gang, the Dempsey Boys, the Breezy Boys, the Oyster Gang, the Tripe Supper Boys and the Cauliflower Gang. (If their names are any guide, some of Govan's gangsters appear to have taken themselves less seriously than their rivals elsewhere in the city.)

The Brigton Billy Boys were still widely recognised as the largest and most powerful gang in Glasgow, and Protestant youths across the city allied themselves with the Billies in the hope of trading on the fear engendered by the Bridgeton gangsters. In return, the Billy Boys periodically intervened in local disputes in other districts. In June 1928, around 500 of them marched from the East End to the dockland district of Anderston on the western fringe of the city centre to avenge the near-fatal stabbing of a member of the Gray Street Gang by one of the Milligan Boys.

Within the East End, gang conflicts continued to be pursued

with greater ferocity than elsewhere in the city – fights in Bridgeton and the Calton tended to be on a larger scale, and severe injuries were more commonly inflicted – and they were more clearly laced with sectarianism than elsewhere in Glasgow. In a tradition established fifty years earlier, religious hostilities were renewed each summer during the parading season. The most spectacular outbreaks of violence took place on the day of the annual Orange Walk, when the Billy Boys escorted the Bridgeton processionists home through 'Catholic' districts in the Calton – gangs routinely accompanied the parades, ostensibly to protect the marchers. Hostile crowds gathered at strategic points on principal thoroughfares, such as the Gallowgate, and violence was easily sparked by the waving of orange or green colours, or by the shouting of party cries and threats.

The Billy Boys' vehement anti-Catholicism was paralleled by anti-Irish agitation by outspoken figures in the Church of Scotland. In July 1928, a deputation of Protestant clergymen met the Home Secretary, Sir William Joynson-Hicks, to plead for restrictions on future Irish settlement in Scotland. Statistical returns from Glasgow formed the heart of the minsters' case: the Irish were disproportionately represented, they claimed, both among the offenders brought before the city's police courts and among the recipients of 'relief funds of all kinds'. (The terms 'Irish' and 'Catholic' were so frequently used as though they were interchangeable during the 1920s and 1930s that the presence of a significant community of Ulster Protestants and their descendants in Scotland, not least in Glasgow, tended to be obscured.)

In the wake of the St Valentine's Day Massacre of 1929, in which seven Chicago racketeers were shot and killed at the behest of Al Capone, Glasgow youths became keenly aware that the connotations of the term 'gangster' had begun to count heavily against them in court. (The atrocity had been widely reported in the British as well as American press.) Edward Glancey of the Romeo Boys appeared before Bailie Brown at St Rollox Police Court in April 1929, charged with assaulting Tommy Goodfellow in a tenement close in Parliamentary Road.

Glancey, aged twenty-one, was jailed for sixty days. The next defendant in the same case was eighteen-year-old John McGrory. According to a police witness, McGrory had kicked Goodfellow in the back. McGrory was fined £3. He protested that he had been had unfairly demonised by the acting fiscal. 'I am not a gangster,' McGrory insisted. 'I have never been convicted of being a gangster, and I object to being called one.' Of course, being a gangster was not in itself an offence, but McGrory's phrasing is revealing nonetheless: police superintendents knew from experience that characterising slum youths as gangsters prompted magistrates to impose harsher sentences.

In an editorial on 'The Gangster' published the following day, the *Glasgow Herald* warned that 'high-pitched' newspaper reports and police attention both served to inflame the hostilities: 'Take away the "glory" and your gangster is a poor creature.' The newspaper claimed that the 'gangster' was a product not of the modern industrial age, but of timeless boyish instinct: 'He is as old as the hills, as old, at all events, as the time when boys first got together in droves with limited resources for exercise and the free-play of their fighting spirit.' Echoing the *Evening Citizen*'s commentary on the gangs two years previously, the *Herald* observed that among boys of the higher social classes, that spirit was 'sublimated' on the playing field: better sports facilities for the children of the slums would solve the problem of 'fighting youth running to vicious seed'. The experience of one of the major English conurbations bears out the *Herald*'s concern: in Manchester and Salford, an epidemic of gang fighting had subsided during the late 1890s due in no small part to the effort of the lads' club movement to promote sport in the districts colonised by the gangs.

The *Herald*'s plea for more restrained coverage of the gangs in the Glasgow press would go unheeded. The following month, the *Evening News* ran a feature article on the city's gangsters and their 'bid to rival Chicago'. Its most startling revelation was that gangs – like professional football clubs – were willing to sell their star performers:

A system of transfers (similar to that which obtains in the football world) is in operation, and when two rival gangs are about to stage a battle, good fighters are transferred from one gang to another. Heavy fees are reported to be paid, and as much as £20 has been paid for a single 'transfer'.

According to the police, the transfer system operated on the South Side, where gangs sold members for profit, while individuals themselves might seek a transfer to obtain a higher rank in a new gang. The system had originally been highlighted by Superintendent Cameron at the Southern Police Court, following a clash between the Liberty Boys and the Nudie Boys, although neither the superintendent nor the *Evening News* appears to have considered the possibility that the transfer system was a hoax. Superintendent Cameron further complained that fights had taken place in the Gorbals 'every Sunday night for the past six months'. The police found it almost impossible to make arrests since the gangs posted lookouts at strategic corners: as soon as the police approached, warnings were given and the fighters dispersed.

Picture Houses and Palais de Danse

By 1930, Glasgow boasted more than 120 cinemas. Most were located in the city's tenement districts, and popular 'picture houses' – such as the 2,000-seater Olympia at Bridgeton Cross – brought Hollywood glamour to the East End and South Side.

Working-class youths, especially, were avid film-goers. The appeal of the cinema for those without work was easily explained: it was 'something to get your mind off things' and offered at least vicarious romance and adventure. Films and film-stars were staple topics of conversation in the home, in the workplace, in the queue at the employment exchange and on the street corner. As social investigator, Charles Cameron, observed:

> Cinema topics are news. It appears just as necessary for many of these young people to be able to discuss the latest film as it is for other people to be able to talk about the best seller in literature.

Audiences were socially segregated, even within districts such as Bridgeton: many of the unemployed took advantage of reduced prices for matinées, while those in work attended the more popular Friday and Saturday night screenings.

If the cinema was one of the symbols of the new, modern age, another was the *palais de danse*, and Glasgow had its share of the ritzy dance halls that sprung up across urban Britain to cater for the dance craze of the 1920s. The Plaza, which opened at Eglinton Toll on the South Side in 1922, had a capacity of 2,000, a coloured lighting system and a fountain in the middle of the dance floor. By the early 1930s, young Glaswegians were said to display a passion for dancing unmatched anywhere else in Britain. Cameron noted that: 'Many young men pass through a phase which has often been described by their parents and friends, and sometimes even by themselves, as "dancing mad".' The young men to whom he spoke were both enthusiastic and knowledgeable, gleaning their knowledge of dance bands and their leaders from radio broadcasts, and trawling commercial stations in search of 'rhythm' and 'swing'.

Cameron also observed that many unemployed youths were too poor to frequent licensed dance halls; even if they could afford the cost of admission, they often lacked the smart, fashionable clothes considered essential for 'the jigging'. Back-street entrepreneurs provided alternative venues that flourished alongside the *palais de danse*, prompting a rash of investigations by the local press from the late 1920s. In the spring of 1930, the *Weekly Record* reported that some of the 'halls' turned out to be cellars or room-and-kitchen tenement houses, where as many as fifty couples gathered to dance by gas-light to records played on gramophones. Entry was cheap ('Gentlemen, threepence; Ladies, twopence!') and lookouts were employed to guard against police raids – many of these unlicensed venues also functioned as shebeens, selling whisky and cheap red wine. The *Record* was appalled to discover girls of sixteen and seventeen 'under the influence of liquor', but acknowledged nonetheless that these 'underground dance halls' provided an important service: 'The youths who go to these places are, as may be guessed, of the poorest class, and in these cheap haunts they find a measure of pleasure that is denied them by the higher prices of respectable dance halls.'

Gang members were determined to take their place in the glamorous new world of leisure. They frequently adopted local dance halls as their headquarters on weekend evenings, often entering 'at the demand' (without paying). The arrival of members of a rival gang – or any party of unknown youths from another neighbourhood – was regarded as an affront. Stories told at the city's police courts attested to both the regularity and ferocity of the fights that ensued: Billy Smith, aged seventeen, was slashed with a razor during a clash between the Botany Boys from Maryhill and 'a crowd from Anderston', while the Romeo Boys from the Garngad were attacked with iron bars when they ventured into a dance hall in Springburn. Territorial rivalries were easily inflamed by sexual jealousy – and both were fuelled by alcohol. In October 1929, Jimmy Kane was charged with assaulting Jimmy Muir during a dance at the Lorne Hall in Govan. Muir told the Govan Police Court that the fight started when the two of them tried to 'lift' the same girl. (Bailie Snodgrass interjected: 'Had she fallen?' 'He means ask her for a dance,' the fiscal explained.) In his defence, Kane told the court: 'Muir said I was just a "big nothing". I said: "Oh, you think you are a fly man!" Then the fight started and I got the first blow.' Kane alleged that Muir was one of the Tripe Supper Boys from Hamilton Street, and that other members of the gang were present at the dance, including the notorious 'Slasher' McGee. Bailie Snodgrass fined Kane £1.

For members of Glasgow's dance bands, outbreaks of violence were an occupational hazard. George Chisholm played in jazz orchestras in a number of the city's dance halls after leaving school in 1929, and one of his first regular engagements was at the Tower Palais in the Cowcaddens on the northern edge of the city centre. Once a notorious slum, the Cowcaddens was generally regarded as a 'quiet' district by the 1930s, yet the Tower was an 'evil place' in Chisholm's recollection:

Every Friday night with sickening regularity, the lights would go out and all hell would be let loose. When the lights came on again, there'd be bodies lying everywhere . . . Once the hooligan element had exhausted themselves and each other, they'd be ejected down some stone steps and a little, self-appointed MC in a muffler and cap would come on and say 'Carry on dancing, please' in a brisk and jovial way that'd almost have you believing you'd dreamt the carnage of a few seconds before.

The licensee of the Tower Palais hired doormen and kept an armoury of wooden clubs to deal with troublemakers, with the tacit approval of the superintendent of the Northern Division. Nor did the Tower's reputation deter dancers from other parts of the city – far from it. Ellen McAllister, who lived in the Gorbals, recalled that she made occasional trips to the Tower during the late 1920s and early 1930s 'for the excitement'.

In common with the wider, youthful populations of Glasgow's poorer districts, many younger gang members were avid film-goers, but they frequently lacked the means to pay for admission. Five youths were fined for breaching the peace after a gang forced their way into the Partick Picture House in February 1929. In court, two of them explained their conduct on the grounds that they were unemployed. Bailie McLellan was unsympathetic: he imposed fines of £5 each with no time to pay and the option of thirty days' jail. 'The whole city of Glasgow seemed to be a crowd of young men trying to stop [other] people going into picture houses,' the magistrate complained. The *Eastern Standard* concurred: the 'gate-crashing' of cinemas had become increasingly widespread, it noted in a report on the conviction of two Bridgeton youths for assaulting the assistant manager of a cinema in the Calton after he attempted to deny them entry. As Superintendent McPherson told the Eastern Police Court: 'The youths were evidently under the impression that they could go into the picture house without paying, at any time.'

The attendance of large numbers of gang members – many of whom routinely carried weapons – ensured that outbreaks of violence at cinemas were commonplace; fights between members of rival gangs erupted in queues for admission, during screenings, or as programmes ended and audiences spilled out into the surrounding streets. Gangs known to frequent a particular cinema were vulnerable to ambushes, or to more direct challenges when rival gangsters turned up in force and interrupted a film. Sudden outbreaks of fighting in darkened auditoriums brought the risk of crushes as terrified non-combatants scrambled for the exits: Lieutenant McDade of the Eastern Division warned of the potentially 'appalling' consequences following a spate of disturbances inside cinemas in Bridgeton during the summer of 1929. Cinema managers instructed their staff to refuse entry to known troublemakers, but retribution frequently resulted. Two weeks after Lieutenant McDade's warning, the manager and attendants at the Picturedrome in Govan were showered with bottles after they refused entry to a crowd of 'rowdies'.

In the wake of a barrage of complaints, Glasgow's magistrates met on 27 August to debate whether police ought to be deployed at picture houses to maintain order. The option was dismissed on the grounds that the preservation of order within places of entertainment was a matter for the proprietors of the premises concerned. Two months later, Superintendent Cameron of the Southern Division alleged that gangs from the Gorbals had targeted the Oatlands Picturedrome. In consequence, 'it was impossible to enjoy the programme after the hour of 8.30, as at that time gangs were in the habit of entering and deliberately causing fights.' Similar tales were heard in police courts across the city. Disturbances were so frequent at the Govan Picturedrome by February 1930 that business was 'ruined', according to the manager. Local gangs, including the Breezy Boys, the Tripe Supper Boys and the Dempsey Boys, had clashed repeatedly both inside the cinema and in the streets outside.

Encounters at picture houses provided opportunities to settle individual as well as collective grievances. In December 1929, George Stokes and Abraham Zemmil of the South Side Stickers appeared at Glasgow Sheriff Court following a 'free fight' in a South Side cinema – only seventeen months earlier, the two youths had stood trial at the High Court charged with the murder of Jimmy Tait. Zemmil was now aged seventeen, Stokes nineteen. They were joined in the dock at the sheriff court by eighteen-year-old Joseph Lucas. Zemmil – born in Glasgow to Russian parents – was identified in court as a 'Pole', Lucas as a Lithuanian. The procurator fiscal alleged that 'it was the habit of members of this gang to visit picture houses in bands and cause trouble under cover of darkness.' On this occasion, they spotted a youth named Solomon in the audience. Solomon had previously got the better of Lucas in a fight, and Stokes and Zemmil encouraged Lucas to take his revenge. All three prisoners confronted Solomon: Stokes drew a razor and slashed him on the face, inflicting a three-inch wound from Solomon's left ear to his neck. In the ruckus that followed, Lucas was stabbed in the neck by an 'unknown assailant' – he was lucky to escape with his life, as the wound narrowly missed his jugular vein. Sheriff Wilton jailed Lucas for six months and sentenced both Stokes and Zemmil to three years' Borstal.

'I gave one of your crowd it solid'

In March 1930, territorial animosity and sexual jealousy would entwine in what became known as the 'Drygate Tragedy'. The Drygate was a steep, narrow, gloomy thoroughfare in the shadow of Duke Street Prison on the edge of Glasgow city centre. The district was not renowned for its gangs, but local youths had banded together to form the Sheiks – a rambling club rather than a gang, according to its members, who made weekly trips into the countryside on Sunday afternoons.

The absence of noted gangsters in the area encouraged members of gangs from the adjacent district of the Calton to venture into the Drygate in search of girls and trouble. During the summer of 1929, furious local youths had chased a group of Sydney Street Billies out of the district; later that year, a group of younger boys from Sydney Street tried their luck, and the Drygate lads repeatedly chased them away. Blows were rarely struck in these encounters, but in January 1930, nineteen-year-old Alec McLellan from the Drygate 'thrashed' one of the more persistent intruders, and the Sydney Street boys warned McLellan that they would return. Next time, they said, they would 'fetch Booth'.

In the weeks that followed, the Sheiks received numerous messages that the boys from Sydney Street were going to come to the Drygate en masse. Most of the messages were relayed by eighteen-year-old Kate McMahon. She had 'run about' with the Drygate lads since her family moved to the district five years previously, and it had been widely noted that she and Paddy Venters of the Sheiks had been 'keeping company' together. In January 1930, however, McMahon had met John Booth, a nineteen-year-old apprentice slater, at a cinema in London Road. Booth hung round with the Sydney Street boys. He and McMahon began courting and Booth quickly became a familiar figure in the Drygate. As McMahon explained: 'He frequently saw me home and stood in the close with me,' while Booth told his friends that he was 'winching [courting] a girl strong'. When his friends asked him if he was not afraid to go to the Drygate on his own, he replied: 'No, I wouldn't let anybody there touch me.' They were not surprised: even Booth's friends were wary of him – they thought him a bully – while others knew him as a 'first-class fighting man' with 'more than a local reputation'.

Both the Sydney Street boys and the Sheiks began to use Kate McMahon as a go-between. According to Booth's cousin, she was 'carrying about reports that the Sydney Street boys were going to get a kicking'. General threats against the Sheiks were mingled with more severe warnings to McMahon's former companion, Paddy Venters: if Booth saw Venters speaking to McMahon, 'he was going to give Venters a doing'.

As Booth walked McMahon home through the Drygate on the night of Monday 10 March they were mocked by a group of local youths, who made farting noises as the couple passed. Booth told McMahon: 'Never mind, we'll get them after.' After he left her, however, he was threatened with a kicking and chased back to the Calton. There, Booth headed to the Paragon picture house in Tobago Street, where he joined three of his friends – John Brown, Paddy Riley and Anthony McVey – who were sitting with a group of girls waiting for the nine o'clock film. Booth told Brown and Riley that he had just been chased out of the Drygate. He was determined to confront his tormentors the following night and appealed to Brown and Riley to join him: 'Get what you can get your hands on and we will go up tomorrow night and give them it.'

At quarter past seven on Tuesday evening, Booth met Brown, Riley and McVey, along with Vincent Kerr, in Trotter's sweet shop in Sydney Street. Booth showed them a dagger with a long, pointed blade, which he had hidden under his jacket, declaring: 'There's what I have got for the bastards.' McVey, who was aged fifteen, was reluctant to join the raid. He told Booth: 'There's not much use of me coming up there. I'll have no chance.' Booth replied: 'Come on, I'll stand by you. I'll give it them solid if they harm you.' McVey relented, fearful both of Booth and of appearing a coward.

The five youths set out from Sydney Street at around quarter past eight. Apart from Booth, only Brown was armed – he was carrying a belt with a heavy metal buckle. As they entered the Drygate, Booth declared: 'If I get Venters I am going to cut the heid [head] off him.' Booth marched up the street and went into one of the tenement closes to see who was about. As he came back out into the street and rejoined his companions, two local youths approached. One of them – Alec McLellan – rounded on Booth. 'You chased Paddy [Venters],' accused McLellan. 'If it's a fight you want, I'll give you a fight.' McLellan and Booth grappled with each other and, moments later, McLellan staggered and fell on his back, bleeding copiously from his mouth and body. Booth and his followers fled. Shouts of 'Stop him! Stop him!' rang out as he ran down the street.

Anthony McVey caught up with Booth back in the Calton, where Booth bragged: 'I gave it him proper that time.' Booth then introduced McVey to his 'bird' – Kate McMahon – before repeating his boast to her: 'I gave one of your crowd it solid.' McMahon was dispatched to 'see how the boy who had been stabbed was getting on'. Before she returned, someone else brought Booth the news he was waiting for: Alec McLellan was dead.

Booth had plunged his dagger into McLellan's chest with such force that the blade almost passed through his body. Two adult neighbours lifted McLellan onto a passing bus and accompanied him to the Royal Infirmary, but he died before they reached the hospital. McLellan's mother learned of his death later that night when her two remaining sons returned from the Infirmary. A reporter from *Thomson's Weekly News* – tipped off, presumably, by the police – was already ensconced in the kitchen of the family's house at 137 Drygate. He described Mrs McLellan's reaction to the news: 'Nothing that her friends could do or say would comfort her. It is doubtful even if she realised that they were speaking to her, she was so overcome.'

Alec McLellan's brothers had called at John Booth's house before returning home, but Booth's mother had told them that her son was not in. When a police sergeant called at the house shortly afterwards, Mrs Booth set out to search for John herself. She roamed the streets round Calton Cross until someone told her that her son was in the house of the McFadyens at 94 Well Street. She found him drinking tea with Alec McFadyen, a twenty-five-year-old bookmaker's runner, and his wife. Mrs Booth asked her son: 'Oh, John, what trouble is this you have got into?' He made no reply. Alec McFadyen's sister, who had gone up to the house a few minutes earlier, spoke instead: 'Now you stick to what I have said to you, John . . . we will do all we can.' Mrs Booth left her son to give himself up to the police. Alec McFadyen accompanied him to the Eastern Police Office.

Detective Lieutenant John Montgomery – the officer who had led police inquiries into the death of Jimmy Tait two years earlier – took charge of the investigation. Detectives dragged Booth's four companions from their beds that night, along with a lad named Jimmy Bole. They appeared at the Central Police Court the following morning. The youngest of the prisoners

– Anthony McVey – was three days short of his sixteenth birthday, so they appeared at the juvenile sitting, where they were all charged with murder. Later that morning, Booth told detectives that Bole had had no involvement in the fight, declaring: 'I am alone responsible and I am taking the blame of this.' Bole was liberated on the basis of Booth's statement.

The funeral of Alec McLellan was held on Saturday 15 March. Thousands of people lined the route from the Drygate to the cemetery at Riddrie. The hearse was followed by four coaches, one of which was laden with floral tributes: 'From women neighbours' and 'Boys in the Street'. Journalists mixing with the crowds heard nothing but kind words for a cheerful and courteous boy, who had preferred to spend his weekends rambling rather than hanging about the streets.

'No wonder people is frightened to come forward'

The Sydney Street boys were held on remand in Duke Street Prison for two months prior to their trial at the High Court. Police efforts to locate the murder weapon initially proved fruitless, then three anonymous letters – written in the same hand over a period of seventeen days – were posted to the Central Police Office by a witness who was keen to assist the search but frightened to do so publically. The first, sent on 14 March, advised the police to call at Alec McFadyen's house in Well Street in the Calton. The letter-writer claimed that McFadyen and his brother, Berty, had supplied Booth with the dagger used to stab Alec McLellan: the dagger had been in the possession of the McFadyen family for many years, but Alec McFadyen had warned Booth not to reveal how he obtained it.

Detectives questioned members of the McFadyen family, all of whom denied the allegation. A second letter, posted four days later, urged the police to pay Berty McFadyen another visit:

> him and his people [family] have got the wind up in case yous get to know where he has buried the Dagger he has broke it up

into pieces and buried it in some place where he think yous cant leave your hands on it so it is up to yous to win . . .

McFadyen's sisters were telling their neighbours that the police could not 'put their hands on' Berty as it was 'his word against the boy Booth'. Local sympathy, according to the letter-writer, lay with the youths on remand:

> we all think if he [Berty] has a heart that he is more to blame than the boys that is in [jail] so let them see what yous can do for if it had not been for him giving the Boys out the Dagger there would be no Murder done . . .

If the boys could be persuaded to speak openly, the writer insisted, Berty McFadyen's role in the affair would soon be revealed. As for the McFadyens:

> they are a family that has given the Eastern Police office a lot of trouble and so has abby kane the one that stays [lodges] with one of the Daughters so keep a eye on them.

The missing dagger was found on 28 March. Acting on 'information received', detectives accompanied two of Berty McFadyen's friends to the suspension bridge at Glasgow Green: James Sweeney and Alec McGregor pointed to the spot where they had thrown the dagger into the Clyde. Watched by a large crowd, a diver retrieved the dagger from the riverbed: it was a foot long, although the seven-inch blade had been bent into an S shape before it was discarded.

A third letter, now addressed to Detective Lieutenant Montgomery, was sent on 31 March. The writer praised the detective's efforts – 'you have done your work well' – but claimed that sympathy still lay with the boys in Duke Street Prison: 'We want to see the right man in [jail].' The writer now provided an account of a conversation that allegedly took place between John Booth and Berty McFadyen when Booth returned from the Drygate on the night of 11 March:

> the words that Berty McFadyen said to him, was, did you do what you went up to do and the young Lad said that he fell at my feet

like a big log so I think he [Berty] is as much the Murderer; as the Lads that is in [jail] . . .

The letter-writer claimed to want to see justice done, but clearly held a long-standing resentment towards the McFadyens, too: it is hard to avoid the suspicion that the police were not the only people in the Calton to have had 'a lot of trouble' from this family.

Another anonymous letter – written in a different hand – was sent to Detective Lieutenant Montgomery at the end of April. The writer, who appears to have been a friend of John Booth's mother, also insisted that Berty McFadyen had supplied Booth with the dagger, but claimed that people were scared to testify against the McFadyens – 'they are a bad lot'. One of the McFadyen sisters had been:

> going about and telling the witness what to say, they are frightened for their own neck . . . She should be under lock and key. No wonder people is frightened to come forward. She is going to give Mrs Booth a doing. I think it is a shame that people will stand up and say what they know is not true. My Boy heard her himself saying she would get out of it and all belonging to her, her old mother is just as Bad.

Older neighbourhood grievances – stretching back a generation – were being aired here, but these had been exacerbated by the intimidation that had stymied the recent police inquiries. This writer revealed part of her address to confirm that she lived in the Calton – but no more: 'I stay [live] in Green Street,' she confided, 'but that is all I can tell.'

Barbarism on Trial

Glaswegians were quick to make sense of the Drygate tragedy. As the solicitor appointed to prepare John Booth's defence noted:

> The tragedy has created a profound impression on the city, and has led to an outcry against Glasgow's gangs. The newspapers

are full of comments on this subject. It is stated that the time has come for the authorities to make an example, and that crimes of this kind must be stamped out without mercy.

The solicitor claimed to have heard many conversations along these lines and wrote to the Secretary of State for Scotland on 18 March, requesting that the trial be moved to the High Court in Edinburgh to ensure a fair hearing. The solicitor's request was referred to John Drummond Strathern, Glasgow's procurator fiscal. Strathern was unmoved, pointing out that if the solicitor's request was granted it would prevent any gang case being tried in Glasgow, since 'the operations of gangs are a more or less constant matter of comment to the public press'. According to Strathern, there was an 'element' of gang warfare in the Drygate case, but it was 'not very strong'. The real motive was Booth's jealousy in regard to Kate McMahon's relationship with McLellan's friend, Paddy Venters. Strathern was confident that there was ample evidence to secure a conviction of murder against John Booth.

The Crown's case was strengthened immeasurably when Anthony McVey elected to turn King's evidence, thereby testifying against Booth. In a sworn statement given on 11 April, McVey provided a detailed account of the fatal expedition from Sydney Street to the Drygate in which he confirmed that John Booth had plotted and led the raid, 'wrestled' with McLellan and subsequently boasted of carrying out the stabbing.

John Booth, John Brown, Vincent Kerr and Patrick Riley stood trial before Lord Alness at the High Court in Glasgow from 6–8 May 1930. Interest in the case in the Drygate and the Calton was enormous: most of those who queued for admission to the public gallery had to be turned away. All four prisoners pleaded not guilty to the murder of Alec McLellan: a further plea of self-defence was entered on behalf of Booth.

At the outset of the trial, Booth's counsel strove to depict the killing as a gang case. Questioning McLellan's brother, Roderick, he demanded:

Have you heard of the Sheik Gang?
– Yes. It is a rambling club.
Is there any other 'club', as you call it, in the Drygate?
– Not that I know of.
I am told that there is one known as the Sheba Gang?
– I have never heard of it.
Have you heard of the Sydney Street Billies?
– No.

Roderick McLellan subsequently admitted that his deceased brother had mentioned the Billies, but insisted that this had been some years ago.

The most dramatic testimony on the first day of the trial came from sixty-seven-year-old Mrs Isabella Scott. She had witnessed the stabbing at close range. She described how she had heard McLellan ask a group of boys: 'What about Paddy?' She continued:

> One of the boys then struck a blow at McLellan's chest. Then he withdrew his hand and stabbed it forward in short, sharp jabs like that – bouf, bouf, bouf! [she thrust her clenched first forward three times]. McLellan threw up his hands, and said: 'I'm stabbed.' I shouted: 'You rascal, you coward!' as the other boy ran down the street.

Several other witnesses to the fight identified John Booth as McLellan's assailant.

On the second day of the trial, Anthony McVey told the court that McLellan had challenged Booth to fight – 'If there is to be any fighting, I'll give you all the fighting you want' – before grabbing Booth by the lapels. McVey's account lent some support to Booth's plea of self-defence, although there was no suggestion that McLellan had intended to fight with anything other than his fists. McVey then caused a sensation in court when he identified the S-shaped dagger as the one that Booth had brandished prior to setting out for the Drygate on the night of 11 March.

There was a rustle of anticipation in court later that day

when 'the girl in the case' – Kate McMahon – was called as a witness. 'Miss McMahon, a pretty girl of eighteen, who wore a navy blue coat with a fur-trimmed collar, was obviously ill at ease in the witness box,' noted the *Scottish Daily Express*. Her discomfort was understandable: grilled on her relationships with both John Booth and Paddy Venters, she confirmed that she had been Booth's 'sweetheart' since the New Year, but denied that she had previously courted Venters. Under repeated questioning, she admitted that she and Venters used to 'stand in the close' together. She confirmed that she had met Booth in the Calton on the night of 11 March: 'He said that he had been up the Drygate, fighting.' Asked how Booth had seemed to her that night, she replied: 'He just seemed his normal.'

Attention then turned to the murder weapon. Two sixteen-year-old girls testified that they had been standing at the corner of Claythorn Street and Stevenson Street in the Calton on the night of 11 March when they were approached by Berty McFadyen and James Sweeney. McFadyen showed them a dagger; Sweeney then put it under his foot and bent the blade. Sweeney, aged twenty-three, was the next witness to appear. He told how McFadyen had asked him to destroy the weapon, and to say nothing if questioned by the police. Sweeney told the court that he had shown the dagger to Alec McGregor, and the two of them had walked through Glasgow Green before McGregor hurled it into the Clyde.

Called as a witness, Berty McFadyen strenuously denied that the dagger was his – he had 'never seen it before' – and further denied that he had supplied Booth with a weapon to 'frighten' anybody who attacked him when he went to the Drygate. Declaring this testimony 'in the last degree unsatisfactory', Lord Alness ordered McFadyen to be detained in the precincts of the court.

Medical evidence was given on the third and final day of the trial. Booth flinched for the first time in the proceedings as Professor John Glaister of the University of Glasgow described the wound to McLellan's chest: the depth of the wound was seven and a half inches. 'The cause of death was loss of blood and shock due to severe wounds on the chest and abdomen,' Glaister confirmed. 'In the whole of my experience,' he added, 'I have never seen a wound on the chest more severe' – one thrust of the dagger had passed through both McLellan's heart and one of his lungs. As the *Sunday Post*'s correspondent noted, this was 'a blow of which a bull fighter might well have been proud'.

The Advocate Depute pressed the jury to return verdicts of culpable homicide against Brown, Kerr and Riley, but urged them to find Booth guilty of murder: his plea of self-defence should be dismissed, the Advocate Depute insisted, since more than one blow had been struck with the dagger. Booth's counsel, meanwhile, depicted the episode as an ill-fated love story. He claimed that a 'collision' between the Drygate boys and his client was inevitable once Booth had starting courting 'a Drygate girl'. In this account, if anyone had the right to feel aggrieved it was Paddy Venters – the rejected suitor – but Alec McLellan 'took on himself another man's quarrel'. Implicitly accepting that Booth's actions had gone beyond self-defence, he claimed that his client had acted in a 'sudden frenzy without conscious intent'. He pressed for a verdict of culpable homicide.

Summing up, Lord Alness described the entire case as sordid. He told the jury that if they accepted Anthony McVey's account of the challenge issued by the deceased, they should opt for the lesser charge of culpable homicide rather than murder against John Booth. As for Brown, Riley and Kerr, the judge stated that they had taken 'no active part' in the affair.

After deliberating for an hour and three-quarters, the jury – by a majority – found John Booth guilty of culpable homicide. They found Brown, Kerr and Riley not guilty.

Addressing Booth, Lord Alness declared that the jury had been 'most merciful'. Nonetheless, the judge proclaimed:

You have been convicted of a most wicked and dastardly deed. You have destroyed a human life. You used a lethal weapon on an unarmed man. That is a cowardly act, an un-British act. The use of razors and other weapons in this city and elsewhere is far too common today, and it must be put down.

He sentenced John Booth to seven years' penal servitude.

The outcome of the trial met with considerable unease in the local press. The *Evening Citizen*, in particular, was dismayed both by the jury's failure to convict Booth of murder and by what it saw as a paltry term of imprisonment. 'The inhabitants of certain districts of Glasgow are living in a state of barbarism,' it warned.

Unlikely Gangsters

Like the South Side Stickers charged with the murder of Jimmy Tait two years previously, Booth and his companions had led remarkably ordinary lives prior to their arrest on suspicion of murder. If anything, the Sydney Street boys were the more unlikely 'gangsters'. Of the four prisoners to stand trial, only John Brown had previously appeared before the magistrates. Convicted of breaching the peace in August 1929 and disorderly conduct four months later, he had been fined 10 shillings on both occasions. For all his reputation as a street fighter, John Booth had no convictions of any kind, although his school record was poor: he had regularly played truant, and the doctor at Duke Street Prison found that – at the age of nineteen – he was 'unable to work the examination paper of a boy of twelve'.

All four were in work at the time of their arrests. Booth was in the final year of his apprenticeship as a slater, for which his weekly wage was 22 shillings. His employer described him as quiet, trustworthy and hard-working: 'He was very efficient at his work and I was greatly astonished when I heard that he had been arrested in connection with the Drygate murder.' Booth's mother testified that he gave her all his wages: she allotted him just a shilling a week as spending money, while he had asked Kate McMahon to purchase tickets for a dance, promising to ask his mother for money to refund her. Nor was he fashionably attired: on the night of his confrontation with Alec McLellan, he was wearing an ill-fitting, borrowed jacket as his own was in pawn. Vincent Kerr earned 15 shillings per week selling sawdust for a merchant in the Gallowgate; John Brown made a fraction less as an apprentice moulder. Paddy Riley, the youngest of the four at sixteen, earned just 7 shillings a week as an apprentice hairdresser.

None of the evidence presented at the trial suggested that the prisoners were gang members. They hung around the corner of Sydney Street and Armour Street and other young people in the district knew them as 'the Sydney Street crowd', but they were not renowned as a fighting gang and did not belong to the better-known Sydney Street Billies. Brown, Riley and Kerr were Catholics; only John Booth was a Protestant.

The religious affiliations of the prisoners were seized on by Alexander Ratcliffe, founder of the vehemently anti-Catholic political party, the Scottish Protestant League. Mistakenly assuming that Booth, too, was a Catholic, Ratcliffe used the April–May issue of the League's journal, *Protestant Advocate*, to rail against what he saw as the Catholic proclivity towards lawless violence. After noting the mere fines imposed – 'by a Catholic Bailie' – against two young Catholics convicted of committing a breach of the peace in a South Side cinema, Ratcliffe turned to the Drygate murder:

> Then we have that terrible stabbing affray when a young man was done to death . . . Youths from 16 to 19. And Roman Catholics again! Sons of 'Holy Mother Church', the great school for rearing criminals! Such is Popery.

As a correspondent to the *Glasgow Observer* (the city's Catholic newspaper) pointed out, such statements – published while the case was *sub judice* – were likely to 'prejudice a Protestant juror'. Ratcliffe's comments were brought to the attention of the Lord Advocate at Westminster, but no action was deemed necessary since the three Catholic youths to stand trial alongside John Booth had been acquitted.

Berty McFadyen – like John Booth, a Protestant – appeared before the Lord Justice General, Lord Clyde, at the High Court in Edinburgh on 20 June. He pleaded guilty to perjury, admitting both to having supplied John Booth with the dagger used to stab Alec McLellan and to having taken the weapon back from Booth later that night.

McFadyen presented himself as a victim of Glasgow's 'reign of terror' rather than one of its instigators, claiming that his life had been threatened prior to the trial at Glasgow High Court six weeks earlier. McFadyen's employer testified that he was 'a good-natured boy, admired for his honesty and cheerfulness', and confirmed that he would be re-employed as a journeyman plasterer on his release from prison. This was a very different portrait from the one gathered by detectives: Booth's companion, Anthony McVey, knew McFadyen as 'a vicious character' and a member of a gang from Claythorn Street, while his family had been the subject of the series of anonymous letters sent to police searching for the murder weapon in the Drygate case. Lord Clyde jailed Berty McFadyen for eighteen months.

The last word on the Drygate murder went to the intended victim, Paddy Venters. In his account of '**MYSELF AND THE DRYGATE DRAMA**', Venters told the readers of the *Sunday Mail* that Alec McLellan had died for no reason at all: there had been no contest for the affections of Kate McMahon; John Booth had no grounds for jealousy – unless 'someone was telling lies'. Venters had lost his best friend. He had also lost his job, having been dismissed on the day following Booth's conviction for culpable homicide: Venters was convinced that he had been falsely labelled as a gang member. In prose carefully crafted by the *Mail*'s feature writer, but poignant nonetheless, Venters protested: 'Certain newspapers in their reporting of the case have inferred that this was a gang murder. It was nothing of the kind.' Venters was adamant that he and McLellan were not members of any gang and neither was John Booth. To reporters, however, the temptation to label McLellan's killing a gang murder had been irresistible. The echoes of the case of Jimmy Tait were too resonant – and the template too sensational – for the story of the 'Drygate Tragedy' to be told in any other way.

5
Razor Thugs and Girl Gangsters

The Drygate murder might not have been a gang case, but it prompted the most intense bout of concern with gangs in Glasgow since the hooligan scare of 1906. Calls for a judicial backlash stoked a rash of sensational press reports – and vice versa – as the city struggled to come to terms with the revelations at the High Court. A series of experts ranging from senior police officials to psychologists debated the causes of the gang problem, offering solutions that veered from compulsory military service to the gallows. Fascination with Kate McMahon – the 'girl in the Drygate case' – led to a renewal of concern with the figure of the 'girl gangster', amidst allegations – never verified – that membership of some gangs was 'exclusively confined to females'. Added to this, all kinds of depravity, from the theft of coal to the raiding of orchards, were attributed to the growing menace of the gangs – according to one exposé in the *Weekly Record*, the recent stoning of swans at the reservoir at Hapton Crags, fifteen miles south of Glasgow, showed the depths to which the youthful habitués of the underworld had plunged: 'There can be no shadow of a doubt but that this wicked and malicious act had been inspired by the desire of . . . misguided youths to emulate the doings of the professional gangster.' In the face of such wanton cruelty, the *Record* concluded, the 'most rigorous punishment' – the gallows – had to be considered.

'War on the Razor Thugs'

After jailing John Booth on 8 May 1930, Lord Alness dealt with three cases of assault by cutting 'with intent to maim or disfigure' at the High Court the following day. In a highly symbolic gesture, the charges were framed under a century-old statute – dating back to the reign of George IV – which prescribed the death penalty for such offences. Two of the prisoners were found guilty. George Clark, aged eighteen, was convicted of slashing Thomas Bradley with a razor in the Casino Picture House in Townhead. Bradley's wounds were not serious: he required three stitches in a scalp wound and two in his left hand. Asked what had prompted the assault, Bradley replied that Clark had accused him of 'talking about the Romeo Boys' – a prominent gang from the Garngad. In a separate case, nineteen-year-old Angus Hunter was convicted of cutting a man on the face with a knife at Bridgeton Cross. The victim required fourteen stitches. Lord Alness jailed both Clark and Hunter for three years.

These were exemplary punishments, as terms of twelve months, or less, had previously been deemed severe enough to deal with most of the razor-slashers brought before the city's courts. The local press was ecstatic: the Glasgow-based *Scottish Daily Express* heralded the sentences as the onset of a '**WAR ON RAZOR THUGS**', noting that the resort to the 'ancient' statute was 'the most drastic move so far taken to deal with razor-slashers and knifers.'

Lord Alness again invoked the spectre of the death penalty in his valedictory address to the High Court on 12 May. In his capacity as Lord Justice Clerk, he told the city's magistrates that his alarm at the number of assaults with lethal weapons was exceeded by his dismay at the difficulty encountered in finding witnesses to testify against the perpetrators:

> I am officially informed that a very large number of cases is reported, but it is found possible to lead evidence only in a very small proportion of cases, and even that evidence is obtained in the face of the very gravest difficulty . . . because of the reign of terror which prevails.

Proclaiming that lengthy jail sentences were inadequate to 'cut out this cancer from the civic body', Lord Alness warned that the death penalty might yet be required – along with a resort to flogging – to safeguard Glasgow's 'good name'. Once again, Alness's pronouncements were seized upon by gleeful journalists. Unease at the verdict and sentence passed upon John Booth gave way to approval for the prospect of harsher punishments for those gangsters and razor-slashers subsequently brought before the courts.

The magistrates met to discuss the Lord Justice Clerk's remarks the following day. They endorsed his call for more severe punishments, and plans were initiated for a petition to the Secretary of State for Scotland for additional powers to deal with those offenders convicted of assaults with lethal weapons. The city's senior magistrate, Bailie William Hunter, told the *Evening Citizen* that the magistrates' existing powers were grossly inadequate: sixty days' imprisonment with hard labour – the maximum penalty at their disposal – was no deterrent to a razor-slasher. The magistrates were divided, however, on how best to deal with such cases. Several of Hunter's colleagues spoke against any increased resort to the death penalty. There was stronger support for flogging, along with longer jail sentences, amid concern that the imposition of fines tended to exacerbate, rather than diminish, the threat of violence. As Bailie Holmes told the *Citizen*:

> Flogging is the only cure or deterrent . . . We have evidence in the police court regularly that shopkeepers and others are blackmailed to pay the fines of these criminals, and in the event of them refusing they are subject to all sorts of terrorism.

An unnamed police officer corroborated Bailie Holmes's account, adding that the police were unable to act since 'the victims were afraid to come forward'.

The most outspoken sceptic was Bailie John Kennedy. A staunch Unionist, or Tory, Kennedy questioned the utility of flogging as a punishment but nonetheless agreed with the Lord Justice Clerk that assaults with weapons such as razors or knives were profoundly un-British. Kennedy told the *Citizen* that the proliferation of such assaults resulted from the growing American influence on 'the mind of the poorer-class boy'.

Kennedy invoked the now familiar racial slant to fears of Americanisation, alleging that literature and films depicting the 'amazing way in which the American negro handles the razor as a weapon' had been especially harmful. In this light, Kennedy complained, the resort to the razor among youths in Glasgow was 'a form of perverted hero-worship'.

The most determined advocate of flogging was the Socialist bailie, William Reid. Describing the prevalence of gangs in Glasgow as a menace, Reid told the *Scottish Daily Express*:

> A man brought to me last week a steel knife which had been dropped by a gangster who was pursued by the police on the South Side. These knives are made in hundreds by gangsters employed in the shipyards, and are distributed among the gangs.

The *Express* made its own inquiries into the gangs' armouries. On a visit to a cinema in Bridgeton, its reporter was shown a drawer full of weapons confiscated from local gang members: they included a steel tube with a knob on the end, which sank into a block of wood with terrifying ease; a metal bar; four bayonets – of regulation size, and recently sharpened; and a cloth cap with a safety-razor blade stitched into the peak.

The call for razor-slashers to be flogged was widely supported in the local press. The staunchly Conservative *Glasgow Herald* applauded the Lord Justice Clerk for his boldness. The *Herald* conceded that it would be difficult to sway public opinion behind the death penalty for offences other than murder, but was confident that the introduction of flogging would encounter much less opposition. The *Evening Citizen* concurred, declaring that while flogging was 'repellent', imprisonment was no deterrent to 'certain types of criminal'. People who carried razors in their pockets, the *Citizen* added, were not 'normal human beings'.

Meanwhile, disquiet at the verdict of culpable homicide against John Booth persisted in Glasgow's legal circles. The *Sunday Post* carried an article by an unnamed barrister, who accused the jurors in the Drygate case of a 'lack of moral courage' in the face of unusually clear evidence of wilful murder:

motive, preparation, the seeking out of an adversary, the use of a weapon against an unarmed opponent and rejoicing in the wounds inflicted had all been proved, the barrister insisted. The city's legal circuit was awash with rumours – that the 'majority' verdict of culpable homicide rested on eight votes against seven; that the majority included all six of the female jurors – women were widely supposed to be especially reluctant to convict for murder. Experienced lawyers were left asking: 'If this is not stark, staring murder, what is?'

Girl Gangsters

Lord Alness's pronouncements at the High Court prompted a flurry of investigations into the nature and origins of the Glasgow's gangs in the Scottish national press. A series of reports in the *Weekly Record* dwelled on the organisation of the gangs, highlighting their hierarchical structures and their ready resort to weapons. The *Record* was especially concerned with the role of girls and young women in the gangs: 'Nearly all of them,' the *Record* reported, 'have "queens" – young girls who are elected by common consent to an important position in the gang. These girls are the cause of most of the trouble that arises.'

Gangs such as the Bridgeton Billy Boys and the South Side Stickers were known to have large numbers of female followers, and it was widely alleged that they incited fights by flirting with lads from rival districts. The *Sunday Mail* put the accusation more starkly than most:

> In true Chicago style the Glasgow gangster has his 'moll,' and in the dance-halls she is frequently the cause of the trouble that leads to razor-slashed faces and bottle crowned heads. The caprice of a tawdry-dressed, prematurely aged looking, over-powdered girl, in a moment of passion, may decide whether or not a youth should live. There is, indeed, a rivalry among the girls connected with the gangs as to how many fights they can get their 'bloke' to engage in.

The *Mail*'s contempt for these modern 'girls' with their mass-produced frocks and cheap cosmetics is clear.

Male gang members frequently made the same allegation, as well. In 1931, a former South Side Sticker, Paddy Cousins, claimed that the women and girls 'attached to the gang' had been wholly responsible for many of the atrocities that the Stickers had carried out. 'The girls often assumed affection for men in other districts,' Cousins complained. His phrasing is revealing: by this account, the Stickers' female followers were attached to the gang, rather than members in their own right. So far as the lads were concerned, the girls were possessions to be guarded as jealously as the territory to which the gang laid claim.

The Stickers' female entourage had gained considerable notoriety in the aftermath of the fatal stabbing of Jimmy Tait in 1928, while the following year, the *Weekly Record* claimed that they outnumbered the female adherents of any other single gang in the city. The *Record* characterised the Stickers' female followers as Eve-like figures, both corrupted and corrupting:

> These girls range in age from as young as fifteen, but even at that age they are prepared to do anything themselves to gain favour in the eyes of the 'strong men' of the gang, or to encourage them in their violence.

The *Record* claimed that they routinely drifted into prostitution: many young women 'of this class' walked the streets nightly – 'powdered and rouged' – with gangsters acting as their 'bullies', or pimps, but these allegations of sexual precocity appeared to owe less to direct observation than to the prevailing fears of young women's heightened independence and assertiveness in the aftermath of the Great War.

More commonly, gangsters' female companions were depicted as molls. They were expected to dress fashionably, in keeping with the status enjoyed by gang members within the city's poorer districts and they were also expected to perform a series of auxiliary roles on the gang members' behalf: acting as decoys and spies, delivering challenges to rival gangs, carrying weapons, and providing alibis and false testimony in court. In the wake of the Drygate tragedy, the *Weekly Record* detailed the role that these 'modern Amazons' were expected to play at the scene of a fight:

> Although these girls are not to initiate any form of physical attack, they are to be close at hand, at critical times, as a kind of Reserve Army behind the lines, ready to assist the belligerents, either by carrying supplies of 'ammunition', such as bottles and stones, or in stepping into the breach in order to strengthen the line of defence or attack, contingent on the progress of the 'battle'.

The *Record*'s account was presented as a startling new revelation from gangland. In fact, it did little more than rehash earlier press depictions of 'girls' as handmaidens and spies.

While girls and women were generally expected to leave the fighting to the men, their occasional participation in 'rammies' (fights) should have come as no surprise as, elsewhere in their day-to-day lives, young women – like young men – sometimes agreed to settle their differences by fighting. In keeping with broader expectations of feminine decorum, stand-up fights among young women were relatively rare. However, when they did occur, they were highly public events – often conducted in the street in front of large crowds: spectators formed rings around the combatants, but did not intervene so long as the fight was conducted fairly. The pretexts for fights frequently appeared trivial – a careless word or an accidental collision – but young women could be as determined as any gangster to seek redress for a perceived slight. They were also sometimes willing to fight for the affections of young men.

On the night of Tuesday, 17 September 1929, Elizabeth Millar and Patricia McCormack had a furious argument over a lad in a Gallowgate dance hall, and agreed to go outside to 'fight it out' in front of a group of their friends. The two young women, both of whom were aged in their mid-teens, fought 'to the point of exhaustion', and Millar was declared the winner. Refusing to let the matter rest, McCormack subsequently brought a charge of assault against her. Police inquiries found that the alleged assault sounded 'more like a prize-fight'. Millar and McCormack were both charged with breaching the peace. Witnesses told the Eastern Police Court that they had not interfered in the fight, as the agreed rules – including no hair-pulling – had been 'fairly observed'. Inquiries into the prisoners' backgrounds revealed that Millar's mother was broken-hearted: 'Elizabeth fought everyone in the house, and came to blows even with her mother.' McCormack had less of a history of violence, but she 'was starting to run about with bad company of late'.

Bailie Matthew Armstrong fined both prisoners 21 shillings, with the option of fourteen days' imprisonment. He also gave the prisoners a stern moral lecture: 'You do not seem to realise what sin means, and if you do not pull up soon you will both head straight for perdition. You will be disgraceful women, and nothing but ruined lives await you.' He further advised them to 'give up frequenting dance halls and the people who hung around those places of brawling and dissipation' – the bailie appeared to be more concerned with the prisoners' spiritual well-being than with any threat they might pose to public order.

Styles of fighting among young women were widely believed to differ from those among men. Few women were charged with using the gangster's weapons of choice – razor, bayonet, hatchet or knife. By contrast, hair-pulling was seen as a typically female tactic, as demonstrated by a smartly-dressed Bridgeton 'girl' named Margaret Dawson. After a lengthy period of ill-will, Dawson and her adversary agreed to fight at one o'clock in the morning in Pirn Street. The bout drew a sizeable, drink-fuelled crowd. The girls 'boxed in the manner of old-time pugilists for several rounds', reported Superintendent McPherson at the Eastern Police Court, 'then they got into grips and rolled together on the ground. It took the combined efforts of two stalwart policemen to separate the girls and release their fingers from each other's hair.' The superintendent's account was lapped up by the *Eastern Standard* under the headline: **'Girls' Stand-Up Fight! AMAZING BRIDGETON SCENES'**.

Such violence was highly visible, even if no arrests were made and no notice taken by the newspapers. For young people of both sexes, fighting was a public performance in which both parties' grievances were aired – and acknowledged by the spectators – and both might emerge with credit so long as they fought bravely, and fairly.

Like their male counterparts, girls and young women did not always abide by the rules of the stand-up fight. In November 1929, a row broke out in the foyer of the Wellington Palace picture house in the Gorbals after a 'little girl' accidentally knocked a cigarette out of the hand of Elizabeth McLeod. Fearing that McLeod was about to strike the younger girl, a fifteen-year-old stepped between them, only to be asked if 'she wanted the same'. McLeod resented the interference, as did her companions: before the peacemaker could reply, she was set upon by a group of between ten and twenty girls who 'dragged her about the floor by her hair, and kicked her.' Three of her assailants – Elizabeth McLeod, Agnes Kerr and Margaret Ryan – were fined 10 shillings each by Bailie Holmes at the Southern Police Court. The leniency of the sentences suggests that the magistrate was not unduly concerned – or surprised – by the prospect of girls brawling in South Side cinemas.

Young women were most likely to take part in fighting between rival gangs when disturbances broke out during religious processions and sectarian parades. When violence flared, young men tended to be at the forefront but girls and young women were also frequently among the combatants. The female contingent of the Bridgeton Billy Boys were famous for their rowdyism and attracted widespread condemnation in the local press, not least for their distinctly unfeminine habit of carrying empty beer bottles on the annual Orange Walks. Much of their violence was directed at other young women, and they were quick to target female members of the crowds that gathered to taunt the processionists.

In May 1927, the Brigton Billy Boys escorted an Orange procession to the Blochairn United Free Church in the predominantly Catholic district of the Garngad. The parade drew an angry crowd of several thousand and police made twelve arrests as the Billies traded threats and blows with local youths. In the ensuing court case, witnesses described how the Billy Boys were accompanied by a group of girls who were equally aggressive in their defence of the processionists. Mary Pritchard struck a Catholic youth named Louis Lennon on the face after he had been grabbed by police as he charged at the procession – one of Lennon's friends told the St Rollox Police Court that they had been 'rushed' by the Billy Boys because they were wearing green handkerchiefs. A police inspector described how Mary Pritchard struck Lennon without any provocation, adding: 'I got hold of her or the crowd would have torn her to pieces.'

The Billy Boys' female champion on this occasion was Isabella McMillan from Nuneaton Street in Bridgeton. McMillan had launched herself at Bridget Cartwright, one of the female members of the angry Catholic crowd, and the two women were arrested as they fought. Cartwright told the magistrate that: 'McMillan had been with other girls, who were egged on by a crowd of youths with blue handkerchiefs' – the colour blue signalled their support for (Protestant) Rangers Football Club. McMillan and Cartwright were fined 42 shillings each with the alternative of twenty days' imprisonment. Mary Pritchard got the same sentence for her assault on Louis Lennon.

Two years later, in the spring of 1929, the *Weekly Record* reported on a clash between the Billy Boys and the Norman Conks under the startling headline: **'BATTLE OF ARMED GIRLS'**. The *Record* told how bayonets, razors, knives, belts and bottles had all been used in the 'terrible mêlée' at Bridgeton Cross on the evening of Sunday 26 May. More shocking still was the participation of 'many girl gangsters, who cut and thrust with as great a will as their male confreres.' The Conks had attached themselves to a procession of boys from Sacred Heart Church, which was returning to Bridgeton following a gathering of the Catholic Boys' Guild at St Andrew's Halls in Glasgow city centre. The boys from Sacred Heart, headed by a band, had set out along London Road towards Bridgeton Cross. The Conks had walked ahead, singing 'popular songs'.

In the clash that followed, fifteen-year-old Patrick Cannon from Dunn Street in Bridgeton was stabbed in the thigh with such force that doctors at Glasgow's Royal Infirmary feared that they would have to amputate his leg. Cannon gave an account of the incident from his hospital bed. As relayed by the *Weekly Record*, it made vivid reading:

> As the procession neared Bridgeton Cross, we saw a sight which rooted us to our tracks.
>
> There, right in front of us, were the Billy Boys, armed to the teeth and stretched in fighting array right across the street from the Olympia Theatre to the car [tram] shelter.
>
> Wisely the procession wheeled to the right down Dalmarnock Road, leaving the two rival factions to fight it out to a finish themselves. Then the leader of the Conks surveyed his army.
>
> 'All you that are stickers [game fighters] follow me,' he said grimly. 'The rest can fly.'
>
> Weapons were produced like magic, and, whooping their war cry, the Conks swooped down on their enemies. They clashed, and a desperate close-quarter conflict ensued.
>
> It was a terrible scene. The whole crossing was in an uproar. Gangsters were struggling on the ground and slashing and kicking at each other.
>
> One young woman just avoided a bayonet thrust while another was being mauled till rescued by force of numbers. Frightened spectators crushed desperately into shops and close mouths [entrances to nearby tenements].

The *Record*'s headline, which appeared to invoke a clash between opposing all-female gangs, owed more to the quest for sensation than to Cannon's description of the scene. And while the newspaper was eager to highlight participation of 'girl gangsters' in the scrum, it nonetheless reassured its readers that other women at the scene had responded in a more delicate – and appropriately feminine – fashion, by screaming and fainting as the fight developed.

The Queen of the Nudies

In the aftermath of the Drygate murder, the elusive figure of the gang 'queen' gripped the collective imagination of journalists on the Scottish national press. Few female gang leaders were identified, however, and feature-writers tended to refer back to the previous spring when seventeen-year-old Mary Mooney reportedly led the Nudie Boys in a series of fights with rival gangs in the Gorbals. The Nudie Boys, or Nudies, of Mathieson Street engaged in regular Sunday night skirmishes with the Naburn Street Billy Boys, the Kidston Street Bruisers, the Liberty Boys and the South Side Stickers. On 21 April 1929, she was arrested during a clash with the Naburn Street Billies – police arrived at the scene to find between thirty and forty young people fighting in front of 400 onlookers. By their account, 'Bottles and belts were used freely in the scrap, and the girl was as active and fierce as any of her battling companions.' Mary Mooney was apprehended alongside four lads. The following morning they appeared at the Southern Police Court, where they were charged with breaching the peace.

Mooney's parents attended the court. Her father stated that he had nothing to say on her behalf: 'Anything he might say would be against her.' Her mother declared that Mary 'was a member of the gang, and had given her parents considerable trouble by not returning home at nights.' Parents seldom testified against their children in this way, and Mooney's parents appear to have looked to the court to discipline their daughter, having found that they were unable to control her behaviour themselves. Mrs Mooney's complaint – that Mary stayed out overnight against her parents' wishes – suggests that she was at least as worried by her daughter's sexual precocity as by her association with a gang. Mooney and her followers disputed the allegations against them, but were found guilty on the basis of police evidence. Bailie Armstrong fined each of the prisoners 21 shillings.

At around nine o'clock on the following Sunday evening, Mooney and her followers gathered in Mathieson Street in anticipation of a raid by the South Side Stickers. Police constables found them 'going about the street shouting and swearing, and stating what they intended to do to the Stickers when they arrived.' The officers made four arrests: once again, Mooney was among those taken into custody.

The prisoners appeared at the Southern Police Court the next morning. Leading the prosecution, Superintendent Cameron pointed out that Mooney was widely recognised as the gang's 'queen'. Bailie Watson jailed her for twenty days.

While Mary Mooney's leadership of the Nudie Boys appears to have been short-lived, her notoriety was more enduring. The *Evening Citizen* recalled her exploits – and her appearance – more than a year later:

> The gang known as the 'Nudies' had a girl leader known as 'The Queen of the Nudies'. She had a striking face and a strong personality, but was not possessed of much beauty either of feature or of form. She was, in fact, very small and bandy-legged. She led her gang in several fights. For this she was arrested twice. The second time she got 20 days. This brought Mary's reign to an end and her kingdom broke up.

The jailing of their 'queen' would do little to deter the gang's younger members, however. They increasingly forged a reputation as thieves as well as street fighters. According to the police, they specialised in raiding shop tills and automated vending machines.

The Queen of the Redskins

Mooney's reputation paled in comparison with that of Agnes 'Aggie' Reid of the Redskins. A legendary figure in Glasgow's underworld, Reid was renowned both for her use of the cut-throat razor and for the vigour with which she resisted arrest. She was not the only young woman to be known as the 'Queen of the Redskins': Annie Rennie held the title in November 1916, but Reid's reputation spread further and was much more enduring. According to the historian of the City of Glasgow Police, Douglas Grant: 'Aggie was a handful. Every time the police laid hands on her, never less than four policemen were required to get her into the van.'

The Redskins' notoriety peaked during the First World War, but even after the gang had been broken up – following a prolonged campaign by plain-clothes detectives – their 'queen' remained one of the city's most troublesome offenders: between 1917 and 1926, Reid spent fifty-nine stretches in Duke Street Prison. More than half of her convictions were for breaching the peace, but she was also jailed thirteen times for assaulting the police. In May 1918, she was jailed for ten days for assaulting a constable 'to the effusion of blood', and the sentences passed on her were soon ratcheted up. She received the maximum penalty for assaulting the police – sixty days – on five separate occasions between 1920 and 1924, but prison was no deterrent to her.

Reid grew up in the Tollcross district of Glasgow's East End. By her early twenties, she was living in a women's lodging-house on the Trongate in Glasgow city centre. She worked as a cleaner, but supplemented her earnings by petty theft and, increasingly, prostitution – Reid provides a rare documented case of a young woman who followed the path from gang membership to street walking, as highlighted by the *Weekly Record*. She amassed six convictions for loitering for the purpose of prostitution and three for indecent behaviour. She also turned to drink.

Following an all-day boozing spree in January 1925, Reid accosted one of the other residents of the lodging-house at 114 Trongate, declaring: 'I have been looking for you and you can have it.' Then she slashed the other woman across the face with a razor; the victim had to have two separate facial wounds stitched at the Royal Infirmary. Reid stood trial at Glasgow Sheriff Court on 5 February. Leading the prosecution, the depute fiscal told the court that Reid was 'addicted to drink, and when under its influence she was very violent,' while police witnesses confirmed that: 'When she was apprehended, Reid was so violent that the police patrol van was brought to take her to the police office.' Reid's counsel told the court:

> The accused was very much the worse of drink at the time, having been drinking from 10 o'clock in the morning. She had little recollection of what had happened, and could not understand why she committed the assault, as the woman was a friend.

Sheriff Lyell was scathing in his summing up. He had never seen a woman of Reid's age – twenty-four – with so many convictions, and he jailed her for six months with hard labour. Eleven days after her release, however, she was convicted of drunkenness and the following month she was jailed for three months for breaching the peace and assaulting the two constables who apprehended her. In 1926, she was jailed no fewer than eight times.

By the time of the Drygate murder, Reid's successors in the East End included Margaret Robinson. Known throughout Parkhead as the 'Sally Queen' – on account of her association with the Sally Boys of Salamanca Street – Robinson was also reputed to carry a razor. She pursued a long-running feud with Annie McGarvie from the adjacent district of Shettleston, which saw both young women brought before the Eastern Police Court following a showdown at Parkhead Cross. Bailie Brown fined Robinson £1 for assault, telling her: 'You women are getting worse than boys. I can understand boys getting into scrapes, but not young ladies. I do not know what kind of mothers you will make.'

'How I Would Deal With the Glasgow Gangsters'

The magistrates' proposal to petition for additional powers in the wake of the Drygate episode was referred to the chief constable of Glasgow, Andrew Donnan Smith, in May 1930. He submitted a report on 'the origins of gangs in the city and the steps which might be taken to end the evil' to the magistrates on 3 June. While echoing the Lord Justice Clerk's conclusion that only flogging would curtail the use of razors and knives, Smith confounded the magistrates by stating that he doubted that Parliament would legislate on their behalf 'in view of the adequate powers that already exist'. The chief constable was adamant that the city's gangs could be wiped out if only the magistrates made full use of existing sanctions: 'All too frequently,' he asserted, 'offenders are dealt with in a lenient way.' Smith was particularly scathing of the magistrates' tendency to deal with assaults with lethal weapons themselves at the city's police courts, rather than referring the offenders to the higher courts, where harsher terms of imprisonment could be inflicted by the sheriffs and judges.

Turning to the origins of Glasgow's gang warfare, the chief constable denied that the current spate of disorder among the city's youths was anything new. Smith acknowledged that overcrowding was one root of the problem, but he insisted that irresponsible parenting was also to blame, not least for exposing children to the 'pernicious' life of the streets. Psychological factors were crucial, too, according to the chief constable's diagnosis: 'Children all play at make-believe,' Smith declared. In 'better localities', he added, this fantasy instinct was controlled and guided. In poorer districts, however, the lack of parental responsibility was exploited by vicious lads, who trained younger boys 'to commit crime and to indulge in habits of disorder and vice'. Of course, shifting responsibility onto working-class parents and the dissolute street life of the city's poorer districts neatly absolved the police of responsibility.

The solution, the chief constable concluded, lay in better guidance for the boys of the city's slums. Smith did not specify the means by which this might be achieved – 'This is a matter outwith my province' – but his report read like a coded appeal for the expansion of the work of organisations such as the Boy Scouts, the Boys' Brigade and the Foundry Boys' Religious Society.

Smith's report effectively quashed the magistrates' plan to petition for the power to flog those offenders convicted of using razors and knives. Other means would have to be found for curbing the city's gang warfare.

A more radical assessment was offered by an unnamed professor of psychology, commissioned by the *Sunday Post* to explain: '**HOW I WOULD DEAL WITH THE GLASGOW GANGSTERS.**' Whether the professor had ever set foot in the city was unclear, but he was confident that its gang members could be divided into two distinct types. The first – weak and easily led – could be steered away from gangs, the professor asserted, through the provision of social clubs and gymnasia. The second – the 'vicious bully' – required discipline. For this type, the professor advocated compulsory military training:

> Why can't we do what the French have done and form a Foreign Legion? On the frontiers of India or among the sands of Mespot the hooligan would soon get all the discipline he needs, and a bellyful of fighting into the bargain.

The professor's diagnosis was geared to converting gangsters into good citizens. As he noted approvingly, two Glasgow ministers had already signalled their intention to establish a social club for youths in the city's East End. His call for the introduction of military service as a form of judicial punishment went unheeded.

Wild Rumours

The chief constable's report to the magistrates helped to dampen the anxieties that had surrounded the city's gangs since Lord Alness's sensational pronouncements at the High Court two months earlier, following the Drygate murder trial. Later that summer, the *Evening Citizen* sought to reinforce the chief constable's position by publishing a four-part series that purported to reveal the '**TRUTH ABOUT GLASGOW'S GANGS**'.

The *Citizen*'s 'special investigator' claimed that Glasgow's growing reputation as a 'city of gangs' was unfounded: in his view, the city was suffering not from a gang menace but from a 'gang scare', fostered by exaggerated and sensational press reports. Refraining from pointing out that if this were the case, the *Citizen*'s own reporters had long been among the chief culprits, the investigator conceded that he had found it difficult to make contact with the gangs – their members, ever wary of strangers, sometimes allowed him to join their street corner card games but they were unwilling to divulge their secrets. He was more thoroughly briefed by the police. As a result, the

Citizen's survey – the most in-depth account of the Glasgow's gangs yet published – presented the 'truth' largely as the police saw it.

The *Citizen*'s investigator was adamant that the gangs were, for the most part, little more than groups of friends who gathered on street corners in search of amusement. While he admitted that their quest sometimes led them to seek fights with rival groups, he claimed that their instincts were natural and healthy: 'A fight is, after all, good fun for youth.'

Few outsiders acknowledged the pleasure to be derived from fighting, and this attempt to understand the appeal of the gangs in their own terms represented a significant departure from the blanket condemnation that generally underlay both judicial pronouncements and press reports. Less convincing, however, was the investigator's claim that the city's gangsters only rarely carried lethal weapons: the *Citizen* had itself published ample evidence to the contrary over the previous five years.

The investigator was determined to dispel some of the rumours that were 'floating around' the city: no district was 'terrorised' by the gangs; shopkeepers were not compelled to pay gang members' fines; no street was unsafe for police to patrol even in pairs. The real situation, he insisted, was utterly different:

> To reassure the public in face of the wild rumours prevalent, it should be made clear that the police can break up any gang any time they wish to do so.
>
> The policemen on any particular beat make a point of getting the names and addresses of every member of the local gang.
>
> This is a very clever piece of work, as the gangs will not let the police within a hundred yards of them if they can help it. How it is done is a secret that must not be given away.
>
> The result is that, should it ever be necessary to do so, our police can have every gangster in the city under lock and key within a few hours.
>
> So far as the police are concerned, the gangster problem is solved.

In a clear echo of the chief constable's complaint, voiced in his report to the magistrates two months earlier, the *Citizen*'s investigator insisted that all that remained was for the magistrates to back up the police efforts with stiffer sentences.

This was all propaganda, of course: the activities of the Billy Boys and their adversaries had long been a source of acute embarrassment to the City of Glasgow Police and the appearance of a succession of prominent Billies at the city's sheriff court had done little to deter their followers. In the wake of the panic engendered by the Drygate murder, however, such unqualified support for the police in the local press must have been a huge boost to Chief Constable Smith and his senior officers.

The *Citizen*'s investigator was equally determined to prove that there was no religious basis to Glasgow's gang conflicts. In practice, he insisted, no gang's followers could be described as devout – even if their names sometimes suggested otherwise:

> They may on an occasion like . . . July 12 seize a glorious opportunity for a fight. But . . . the Protestant members of gangs are not in any church. The Catholic members of gangs are not in any chapel. They are neither good Protestants nor good Catholics. They have no religion of any kind except in name.

Even though he doubted the sincerity of their convictions, the investigator still acknowledged that gang rivalries were shaped by both religious and territorial affiliations. 'Roughly,' he conceded, 'it may be said that the Bridgeton gangs are Protestant, while the Calton and South-side gangs are Catholic.' What he failed to acknowledge was that the reputations of particular locales as 'Protestant' or 'Catholic' were vigorously maintained by gang members, for whom the wearing of orange or green colours in the 'wrong' place was frequently deemed to be sufficient grounds for an assault.

Turning to the vexed question of how to deal with the gangs, the *Citizen*'s investigator advocated the appointment of full-time, paid magistrates for the district police courts in lieu of the bailies who, as elected councillors, could be seen to administer justice in a way that was tempered by their understandable concern with maintaining their popularity among the electorate. A deeper remedy, he concluded, lay in the establishment of classes in good citizenship – including respect for the law and its guardians – in schools. By that means, he concluded, 'our present problem' would be solved within a generation.

With its blend of cynicism and sympathy, propaganda and insight, the *Citizen*'s series offered not so much an unvarnished truth as a corrective to some of the wilder accusations unleashed by the killing of Alec McLellan in the Drygate five months earlier. The investigator's call for training in citizenship was soon taken up, however – not by Glasgow's schools, but by energetic and socially conscious ministers in the Church of Scotland.

How Glasgow Gangsters Terrorise Shopkeepers

Scottish Daily Express Staff Reporter.

RIGHT at the start of this article I should like to point out that, although practically every working-class area in Glasgow has its gangs, they form a minute fraction of the community.

The great majority of the population in areas like Bridgeton, Parkhead, Anderston, the Gorbals, Garngad, Plantation, and so on, are decent people who have their own decent homes, their own decent ambitions, and are upholders of the authorities. They are Glasgow people and are proud of their city.

Now let me tell you of the gangs. Each part of the city that is infested is strictly split up into areas ruled by one of the gangs.

There are more than fifty gangs, but the principal ones are:—The Nunny Boys, the Stickits, the Derry Boys, the Billy Boys, the San Toys (second generation of the famous old Glasgow knuckle-duster bullies), the Kent Star, the Shanley Boys, the Steens, the Norman Conquerors, the Calamity Boys, the Baltic Fleet (from Baltic Street area), and the Shang Boys, from

Glasgow's 'gang menace' as seen by the *Scottish Daily Express* in August 1936. The *Express*'s montage features a rare photograph 'taken during a typical street gang battle in Glasgow's East End'.

George Square, Glasgow, on 'Bloody Friday', 31 January 1919. A strike among the city's engineering and shipyard workers saw 10,000 troops posted to Glasgow and helped to forge the legend of Red Clydeside.

The Garngad, or 'Little Ireland', in 1925. Glasgow was the most congested place in Britain. The proliferation of gangs in the 1920s and 1930s was widely ascribed to the conditions of life in the city's slums.

The National Unemployed Workers' Movement campaigned tirelessly on behalf of those without work during the early 1930s. In Glasgow's East End, the N.U.W.M. met fierce opposition from the Brigton Billy Boys, whose loyalty to the crown was manifested in their repeated disruption of left-wing demonstrations.

The launch of the Cunard liner, the *Queen Mary*, at Clydebank in 1934 provided a poignant reminder of Glasgow's former glories. As recently as 1913, Glasgow – 'Second City of the Empire' – had been the shipbuilding capital of the world.

Sauchiehall Street in 1925: department stores as enticing as
any in Bond Street in London.

The 'other Glasgow': dilapidated tenements in Roslin Place and
Burnside Street in the Cowcaddens in the 1920s.

Street corner society: Hamilton Street, Govan, 1924.

In the 'backlands':
Garngad Road,
around 1920.

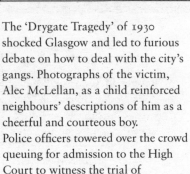

The 'Drygate Tragedy' of 1930 shocked Glasgow and led to furious debate on how to deal with the city's gangs. Photographs of the victim, Alec McLellan, as a child reinforced neighbours' descriptions of him as a cheerful and courteous boy.

Police officers towered over the crowd queuing for admission to the High Court to witness the trial of his assailants.

McLellan's funeral saw a huge crowd gather outside the family home in the Drygate.

Sixteen-year-old James McCluskey of the South Side Stickers, sentenced to five years' penal servitude in 1928 following his fatal stabbing of Jimmy Tait during a clash between the Stickers and the Young Calton Entry.

Reverend J. Cameron Peddie, minister of Hutchesontown Parish Church, with members of the South Side Stickers' Club in 1931. Club secretary and 'ex-gangster', Paddy Cousins, sits at Peddie's side.

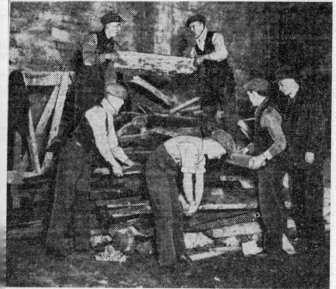

Peddie supervises a group of Stickers at work in the firewood 'factory' in the basement of their temporary clubroom in Naburn Street in the Gorbals.

WHY GLASGOW GETS A BAD NAME

A Word In Season To The Magistrates

DO you know, Magistrates of Glasgow, that your great city is rapidly gaining the worst name in Britain, that while business men are striving to attract new industries and bring the city back to prosperity their work is being instantly undone by the spreading abroad of the notoriety of Glasgow's gangsters?

Glasgow's notoriety spreads abroad: a gangster looms over the City Chambers, ready to swoop with dagger and claws, in the *Sunday Mail*, 1935.

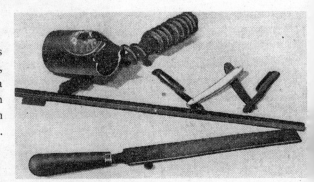

The weapons of 1930s 'gangsterdom': razors, a broken bottle, a heavy file, a stick with a razor-blade stuck in the end, and a cosh.

GLASGOW GANG WARFARE REVIVAL

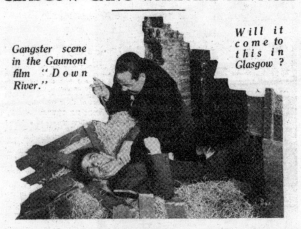

Gangster scene in the Gaumont film "Down River."

Will it come to this in Glasgow?

'Will it come to this in Glasgow?' The *Glasgow Weekly Herald* uses a still from a British crime 'movie' to warn of the revival of Glasgow's reign of terror in 1932.

New Outbreak of Terrorism Threatened

6

Saving Hooligans from Hell

In the wake of the Drygate murder, Major A. B. Meikle, the governor of Polmont Borstal in Falkirk, declared that the solution to Glasgow's gang problem was simple. In a speech to his local Rotary Club, Meikle proclaimed that if lads' clubs and municipal playing fields were established throughout the city: 'There would be none of this gang warfare and razor-slashing at all.' According to Meikle, many of the lads in Polmont had said the same thing themselves.

Meikle's call-to-arms, which was widely publicised in the Scottish national press, prompted a flurry of responses by youth workers, councillors and church leaders. Representatives of existing juvenile organisations pointed to the work already undertaken by groups such as the Boys' Brigade, Boy Scouts and Foundry Boys' Religious Society, but were forced to admit that 'unattached' youths were prone to fall prey to the evils of the street corners. Added to this, these organisations were most active in the city's middle-class and 'artisan' districts; they were notably weaker in the poorer areas, where gangs generally flourished.

The most forceful response came from the Moderator of Glasgow Presbytery, Reverend Dr Lauchlan MacLean Watt, who told the *Scottish Daily Express*:

> It is time that the Church concentrated on finding some means of stopping this orgy of gang violence. We should make a determined effort to reach the hearts and minds of these young men to prevent them developing into jail birds and murderers.

Watt promised to urge his fellow churchmen to 'save these hooligans from going to hell'. His call was taken up by William

Whitelaw, chairman of the London Midland and Scottish Railway Company, at a meeting of the Home Mission of the Church of Scotland in Edinburgh later that month. 'Glasgow gangs may be attributed to the outcome of neglect,' Whitelaw declared, 'and it will not do for the Church to assume that it has no responsibility.' Whitelaw proposed a novel alliance of clergymen and professional footballers: 'A gang must have a hero of some kind and the only idol they know is a football player. If one of the leading Rangers players started a boys' club in the East End of Glasgow, they would find queues of lads outside the door.'

From Gangsters to Pals

While the city's footballers proved reluctant to heed Whitelaw's call, two Church of Scotland ministers were eager to take the lead: Reverend J. A. C. Murray of Park Church in Glasgow's West End and Reverend Sydney Warnes of St Francis-in-the-East, Bridgeton. Warnes had moved to Bridgeton early in 1930 to devote himself to rescue work among the 'non-churchgoing lads' of the East End. St Francis-in-the-East, located close to the Billy Boys' gathering-place at Bridgeton Cross, was the perfect spot for his scheme. His alliance with Murray – minister of one of the city's wealthiest parishes – promised to bridge the 'two Glasgows' in a determined effort on the part of the Church to eradicate the gangs.

The two ministers outlined their plans at a meeting of Glasgow Presbytery on 10 June 1930. As Murray reminded the assembled church officials, the Drygate murder three months earlier had focused the attention of the entire city on the gangs. 'Since then,' he complained, 'every day had seen an increase in the talk and in the action advocated, but nothing had been done.' Together with Warnes, he had conducted a survey of the district within a 200-yard radius of St Francis-in-the-East; they had found ten named gangs with a combined membership estimated at between 250 and 300, with the members' ages ranging from fifteen to forty. They were well organised, the ministers confirmed, 'not only for the purpose of discipline, but for the purpose of finance.'

Murray told the Presbytery that the gangs were a product of economic conditions in the East End. He derided the suggestion made in Chief Constable Smith's report to the city's magistrates that 'a great deal of the element of make-believe' lay behind the formation of the gangs. According to Murray, the forces that drove young men to band together were all too real: unemployment, depressing and insanitary surroundings, and the 'vicious' example set by their elders. Under these circumstances, Murray proclaimed, the wonder was not that gangs were so numerous, but that there were so few. Murray and Warnes also identified three healthy instincts among Bridgeton's gangsters: loyalty, gregariousness and independence. Viewed in this light, the youths' fierce territorial rivalries were not intrinsically harmful. Quite the reverse: channelled into the right outlets – football, athletics, gymnastics and boxing – they could be both healthy and profitable.

The ministers made two proposals. Initially, they wished to organise a football league composed of teams drawn from rival gangs. In the longer term, they proposed to make structural alterations to the building at St Francis-in-the-East to incorporate rooms for recreation and reading, along with a gymnasium and a set of baths. Responding to Murray's address, a member of the Presbytery urged that the ministers' campaign should make 'no denominational differences between the gangsters'. This was a bold call. Just seven years earlier, a report to the General Assembly of the Church of Scotland had warned of 'The Menace of the Irish Race to our Scottish Nationality', and anti-Irish sentiment was generally merged with anti-Catholicism in debates on the racial purity of the Scots.

Murray and Warnes, however, had already agreed that any scheme to combat gangs must be non-sectarian: the new facilities at St Francis-in-the-East were to be open to Catholics as well as Protestants. As Warnes explained to the *Scotsman*: 'No religious differentiation would be made. The desire was to render Christian service in that spirit of brotherhood which recognised every man a brother man.' In a statement to the local press, they insisted that their stance was consistent with the aims of the Church of Scotland: 'not so much to proselytise for any particular communion as to do something productive of Christian citizenship.'

Murray estimated that the building works would cost £2,000. He was confident that the funds could be raised by a public appeal, and announced that he planned to enlist some of Glasgow's younger businessmen in the future running of the scheme. The Presbytery offered its wholehearted support.

Newspaper coverage was equally enthusiastic. The two ministers gave a series of interviews in which they detailed the origins of their scheme. Murray, especially, appears to have relished the thrill of venturing into gangland. He told reporters that he and Warnes had waited for several months for an opportunity to approach the leaders of the gangs; as soon as contact had been made, they embarked on their 'secret mission'. The gang members proved surprisingly affable. 'We interviewed them,' Murray explained, 'and found them very approachable fellows.' The ministers' offer to arrange football matches had met with immediate approval. As Murray confirmed: 'Football is the gangsters' principal recreation. They talk it and play it, and follow the form of the noted Scottish clubs.' Warnes, too, took great encouragement from these first encounters: 'Gangsters as a rule possess a sense of humour,' he told the *Scottish Daily Express*, 'and because of that I feel there is great hope of directing their energies in the right direction.'

Murray and Warnes began to host weekly meetings for local youths at a Bridgeton school on Tuesday nights. On 26 August, they launched a formal organisation: The Bridgeton, St Francis Own, Pals' Association.

In naming their members 'Pals', the ministers invoked the heroism – and intense local pride – of the Pals' battalions of volunteers in the Great War. Within three weeks, more than 400 boys and young men had registered as members. Each meeting concluded with a recital of the 'Pals' Promise': a solemn declaration of loyalty 'to my King and Country, [and] to every brother Pal.'

The Bridgeton 'street-corner' football league was launched the following month. Eight teams of young men, drawn from the corners between Bridgeton Cross and Main Street, played matches on a patch of vacant ground adjacent to a local park on Saturday afternoons and Wednesday evenings.

The structural alterations to St Francis-in-the-East were completed three months later, and the first public meeting of the Bridgeton Pals' Association was held on 30 December. Between 200 and 300 Pals attended. As the *Evening Citizen* noted, most were members of 'a huge Glasgow gang' – the journalist was reluctant to identify them as Billy Boys – and they 'listened attentively through numerous addresses, sang community songs, and in the end promised on their honour to observe the unselfish rules of the Pals' Association.' A former Socialist councillor, W. G. Hunter, told the meeting that Murray and Warnes had put Glasgow's civic leaders to shame by their work in Bridgeton. In a thinly veiled jibe at the 'Moderates' (Tories) in control of Glasgow Corporation, Hunter declared: 'I think some of our big men in the city are afraid of the East End. They seem to think it is the Chicago of Scotland. It is nothing of the kind. There are no Al Capones here!' Hunter's remark drew a lusty response from the assembled Pals. The *Citizen*'s reporter was only too eager to record their 'shout of complete agreement'.

Murray and Warnes's scheme to reform the gangs of the East End inspired a parallel project in Govan under the energetic leadership of Robert Black, the district's police court missionary (an early form of probation officer). Black canvassed the district's Church of Scotland ministers for support. Some were sceptical, even hostile. One warned: 'You can't reform that rabble. You'll simply drive the rats from the streets back to their holes. In fact, you'll be opening up new ground for them.' Three others ministers offered their support, however, along with the local Catholic priests. Black arranged a public meeting for 15 September to launch a new body to be known as the 'Govan Street Corner Movement'. Notices were posted inviting the young men of the district to attend.

More than 500 lads turned up, including delegations from nine different groups of corner boys – the *Scotsman* noted that many of those present already 'had experience of prison life'. They listened to a series of speakers, including the district's socialist MP, Neil MacLean, who urged that the lads should be granted the use of the local public halls for recreational purposes. Councillor Tom Kerr agreed, but added that the Rangers Football Club should likewise make its pitch and dressing rooms available. The meeting established a committee to oversee the provision of new facilities, and each group of lads in attendance was asked to nominate a representative. In a ringing endorsement of the work of Murray and Warnes, it was agreed that the new body would be known as the Govan Pals. As the secretary of the Glasgow Council of Juvenile Organisations pointed out, this would remove 'any stigma associated with street corner boys'.

Within a fortnight, Black was issuing glowing reports on the movement's progress. 'Practically every group or street has its committee for the establishing of a club,' he told the *Sunday Post*, 'and the boys are already considering an interchange of friendly visits.' By October, fourteen clubs had been established with a combined membership of close to a thousand. A reporter on the *Sunday Mail*, who toured the district with Black as his guide, described the startling transformation that had taken place. Under the headline **'GOVAN GANGSTERS GIVE UP WAR!'** the journalist described how formerly lawless young men had organised the new clubs themselves – with Black's assistance – instituting programmes of concerts and dances, forming the Govan Pals' Amateur Football League and planning boxing tournaments and a whist league – the prospect of these much-feared youths challenging each other to card games rather than armed combat delighted the *Mail*'s correspondent. He was equally impressed by the Govan Pals' pledge:

> Never again to stand at street corners, argue or sing in the streets. To be always law-abiding, help the defenceless in time of need, assist the police in the maintenance of order, and to endeavour

to obtain a higher conception of life by social intercourse, reading and debating in their own clubrooms.

This was an altogether loftier undertaking than the Bridgeton Pals' promise, but the managers of Govan's cinemas and dance halls took the local Pals at their word, and opened their premises to groups of lads who had previously been barred on account of their rowdyism.

Black introduced the *Mail*'s reporter to as many of Govan's Pals as possible, and the journalist was surprised to encounter youths who seemed to be both responsible in outlook and highly articulate. They had established a subscription system, whereby those currently in employment subsidised those without work, and had made a determined collective effort to spruce themselves up – jackets with holes in the elbows had been carefully brushed and pressed. The *Mail*'s correspondent confirmed that 'a big percentage' of the young men with whom he spoke were 'anything but vicious'. (Some of the others must have intimidated him, however benign their disposition.) One 'bright young fellow' made an eloquent plea for assistance:

> We are now convinced that the old mode of life could lead us nowhere. All we want is a chance in life. Let those who have condemned us come forward and lend a helping hand. We are not really bad. Most of our gang simply drifted into wrongdoing, not because they wanted to, but because they had nothing else to do.

Black endorsed the Pal's plea. Proclaiming that 'so far as Govan is concerned, gang warfare is a thing of the past,' he lamented the difficulties that the clubs had encountered in finding appropriate premises and appealed to the *Mail*'s readers to donate any unwanted clothes that might enable the 'ex-gangsters' to smarten their appearances, in keeping with their behaviour.

Good Citizenship in the Gorbals

On Glasgow's South Side, as in the East End, the attempt to reform the gangs was led by an enterprising minister of the

Church of Scotland. Reverend J. Cameron Peddie had taken up his post at Hutchesontown Parish Church in the Gorbals in 1928. His interest in the local gangs had been sparked by reports of the trial of four members of the South Side Stickers at Glasgow Sheriff Court in July 1930. The youths had been charged with riot and assault following a pitched battle on the night of the Scottish Cup Final replay between Rangers and Partick Thistle at Hampden Park. The match had attracted a crowd of 103,000 but only around one-fifth of the crowd had been able to squeeze onto the trains, buses and trams back to the city centre after the game, leaving tens of thousands – most of whom were (Protestant) Rangers supporters – to walk. Their route had taken them through the Gorbals.

One group of between forty and fifty Billy Boys had paraded through Crown Street, one of the main Gorbals thoroughfares, waving orange and blue banners and flags along with Union Jacks and a cardboard replica of the Scottish Cup. Their conduct could hardly have been more provocative. As they reached Govan Street, they entered the territory of the South Side Stickers, the largest of the Gorbals gangs. A fifty-strong group, led by eighteen-year-old Arthur Boyle, was waiting. The Stickers rushed at the Billy Boys and, in the fight that followed, weapons were used by both sides. The street quickly filled with 'a seething mass of men fighting', traffic screeched to a halt and passers-by dived into nearby shops for cover. Robert Cotton, a twenty-year-old Rangers supporter easily identified by his blue rosette, was felled by a blow to the back of the head. More than a dozen Stickers swarmed around him, kicking him as he lay on the ground.

Four Stickers – including Arthur Boyle – were arrested at the scene. They stood trial on 11 July. Sheriff Boyd Berry jailed them all for nine months for assault and 'forming part of a riotous mob'.

Procurator Fiscal J. D. Strathern caused a sensation in court when he alleged that some of the prosecution witnesses were afraid to testify: 'Be as careful as you can. I know exactly your difficulty,' he told a young woman who had been in charge of her mother's shop in Crown Street on the night of the disturbance. Prompted by Strathern, a detective from the Southern Division confirmed that the shopkeepers in the district lived in terror of the Stickers. When the police had first asked them to testify, the detective added, the shopkeepers had seemed to 'turn white with fear'.

Shocked by the procurator fiscal's allegations, Reverend Peddie set out to investigate their veracity. He quickly learned that the South Side Stickers – the largest of the Gorbals gangs – was based in the neighbourhood of his church. He spent the next few weeks trying to make contact with them, but none of the groups he approached on nearby street corners would admit to any knowledge of the gang.

Peddie's introduction to the Stickers came about by chance when he walked into a gang fight in one of the streets near his church. A group of Stickers had been attacked by a much larger contingent from a rival gang and while the Stickers stood their ground, they were getting much the worst of the fight. Peddie made towards one youth who was desperately struggling to ward off several opponents, and the other lads fled as the clergyman approached. Peddie led the beleaguered youth – who turned out to be one of the Stickers – into a nearby tenement close and tried to tend his wounds. As other Stickers approached, Peddie drew them into conversation, explaining his interest in establishing a social club on their behalf.

Peddie asked the Stickers to come to his church on the night of Monday 4 August. No one showed up at the appointed time, so at nine o'clock, Peddie went out to look for them. A group of corner boys told him that several of the youths he had spoken to were 'on holiday' [in jail]. When Peddie asked them about their plans for the night, they told him that the Liberty Boys had 'done serious harm to one of our boys' – the Stickers were intent on vengeance. When Peddie tried to persuade the youths to come to the vestry at his church 'to talk over a plan of action', to his astonishment, they agreed. As they walked towards the church, numerous small clusters of youths appeared from various points to join them – the minister realised that this was the gang members' custom when mustering for a fight, to avoid raising the suspicions of the police. Forty youths crowded into the vestry: some were armed with razors and iron bars, while one brandished a sword. Peddie spent half an hour outlining his proposal for a social club before the Stickers took over the discussion as to how to run it. The raid on the Liberty Boys was called off.

A 'free and easy' concert evening was arranged for Friday 8 August, and with a keen eye for publicity, Peddie invited a local dignitary to attend. The observer, who remained anonymous, supplied a glowing account to the *Evening Citizen*. His praise for the performers – 'The Stickers are great singers' – was overshadowed by a rapturous description of the extraordinarily cordial welcome the gang members had extended to him. His only regret was that the Stickers had been unable to turn out in full: no fewer than fifteen of them were in prison.

The *Citizen*'s correspondent reported that Peddie, in his role as the club's leader, had used the meeting to introduce a set of by-laws. These prohibited drinking, betting and swearing on the club's premises. The minister had also announced the club's guiding principle – 'Brotherhood and Good Citizenship' – and reassured the Stickers that no attempt would be made to use the club to proselytise:

> I do not know what your religion is, and I do not want to know. If you are Catholics, be good Catholics, and if you are Protestants, be good Protestants. I will never ask a boy here what his religion is, or whether he has any religion at all.

Peddie's plans for the club were closely modelled on those of Warnes and Murray in Bridgeton, with boxing and football tournaments envisaged as alternatives to 'scraps' in the street. Asked to suggest a colour for the club's membership cards, the correspondent had suggested a neutral white with gold trim, 'to obviate any possible semblance of party feeling'.

The South Side Stickers' Club quickly received enthusiastic backing from the police and magistrates, as well as the press. On 15 August, two Stickers appeared at the Southern Police Court charged with committing a breach of the peace and causing wilful damage during a disturbance in Caledonia Road two weeks previously: plate-glass windows valued at £16 had been smashed. The acting fiscal, Superintendent Cameron, stated that the prisoners, Andrew McCarthy and Alec McLean, had 'unenviable reputations as gangsters' and were recognised as leading figures in the Stickers – McCarthy had appeared as a Crown witness at Glasgow High Court in June 1928 when six of the gang's members had stood trial following the killing of Jimmy Tait. However, rather than pushing for exemplary sentences – as was his wont in gang cases – the superintendent explained that the Stickers had undergone a dramatic change during the past week under Peddie's guidance: 'It is quite obvious that the boys themselves have caught on with the scheme, and I firmly believe that they are trying to do better and lead decent lives.' In a remarkable show of faith, Superintendent Cameron advocated probation for McCarthy and McLean rather than imprisonment. The magistrate assented.

By 16 August, membership of the South Side Stickers' Club stood at 154. The *Evening Citizen* reported that all 107 of the Stickers had joined, along with 47 members of a smaller Gorbals gang called the Bon Accords. John Murphy, the Stickers' former leader, had been elected chairman of the club, while two former bailies had accepted honorary positions. Membership fees were set at twopence per week for those in work, and a penny for the unemployed.

Peddie's initiative was acclaimed in the British national press. *The Times*'s Glasgow correspondent reported that: 'The Stickers and the Bon Accords have intimated to other gangs in the district that they do not intend to indulge in street fighting again unless they are attacked, and have invited these gangs to organise clubs similar to their own.'

The Stickers' pledge to avoid confrontation was to be continuously tested by their former rivals, however – in the months that followed, gangs from the Calton made repeated raids on the Gorbals, challenging the Stickers to fight. On the night of 23 November, police arrested three Calton youths who had been part of a marauding pack 'shouting and bawling' outside the

Stickers' temporary clubroom in Naburn Street. The Gorbals lads ignored the intruders, earning resounding praise from Superintendent Cameron at the Southern Police Court: 'I must say that the Stickers have risen to the occasion very well. These [Calton] youths were just out to try and bring strife to this gang which is trying to keep the peace.' The police carefully acknowledged the Stickers' pride – an important concession to any scheme of this nature. When another group of Calton youths was brought before the same court, Superintendent Cameron explained that the prisoners had been taken into custody for their own safety: 'While the police knew that most of the South Side gangsters were now reformed, they also knew that they would not allow other gangsters to enter their district, challenge them to fight, and let them go scot free.'

On Christmas night, the South Side Stickers' Club organised a dance for 200 young men and women. Among the guests was Bailie Kate Beaton, who applauded the club's work in an interview with the *Scottish Daily Express*. Mrs Beaton was adamant that she saw nothing to suggest that the young people present had been 'bitter enemies of law and order' just six months earlier.

What impressed Peddie most about the Stickers was their 'amazing loyalty to their class'. Under no circumstances, the lads declared, would they collaborate with the police – even if one of their own men faced the gallows for a crime he did not commit: 'We hang rather than tell,' they insisted. Peddie was determined to abide by the Stickers' code. He resolved 'not to let them down. I never gave away any of them and they knew it.' The minister was struck, too, by the youths' generosity: 'When up against it, they would share their last fag-end and their last bite with each other.'

Convinced that poverty and unemployment were the chief causes of the Stickers' resort to crime, Peddie experimented with a number of schemes to provide them with jobs. Many of the lads lacked the physique for labouring work – they tended to be 'underfed, pinched and stunted in growth' – so Peddie established the Lightning Distribution Agency, for which they could go out delivering hand-bills from door to door.

Unfortunately, the enterprise floundered in the face of stiff competition. A firewood 'factory' in the basement of the club's temporary premises in Naburn Street fared rather better after Peddie installed a power-driven circular saw and a bunching machine. Two 'well-known thieves' helped to run the business, buying old wood to be chopped, bundled and sold to shops.

After six months, the factory was employing twelve full-time workers. Peddie attempted to expand the firewood business, renting larger premises to accommodate up to forty employees. However, the strain of running the factory proved too much even for a man of Peddie's dedication. As he later recalled: 'I became convinced that it is impossible to carry on such an undertaking with this class of employee other than on a charitable basis. They need careful and constant supervision which only men of leisure and means achieve.' Peddie had been obliged to call at some of the lads' houses at seven o'clock every morning to make sure that they turned up for work: while he trusted the Stickers to refrain from gang warfare, he was unconvinced by their work ethic. When the factory closed, he ruefully admitted, some of the workforce 'returned to their old ways'.

The Official History of the South Side Stickers

The secretary of the Stickers' Club, Paddy Cousins, wrote a history of the South Side Stickers for the *Weekly Record* in March 1931. Cousins's account, which was prefaced by a glowing testimonial from Peddie, was carefully crafted to culminate in an appeal for donations towards the sum of £4,000 required for new, purpose-built club premises.

Cousins made almost no mention of the Stickers' street fights – those had already been extensively reported in the local press even before the death of Jimmy Tait in 1928 – preferring instead to introduce some of the gang's more colourful members, and detailing their more outlandish exploits, in a series of humorous vignettes. His history of the Stickers was far from complete, but it nonetheless provided a rare glimpse of a Glasgow gang from the inside.

Cousins revealed that the Stickers had been formed in 1921. Peddie had been surprised to discover that the Stickers had both Catholics and Protestants in their ranks; Cousins pointed out that the gang contained Jews and atheists, too. In that sense, the gang's membership was entirely in keeping with the wider population of the Gorbals. Hundreds of men, youths and boys had passed through their ranks since 1921, and a sizeable number of women and girls had 'attached themselves' to the gang. Members had been graded according to age and physique – effectively confirming the claim by Murray and Warnes that Glasgow's gangs were tightly organised. Cousins also dwelled on the Stickers' exploits as thieves rather than their reputation as street fighters: by his account, the gang had boasted a dedicated housebreaking section. This was organised by 'the Traveller', who – in the guise of a pedlar – roamed the surrounding districts to identify houses and commercial premises to be burgled. Junior members concentrated on petty thefts from city centre stores and on plundering outdoor displays from shops and warehouses.

While reluctant to detail the Stickers' history of violence – 'There are many crimes and atrocities which cannot be allowed to appear in these pages' – Cousins did confirm that the Stickers had routinely fought with razors and daggers, while on occasion, he added, the city's gangs resorted to still deadlier weapons: 'I have seen times when firearms and corrosive acids were used' – no shootings were reported by the police or local press, however. Unsurprisingly, many of the Stickers bore the marks of hand-to-hand combat on their faces: 'Many have lost a part of their ear, one or two of them are devoid of an eye, and scars four and five inches long are common.'

Thieving and fighting were by no means the gang's only preoccupations: their parties were huge, riotous affairs, fuelled by stolen liquor. Entertainment was provided by dance bands, which routinely performed without payment.

Cousins devoted a significant portion of his story to the gang's 'characters', including 'the Cadger' and 'the Swank', both of whom embodied the Stickers' ability to live by their wits: the Cadger made sizeable sums by swindling racecourse bookmakers, while the Swank was an expert all-round conman. The Swank's escapades – in the guise of clergyman, doctor, army or naval officer, gas account collector and property agent – were the stuff of Gorbals legend. According to one of the gang's most treasured tales, he had even posed as a detective to liberate two fellow Stickers – along with their haul of stolen goods – from the clutches of a pair of beat constables. Another of the gang's leading members, known as 'Dead-Eye', was a ship's fireman, and was responsible for the accumulation of the Stickers' armoury of revolvers. Cousins told how Dead-Eye had once made a drunken attempt to stow away on a ship he believed to be bound for the USA. He awoke to find the vessel stationary and empty and that he was still in Glasgow: the ship was berthed in a dry-dock, awaiting repairs.

Cousins himself was known as 'the Emigrant', following a spell in Canada. He relayed how, following a brief and unhappy stint as a farmhand, he had spent an enjoyable few months as part of the crew of a passenger ship plying between Toronto and New York. Laid off at the end of the summer season, he joined 'a well-known crook organisation in Toronto', but the gang disbanded when police attention became 'too hot' and Cousins headed to Montreal. There he met two fellow Stickers, who persuaded him to return home.

Cousins's tales celebrated the Stickers' endless capacity for mischief and adventure, along with their ability to laugh at themselves and everyone around them. In this vivid 'human document', the Stickers were not mindless brutes, but streetwise, fun-loving rogues.

The month after Paddy Cousins's history of the Stickers was published by the *Weekly Record*, Peddie appeared at the Southern Police Court as a character witness on behalf of another of the club's members, who was convicted of assaulting his wife with a hatchet. The victim, who appeared in court with her head heavily bandaged, claimed that she had repeatedly been forced to send for the police to deal with her husband's drunken outbursts. He admitted that they had argued, but denied striking his wife with the hatchet produced in court: he had 'shoved her against a door,' he explained, 'but there were nails in the door, which had caused the injuries.' Superintendent Cameron told the magistrate that the prisoner was a 'reformed gangster', adding that Reverend Peddie wished to speak on the prisoner's behalf. Peddie confirmed that the accused was a member of the South Side Stickers' Club and employed in his factory, where he had been doing 'exceedingly well' (so much so that without him, 'the scheme could hardly carry on'). Superintendent Cameron requested that the prisoner be put on probation for twelve months. With some reluctance, the magistrate concurred.

It would appear that Cameron and Peddie were both more concerned with suppressing gang fights than with protecting women from violent husbands. To the police, outbreaks of gang warfare were a highly public challenge to their authority, whereas domestic violence – so long as it was not fatal – could be more leniently dealt with. Peddie, who clearly formed a very close bond with the Stickers but appears to have had little day-to-day contact with their wives or sweethearts, in effect shared the police's priorities. When Peddie recalled the case more than twenty years later in an article for the *Evening Citizen*, he told how he had escorted the prisoner home following the court hearing, only to be confronted in the street by his wife. She had given her husband 'as good a mouthful of language as I'd ever heard' and Peddie had had to restrain him from renewing the assault. She had continued to 'abuse' her husband when they arrived home, shouting: 'I'll get you yet. I won't rest till I see you hanged.' Peddie's sympathies appeared to lie with the exasperated husband. The minister advised the couple to separate, but reported with some satisfaction that they were later reunited. According to Peddie, the husband went on to become a steady worker and a good citizen. How the 'reformed' gangster's wife fared over the subsequent years of their marriage, Peddie did not remark.

The Rehabilitation of James McCluskey

James McCluskey of the South Side Stickers had been jailed for five years in June 1928 after pleading guilty to the fatal stabbing of Jimmy Tait. McCluskey, then aged sixteen, spent the first two weeks of his sentence 'teasing' cotton in his cell at Duke Street Prison in Glasgow. He was then moved to Edinburgh Prison, where he was held alongside the adult prisoners and put to work in the blacksmith's shop. McCluskey proved to be a model prisoner. Three months after his arrival at Edinburgh, warders reported that he was 'shaping very well' and that his work was 'a credit to him'. The prison governor, R. M. Dudgeon, permitted him to attend the educational classes held in the prison's Borstal department, and to play football with the Borstal inmates on Saturday afternoons. Six months later, McCluskey was transferred to the Borstal section after Dudgeon vouched for his exemplary conduct: 'I am of the opinion that McCluskey will do well in the future and make good,' the governor reported. 'He readily responds to encouragement, and is really a nice lad.'

In June 1930 – two years into his sentence – McCluskey was interviewed by the prison's visiting committee. They recommended that he should be liberated on licence under the terms of the 1908 Prevention of Crime Act, so long as suitable employment and an appropriate guardian could be found for him. The 1908 Act sanctioned the early release of Borstal inmates, under supervision, in cases where the prison commissioners were satisfied that there was a 'reasonable probability' that the offender would 'abstain from crime and lead a useful and industrious life'. The visiting committee was swayed by McCluskey's record since his arrival at Edinburgh – six good-conduct badges and not a single record of misconduct – along with a series of glowing reports prepared by prison staff. McCluskey was 'always willing' and 'naturally intelligent' observed the prison schoolmaster, while the Catholic chaplain could find no fault in his character: 'A most obliging and courteous youth: self-reliant and yet without presuming.' The governor was adamant that the prisoner 'realises to the full the mistake he has made', and insisted that McCluskey would make a law-abiding and industrious citizen upon his release.

Inquiries into McCluskey's family circumstances were less promising. By July 1930, his father, Michael, aged sixty-three, had been out of work 'fully eight years' – the household income totalled just 42 shillings per week. James's fifteen-year-old brother was the sole wage earner; a grocer's message boy, his weekly wage was 10 shillings. Neither of his sisters was in paid work, although one was fully occupied in looking after the house. Not surprisingly, police inquiries revealed that the family's tenement home had 'a comparatively poor appearance', while there was no immediate prospect of James finding employment were he to return to the Gorbals.

James McCluskey was released on licence on 13 November 1930, almost halfway through his five-year sentence. He undertook to abstain from any violation of the law, to refrain from associating with persons 'of bad character' and to lead 'a sober and industrious life'.

Having stated a desire to go to sea, McCluskey was taken by Alexander Thomson of the Scottish After-Care Council to join the SS *Melrose* at Leith – as an ordinary seaman, his wage would be 44 shillings per week. But McCluskey's stint at sea was to last just twelve days: he complained of seasickness, and persuaded Thomson to recommend that he should be permitted to return to his family home in Glasgow. On 27 November, James McCluskey made his way back to the Gorbals.

He found the district little changed: unemployment and poverty were still rife, and his own family was suffering more than most. Yet many of his friends had renounced gang warfare, and now gathered under the watchful eye of Reverend Cameron Peddie at the South Side Stickers Club, where a bemused McCluskey was welcomed home with a celebratory concert party.

Despite all his displays of repentance, McCluskey had returned to the Gorbals with one grievance in mind – Peddie later recalled how McCluskey rounded on Andrew McCarthy at a subsequent meeting of the club, declaring: 'This man gave me away at my trial.' His fury was understandable: McCarthy's testimony at the High Court in 1928 was the clearest breach imaginable of the Stickers' boast that they would hang before giving away even an enemy, and McCluskey vowed that he would 'have his revenge yet'. Only Peddie's intervention – and the minister's formidable skills as an arbitrator – prevented bloodshed.

In February 1936, James McCluskey – now aged twenty-four, and working as a road contractor's labourer – married nineteen-year-old Barbara Docherty, and the couple settled in Cleland Street. McCluskey's supervision had by now expired: his record, since his release on licence, was unblemished. His hair, however, had turned prematurely white. To the once dapper former gangster, and all those who knew him, it was a lasting reminder of McCluskey's culpability for the slaying of Jimmy Tait.

The Unfortunate Gardener of the Garngad

Not all such 'club' schemes were successful. In the Garngad, Great War veteran Harry Bonar converted some of the rooms in his tenement house in Villiers Street into a club house for the Romeo Boys – local gangsters who had enjoyed citywide notoriety for several years after they derailed a tramcar by placing pieces of metal on the line. Bonar, who worked as a gardener at a private house in Thornliebank six miles south of Glasgow, had incurred their wrath after complaining about repeated disturbances in his tenement close. As he explained to *Thomson's Weekly News* in November 1930: 'Free fights in the close occurred every other night, and I would not get more than an hour or so of undisturbed sleep.' The weary gardener had reported the youths to the police, only for them to retaliate by hammering on his door night after night in the early hours of the morning.

Bonar, who had 'gone all through the war in France, Belgium and Mesopotamia' with the Royal Artillery, had approached the Romeo Boys in the street. He had offered to form a club on their behalf and, to his surprise, they had accepted. His former tormentors began to congregate in his house most evenings, playing dominoes or cards and organising 'socials' to which girls were invited. They paid threepence per week towards the club's funds and appointed a secretary, who issued a monthly balance sheet. Bonar acted as their president.

It was not all plain sailing, however. Some of the Romeos rejected Bonar's hospitality, and his recruits were given a torrid time by their former companions. As he recalled:

> When our club first started the boys who joined me had a terrible time. The old members of the gang not only hurled abuse, but also missiles at them, and I was terribly afraid that some night there would be a riot. That would have finished our club, of course. The boys weathered the storm without retaliating, but it must have been hard for them.

Bonar helped several of the club's members – previously regarded as 'unemployable' – to find work, and set out to recruit prominent local sportsmen to act as coaches to the club's members. His own employer promised to supply a punch ball for boxing training, while another 'gentleman' offered to provide Sandow developers – bodybuilding apparatus – so that the Romeos might be encouraged to demonstrate their virility by peaceable means. Bonar was also keen to start reading classes, and cited the local police superintendent – 'He only wishes there were more clubs like ours' – in support of his appeal for assistance from the readers of the *Weekly News*.

Bonar's venture made the pages of the national press for a second time in July 1932. Speaking now to the *Scottish Daily Express*, Bonar told how his endeavour to reform the gangsters of the Garngad had ended in disaster: the Romeo Boys' Club had closed, while Bonar had lost his life savings along with his job. He was now living in penury and fear in a single room. A few days prior to his interview with the *Express*, he had been assaulted and severely kicked by an 'ex-gangster' to whom he had previously given food and shelter. He had reported his plight to the police, but was unable to prosecute his assailant, as no one was willing to act as witness on his behalf. Bonar was eager to warn of the perils of working with 'ex-gangsters':

> Gang reformation, to my mind, is impossible. I struggled for two years to keep the club open. I gave the men food, lent the club

for marriages of the ex-gangsters, and gave them money to start in small businesses.

It was all futile. There was no gratitude shown. The men got angry when I checked their swearing. They wanted to run wild.

Bit by bit my Queen Anne suite of furniture, my carpets, pictures, boxing gloves, cutlery and clothes were sold to help them.

Now when I am heart-broken no one comes near me.

Bonar's experiment had been a disaster. Other observers, however, remained convinced that converting gangs into social clubs was the only method of curbing Glasgow's gang menace.

A City's Youth Saved?

In 1933, Donald Brown of the *Scottish Daily Express* hailed Glasgow's 'gangster clubs' as a triumphant success. Brown claimed that 'hundreds' of such clubs had been formed across the city during the previous three years, all of them resolutely non-sectarian – other commentators spoke of dozens: Reverend Sydney Warnes counted sixty. Brown toured a number of the South Side clubs with Reverend J. Cameron Peddie. He was impressed to discover that clubs that had been started by clergymen and social workers were now run quite effectively by the youths themselves.

The young men to whom Brown spoke did not want charity. They also resented the label 'gangster'. Their premises – disused shops, obsolete factories and dilapidated former public houses – were frequently shabby and poorly furnished, but Brown was deeply impressed by the lads themselves. 'They are slowly but steadily taking their places as citizens,' he concluded.

In speaking up for the youths of Glasgow's slums, Brown added his voice to those of Peddie, Warnes, and Govan's police court missionary, Robert Black, all of whom repeatedly championed the virtues of the 'ex-gangsters' with whom they worked. In a series of speeches delivered in Glasgow and Edinburgh during 1932, Warnes appealed for additional funds to support his work in the East End, telling of the spiritual awakening taking place at St-Francis-in-the-East, while reminding his audiences that 'if there was a war tomorrow', the Bridgeton Pals were 'just the type who would be recommended for medals'. Peddie was more effusive still. In November 1932, he told a meeting of the Speakers' Club in Glasgow's Grand Hotel that he had found the South Side Stickers to be 'a splendid set of lads, at heart'. They had renounced gang warfare, Peddie insisted, and were 'anxious to exchange their fighting and squabbling for something better'.

Peddie claimed that since the formation of the South Side Stickers' Club, 'the gangsters in that district had not been involved in a single fight'. The minister was eager to cite police support for his work, as was Paddy Cousins, secretary of the Stickers' Club.

The local superintendent was more circumspect, however, noting that 'most' of the Gorbals gangsters were reformed. In fact, while the South Side Stickers appeared to be keeping the peace, some of them at least were still engaging in periodic clashes with their traditional enemies, the Liberty Boys. On the afternoon of Sunday, 11 January 1931, members of the two gangs assembled at a field in Rutherglen on the outskirts of the city, where two youths – one from each gang – took part in a square-go. Police rushed to the scene and managed to arrest one of the combatants: John Boyle of the Liberty Boys. Boyle told the Southern Police Court that: 'The other chap said he got a kicking on Hogmanay. He said I was there, and he claimed me.' Police witnesses alleged that the square-go was merely the prelude to a general fight between the two gangs.

Peddie was no doubt conscious that outsiders tended to bracket slum youths as either virtuous or vicious. Little was to be gained by admitting that some of the South Side Stickers had quickly returned to their old ways, or that the club's formation had simply meant another Gorbals gang – the Beehive Boys – had eclipsed the Stickers as the leading force on the South Side.

Fewer in number than the Stickers, but more tightly knit, the Beehive Boys saw themselves as a new type of gang: capable of ferocious violence, but more interested in the pursuit of profit than in territorial or sectarian skirmishing. In Bridgeton, too, gang rivalries persisted, despite the considerable efforts of Sydney Warnes. The Pals' Association provided a welcome route out of gang life for dozens, if not hundreds, of East End youths but, ultimately, Warnes's dream of eradicating Bridgeton's gangs was never realised. As with Peddie, the obstacles facing this energetic and ecumenical minister were simply too great: the Billy Boys and their adversaries were too numerous, the bitterness forged by their years of skirmishing too deep and, despite the successes of the clubs, gangs proved to have a continuous and ongoing presence on the streets.

7

Billy Boys and the San Toy

On the morning of Saturday, 10 July 1926, an Orange procession set out from Bridgeton Cross for St Enoch railway station in Glasgow city centre. From there, they travelled by train to Dalry in Ayrshire, site of the annual parade of the Grand Orange Lodge of Scotland in commemoration of the victory of 'King Billy' at the Battle of the Boyne. They were accompanied by a contingent of Billy Boys, most of whom travelled to Dalry to take part in the parade.

Two of the Bridgeton gangsters did not board the Dalry train. Instead, shortly before noon, they set out to walk back to Bridgeton. In London Road four men accosted and then attacked them. Both of the Billies suffered severe cuts: one on the arm; the other on the head, face and arms, 'his right ear being almost severed from his head'. The assailants ran off, but two of them were arrested later that day: Dan Hands, aged eighteen, and nineteen-year-old Joe Willis. Both were found to be in possession of razors as well as knives, and Hands 'practically admitted what had been done'.

The two youths stood trial at Glasgow Sheriff Court three weeks later. Both pleaded guilty. The Billy Boys alleged that the assault had been entirely unprovoked, claiming that they had been targeted merely for wearing orange rosettes. The prisoners told a different story: the Billy Boys had been singing 'party songs' and shouting: 'Kick the Pope!' When asked to stop, one of them motioned as if to draw something from his pocket. Willis and Hands drew their razors in response. Willis claimed that he, in particular, had reason to be fearful as he was 'keeping company' with a girl who had been a member of the Orange lodge in Bridgeton and she had been given an ultimatum: give up Willis or leave the lodge. She had left the lodge and, on a subsequent visit to Bridgeton, Willis had been assaulted by members of the Billy Boys. Willis's counsel explained to the court that any threat posed by the Bridgeton gangsters could not be taken lightly since 'the Billy Boys were about 400 strong.' Sheriff Macdiarmid was not swayed by any of this, however. He jailed both prisoners for nine months with hard labour.

The claim that the membership of the Billy Boys had grown to 400 was widely noted in the local press, particularly as few gangs had been mentioned by name in previous accounts of Bridgeton's 'gang warfare'. The *Evening Citizen* had identified the Billy Boys and a rival 'Fenian' gang in March 1926, while the Billy Boys and the Norman Conks had made the headlines following a clash at Bridgeton Cross the following month, but few people outside the ranks of the gangs themselves had been aware that the Billy Boys had amassed so many followers.

No mention was made in court of any gang affiliation on the part of Dan Hands or Joe Willis, but the location of the assault – at the junction of London Road and Charlotte Street in the Calton – suggests that they were members of the San Toy. In its original incarnation, during the 1900s, the ranks of the San Toy had contained Protestants as well as Catholics. By the mid-1920s, however, Protestant youths from the Calton had begun to flock to Bridgeton Cross to swell the numbers of the Billy Boys, and the San Toy, along with the Kent Star, the Calton Entry Boys and the Norman Conks, were firmly identified as 'Catholic'.

No one doubted that the gangsters who congregated at Bridgeton Cross were Protestants. Their anthem borrowed the most inflammatory line – 'up to his knees in Fenian blood' – from the unofficial and highly combative version of the traditional Orange song, 'Boyne Water'. To the tune of 'Marching through Georgia', the Brigton Billy Boys sang:

Hello! Hello!
We are the Billy Boys
Hello! Hello!
You'll know us by our noise
We're up to our knees in Fenian blood
Surrender or you'll die
We are the Brigton Billy Boys.

Bellowed in the streets of Bridgeton or the Calton on a Saturday night, the Billies' anthem could all too easily provoke a riot, as police officers ruefully testified at the Eastern Police Court.

Orange Walks

The Brigton Billy Boys earned much of their notoriety through their participation in parades organised by the Orange Order. By the 1920s, the annual Orange Walks – staged on the Saturday before 12 July – were held in a town or village outside Glasgow. The Billies claimed that their role was to protect the processionists from crowds of hostile Catholics, not least on their return to the city on the Saturday night, while Catholic residents of the East End inevitably viewed the presence of this band of Protestant street fighters as hugely provocative. In districts such as the Calton, Catholic youths felt obliged to turn out to oppose the Billy Boys and confrontations between opposing street gangs inflamed what were already highly volatile occasions. Newspaper reports of the clashes that marred the parades did much to burnish the Billy Boys' reputation.

In July 1927, 40,000 people assembled for the annual Orange Walk at Cambuslang. The *Sunday Mail* reported how:

A crowd of young men, about two hundred in number, their ordinary clothes hardly to be seen by reason of their many orange coloured decorations, marched down Glasgow Road West, apart altogether from the procession.

As they walked along they sang raucously, 'We are the Bridgeton Billy Boys.'

After exchanging abuse with local residents, the Bridgeton gang besieged a public house, launching a 'perfect fusillade' of bottles at the premises, before one youth ran forward to smash the pub windows with a cricket bat bound with steel wire.

Violence was by no means confined to the Twelfth of July celebrations: within Glasgow's East End, the Billy Boys attached themselves to local processions, including children's parades. On Sunday, 10 June 1928, a 750-strong procession, including around 100 children, wound its way through the East End from Bridgeton to the city centre. The parade, which was headed by the Argyle band, included a sizeable contingent of Billy Boys. Both the outward and return journeys through the Calton saw skirmishes between the Billies and local Catholic gangs.

Police identified prominent members of the (Catholic) Kent Star, including Ross Prete, who was armed with a piece of rubber tubing, and James McLaughlin, who was waving a bayonet above his head, as the gang made a series of rushes at the procession. On the return journey, the band pointedly marched along Kent Street to the fury of residents, including John Hotchkiss and William Mills, who hurled missiles into the middle of the crowd from the tenement windows. 'The Billy Boys came down the street, and they began to "pap" bricks at the window,' according to one of Mills's neighbours. In Well Street, weapons were brandished, missiles were thrown, a plate-glass window was broken and one Orangeman was stabbed.

Matthew Hotchkiss was charged with the stabbing. He stood trial at Glasgow Sheriff Court, where the victim, Alexander Torrance, confounded the procurator fiscal by claiming that he had not been stabbed at all. In accordance with gangland's code of non-cooperation with the police and courts, Torrance insisted that: 'He and the accused were "catapulted" through the plate-glass window by the rush and pressure of the crowd.' The prosecution was abandoned.

Ross Prete fared less well in court: he was jailed for sixty days with hard labour, along with two other members of the Kent Star, for rioting and committing a breach of the peace.

Such clashes were the stuff of legend. This episode – or one like it – was recalled more than sixty years later by Larry Johnson, a former member of the Beehive Boys from the Gorbals. Johnson recalled how:

> The principal gang in Glasgow at that time was the Bridgeton Billy Boys. Now this was a Protestant gang, Rangers supporters, they were so strong at the time that no other gang could come near Bridgeton Cross . . . Then there was Orange Walks used to take place . . . and as they were marching through Glasgow they had to get some support. So the Billy Boys supported them, and it was all hell let loose, it was terror for anybody who interfered . . . it was possible that Roman Catholic gangs would attack them if they could, and the Billy Boys would intervene because they were more powerful, and there would be slaughter. They would smash the Roman Catholic gangs going through the Calton. There was always a number of arrests – the police accepted that it would happen. I remember one particular time, there was one well-known Roman Catholic gangster, they called him Ross Prete, they caught him one time because he was leading off the gang that was attacking the Billy Boys. They lifted him up and smashed him right through a big plate-glass window, his head first. That was the sort of thing that happened.

At the time of his appearance at Glasgow Sheriff Court in June 1928, Ross Prete was seventeen years old.

The King of the Billy Boys

Within the East End, incessant feuding between the Billy Boys and the Catholic gangs of the Calton and Bridgeton saw the emergence of a clutch of notable 'fighting men', including the 'leader-off' of the Norman Conks, John Brogan, and Eli Webb and Billy Fullerton of the Billy Boys. Webb appeared at Glasgow Sheriff Court in June 1927 following an assault on William McIlhinney in Charles Street, Bridgeton. McIlhinney had been making his way home from a football match between Clyde and Rangers when he was attacked by a group of Billy Boys, one of whom slashed him on the back of the neck with a razor.

The motive for the assault was simple: McIlhinney was displaying a green handkerchief in his jacket pocket.

Six Billy Boys were charged with assault by stabbing. Proceedings against John Ross and Robert Gibson were dropped following an identity parade, but Webb and three others – Edward Livingstone, Donald Gemmell and Richard Purdon – stood trial at the sheriff court. Leading the prosecution, Procurator Fiscal J. D. Strathern described the attack as both random and cowardly: the unsuspecting victim had been 'deliberately slashed on the neck without having the opportunity of defending himself or identifying his attackers'. The court heard that Webb carried out the slashing after Livingstone handed him a razor.

The proceedings took an unexpected twist when John Ross, who had been held in Duke Street Prison in connection with the assault, appeared as a witness for the defence: Ross told the jury that he had slashed McIlhinney. Under cross-examination, Ross insisted that none of the prisoners in the dock had been present. The jury was unimpressed. They found Webb, Livingstone and Gemmell guilty, although they found the case against Purdon not proven. Sheriff Robertson jailed Webb and Livingstone for twelve months with hard labour. Gemmell got nine months.

The trial had aroused considerable interest in the East End and a large crowd gathered outside the sheriff court to await the verdict. It was dispersed by police before any protest could be mounted. Webb, Livingstone and Gemmell appealed against their convictions, but their pleas were rejected by the Court of Criminal Appeal in Edinburgh on 19 July. Two days later, John Ross was tried at Glasgow Sheriff Court: he, too, was jailed for twelve months.

At the time of the trial, Eli Webb was reputed to be the 'King' of the Brigton Billy Boys. Aged twenty-five, he was already a veteran of violence – nine months earlier, he had been admitted to Glasgow Royal Infirmary with head injuries following a fight with members of the Norman Conks in Dale Street. Webb had joined the army in October 1919 at the age of seventeen. He returned to Glasgow in June 1921, moving back into the house of his mother and stepfather in Bernard Street in Bridgeton. He found work locally as a rivet-heater at Sir William Arrol's engineering works, and the following summer he married Rose McAllister, a mill worker two years his junior. Their life together did not run smoothly. Within six months, Webb had lost his job and his dole payments of 15 shillings per week were insufficient for them to set up home on their own, even with Rose in regular work. They lived first with his parents, then with hers, before settling in Webb's sister's house in Boden Street, Bridgeton.

Shortly before Webb's trial at the sheriff court, in June 1927, Rose was laid off from her job. With her husband in prison, she was obliged to apply for poor relief. The parish officer's case-notes recorded: 'Husband to prison for 12 months for razor slashing. He is a notorious criminal and is said to be "<u>King of the Billy Boys</u>."' Eli Webb might not have been master of his own house, but on the streets of Bridgeton his authority was palpable.

The Billy Boys' power rested on their capacity to gather support from a much wider catchment area than any rival gang: of the three young men to stand trial with Eli Webb following the assault on William McIlhinney, only Edward Livingstone hailed from the East End – Donald Gemmell came from Cumberland Street in the Gorbals, while Richard Purdon lived in Rutherglen. Youths from across the East End and nearby districts on the South Side gathered in huge numbers at Bridgeton Cross. In effect, the Billies took possession of the Cross, with its cinema and numerous public houses, so that Bridgeton – by no means an exclusively Protestant locality – became renowned as the symbolic heartland of the Protestant East End, while those Billy Boys based in districts outside Bridgeton frequently became embroiled in bitter sectarian feuds in their own neighbourhoods. Richard Purdon was a notable example: in September 1928, fifteen months after standing trial in the McIlhinney case, he was one of three men charged with the attempted murder of John McKernan, a twenty-one-year old Catholic, in Rutherglen.

McKernan recovered sufficiently to testify against his assailants at Glasgow High Court the following month. He told the jury that there had been 'considerable ill-feeling' between Catholics and Protestants in the district, leading to a number of fights. McKernan's mother told the court that she had witnessed the assault. She had begged Purdon not to murder her son, but he had replied: 'You are only a Papish —'

Purdon entered a plea of self-defence, but he was convicted of assault along with his two co-accused. They were each jailed for twelve months. The feud persisted, however, re-ignited by threats posted on the walls of public houses. On the night of 3 November, sixteen-year-old James McKernan fought the nephew of one of his brother's assailants after pointing to a poster which read: 'Notice to all cowards. Dead men tell no tales.' A photograph of John McKernan, taken from a newspaper report, had been attached to the poster. James McKernan and his adversary were both fined £1.

The Razor King

John Ross, who had been jailed for twelve months in July 1927 after confessing to assaulting William McIlhinney with a razor, was jailed again in August 1930. Now aged twenty-two, he was convicted of assaulting two of the Billy Boys' female followers in Glasgow Green. According to the police, Ross was 'in the habit of carrying a razor, and was known as the Razor King.' On the night of Saturday 26 July, he entrusted one of his weapons to a girl named Hyndman. When he asked for the razor back, four nights later, Hyndman told him that she had thrown it away. Ross punched Hyndman in the face and then kicked her. When one of Hyndman's friends protested, he struck her too. A detective constable told the Eastern Police Court that Ross 'was well known to the police in the vicinity of Bridgeton Cross as one of the ringleaders of the Billy Boys'. Ross was jailed for sixty days with hard labour.

The Billy Boys' female adherents could be quick to use the gang to settle their grievances. On the night of 17 November

1930, two of them got into an altercation with William Rankin in the King's Picture House in James Street, Bridgeton: Rankin grew irritated when the girls chattered to each other during a 'talkie'. When he asked them to stop talking, they did – but one of them warned: 'I will laugh in your face for that.' Rankin thought nothing more of it, but on his way out of the cinema he was pushed from behind and then struck on the back of the neck. When he turned to see who had struck him, he received another blow from behind and was knocked down. He was immediately surrounded by a group of young men who kicked him about the face and body. Fearing that Rankin would be kicked to death, nineteen-year-old Isabella McLaughlan pushed her way through the crowd and threw herself on top of him. Surprised by McLaughlan's action, the crowd scattered.

Police inquiries led to the arrest of several Billy Boys, including John Ross – only just out of jail. After initially denying any knowledge of the incident, Ross admitted to detectives that he had been involved but named another man as the instigator of the assault. The man was questioned by detectives, but no witnesses could be found to verify Ross's account and the man was released. Ross stood trial at Glasgow Sheriff Court on 11 December, when he pleaded guilty to the charge of assaulting William Rankin 'to his serious injury'.

Press reports of the proceedings were dominated by a background report on the Billy Boys prepared by the procurator fiscal, J. D. Strathern, as part of the case against John Ross. According to the report, which was presented in court by Strathern's deputy, the gang's membership had peaked 'four or five years ago' at around 800, but now stood at about 400. The remaining members were organised into sections thirty to forty strong, each with its own leader. Strathern alleged that the gang exerted a system of terror whereby anyone who annoyed one of its members was waylaid and severely assaulted.

Strathern's report highlighted the Billy Boys' eagerness to profit from the fear they inspired. On the basis of information supplied by the police, he alleged that:

Frequently members of the gang, who are unemployed, 'tap' persons who are employed and if they refuse to give the small sums of money asked for they are assaulted by members of the gang at the first favourable opportunity. If a member of the gang is arrested by the Police, it often happens that the shop keepers in that district are asked for a small sum of money towards the defence of that member and they are afraid to refuse to contribute.

There are a number of smaller gangs in that district but they are not so powerful as the 'Billy Boys'.

The police have endeavoured to suppress the gangs but as the persons in that district are afraid to assist, the difficulty of so doing is evident.

Strathern's deputy told the court that Ross's admission of guilt presented the judicial authorities with an opportunity: for once, exemplary punishment could be meted out without fear of witness intimidation. Sheriff Wilton agreed. He remitted John Ross to the High Court.

Strathern's report on the Billy Boys was aired for a second time at the High Court on 16 December. Pressing for an exemplary sentence, the Advocate Depute highlighted Ross's status as a section leader in the Billy Boys, along with his nickname. To demonstrate the menace posed by 'these gangs of brutal and cowardly hooligans', the Advocate Depute pointed out that Isabella McLaughlan had been harassed by several members of the Billy Boys, culminating in an assault on her the day after Ross appeared at the sheriff court. Declaring that Ross was 'addicted to violence', Lord Anderson jailed him for eighteen months. Had Ross used his razor against Rankin, the judge warned, the penalty would have been much more severe.

The jailing of the 'Razor King' was greeted with sensational headlines in both the local and the Scottish national press, the *Weekly Record* commissioning a special investigator to follow up Strathern's report on the Billy Boys. Briefed by the police, he reported that the gang had been founded 'for the sole purpose of making trouble with the Roman Catholic population of Bridgeton and Calton'. Their song, 'We are the Billy Boys', was 'really a challenge to all and sundry to fight', while their reputation as the best-organised of Glasgow's gangs rested on military-style discipline:

> it is part of the constitution of the 'Billy Boys' that members must implicitly obey the commands of their leaders. Periodically there are held 'courts-martial,' and several kinds of punishment are meted out to the disobedient, from a fine, which goes into the gang's exchequer, to expulsion.

Those who were expelled generally left the East End rather than risk the wrath of their former comrades.

To the English press, the revelations at the High Court pointed to one thing: the emergence – as yet on a minor scale – of a Chicago-style terror in Scotland. As the *Empire News* grimly warned: 'Gangdom must be ground into the dust it came from if we are not to be classed with the Chicago impotents.' The ire of the press was further roused when details emerged of the Billy Boys' continued persecution of Isabella McLaughlan: one of her chief tormentors, Robert Kelly, followed her into a shop where he sang: 'John Ross is in jail through you' to the tune of a current popular song; the following night, Kelly took the seat behind McLaughlan in the Olympia cinema at Bridgeton Cross. McLaughlan was terrified, and with good cause: when she got up to leave, Kelly punched her in the face. McLaughlan refused to press charges, but the police arrested Kelly nonetheless. He was jailed for nine months at Glasgow Sheriff Court.

Despite his reputation as the 'Razor King', John Ross was not an imposing figure. According to the *Empire News*, he 'did not look much of the hero' when he appeared in the dock at the High Court: his face showed 'signs of green' and he visibly trembled as his sentence was pronounced. Ross gave his occupation as baker. He had worked for three years as an apprentice to a baker in the Calton after leaving school, but had been laid off in 1925 due to bad trade. By the time he served his first prison sentence, in 1927, he had been out of work for two years. He was living with his brother, two sisters and their widowed mother in a 'single-end' in Mile End, the district to the north of Bridgeton Cross. As he awaited trial in July 1927, he told the governor of Duke Street Prison, Robert Walkinshaw, that he had 'broken away' from the Billy Boys. Ross claimed that: 'The members of the gang had in consequence been trying to do him physical injury, and he is afraid that his life is in danger.' This appears to have been a ruse as, following his release from prison in 1928, he returned to the ranks of the Billy Boys at Bridgeton Cross. By the time of his appearance at the High Court in December 1930, he had been unemployed for a further two years, was single and still living with his mother.

The Trials of Billy Fullerton

The most notorious Billy Boy was not the 'Razor King', John Ross, nor Eli Webb, but Billy Fullerton. A more imposing figure than Ross, and a more charismatic leader than Webb, Fullerton was both a fearsome street fighter and a bold general. Fullerton's early court appearances were unremarkable. In May 1926, he was fined £5 for disorderly conduct and committing a breach of the peace in the Calton. A police officer described him in court as 'the head of a body of young men known as the Fullerton gang.' His father paid the fine. Five months later, Fullerton was convicted of assault: Glasgow Sheriff Court heard that Fullerton and another man had struck their victim with a baton and attempted to stab him with a sword. They were both jailed for three months, after Sheriff Blair railed against what he termed 'meaningless' disputes between Orangemen and Catholics. Fullerton served another stretch of three months for assault during the spring of 1927. No further convictions were recorded against him for three and half years.

In October 1930, Fullerton appeared again at Glasgow Sheriff Court. On this occasion he stood trial alongside one of his henchmen, Edward Livingstone, and Livingstone's brother, James. They were charged with assaulting John Evans, a forty-two-year-old cinema doorman, in a back-court in Green Street in the Calton. Evans worked at the Queen's Theatre – 'The Alhambra of the East' – near Glasgow Cross. He told the court that he had been approached by James Livingstone at around quarter to ten on the night of Wednesday 3 September. According to Evans's account, Livingstone was drunk and they got into an argument, which quickly led to a fight. Later that night, Evans heard someone shouting up at his window, challenging him to come down as 'the boys were there now'. Evans looked down to see James Livingstone 'with his sleeves up and jacket off'. When Evans went downstairs, Livingstone rushed at him. As they began to wrestle, Livingstone's brother joined in, striking Evans over the head with a bottle. Evans was then bombarded with more bottles, including one thrown by Billy Fullerton.

John Evans was no stranger to Glasgow's courtrooms himself. A former Redskin, he had been jailed for six months in 1919 after extorting money from bookmakers. Under cross-examination, he admitted to eight previous convictions for assault – the first dated back to 1905, the year before Billy Fullerton was born. Edward Livingstone, for his part, vigorously denied smashing a bottle over Evans's head. Fullerton also pleaded not guilty, telling the court that he had been at the National Sporting Club at the time of the fracas. Asked how he came to be implicated in the case, Fullerton replied: 'Evans wanted easy money. He asked me for two pounds to drop the case.' Other witnesses confirmed that they had heard a conversation between Evans and Fullerton at Bridgeton Cross, in which Fullerton stated: 'You will get no money from me.'

Despite this, Sheriff Welsh declared that he saw no reason to doubt Evans's account. He passed sentences scaled according to the prisoners' previous convictions: Fullerton got four months' hard labour, Edward Livingstone three months and James Livingstone sixty days. Fullerton was furious. He struggled with the police officers who led him from the dock and, as they dragged him out of the court-room, he shouted: 'Is this justice?'

Fullerton was released from Barlinnie, the grim Victorian prison on Glasgow's eastern outskirts, on 4 February 1931. On the afternoon of Saturday 7 February, he joined the ranks of Billy Boys at Ibrox Park, where they watched Rangers lose one-nil to Airdrieonians. After the match he made his way to the pubs at Bridgeton Cross. At around half past eight, Fullerton's wife, Rose, came to meet him with their two young children. They set out for their home in Loom Street in the Calton, escorted by a forty-strong group of Billy Boys. Fullerton was carrying his three-year-old daughter in his arms.

The crowd was soon spotted by two plain-clothes detectives, who followed them along Orr Street. Seeing that Fullerton was drunk, one of the officers seized him by the shoulder, turned him sharply around and told him to 'Lay down that child.' Fullerton refused, telling the detective that he was 'doing no harm'. The detectives continued to shadow the group. At the corner of Crownpoint Road, Fullerton was stopped by a uniformed constable, who repeated the demand that Fullerton put the child down. When Fullerton refused, the constable struck him with his baton. As the police gathered round, Fullerton lashed out at them, urging the rest of the Billies to 'give the "busies" a kicking'.

In the scrum that ensued, Fullerton kicked one constable in the face, knocking him unconscious, while a second officer suffered a broken jaw when he was struck by a bottle. Fullerton was dragged face-down towards the police station in Tobago Street as his followers tried desperately to rescue him, prompting two passers-by to run into the station, shouting that 'the police were being murdered'. More police rushed out to the aid of their beleaguered colleagues and Fullerton was eventually lodged in the cells. There, the violence he had meted out was returned in kind. As Fullerton recalled: 'When I wakened up in the cell every bone in my body was sore, and my nose had been bleeding. My clothes were almost in stitches.'

Fullerton stood trial at Glasgow Sheriff Court on 7 April. Described by Procurator Fiscal J. D. Strathern as 'one of the principal leaders of a gang in the East End', Fullerton pleaded not guilty to charges of committing a breach of the peace and assaulting the police. A witness for the defence described how one of the plain-clothes officers pushed Fullerton and struck him on the face when he refused to let go of his daughter.

'He staggered along towards Stevenson Street,' the witness continued. 'He had done nothing to justify the treatment he received.'

Cross-examined by the procurator fiscal, Fullerton denied that he had a reputation as a fighting man but admitted that 'he had gone in for boxing when he was younger, and had won a prize.' Asked whether he had ever been associated with the Billy Boys, Fullerton replied: 'No, sir.' He then invoked the work of Reverend Sydney Warnes in Bridgeton: 'I can tell you that there are no Billy Boys now, owing to the activities of the police and a minister in the East End.'

Fullerton's protestations counted for little when set against the graphic accounts of his resistance to arrest, however, and the jury found him guilty on both charges. Sheriff Robertson jailed him for twelve months with hard labour. A second Billy Boy, David Black, got four months for attempting to rescue Fullerton from the police.

The manner of Fullerton's arrest, along with its timing – only three days after he had been released from prison – suggests that the police were determined to snare him before he could re-assert his authority over the gang. No doubt they were still smarting from the publicity that had surrounded the trial of John Ross at the High Court in December 1930, and were also determined to assist Reverend Sydney Warnes's crusade to convent Bridgeton's gangsters into civic-minded 'Pals'.

To Fullerton, police attention was nothing new. As his agent (solicitor) had pointed out at the sheriff court, Fullerton's tally of just four previous convictions bore little relation to the frequency of the interrogations to which he had been subjected:

> He had been apprehended by the police on no fewer than thirty-five occasions in respect of offences alleged to have been committed by him, but in most of these it was found that there was no evidence against him, and he was liberated.

In Glasgow police lore, the arrest of Billy Fullerton in February 1931 features as one of the most heroic episodes in the history of the Eastern Division. Fullerton's capture is ascribed to

Sergeant Tommy Morrison, who is said to have felled Billy Boys like skittles during the fracas.

The jailing of Billy Fullerton did not bring peace to the streets of the East End, however: the following month, 200 people took part in a pitched battle in Norman Street when the Billies escorted an Orange procession, headed by a band, right through the territory of the Norman Conks.

Catholic Gangs of the Calton

In August 1930, the *Evening Citizen* identified the Calton Entry – known by the street where its members congregated – as the leading Catholic gang in Glasgow. In an interview with the *Sunday Dispatch*, Billy Fullerton had acknowledged two other gangs as the Billy Boys' principal adversaries: the Kent Star and the San Toy. In practice, members of the three gangs frequently fought side-by-side in the long running 'faction fights' that blighted the city's East End, their alliance testament in itself to the respect – and fear – commanded by the Protestant gang that gathered at Bridgeton Cross.

While large-scale disturbances tended to follow the religious calendar, culminating each year in the Twelfth of July parades, smaller skirmishes took place all year round in tit-for-tat raids on each other's territory, and brutal violence was sometimes inflicted on lone passers-by identified by the colour of a hand-kerchief, pullover or tie as members of the rival faith. In June 1931, five youthful members of the Kent Star were arrested following a confrontation in Kerr Street in Bridgeton. Police discovered two gangs, numbering thirty to forty on each side, brandishing weapons and hurling missiles at each other as 'religious' cries and threats echoed across the street. The officers drew their batons and ran between the opposing groups, who immediately scattered: some not quickly enough, however. The youths apprehended were aged between seventeen and twenty, and their trial at Glasgow Sheriff Court drew huge crowds: several hundred people were cleared from the court prior to the morning session, while every seat in the public gallery was taken and additional spectators had crammed into the aisles. More than a thousand people flocked to the court that afternoon: amidst 'ugly' scenes, police reinforcements managed to prevent the crowd from forcing its way into the building.

Weapons discarded at the scene of the skirmish were exhibited in court, where they made quite a spectacle. The display included:

A murderous-looking Kaffir knobkerrie, an almost theatrical Gurkha knife, a swordfish 'spear', a battered pot-holder, hooked pieces of iron, lengths of lead piping, a big file, a grenade-shaped ball of metal, pokers, thonged batons, and a miscellaneous collection of iron scrap.

The armoury testified to the youths' capacity for improvisation as much as to their apparently murderous intent. As the *Eastern Standard* drily noted: 'The productions looked like an antique shop.' To prove that the fight was a 'religious' one, a police inspector showed the knobkerrie to Sheriff Boyd Berry. The weapon – a souvenir from the South African War of 1899–1902 – had been inscribed with 'certain uncomplimentary remarks towards "King Billy".' Daniel McLaughlin and Robert Russell were jailed for three months with hard labour after the court heard that they had wielded the knobkerrie and the swordfish bone respectively. Bernard Kiernan, Patrick Smith and Francis Reid got two months.

The arrest of the Kent Stars did nothing to deter their fellow gangsters in the Calton, however, and members of two other Catholic gangs ambushed a smaller number of Billy Boys who were returning to Bridgeton following an Orange procession in Glasgow city centre on Sunday 5 July. The Billies had been warned that a gang of youths was interrogating everyone passing through London Road and had taken an alternative route through Glasgow Green, but they were quickly spotted. A crowd of about forty young men rushed at them, shouting: 'Come on the Calton Entry! Get into these bastards!' Heavily outnumbered, the Billy Boys fled. Seventeen-year-old John Riddell fell behind his companions. He later recalled:

I felt something strike my heel and I fell on my side and rolled over on my back. The youths who had been following then gathered round me and began kicking me on the body and legs. I was also struck a blow on the forehead with something, but I don't know what it was. I put my hands up to save my face and then felt blood coming from a wound on my forehead. The gang then ran away.

Riddell claimed that he did not recognise the youths who attacked him, but his companions were less reticent. William Watson identified two of Riddell's assailants as Vinny Wallace and 'Dagger' Kane – in many cases, members of rival gangs recognised each other or knew each other through contacts made in workplaces and places of amusement, while myriad personal connections were made as members of rival gangs were thrown together in reformatories, borstals and prisons. According to Watson, Wallace had struck Riddell with a cleaver, while Kane had hit him with an iron bar. Kane then shouted: 'That will do the Orange bastards.' The crowd ran off towards the Calton, leaving Riddell lying on the ground. Five of the Billy Boys escorted Riddell to the police office in Bridgeton, where they reported the incident and named Kane and Wallace as Riddell's assailants.

Kane and Wallace stood trial at the High Court on 24 November. A house surgeon from the Royal Infirmary testified that Riddell was fortunate to have survived the attack: the wound on his forehead 'went so completely to the skull . . . that it was within very little of killing him at the moment of impact.' Sergeant James McKenzie of the Central Division testified to the prisoners' gang affiliations, explaining that the Catholic gangs of the Calton regularly joined forces:

Both are members of gangs – Kane of the Calton Entry and Wallace of the San Toy – operating in the Eastern district of the city. These gangs are composed principally of Roman Catholics, and while they are separate concerns, they frequently combine forces when an attack is to be made upon persons of different religion.

Albert 'Dagger' Kane was eighteen years old. He had been unemployed for the past two years and police inquiries suggested that, at the time of his arrest, he had no fixed place of abode. Vinny Wallace was aged seventeen, and lived with his mother at 165 Gallowgate. He, too, was unemployed, although he sometimes assisted his mother in her occupation as a 'general dealer'. Wallace was a precocious fighter: convicted of assault at the age of twelve, he had spent four years in Parkhead Reformatory. At the time of the assault on John Riddell, he had been home for just nine months.

Pat Deary of the San Toy provided Wallace with an alibi, swearing that they had been standing together at the gang's adopted corner of Charlotte Street and the Gallowgate at the time John Riddell was assaulted. The jury dismissed his account. They found both prisoners guilty of riot and assault 'to the danger of life'. Lord Morison sentenced both Kane and Wallace to fifteen months' imprisonment, commenting that only their youth spared them from more severe punishment.

'"Gangsters" as Tory Stewards'

The Billy Boys issued membership cards bearing two pledges: 'To uphold King, Country and Constitution' and 'To defend other Protestants'. At general elections, the first pledge translated into support for the Tories (or Unionists, as they were known in Scotland.) Their staunch Toryism left them at odds with mainstream Protestant feeling: Jimmy Maxton held the Bridgeton constituency for the Independent Labour Party (ILP) from 1922 until his death in 1946, and his enduring success rested in large part on Protestant support. The Billies' commitment to 'uphold the constitution' manifested itself in their persistent disruption of left-wing meetings and marches, especially those organised by the Communist Party. The Protestant gangsters might not have been able to topple Maxton, but they significantly hindered Communist attempts to mobilise the district's unemployed.

Nor were their endeavours confined to Bridgeton. In February

1929, the Billy Boys turned out in force at an ILP meeting in Govan. Their intention was to interrupt a speech by Arthur Cook, leader of the Miners' Federation of Great Britain and a close ally of Maxton. Cook was livid: he told the *Evening Times* that the Billy Boys had been acting on the instruction of local Unionists: 'My candid opinion is that the row was an organised attempt on the part of the Tories to break up my meeting,' and insisting that this 'nefarious bargain' was no figment of his imagination. He warned that the Tories would suffer if tit-for-tat reprisals ensued. The secretary of the Bridgeton Division of the Glasgow Unionist Association issued a statement refuting Cook's allegation.

Communist meetings faced more aggressive interruption. In September 1930, the *Evening Citizen* reported that a Communist Party meeting in Bridgeton had been broken up by an unnamed 'East End gang'. The Communists had marched eastwards from the city centre, 150-strong, bearing banners and placards, but before they reached Bridgeton Cross – the Billies' heartland – police diverted them into Anson Street, a cul-de-sac, where the marchers set up a temporary platform for an open-air meeting. Before the meeting could commence, however, a crowd of young men and women arrived and began to sing 'patriotic songs'. Scuffles quickly broke out and, on the advice of the police, the Communists regrouped and marched back towards the city centre along London Road. A 'large crowd' followed. When the marchers reached Albion Street, they made a second attempt to hold a meeting, only for fighting to erupt once again. The Communists fled, 'leaving their placards and banners in the street'. The incident was later described by Harry McShane, one of the most prominent Communist Party activists in Glasgow and leader of the local branch of the National Unemployed Workers' Movement (NUWM). As he recalled: 'We were completely cordoned off by Billy Boys in the cul-de-sac where we held our meeting. We had to hit our way out with our slogan-boards, and then they followed us throwing bottles and stones.'

During the 1930s the NUWM worked tirelessly to uphold

Glasgow's tradition of militancy, organising repeated marches and rallies on behalf of those without work. On 1 October 1931, a crowd of between 40,000 and 50,000 gathered at Glasgow Green in readiness for a march through the city centre in protest against the Labour government's proposal to cut unemployment benefits. The organisers were asked by the police to cancel the march as no permit had been issued by the magistrates; when they did not immediately comply, they were arrested, among them Harry McShane and John McGovern, Independent Labour MP for the East End constituency of Shettleston. Mounted police then charged the crowd, clearing the Green within five minutes.

The following night saw widespread outbreaks of looting in the Calton, the police having to patrol the 'storm centres' throughout the night. They made forty-eight arrests, but came under repeated attack themselves – flying-squad vans were even bombarded with missiles thrown from tenement windows in Charlotte Street. Some of the leading figures in the San Toy, including Owen Mullen and Alexander Moore, were arrested before order was restored around midnight.

In the series of court cases that followed, McGovern was acquitted of disorderly conduct. Mullen and Moore got sixty days' hard labour.

Coverage of the disturbances in the international press caused dismay among Glasgow's industrialists. The fiercely pro-Tory *Evening Citizen* published an angry front-page editorial featuring an extract from a telegram sent to a Glasgow firm from Durban in South Africa on 5 October. It read: 'Very disturbed news riots Glasgow. When will you ship all machinery?' To the *Citizen*, this was an appalling example of the damage done to Glasgow's economic prospects by the belief – commonly held in England and overseas – that the city was a hotbed of revolution: 'Thus our foolish MPs, our processions and Communist agitators drive away work from the Clydeside and drive our workers to despair and to the "dole".'

The Billy Boys attracted remarkable headlines during the general election campaign later that month. With dole cuts in prospect, the two-week campaign was fought amidst considerable rancour. Unionist election meetings in Glasgow's East End suffered widespread disruption: in both St Rollox and Shettleston, successive meetings were abandoned, as stewards were unable to deal with the hostile crowds.

In Bridgeton, where Unionist candidate Miss Catherine Gavin was the sole challenger to the sitting MP, Jimmy Maxton, opposition was especially fierce. Gavin gave her opening address at a meeting in Tobago Street on 12 October 1931. At the end of the meeting, she was surrounded by a crowd of thirty women, who alleged that the candidate had declared that 2 shillings per week 'was enough to keep a child in milk, etc.' Gavin claimed to have been misheard: she had declared that 2 shillings was not enough, but she 'preferred giving work to giving dole'. The following night, Gavin ended her meeting early due to 'constant interruptions, cat-calls and Communist choruses in which the slogan "Not a Penny off the Dole" loomed large.' As the meeting 'broke up in disorder', Gavin was escorted from the hall by the police – aided by gallant journalists – and whisked away in a car driven by a reporter from the *Evening Times*.

On the night of 16 October, Unionist meetings across Glasgow were subjected to sustained disruption, but the most orderly meeting was Catherine Gavin's at Bridgeton Public Hall. Here, as the *Evening Citizen* was pleased to report, 'interrupters got short shrift'. As the *Citizen* explained: 'Members of the "Billy Boys" had offered their services as stewards, and assisted the regular stewards in maintaining order. One man was removed from the gallery.' The *Evening Times*, too, was quick to praise the 'gang youths' who had 'offered their services to maintain order at Miss Gavin's meetings, and thus uphold Bridgeton's reputation for fair play' – in fact, the incessant coverage of the district's gangs by the city's evening newspapers meant that Bridgeton enjoyed no such reputation but, momentarily, the Billy Boys stood for fair play and free speech rather than violence and intimidation.

Headlines in the local press nonetheless embarrassed the Unionists. The *Evening Times* proclaimed: '"BILLY BOYS" IN

NEW ROLE: Stewards at Tory Meeting' while its sister paper, the *Bulletin*, announced: '"GANGSTERS" AS TORY STEWARDS: Billy Boys Rally Round Glasgow's Girl Candidate'.

As the *Bulletin* hinted at the Billy Boys' unexpected chivalry, news of the Bridgeton gangsters' role filtered through to the London-based, British national press. The *Daily Mirror* praised Catherine Gavin for her 'pluck' in the face of 'the women in shawls' who had 'pulled her dress off, slapped her face, and subjected her to every kind of vituperation.' It was little wonder, the *Mirror* implied, that Gavin 'now goes about protected by a bodyguard of those gentlemen of leisure known in the northern city as Billy Boys.' Stung by the association – headlines that connected politicians to gangsters were far too reminiscent of Chicago for comfort – the Unionist Party turned to an alternative pool of stewards: students from Glasgow University. To the impoverished voters of the East End, however, well-heeled undergraduates were less palatable as stewards than gang members, and hostility to their presence was so vehement that the students were forced to withdraw from Gavin's meeting in the Tobago Street police hall on 21 October.

The general election, held on 27 October 1931, resulted in a crushing defeat for the Labour government and the formation of a 'National Government' (Tory-dominated coalition). The following day, Glasgow turned its attention to the forthcoming municipal elections. Here, the Billy Boys abruptly switched allegiance to the Scottish Protestant League (SPL), the vehemently anti-Catholic party led by Alexander Ratcliffe. The SPL contested three wards: Dalmarnock, Dennistoun and Partick East. Dalmarnock, situated immediately to the south of Bridgeton, was home to the (Catholic) Norman Conks.

The SPL candidate for Dalmarnock, Charlie Forrester, received letters warning that if he attempted to address public meetings in the district, violence would result. Forrester had turned to the Billy Boys, who provided him with a twenty-strong bodyguard.

Police were called to restore order at Forrester's campaign meeting on 29 October. The following night, 400 people attended his meeting at a school in Rumford Street. The moment Forrester began to address the crowd, a voice cried: 'Up the Conks and at him!' A group of young men led by Patrick Brogan then rushed the platform. In the struggle that followed, bottles and other weapons were used on both sides, while the crash of windows smashing added to the 'din and confusion'. Forrester was among those floored, but his bodyguard held their ground. 'The fight was at its height,' reported the *Bulletin*, 'when a series of shots cracked out. It could not be established whether these were fired from a real or toy pistol. Great panic ensued.' There were no reports of gunshot wounds, but the meeting was abandoned. Forrester and his bodyguard headed to Bridgeton Cross, where an open-air meeting was held without interruption, and Patrick Brogan and two other men subsequently stood trial at Glasgow Sheriff Court, where Brogan's counsel alleged that the SPL stewards had been readily identified as Billy Boys by their blue jerseys. The charges were dropped.

The Billy Boys also provided stewards for the SPL candidate for Partick East, Mrs Susan Cameron. Their presence was fiercely resented by local gang members, notably the Plum Boys, who scattered the Bridgeton youths after Cameron's meeting on 28 October. On 2 November, the Billies hired a corporation bus to take a larger troop of stewards to Cameron's final campaign meeting at Partick Burgh Hall. After a hostile crowd – said to number several thousand – surrounded the hall, the bus driver decided to return to Bridgeton while the meeting was still in progress. Bereft of transport, the Billy Boys remained in the hall for an hour after the meeting had finished before police attempted to escort them through a back-court into Dumbarton Road. The Billies were showered with missiles as they boarded a tram, while one Bridgeton youth was caught: he was bludgeoned and badly injured before he was dragged to safety.

The Billy Boys wasted no time in seeking revenge. Around 200 of them set out from Bridgeton Cross to Partick later that night, 'vowing vengeance on the Plum Boys', only to be intercepted by a police patrol van before the Partick gang had been found. The Billies made their way back to Bridgeton, where their numbers swelled to 400. They headed to the Sacred Heart League of the Cross hall in Muslin Street, where they hurled volleys of bottles and pieces of metal at the windows. Encountering no opposition, the Billy Boys contented themselves by swarming through nearby streets, to the alarm of local residents.

The Billy Boys' harassment of the Communist Party would persist into the 1930s. In October 1932, fifty youths – said by police to be 'members of a gang' – attended a Communist meeting held in the London Road public halls, close to Bridgeton Cross. The youths 'resented the views expressed by some of the speakers' and waited outside the halls at the end of the meeting to hurl missiles at the rest of those leaving. Some attendees scattered into nearby tenement closes; others escaped by jumping onto a passing tramcar. Tommy Hastings was unlucky. The gangsters chased him into Heron Street, where he was struck on the head with a piece of wood and stabbed in the arm with a bayonet. Hastings managed to flee his attackers and ran into a nearby house, whose occupants sheltered him and tended to his wounds until he could be taken to the Royal Infirmary.

Thomas Davidson, a member of Bridgeton branch and a keen fighter in his youth, acted as a doorman at party meetings. He recalled how: 'Men would come to the door and they would be mad and threatenin' ye wi' getting' your throat cut! That wis the kind o' language – they were kind o' rough.'

8

The Abdication of Billy Fullerton

On 18 February 1932, a petition containing 600 signatures was sent to Glasgow's new chief constable, Captain Percy Sillitoe:

> We, the undersigned ratepayers of Bridgeton district, appeal to you for protection from this East-end gang that frequents the Cross and surrounding district.
>
> We, as citizens, are insulted, and our sons are not safe to be in that vicinity when they go to places of amusement if the gang know them to differ from their views.
>
> We trust that you, as police chief, will find ways of dispersing them, if not, then we will bring it to the notice of the Scottish Secretary.

The petition was delicately worded, but every reader of the local press was familiar with the name of the gang that frequented Bridgeton Cross and their fierce attachment to the cause of King Billy.

The timing of the petition was significant. Sillitoe had arrived in Glasgow two months earlier, having secured the post of chief constable in the face of stiff competition. In his previous post, in Sheffield, Sillitoe had been widely acclaimed for suppressing the violent feuds between gangs wrestling for control of the city's illegal gambling rings. His methods were unorthodox: police across Britain readily resorted to force when dealing with disorderly youths and drunks, but few chief constables gloried in the 'strong arm of the law' as much as Sillitoe. As he saw it, the only way to deal with Sheffield's gangsters was to 'play [them] at their own game'. To that end, he asked his senior officers to pick the toughest men under their command to be trained in ju-jitsu and 'various other methods of attack and defence'. Sillitoe did not rely solely on his men's brawn, however. Drawing on his experiences in the Northern Rhodesia Police during the Great War, he placed considerable emphasis on information gathering.

Sillitoe knew that he owed his appointment in Glasgow to his reputation as a 'gang-buster'. Upon his arrival, he asked long-serving local officers to brief him on the composition and organisation of the city's gangs, and he also instructed each police division to record every reported outbreak of violence, logging the dates, times and locations on large-scale maps to reveal the patterns of gang conflict. As part of a general scheme to overhaul police communication systems, police boxes were upgraded: telephone links to divisional headquarters were installed to enable more rapid responses. Under Sillitoe, the Glasgow force also invested heavily in motor technology, increasing the use of patrol vans and cars, some of which were equipped with radios so that flying squads could be mobilised to deal with incidents anywhere in the city. Within three months of Sillitoe's arrival in Glasgow, 'war' had been declared on housebreakers, gangsters and resetters – those who received stolen goods – in turn.

Sillitoe's technological innovations were widely trumpeted in the local press; he was more reticent about his personal pool of informants. He recruited an extensive network of barmen, barmaids and publicans along with ex-convicts and prostitutes – including Aggie Reid, former 'Queen' of the Redskins – all of whom were instructed never to speak to a police officer in person, nor to attend a police station. Sillitoe's spies were required to pass on information only by telephone: most of it reached him directly.

Sillitoe's informants were augmented by his 'C Division Specials'. C Division covered Glasgow's East End. Here, according to police lore, Sillitoe recruited a squad of 'special irregulars', including a number of ex-boxers, whose role was to assist the police in beating the gangs at their own game. Prominent among the irregulars was said to be the former Scottish feather-weight boxing champion, 'Deaf' Burke.

As a challenge to the new chief constable, the petition addressed to Sillitoe in February 1932 could hardly have been more direct, but the petition was timely in a second sense: Billy Fullerton had been released from Barlinnie Prison just ten days earlier, having served ten months of his twelve-month sentence for assaulting the police. The petition's organisers courted the press, releasing the text of the petition on the night it was posted to the chief constable. It was lapped up – not least by the *Scottish Daily Express*, whose coverage of it read like an excerpt from the script of a Hollywood gangster film: 'The protest was organised secretly by twelve men and women who have pledged themselves to break the gang.' An *Express* reporter interviewed one of the organisers (on condition of anonymity), who explained:

> It would not have been safe to try to get public signatures on the streets. We canvassed houses and shops. All the time we were in danger. We had to work as stealthily as possible, because if the gang knew . . .

While the petition referred to the harassment of young men at Bridgeton Cross ('our sons are not safe to be in that vicinity'), the organiser told the *Express* that women, too, had been subjected to abuse.

The *Sunday Mail* and *Sunday Post* covered the petition on 21 February 1932. Both linked the allegation of 'gang terror' to the long-standing practice whereby gang members extorted money for bail payments and fines from local shopkeepers, with the *Post* dispatching a reporter to Bridgeton and the Calton to gather its own 'remarkable revelations'. One shopkeeper, whose premises stood fifty yards from Bridgeton Cross, confided that he paid 2 shillings per week into the gang's 'fines fund'. The payments were necessary, he explained, to protect his family as well as his premises. On one occasion when he had refused to 'loan' 2 shillings towards the payment of a gangster's fine, the consequences were dire: his windows were smashed during the night and his wife and children were subjected to threats and insults in the street. Another trader told the *Post* that he had been harassed because he was Jewish. He had not been asked for money, but had suffered on account of his religion: 'I am Jewish, and that seems enough for the gang. They seem to have it in for me. I can scarcely go along the street but some of them shout foul epithets.'

The police moved quickly to respond to the allegations. Like the organisers of the petition, they used the *Scottish Daily Express* to publicise their endeavour. On Tuesday 23 February, the *Express* reported that arrangements were already in hand for 'dramatic' action:

> Plans have been made by Glasgow police for the breaking-up of a gang in the Calton and Bridgeton districts . . . A force of detectives has been specially detailed to trace the ringleaders of the gang and secure every available piece of evidence.

Fresh detective work was required, the *Express* explained, because the gang had devised elaborate means of disguising its activities:

> It has been discovered that the gang have compiled a slang vocabulary which baffles the uninitiated, and have an elaborate system of signs which they employ to convey messages, chalked on walls and closes.

By this account, the gang – still unnamed in the recent flurry of press reports – represented a formidable challenge to the Glasgow police. Readers were assured that measures had been put in place to protect the organisers of the petition and, while the newly formed squad of detectives went about its work, regular police patrols had also been increased. The *Express*'s headline made gratifying reading for Sillitoe: '**WAR ON A GANG BEGINS**'.

Billy Fullerton's Life Story

With detectives under orders to target the 'ringleaders' of the Billy Boys, the recently liberated Billy Fullerton was sure to receive a visit. The notorious gangster's prospects were already bleak – unemployment in Glasgow stood at just under 40 per cent among men aged eighteen and above. Now he was warned that if he got mixed up in gang warfare again, he should expect nothing less than penal servitude – a minimum term of three years in Peterhead Convict Prison. This was a much tougher prospect than a stretch of 'hard labour' in Barlinnie. Situated thirty miles north of Aberdeen, and more than 160 miles from Glasgow, the sense of bleak isolation at Peterhead was heightened by restrictions on communication with family or friends: convicts were allowed to send and receive only one letter every two months during the first two years of their sentences.

Peterhead had more than 350 cells, but by the early 1930s was only around one-third full. Housebreakers formed the largest group among the inmates, followed by those convicted of murder or culpable homicide, or sexual offences. They were watched over by forty-six warders. The daily regime was unforgiving: convicts laboured either on the construction of the breakwaters at Peterhead Bay or in the quarry at Stirlinghill, three miles from the prison. Those put to work in the quarry were conveyed back and forth in cattle trucks. They worked from 7.15 to 11.15 a.m. and from 12.30 to 4.30 p.m. Discipline was unforgiving, too: warders at Peterhead carried cutlasses, and work parties were guarded by officers armed with rifles.

Fullerton's response to his warning was twofold: he renounced his membership of the Billy Boys and, six weeks later, he sold his story to the popular Scottish paper, *Thomson's Weekly News*.

Declaring that his days as a gang leader were over, he begged to be left in peace: 'I want a chance for the sake of my wife and children. I am tired of this eternal fighting.' The *Weekly News* introduced Fullerton – under the pen-name 'Bill Fulton' – as the 'ex-leader' of the Bridgeton Billy Boys. Prior to that, readers were told, 'Fulton' had been 'as powerful a personality in his own sphere as the Al Capones and Spike O'Donnells of the U.S.A.'

By Fullerton's account, his early life was trouble-free. Born in May 1906, he grew up with his parents and three brothers in the Calton. He left school at fourteen and, following in his father's footsteps, started an apprenticeship as a boiler-maker at John Brown's shipyard at Clydebank. He completed his apprenticeship at a different boiler shop in the East End of Glasgow, only to be laid off at nineteen – once he qualified for adult wages, it was cheaper for his employer to replace him with another apprentice. As Fullerton recalled, work for a time-served boiler-maker was difficult to find in Glasgow in the summer of 1925: 'Work was scarce. Try as I might, I could not get another job. So rather than go idle, I decided to try my luck in Canada.' He found employment as a ship's fireman and spent several months at sea off the Canadian coast before he was laid off due to poor trade. He managed to work his passage back to Scotland and returned to his parents' house in the Calton, where he found a part-time position as a cinema attendant.

As Fullerton had anticipated, this was no job for the faint-hearted. Shortly after taking up the post, he had to assist an older attendant in ejecting a number of youths who had started a fight in the lower tier (the 'pit'). Twenty-four hours later, he learnt that the trouble-makers were gangsters:

> The next night I was standing at the mouth of the close leading to my house when some members of a gang came over and talked to me. They started by asking me about the pictures. Then they did a cowardly thing – a thing that resulted in me becoming a gangster.
>
> One of them drew a hammer. I dodged, received a glancing blow, and fell dazed to the ground. The scar is on the back of my head to this day.

Fullerton was so enraged that he waded into his attackers – all of whom, by his account, were armed – using only his fists. He chased one of his assailants into the Eastern Police Office, where Fullerton knocked him down in front of the startled desk sergeant, subsequently claiming that his subsequent fine of £5 was 'well worth the money'.

News of Fullerton's exploits had quickly circulated around the East End, and a deputation from the Billy Boys had approached him a few evenings later:

They told me that they had heard of my fight with the other gang and they offered me protection against its members. It seemed that the others were out to get me so I was glad to accept the Billy Boys' offer and join up with them.

In recounting the fight, Fullerton appears to have allowed himself a hefty dollop of dramatic licence – although there were many in Glasgow willing to testify both to his fighting prowess and to the ferocity of his temper. More than twenty years later, he repeated the claim that he first became a gangster after he was himself targeted by another gang. Emboldened by the passage of time, he identified his assailants as members of the Kent Star – although he amended his story at this point, claiming that he had been attacked with a hammer following a football match on Glasgow Green.

Fullerton quickly made himself indispensable to the Billy Boys. After proving his mettle in a series of street fights, he demonstrated his skills as an organiser, first by running the gang's trips to Rangers matches, and then by assuming responsibility for collecting the gang's funds. 'A few months later,' Fullerton recalled, 'I found myself the chief of the 500 young men who formed the Billy Boys gang at that time.'

Running a gang of this size proved to be a full-time job: 'It meant a big lot of work for me. I had to make plans for fights, look after the funds, and attend to a hundred and one other matters connected with the gang and its members.'

The gang's funds came from a variety of sources. Members of the Billy Boys paid subscriptions of sixpence or a shilling per week, according to whether they were in or out of work, while some of the gang's female followers contributed as much as 5 shillings in return for 'protection' from rival gangs. Shopkeepers, too, made regular payments to the Billies, although Fullerton resented the allegation that small traders were victims of extortion:

Shopkeepers give willingly each week. Don't think it is a form of blackmail. There is no question of that. The money they pay is for protection against other gangs. I can assure you I have never intimidated a shopkeeper in my life.

Payments of as much as £1 per week were received from book-makers, and some of Glasgow's 'businessmen' were equally generous. Fullerton was coy about the identity of the gang's wealthier backers, but claimed that: 'The names of some of the people who have sent money to the Bridgeton Billy Boys would surprise you.'

Fullerton insisted that he had not personally profited from the gang's activities: 'I never made a penny out of the gang business all the time I was a gangster' – in this light, the *Weekly News*'s predictable characterisation of the Billy Boys' former leader as the Al Capone or Spike O'Donnell of Glasgow rang hollow.

He confirmed that the Billy Boys had provided 'unofficial' stewards at political meetings – in return for subscriptions to the gang's funds. However, he was keen to stress that the Billies acted out of a sense of patriotic duty as well as pursuit of profit:

> It should not be forgotten that the public owes a good deal to the Billy Boys for their work in the General Strike. More than fifty of them did duty as special constables. Their knowledge of how gangs worked came into use there. They cleared the Bridgeton area in a few days, and for the time worked hand in hand with the police, who had been their bitterest enemies.

This rapprochement between the gangsters and the police was short-lived, but the story served Fullerton well, not least since it demonstrated the Billy Boys' loyalty to the crown.

Billy Fullerton had married Rose Ann Farmer at Guthrie Memorial Church in the Calton in October 1926. He was aged twenty; she was two years his junior. Ironically, given his standing as a Billy Boy, Rose was a Catholic. In her subsequent dealings with parish officials, however, she stated her religion as Protestant, which suggests that she was keen – or perhaps felt pressured – to appease her husband's staunch Orangeism. (Fullerton's mother, who had also been brought up as a Catholic, had done likewise.) Prior to their wedding, Rose encouraged him to 'go straight'. According to Fullerton, he was already disposed to leave the gang:

Truth to tell I was getting more than a little fed up with the whole business myself. The gang was taking up all my time. I had no prospects of getting a job and I felt that I would have absolutely no chance of getting work until I cut myself adrift from the Billy Boys.

Four days after their wedding, Fullerton stood trial at Glasgow Sheriff Court on a charge of assault. He was jailed for three months with hard labour. A refusal to show emotion in the dock was essential to maintain his reputation as a 'fighting man', and Fullerton played the part, but by the time he sold his story to the *Weekly News*, he was ready to reveal the turmoil he had felt as the sentence was pronounced:

> I heard my wife cry out in despair. I did not show any emotion, but for the first time in my life I was on the point of breaking down as I stepped from the dock.
>
> When I came out of prison my wife was waiting for me. For her sake . . . I determined to leave gangdom.

Fullerton declared that the prospect of imprisonment had not worried him in the least as a single man. Now that he was married, it was an agony to him – or so he assured the readers of the *Weekly News*.

When he returned from prison, Fullerton kept his distance from the Billy Boys. He knew that leaving the gang would not be easy – if reputations in Glasgow's gangland were hard-won, they were harder still to shed: 'For nights I stayed indoors,' Fullerton confided, 'knowing that if I showed myself in the street I would have hundreds jeering at me. That sort of thing I simply could not stand.' When he finally ventured out, he was met by one of his former followers, who begged him to return to the gang. Affairs were becoming disorganised, the Billy Boy reported, and collections falling off.

Fullerton's vanity would prove to outweigh his desire to do right by his wife:

> I always had a certain pride in my leadership of the boys. They trusted me, and would do anything for me. At last I gave in. I went back to my old position as secretary and chief.

By his own account, Fullerton was a charismatic leader as well as a skilled organiser. He worked the gang back up to its full strength of 500, regular meetings were arranged, and the gang's 'committee' began to function efficiently again. According to Fullerton, the Billies had 'agents' (local representatives) in every district in Glasgow: 'I had only to say the word, and within a few hours I could learn all there was to know about the movements of any other gang.'

This time, Fullerton had only been at liberty for three months when he was jailed again following another conviction for assault.

His spell in Barlinnie during the spring of 1927 brought him into contact with Major Malcolm Speir, a pioneer of the Boy Scout movement in Scotland and veteran of the Great War. (He had served in the Royal Engineers, and had been awarded the Military Cross in December 1916.) Now working as a senior administrator in the Glasgow office of the London, Midland and Scottish Railway, Speir retained his interest in the Scouts, and was a dedicated prison visitor. Fullerton spoke highly of him, as a 'gentleman' who had been 'a friend to hundreds of men in the same position as myself'. At Barlinnie, 'the Major' dispensed stern moral guidance along with occasional offers of employment. In Fullerton's case: 'He taught me the error of my ways, and, what was just as important, he got me a job as a surfaceman [labourer] on the railway.' The wages of £2 and 3 shillings per week were low but regular, and Fullerton topped them up by returning to his old part-time position as a cinema attendant.

Fullerton had just turned twenty-one. Under the combined influence of his wife and the major, his life briefly took a new course. The former leader of the Billy Boys joined the Rover Scouts, and began to do his fighting in the ring:

> When I was released my wife was waiting for me at the gates. Once again I vowed to run straight. I became a Rover Scout. I took to boxing, and won several competitions. I thought I could drop the bad old life for once and for all.

Fullerton held the job on the railway for three years. However, his notoriety once again proved impossible to shrug off:

> There were folk – not always gangsters – who apparently did not like to think I was doing so well. I was bullied and baited at every turn. I have a quick temper, but for the sake of my wife I stood a lot. In the end things were made so hot for me that I went back to the gang.

Fullerton did not name his tormentors, but he clearly felt better able to deal with them with the Billy Boys at his command.

As leader of the most powerful gang in Glasgow, Fullerton enjoyed considerable kudos, but prominence came at a price: he was a 'marked man', and constantly at risk of being ambushed by his enemies:

> One night when I arrived home I found five members of a rival gang waiting for me in the close. After a struggle in which I was slashed with a razor across the forehead I managed to get into my house. Armed with a hatchet I chased my enemies into the street.

Fullerton gathered 'some of the boys' and set off to the house of one of the rival gangsters, bent on revenge, only to be greeted by a pail of boiling stew, which left one of the Billies badly scarred. According to Fullerton, his enemies possessed no scruples – he was even vulnerable when he went out with his children:

> Walking home [another] night with my little girl in my arms, I was attacked from behind and struck down. I could not turn on my assailants in case my child should be injured. All the way home I had to stand a terrible thrashing. When I got into my house, I was slashed by a razor across the knuckles. Both my eyes were split. I had to get two stitches in my head.

Fullerton's fighting prowess did not so much deter his enemies as spur them on to more calculated – and callous – attempts to maim him.

Speaking to the *Weekly News* in 1932, Fullerton was adamant that his latest prison sentence – twelve months for assaulting the police – would be his last. He still felt aggrieved at his conviction: 'I have my own version of the affair, but there is no use at this time going into the rights and wrongs of the jury's verdict.' What mattered now, Fullerton insisted, was that his days as leader of the Billy Boys were over for good:

> It is enough to say that this last spell [in Barlinnie] has sickened me at the gang game. I have now got two little girls – aged four years and fifteen months – and for their sakes, if nothing else, I am finished with the Billy Boys.

Selling his story must have been part of Fullerton's plan to ensure that, this time, his vow to go straight would be fulfilled. His former comrades were unlikely to be pleased by his revelations: while he did not name any of his fellow Billy Boys in his account, he effectively confirmed that much of what had been alleged about the gang in Glasgow's courtrooms – and in the press – over the past six years was true. From the point of view of the city's chief constable, Percy Sillitoe, Fullerton's revelations served both as indictment of the old police regime and as further justification for Sillitoe's bold declaration of 'war' on the gang.

Asked by the *Weekly News* to give an assessment of the current state of Glasgow's gangs, Fullerton insisted that at least a dozen remained 'on active service', despite the efforts of ministers in setting up social clubs in the East End and South Side. The combined membership of the remaining gangs – as distinct from social clubs – still stood at over 1,500, including 500 Billy Boys. Fights between rival gangs were no less frequent than in the past; however, they attracted less publicity as much greater care was taken to avoid the police:

> Only a short time ago, two gangs clashed in the Mile-End district. There were 300 young men engaged in the battle. Broken bottles, knives, razors, batons, and hatchets were amongst the weapons used. But as soon as the police appeared on the scene, the streets were cleared as if by magic. There were no arrests. And although

there were many casualties, none of the injured went into the infirmary. Past experience has taught the gangster that to land in the infirmary is to risk landing in jail. So, unless he is very seriously injured indeed, he just goes home and patches himself up with sticking plaster.

Fullerton was far from dismissive of the ministers' efforts. However, he warned that the 'gang business' would be very difficult to stamp out. 'The trouble is,' he confided, 'that the young chaps fight more for devilment than anything else. And you can't stop it by removing the causes of the quarrels, because they will quarrel over anything at all.'

Restating his plea to be left in peace, Fullerton revealed that in the six weeks since he had renounced his membership of the Billy Boys, he had been waylaid and 'beaten unmercifully' in the entrance to his tenement close. His tormentors were brutal and persistent in equal measure:

> At night, old enemies come to my door and knock me up. They invite me out to fight. When I refuse, they try to anger me by smashing my windows and hammering on my door. They laugh and jeer at me in the street.

Worst of all, Fullerton revealed, two half-bricks thrown through his windows had just missed his 'bairns' as they were sleeping.

Fullerton was desperate to leave his house in Loom Street in the Calton. Employment was still hard to find, and his former mentor, Major Malcolm Speir, had moved to Belfast. Yet Fullerton insisted that he remained optimistic: 'I have hopes of work, and if I get a job, the first thing I will do is look for a new house in different district – far away from the centre of the city and the gangs.'

The Gangster and the Major

As told to *Thomson's Weekly News*, Fullerton's story contained some surprising omissions: no mention was made of the Billy Boys' identity as Protestants and, while the gang's support for the Orange Order – and Glasgow Rangers Football Club – was well known throughout Scotland, Fullerton's claim that 'the young chaps fight more for devilment than anything else' deflected readers' attention away from the sectarianism that laced gang conflicts in Glasgow's East End.

Fullerton also chose not to divulge the full extent of his dealings with Major Malcolm Speir. After more than twenty years as a prison visitor, Speir enjoyed a rapport with police as well as prison officials, many of whom shared his belief that what Glasgow's hooligans needed most was 'a jolly good hiding'. With the surreptitious support of senior officers in the Eastern Division of the City of Glasgow Police, Speir administered corporal punishment – in the tradition of the British public school – to some of the district's repeat offenders. Speir's methods were both unorthodox and illegal.

When Speir left Glasgow for Belfast in February 1931, the *Weekly Record* published a remarkable profile of his work. Speir confided to journalist Harold Bishop Dickson that he had given 'one of the leaders of the Billy Boys' a 'sound thrashing'. Speir claimed that the police were unaware of the punishment, and the *Record* refrained from naming its recipient. In an interview with the *Evening Citizen* in 1955, however, Billy Fullerton divulged that the recipient had been none other than himself. Once their secret had been aired, Speir eagerly described the incident to a *Citizen* reporter:

It was in 1929 that I learned that Fullerton was in custody again. If I remember alright he had been in a melee outside a cinema. He had taken on three policemen single-handed, which gives an idea of the tough and powerful fellow he was.

Knowing that his latest exploit would bring a prison sentence of anything up to six months, which would only make him more bitter and recalcitrant, I determined to do what I could for him.

Speir now revealed that the police had in fact known of the arrangement. They agreed to entrust Fullerton's punishment to him – so long as Fullerton agreed – and took no action when the leader of the Billy Boys failed to surrender to his bail. Speir recalled:

I put my proposition to Fullerton. He made his choice straight away – for corporal punishment. This I duly administered in my private office. I used a clothes brush on him and I certainly did not spare him . . . Fullerton took it, although he was strong enough to have knocked me into the middle of next week.

By Speir's account, the gangster's father had been in the next room when the thrashing took place, while Fullerton told the *Evening Citizen* that he remembered this incident 'more clearly than others when he was the target of lethal weapons'.

Fullerton was by no means the only notorious offender to suffer a spanking from the major – the 'Dennistoun Cat Burglar' of the 1920s volunteered for the same punishment.

The extraordinary relationship between the gangster and the major might help to explain the alleged links between the Billy Boys and the Tories that surfaced during the visit of miners' leader, A. J. Cook, to Glasgow in 1929. Prior to his move to Belfast two years later, Speir served as chairman of Glasgow Conservative Club. In the light of his long-standing connection to Billy Fullerton, it seems highly likely that it was Speir who harnessed the Billies in the fight against the 'Reds' on the Clyde.

Two weeks after the publication of his life story in *Thomson's Weekly News*, Billy Fullerton appeared as a witness for the prosecution at the Eastern Police Court, where he described how Hugh Stirling had jabbed a nineteen-year-old youth in the face with a broken bottle during a dance in the pavilion of Bridgeton Waverley Football Club. Under cross-examination, Fullerton explained that he used the name Bill Fulton when 'writing for the newspapers'. Asked about his status as a gangster, Fullerton declared: 'I used to be the leader of the Billy Boys, but that is all past now. I am married and settled down.' The agent for the defence handed the magistrate a copy of the *Weekly News* before proceeding:

> *Are you the self-confessed hero whose story is in this newspaper?*
> – I am.

> And in your own sphere you are as powerful as the Al
> Capones and Spike Donnellys [sic] of America?
> – I was, but I want to lead a new life.

The agent's strategy worked. With Fullerton's credibility as a witness undermined, the prosecution case fell apart. The magistrate found the charge against Hugh Stirling not proven.

Fullerton's New Life

In July 1933, as the police courts across Glasgow dealt with the aftermath of the annual Orange Walk, the city's *Eastern Standard* newspaper proclaimed: '**THE "BILLY BOYS" HAVE REFORMED!**' The *Standard* reported that a group of young men headed by Billy Fullerton had worked tirelessly for three weeks to convert a dingy flat in Kerr Street in Bridgeton into 'airy and spotlessly clean' rooms for a social club. The premises had been equipped with a grand piano, gifted by 'a Dennistoun lady who has interested herself in the club', and plans were in place for the installation of a billiard table and a full-size boxing ring.

As president of the new venture, Fullerton enjoyed the prospect of renewed authority and influence, without the hassle of constant attention from the police. Not only that, but various local dignitaries lent their support to Fullerton as the club's first president, effectively endorsing the former gang leader's claim to be living a 'new life'. Reverend J. Cameron Peddie, doyen of the Pals' movement in Glasgow, presided over the formal opening of the premises on Friday 14 July. Reverend Sydney Warnes, whose work with the Bridgeton Pals' Association at St Francis-in-the-East was ongoing, was a notable absentee. His absence was unsurprising, however: the launch of Fullerton's club signalled all too clearly that Warnes's own venture had failed to bring calm to the streets around Bridgeton Cross. Another, much more militant, East End churchman did attend: Thomas Lyons, a fiery Independent Methodist minister and president of the Bridgeton branch of the Scottish Covenanters' Defenders. The club's other backers included several town councillors and magistrates, along with Superintendent Gordon of the Eastern Division of the City of Glasgow Police, all of whom were understandably eager to see Fullerton's new venture succeed.

The *Standard* was sympathetic, noting that the club's members – many of whom were unemployed – had put their skills to good use: they had fixed the water supply to the premises, installed electric lighting and built cloakrooms. If the formation of the Billy Boys' club helped to bring peace to the streets of the East End, it would eclipse even Peddie's legendary work with the South Side Stickers.

Defenders of John Knox

Reporting on the opening of the Billy Boys' club on 14 July, the *Eastern Standard* commented approvingly that Billy Fullerton and his henchmen had devoted their 'full attention' to the preparation of their new premises in Kerr Street for several weeks, and readers were encouraged to view the Billies as 'reformed' gangsters. However, a glance at the *Standard*'s own columns in the preceding weeks suggested that the threat posed by the gang's members was far from over: Fullerton and his closest associates might have been sincere in their vow to go straight, but many of his long-standing followers remained committed to the 'cause', while a younger generation of Billy Boys were beginning to forge reputations of their own.

The *Standard* reported on 3 June that 'an astonishing number of serious disturbances in connection with religious meetings and processions' had occurred in the past week. In the most serious incident, 600 Billy Boys ran from Bridgeton Cross to attack a crowd following a Catholic children's procession as it approached Sacred Heart Church in Muslin Street. According to a police witness: 'Orange handkerchiefs were raised, bayonets flourished and stones and bottles thrown.' Later that night, 200 Catholic youths headed to Bridgeton Cross in search of revenge. The parish priest appealed to local youths to 'stop the sectarian gang warfare'. As counter-accusations flew back and forth, he was forced to deny the allegation that his League of the Cross hall was being used as the headquarters for a Catholic gang.

At a subsequent meeting of Glasgow Corporation, the town clerk confirmed that complaints from numerous 'organisations and individuals' in the East End had been forwarded to the chief constable, who was preparing a report for the magistrates on police plans to deal with the latest spate of 'sectarian gang fights'.

One of those keen to assume Fullerton's mantle was eighteen-year-old James McKay. McKay was arrested at the corner of Main Street and Dale Street in Bridgeton at eleven o'clock on the night of Saturday 24 June – police spotted him brandishing a South African War-issue bayonet and shouting: 'Come on, the Billy Boys.' According to the arresting officers, McKay was 'very much the worse for drink'. Superintendent Gordon told the Eastern Police Court that: 'These youths got drunk, and made a bee-line for a part of Main Street where a Catholic community resided. It was intolerable.' Gordon also complained that a local scrap-metal merchant was supplying the Billy Boys with many of their weapons. McKay pleaded guilty to committing a breach of the peace and was fined £5, with the option of thirty days' imprisonment. He served the time. It was his third spell in Barlinnie, and he missed the annual Twelfth of July celebrations, which that year saw 'lively' scenes across Glasgow.

Bridgeton's militant Protestants did not confine their activities to the East End. On the evening of Tuesday, 13 June 1933, a group of them set off from Bridgeton to Clydebank, eight miles west of Glasgow, where they had arranged an open-air meeting to launch a local branch of the Scottish Covenanters' Defenders. The meeting drew a crowd of 400. The first speaker was Reverend Thomas Lyons, who addressed the crowd for forty minutes, apparently without interruption. He was followed by a fiery Bridgeton gospel preacher named Isaac Queen, who had stood unsuccessfully for the Scottish Protestant League in the last municipal election. Queen had barely begun his address when he pointed at a section of the crowd and shouted: 'I will take any six of you fellows, one after the other.' According to a watching police sergeant, Queen was 'very aggressive in his attitude'. Members of the crowd surged forward and the meeting descended into a free for all in which Queen was knocked to the ground and Reverend Lyons took shelter in a nearby police station.

Queen was arrested and charged with using threatening words calculated to provoke a breach of the peace. When he stood trial at Clydebank Police Court, he claimed that he had challenged the men in the crowd to debate rather than fight. The meeting's chairman corroborated Queen's story, stating that the preacher had offered to debate with two Communists, two socialists and two Catholics in turn. Reverend Lyons claimed that the audience had been hostile from the outset, threatening: 'We will give them hell tonight!' and shouting: 'Up Dublin!' and 'Up Soviet!' as the meeting commenced.

Henry Watson from Lily Street in Bridgeton also returned to Clydebank to testify in Queen's defence. Watson alleged that 200 people had gathered to oppose the meeting, some of them armed with claw hammers and bayonets. The case against Queen was found not proven, although the preacher was admonished and the case made the front page of Glasgow's *Eastern Standard*.

Watson's younger brothers, William and Robert, were Billy Boys of some note – a reminder that gang affiliations and family ties were frequently entwined. They had appeared at the High Court two years previously to testify against Vinny Wallace and 'Dagger' Kane. During the summer and autumn of 1933, William Watson, now aged eighteen, made a series of court appearances, as both the alleged perpetrator of violence and its victim. On 30 June, he stood trial alongside Robert Burnside at the Eastern Police Court, charged with assaulting Philip Malloy with a razor and bayonet in Dalmarnock Road. Both prisoners had alibis: Burnside's was provided by an Orange Lodge official, who confirmed that he knew him as a member of a Bridgeton flute band. The case was found not proven.

William Watson then returned to the Eastern Police Court three weeks later to testify against Louis Barr. Superintendent

Gordon told the court that Barr had struck Watson on the head with an iron bar in retaliation for the assault on Philip Malloy.

On 12 August, William Watson formed part of the escort for an Orange procession which was attacked by a 200-strong crowd in Dale Street, described by police as one of Bridgeton's Catholic 'strongholds'. In the fierce fighting that followed, Thomas Moreland from Dale Street was struck with a hatchet and a bayonet, one of the blows fracturing his skull – Moreland would subsequently claim that he had run into the street to get his children out of the way, only to be 'knocked senseless' as the fighting erupted. Police recognised Watson along with a fellow Billy Boy named John Traquair among those taking a prominent part in the fighting. They stood trial at Glasgow Sheriff Court on 7 September alongside one of the Billy Boys' female followers, Elizabeth Gilfillan. They were found guilty of assaulting Moreland 'while acting in concert', but the sentences imposed by Sheriff Welsh were remarkably light: Traquair was jailed for three months with hard labour and Gilfillan fined just £3, while sentence against Watson was deferred.

William Watson appeared at the sheriff court again the following month. He was now charged alongside two other Billy Boys with assaulting a man with a hatchet during a gang fight in Bridgeton on 28 September. Reverend Sydney Warnes, minister of St-Francis-in-the-East and founder of the Bridgeton Pals' Association, appeared in court to plead for leniency on behalf of Watson's friend, Samuel Kelly Campbell: according to Warnes, Campbell had been 'led astray by bad associates'. Campbell was jailed for three months; Watson got thirty days.

Two days after the trial, a gang of youths gathered outside the Watsons' tenement house in Lily Street, Bridgeton, and hurled bricks and bottles at the windows. When Watson's mother, Sarah, went out to confront them she was met by twenty-two-year-old James Leadingham. According to Mrs Watson, Leadingham drew a sword from his trousers and 'threatened to cut her — Orange head off.' She told him that 'if her sons had been there he would not annoy her'. Leadingham was fined two guineas.

Protestant and Catholic youths alike possessed a keen sense of history – stretching back further, even, than the Battle of the Boyne. At around eleven o'clock on the night of Saturday, 29 July 1933, two beat constables received a message that a gang fight was brewing at Bridgeton Cross. As they rushed to the scene, they spotted a Calton youth named Robert Bowes in London Road surrounded by a large crowd. Bowes, who was clearly drunk, was flourishing a hammer in one hand and a hatchet in the other. The constables took him into custody and charged him with committing a breach of the peace. Bowes told the officers: 'I am a defender of John Knox!' At his trial at the Eastern Police Court, Bowes denied that he was a member of the Billy Boys. Pressing for a salutary sentence, Superintendent Gordon pointed out that the prisoner's invocation of John Knox – widely considered to be the founding father of the Protestant Reformation in Scotland – showed him to be 'one of those people whose intolerance for the views of others was a menace to the peace of the city.' Bowes was fined £5, with the option of thirty days' imprisonment.

Bowes no doubt saw himself as a martyr, while his willingness to fight for his faith was widely shared among Protestant and Catholic youths alike in Glasgow's East End. It also meant that Billy Fullerton's 'abdication' – however welcome to the police of the Eastern Division – was no guarantee of order on the streets of Bridgeton and the Calton.

Part III

Glasgow's Reign of Terror
1932–1935

9

Gangs, Rackets and Crime

Fears of a 'crime wave' – with Glasgow as the epicentre – gripped the Scottish press during the winter of 1931–2. Across the city, adult male unemployment stood at just below 40 per cent, but even this stark statistic masked much denser concentrations of unemployment – and poverty – in Glasgow's poorer districts, where the introduction of the means test in November 1931 left many young men facing severe cuts to their dole.

The city's magistrates met with the chief constable, Captain Percy Sillitoe, to seek his explanation for the reported upsurge in hold-ups, smash-and-grab raids and bag-snatching, and police officials and magistrates presented a united front in subsequent briefings to the press. The crime wave, they insisted, was due to unemployment and the resulting destitution, greatly exacerbated by the means test. Bailie W. T. Docherty told the *People's Journal*:

> The reason for the recent numerous hold-ups and the series of burglaries is not far to seek. The perpetrators are those who have been hard hit by unemployment; they have no money, and rather than go without food, they resort to crime.

An unnamed police officer admitted to the same newspaper that crime was increasing, but insisted that recent criticisms of the Glasgow force were unjustified. He was keen to blame gangster films for provoking copycat crimes, but then offered a second explanation which revealed some sympathy for the 'new' breed of criminal:

> If the story of some of the men figuring in hold-ups were known the public would not be so severe on us [the police]. Some of them have not worked for years. They suddenly lose all sense of balance, go right off the rails and commit crimes.

The relationship between unemployment and crime was viewed as axiomatic in these reports. As the *Sunday Mail* put it, those responsible for Glasgow's 'crime wave' were 'invariably young lads out of work'.

Sillitoe himself was in no doubt that unemployment bred crime. In his first annual report to Glasgow Corporation, for the year to 31 December 1932, he asserted:

> There can be little doubt that the increase of crime in the City is due in some measure to the difficult times through which we are passing, and that unemployment is the main factor, especially in the case of crimes involving the dishonest appropriation of property.

Sillitoe echoed the press in highlighting the plight of the rising generation of young men:

> Many of the younger generation have drifted into crime owing to present-day conditions. Their parents may be able to provide them with a home and clothing, but are unable to supply them with the pocket-money they require for amusements, and, as they have never known the discipline of work, they fall into criminal habits as the opportunity offers.

The close correlation between police and press commentaries was no accident. Journalists on local and national newspapers alike still relied heavily on police briefings, especially when compiling feature articles on the state of crime and its causes, and while the police were constantly vulnerable to criticism in the wake of increases in reported crime, Sillitoe was highly adept at manipulating the press – headlines proclaiming crime waves were quickly followed by positive coverage of police campaigns to target those responsible.

Scots and the American Underworld

Alongside unemployment, 'Americanisation' was still widely invoked by those seeking to explain the growing menace of crime in Scotland, with films such as *Scarface* and *20,000 Years in Sing Sing* said to be providing explicit instruction in the art of gangsterdom. Further problems were said to be posed by young Glaswegians who had journeyed to the United States in search of work, only to become immersed in American crime methods, which they duly brought back to Glasgow.

In April 1929, the *Weekly Record* had told the story of Al Capone's Scottish bodyguard. Two months after the St Valentine's Day Massacre, Capone was reported to be living in Miami in constant fear of reprisal. Ensconced at his house in Palm Beach, he was watched over by a handpicked group of ten gunmen, who were commanded by Ronald Kerr, a 'sandy-haired Glaswegian' and former King's Own Scottish Borderer, said to be 'the only man whom Capone will trust'. According to the *Weekly Record*, Capone had encountered Kerr by chance during a trip to Canada and had been impressed by the Glasgow man's 'rugged honesty and natural shrewdness', as well as his military bearing. Kerr had no criminal record and had previously been employed as a clerk in the accounting department of the London, Midland and Scottish Railway company. The *Weekly Record* took some delight in contrasting Kerr's upright manliness with the vicious duplicities of 'Chicago gangdom'.

Other Scots, it transpired, had played more active roles in the American underworld. In March 1930, the same newspaper ran a series of articles by James Gilzean entitled 'A Scot in Chicago's Gangland'. Gilzean claimed to have been closely associated with many of the leading Chicago gangsters throughout the Prohibition era, and he gave a graphic account of bootlegging, turf wars, ruthless killings and the corruption of police and politicians. Having returned to Scotland, Gilzean was keen to trade on the global notoriety of the 'wild men' of Chicago, and he provided sketches of John Torrio, Al Capone and Dion O'Banion, helpfully adding a gangland glossary peppered with terms such as 'Big Shots' and 'rackets', which were increasingly being deployed in newspaper features on Glasgow's own 'gangsters'.

The most urgent threat was signalled by reports of gunmen decamping from the United States to Britain. In October 1932, the *Glasgow Weekly Herald* claimed that more than 100 criminals deported from the United States and Canada had returned to Glasgow and the West of Scotland in the previous twelve months. An unnamed 'leading Glasgow police official' told the *Weekly Herald* that some of the deportees had been sentenced for serious offences: one was a released murderer. According to the police briefing, a number of the deportees had left Scotland for the United States as teenagers in search of work but, having lost their jobs as a result of the Depression, had turned to crime: 'holding up shops and men and women at the point of a pistol and robbing them'. After serving prison sentences in the United States, they returned to Scotland to find themselves with no prospect of work and little option but to turn once again to crime.

The result, in Glasgow, had been the spate of smash-and-grab raids and armed hold-ups noted by Sillitoe. Most worrying of all for the police was the deportees' ready resort to firearms:

> Few criminals in Scotland and England run the risk of carrying guns for they know that if they are caught, the penalties are much heavier. But these Chicago-fed and New York-brained criminals do not consider that. Consider the remark made by [one such] man to the Glasgow police constable who was attempting to arrest him. 'I have a cannon' (meaning a gun) is typically American.

The police fed such stories to the press for their own ends. On this occasion, the *Weekly Herald* made a graphic case for new police powers of supervision of deportees under a 'ticket of leave' (probation) system.

Glasgow's 'Reign of Terror'

The claim that Glasgow's gangs were operating Chicago-style rackets came to a head in the summer of 1932, when reports of a 'Reign of Terror' across the city's poorer districts caused considerable embarrassment for the police. Extortion took two forms: systematic, ongoing protection rackets were operated by some of the more powerful and well-established gangs such as the Billy Boys, the Kent Star and the Beehive Boys, while more sporadic, *ad hoc* demands were made by large and small gangs alike for contributions towards the payment of their members' fines and the cost of hiring defence lawyers.

Police superintendents, who led prosecutions in the city's police courts, frequently alleged that fines were levied from local shopkeepers under the threat of violence. The superintendents hoped to persuade magistrates to issue mandatory jail sentences for gangsters, but highlighting the 'gang levy' appeared to signal that the police had effectively lost control of large swathes of the city. Repeated claims that shopkeepers and publicans paid gangsters for protection and did not dare to complain to the police did nothing to bolster the image of the Glasgow force.

The fiercest controversy broke out in June 1932 when Superintendent Thomas McClure stated in the Western Police Court that shopkeepers at Partick Cross had been terrorised into paying fines that had been imposed upon the Plum Boys. McClure had been Sillitoe's closest contender for the post of chief constable the previous autumn and it is possible that he enjoyed the prospect of embarrassing Sillitoe by unleashing a new wave of gang revelations. In any event, the *Glasgow Weekly Herald* duly reported that the city was threatened by a 'renewed outbreak of gang warfare'. The *Weekly Herald* cited a 'high police official', who admitted that protection rackets were a recurring problem.

The official claimed that the city's gangs had been temporarily quelled by the intense police campaign in response to the petition four months earlier demanding action against the Bridgeton Billy Boys. However, a recent upsurge in gang activity had led to 'almost daily' complaints from shopkeepers in the affected areas:

> 'Terrorism' is common among shopkeepers in Bridgeton and the Southside. They are approached by gangs who offer 'protection' in exchange for the 'services' of the shopkeeper! In this way

money is extorted from unfortunate shopkeepers in order to pay the fines imposed on 'gangsters' for minor offences! The shops are also held by the 'protecting' gang as places of refuge when they are being chased by the police or the 'enemy'! Failure to co-operate on the part of the shopkeeper always has the same result – a 'beating-up'.

The *Sunday Mail* was quick to latch on to the *Weekly Herald*'s story. The following day, the *Mail* published an open letter to the chief constable demanding better protection for Glasgow's shopkeepers, arguing that systematic extortion threatened to choke the livelihoods of small traders.

To the dismay of local civic leaders and the police, the London-based British national press once again picked up the story. *John Bull* published a sensational account of **'GLASGOW'S REIGN OF TERROR'**, warning that if the evil was left unchecked, 'the methods of the American racket' threatened to 'corrupt the life of Glasgow'. In *John Bull*'s account, the lawlessness of the gangs was linked to an epidemic of thefts and small burglaries, which resulted from the mass unemployment that had left thousands of the city's young men with little or no paid work since leaving school.

Three weeks later, the *Sunday Mail* exposed a sinister new form of blackmail, which the gangs of Glasgow's South Side and East End had borrowed 'from Chicago'. It was no longer just the traders themselves who were threatened with assault should they refuse to pay for protection: 'Typical of the American gangster method is the trick employed of threatening the women members of the victim's family.' Nor were shop-keepers the only targets for the racketeers:

> In the East End of Glasgow publicans have been picked out for special attention, and a big number of licence-holders have preferred to pay rather than leave themselves open to the threats made by the gangsters.
>
> One victim told a *Sunday Mail* representative that within a month the threats made to him cost him over £20.

The publican had initially been asked for money to secure the release of a local 'gangster' on bail. He had refused, and the windows of his public house were duly smashed. The following day, he was told that he or a member of his family would be 'smashed' in turn. He made the payment requested, only to find that he was subsequently required to hand over a weekly sum for protection. The *Mail* claimed that the publican was too frightened to go to the police.

Senior officers in the City of Glasgow Police were appalled by the allegations. Complaining that irresponsible reporting had made Glasgow 'notorious throughout the land as a perfect hotbed of gangdom and hooliganism', they fed an alternative account to the *Evening Times* in an attempt to dampen speculation on the extent of racketeering and thus restore public confidence in the ability of the police to deal with the gangs. Three days after the *Mail*'s report, the *Evening Times* published a direct riposte that curtly dismissed the allegation that the East End was terrorised by American-style racketeers. The *Times* claimed to have interviewed 'several experienced and responsible police officials and detectives in different districts of the city', as well as publicans and shopkeepers over a wide area in the East End. The shopkeepers were 'incredulous', and refuted the suggestion that they would be afraid to request police assistance. A detective stated that he had never encountered a single complaint of 'racketeering' or blackmail, adding that attempting to obtain money by menaces was punishable by sentences of penal servitude. However, he severely undermined the police's alternative version of events by conceding that it was common knowledge that shopkeepers were canvassed to contribute towards gang members' fines. As he indignantly pointed out: 'That sort of thing has been going on since long before the war.'

Gang members exploited their notoriety, using their individual and collective reputations for violence to extort goods and services as well as money from a wide range of both legitimate and illicit businesses. Shopkeepers and publicans were not the only sufferers: café owners, market stallholders and the managers and proprietors of cinemas and dance halls also faced the unwelcome attention of gang members calling 'at the demand'. Illicit enterprises were equally at risk, leaving street bookmakers, gaming houses, brothels and shebeens facing simultaneous harassment from both the forces of the law and those of disorder.

For some leading figures in the gangs, protection rackets sustained a way of life characterised by conspicuous consumption. Fashionable clothes, regular displays of largesse in local public houses and freedom from the discipline of waged labour were the traits of the 'clever' gangster, whose reputation for violence was deployed for monetary gain. A rare insight into racketeering from a gang member's perspective was provided by a member of the Kent Star in an interview with the *Sunday Dispatch*. A journalist from the *Dispatch* told how, 'having paid for protection', he was taken to a private room in a tiny public house in the Calton:

> F. is about 24, Irish-born, small. He is regarded as one of the 'clever' men. He is intelligent and speaks well.
>
> A year or two ago he had a good job as a shop manager. He had been 'in tow' with the Kent Stars since he was 14 because he had the reputation of being good in a rough house.
>
> This is how he lives. He is 'on the parish' – as they call the Public Assistance Committee. But he never gets up until 11 in the morning.
>
> He dresses better than I do. And he can always buy a drink, because bookmakers, shopkeepers, tipsters, auctioneers, and stall-holders on open markets pay him a 'pension'.
>
> That means he calls on his clients once a week and receives ten shillings here, five there . . . for 'protection'.
>
> A refusal to pay a 'pensioner' means that there is no 'protection' and one's stall is overturned, one's goods are smashed or ruined, accidents happen to one's windows. And there is always the threat of a personal attack.

By this account, given the local prevalence of long-term unemployment, 'F' was one of the most prosperous young men in the Calton.

Most gangs across the city made sporadic demands for contributions towards the payment of fines, bail monies and legal fees. Press coverage of the gang levy tended to highlight the intimidation of small shopkeepers, but here again the gangs targeted a wide range of both legitimate and illicit local businesses. In many cases, gang members called casually 'at the demand' but in its more organised form, the gang levy was raised through a subscription list, as an anonymous 'ex-gangster' confided to the *Weekly Record*:

> If any gangsters are fined, the other members of the gang soon raise the cash. And the worse the gang, the easier it is for them to get the money.
>
> A subscription sheet is started, often with a fictitious name at the top to start it off. If possible, however, they get a bookmaker to head the list.
>
> Then the collectors visit the shopkeepers and anyone they meet in the district, and, strangely enough, nearly everyone seems quite eager to contribute.
>
> If they don't, of course, they are liable to get a 'dig on the chin' then and there, or at a later date. On the other hand, if they 'drop' good and plenty they may be able to call on the gang for service some time.
>
> The gangs can get money so easily in this way that they sometimes get up 'dud sheets' and have a blowout on the proceeds.

The ex-gangster's claim that gang members might provide services in return was echoed by Billy Fullerton in his account of the modus operandi of the Billy Boys in April 1932. Fullerton had been clear that the Billies had been willing to settle local disputes without resort to the courts for as little as £2.

'F' of the Kent Star told how gangs used subscription lists to maintain an informal welfare system, whereby legal costs were met, the families of jailed members were supported, and those newly released from prison were offered financial assistance. For those facing trial at the higher courts, the cost of hiring legal counsel was an urgent priority:

He gets the best lawyer. A subscription list is started. It is taken round by members of the gang to shopkeepers, dance-hall proprietors, and publicans.

They are very glad to pay. If they do not – accidents happen to shop windows; fights which cause a lot of damage and scare patrons away happen in bars and dance halls.

The average dance hall proprietor is quite happy to have you go round with a subscription list among the dancers. I myself have collected £20 in a night in this way.

Similar subscription lists are taken round to pay a man's fine, to keep his family while he is away in prison, or to buy him clothes and boots when he comes out after a long stretch.

As this account suggests, the welfare and legal defence of local gang members was deemed – at least by the gangs themselves – to be a matter of collective responsibility within the neighbourhood.

The resentment this provoked in districts already blighted by poverty and unemployment occasionally surfaced in the local press. 'When these ruffians are fined,' complained an anonymous reader of the *Evening Citizen*, 'their confederates come gathering round our doors to get their pals out.' In August 1929, the *Eastern Standard* reported that the door-to-door collection of fines had become a 'serious nuisance' in the East End: shopkeepers and householders alike were confronted with requests to contribute. Refusing the gangsters' demands was unwise, the *Standard* noted, while 'peaching' – informing the police – ran the risk of retribution.

The *Standard*'s condemnation of what it termed 'subsidised crime' was prompted by the example of Walter Scott of the Billy Boys. Scott was apprehended during a Saturday night disturbance at Bridgeton Cross. His supporters toured the district the following day 'armed with sheets in the most business-like fashion' – even though Scott was not due to appear at the Eastern Police Court until the Monday morning.

In addition to demanding payment for protection and contributions towards fines, gang members were also notorious for helping themselves to goods and services, demanding cigarettes and drinks without payment from local shops and public houses and taking rides in taxis with no intention of paying the fares. In one mundane – and yet subsequently notorious – incident in the spring of 1930, members of the South Side Stickers demanded suppers from a local fish and chip shop, claiming that they had no money but would make payment at a later date. The proprietor refused, and five Stickers were convicted of assault and fined for their part in the altercation that ensued. To the outrage of the police and local press, it was widely acknowledged that these fines were raised from local shopkeepers, with the bulk of the money raised from the unfortunate fish and chip shop owner himself, following threats to his wife and children. Beat constables tried as best they could to assist the shopkeepers, but were mindful that the traders could suffer reprisals if criminal charges were brought. Officers routinely advised shopkeepers and café owners to arm themselves and fight back. Those who did so were applauded by the police, many of whom believed strongly that gangsters were more deterred by a beating than they would ever be by fines.

The legion of illicit bookmakers whose patches criss-crossed the city's poorer districts were constantly vulnerable to extortion. Under the terms of the 1906 Street Betting Act, betting on horse races was only legally permitted at racecourses, or if it was conducted on credit by telegram, letter or telephone, through a licensed bookmaker. In practice, this penalised working-class punters, who were forced to resort to illegal 'street bookies' – in Glasgow, these operated out of the tenement closes. Their illicit status allied to their access to relatively large sums of ready cash made them obvious targets, and some paid regular sums for protection. They were also approached when gang members required additional funds for the payment of fines or bail monies: when Peter Williamson, leader of the Beehive Boys, was charged with assaulting a police officer in the Gorbals in November 1933, a local bookmaker paid his bail of £10 in full. Some prominent gang members – including Williamson's henchman, James Crearie – worked for bookmakers as clerks, whilst the requirement for lookouts to guard against police raids ensured that bookmakers employed a steady stream of casual labour. The distribution of work among gang members might well have made 'protection' run more smoothly.

The only alternative was for bookmakers and their staff to cultivate reputations as fighting men in their own right. John Prendergast, who ran a pitch in the Gorbals during the 1930s, described extortion as an enduring occupational hazard; his own predecessor was savagely beaten by members of the South Side Stickers who had come calling 'at the demand'. Prendergast's reputation as a game fighter served him well: 'Having established, when I took over the pitch, that I was capable of looking after myself, over the years I had no problems with the "hard men" in the district.'

In local bookmakers' lore, the plucky bookie who stood up to the local gangsters is frequently lionised. John Burrowes described how another Gorbals bookmaker stood up to Dan Cronin of the Beehive Boys. Few in the district dared to defy Cronin, and the bookmaker's willingness to face him in a square-go was enough to guarantee that the Beehive Boys left him alone.

The relationship between the illegal bookmakers and the police was highly ambiguous. The police periodically carried out surprise raids on the pitches, yet day-to-day relations were smoothed by a constant flow of bribes paid both to detectives and to beat constables, who duly ignored the bookmakers on their rounds. Police officers encouraged bookmakers, like shopkeepers, to fight back if they were molested by gang members and even spoke on their behalf in court when breaches of the peace subsequently arose. In June 1935, a Garngad bookmaker named Burniston was arrested, along with his brother, following a fight with members of the Cheeky Forty. In court, the bookmaker defended his part in the brawl quite openly, calmly telling the magistrate: 'I refuse to be terrorised [and] this is the result.' The superintendent leading the prosecution supported Burniston's claim and the magistrate duly imposed only a light fine.

The ongoing collusion between bookmakers and the police perhaps helps to explain why Glasgow's gangs never monopolised the illicit bookmaking pitches themselves: in effect, it was the police who determined who ran the pitches.

'Never a criminal in the accepted sense of the word'

Interviewed in 1955, Billy Fullerton was adamant that the Bridgeton Billy Boys had observed a rule that: 'At no time was theft to become a part of [their] activities.' Percy Sillitoe, whose memoirs were published later that year, drew a distinction between Fullerton and his followers. The former chief constable commented: 'Fullerton, I must say, was never a criminal in the accepted sense of the word. He was a fighting man, who . . . left the thieving to others, and his only conviction was for assault.'

Sillitoe's judgement on Fullerton's followers is amply borne out by their criminal records: many of them had serial convictions for theft as well as violence, while Fullerton himself was charged with two counts of housebreaking in June 1932 – just two months after his vow to go straight appeared in *Thomson's Weekly News*. Fullerton was released on bail and by the time he stood trial at Glasgow Sheriff Court, three months later, the charge had been amended to reset (receiving stolen goods). The evidence against him was inconclusive and he was admonished, but while Fullerton's own convictions were for assaults and breaches of the peace, he must have been well aware of the regular thieving expeditions undertaken by many of his associates.

David Turnbull, one of Fullerton's most trusted lieutenants, is a case in point. Turnbull, who was a year older than Fullerton, worked for his father as a steeplejack. Like Fullerton, he had convictions for assault stretching back to 1926; unlike Fullerton, he acquired a string of convictions for theft during the early 1930s. In May 1930, David Turnbull appeared alongside his brother, Robert, at Glasgow Sheriff Court charged with stealing bottles of whisky and brandy from a pub in Dalmarnock Road

– police had spotted them near Bridgeton Cross with bottles protruding from their pockets. The brothers fled as the officers approached, but they were chased and caught. In court, their lawyer depicted them as previously honest working men who had fallen on hard times: 'Both are well-known steeplejacks who have been engaged on some of the most hazardous structural work in Glasgow. For some time they have been unable to find work, and their present lapse is attributed to a long spell of idleness.' The two brothers were each jailed for six months with hard labour. David Turnbull had already served two terms of hard labour in the past year: six months for breach of the peace and assault, followed by three months for theft by housebreaking.

Contrary to the assertions of both Fullerton and Sillitoe, other members of the Billy Boys were more ambitious criminals. Edward Livingstone and James Rennie, both of whom were long-standing associates of Turnbull and Billy Fullerton, were known to detectives in Glasgow as safe-blowers as well as street fighters. According to Glasgow police lore, 'schools' for safe-blowers were periodically organised in the city so that novices might learn the trade from experts. Successful raids – in which a firm's wages or a cinema's takings were stolen – might yield small fortunes. Even labour exchanges were targeted. John Louden, aged twenty-four, broke into Bridgeton Employment Exchange in December 1933, blew open a safe, and stole £32. At his trial at Glasgow Sheriff Court, Louden protested that he had spent the night in question at a billiard hall, but his fingerprints had been found at the scene. He was jailed for fifteen months.

When members of the Billy Boys broke into pubs, shops or houses close to the gang's headquarters at Bridgeton Cross, their audacity could be startling. At the trial of John Traquair at the High Court in Glasgow in April 1934, Detective Lieutenant William Paterson of the Eastern Division was asked about the difficulties encountered in obtaining witnesses in the district:

> *(The Advocate Depute): Is it your experience that you have difficulty in getting a witness to speak there?*
>
> (Paterson): It is practically impossible. We have housebreakings there in an afternoon even and with hundreds of witnesses, and they would not even describe or admit seeing the men.
>
> *(The Advocate Depute): What is the reason?*
>
> (Paterson): Pure terror.

Questioned by the judge, Lord Moncrieff, Paterson acknowledged that the Billy Boys were not the only gang members in Bridgeton to intimidate witnesses. Asked whether this amounted to 'a general campaign of terrorism to prevent people giving evidence', Paterson replied: 'So far as local shopkeepers and residents are concerned.' Once again, the British national press seized on the detective's testimony. A headline in *The Times* screeched: '**GANG TERRORISM IN GLASGOW**'.

The Trial of the Beehive Boys

Mass unemployment fuelled the demand for cheap cigarettes and alcohol in Glasgow during the early 1930s, and the city's back-street entrepreneurs – and opportunistic thieves – were eager to meet it. As these illicit markets flourished, police and journalists highlighted the operations of 'shady traders' – unscrupulous shopkeepers, who readily bought stock they knew to be stolen. When two youths appeared at Glasgow Sheriff Court in November 1932 charged with resetting 54,600 cigarettes, the court heard that a new class of cut-price tobacconist was threatening to drive established shopkeepers out of business in the city's poorer districts. Public houses were viewed as fair game, and break-ins peaked in December each year when whisky was stolen in large quantities and sold on for consumption at house parties.

On the South Side of the city, much of this activity was carried out by the Beehive Boys from the Gorbals. The Beehive gang enjoyed a formidable reputation as both street fighters and thieves. Like their local rivals, the South Side Stickers, the Beehive Boys contained Catholic, Protestant and Jewish members. The gang's central figures, including Peter Williamson, Harry McMenemy and Herbert Howie, were Catholics, but they did not hesitate to recruit Protestant youths from Thistle Street and surrounding streets, while one of their fiercest street fighters, Louis Scragowitz, was a Jew. According to Percy Sillitoe, the core of the gang consisted of a group of house-breakers, around whom moved 'a much larger group of men who could be called upon to take part in fights, intimidations, and occasionally mob attacks and robberies.' Their leader, Williamson, was described by Sillitoe as a dangerous street fighter, skilled at evading arrest and 'a highly intelligent and fluent speaker' who could put up 'a creditable show' defending himself in court. His second-in-command, McMenemy, was so loyal to Williamson that he once pleaded guilty to an assault that had been committed by Williamson and a fellow Beehive Boy, Dan Cronin, serving a nine-month prison sentence on their behalf.

While Williamson led the Beehives into battle, the criminal master-mind behind the gang, was Herbert Howie. Sillitoe described Howie as:

> The real brains of the outfit . . . who planned and executed numerous clever, ingenious crimes but seldom took part in the unprofitable raids. He was a skilled burglar, and at one time Howie and the 'inside circle' of the Beehive Gang teamed up for their robberies with an English safe breaker, who was associated with them for several months.

Sillitoe attested to the fighting prowess of the Beehives by pointing out that one of the mob of street fighters around the gang's inner circle was Frank Murphy, who – as Frank Erne – later became Scottish welter-weight boxing champion. Sillitoe noted that Murphy possessed 'no great standing' among the Beehives, adding that it required more than fists to become an outstanding fighter among Glasgow's gangsters.

During the early 1930s, the Beehive Boys formed the largest network of housebreakers known to the City of Glasgow Police. Thirteen of them, including Peter Williamson and Herbert

Howie, featured in a detectives' mug-shot album compiled in 1934. Their average age was just under twenty-four; Williamson was the eldest, at thirty. They bore the marks of street fighters: seven of the thirteen had scars on their faces or necks, and one had lost an eye.

The Beehive Boys enjoyed considerable kudos within the Gorbals, as did their female contingent – the Queen Bees – and their junior section, the 'Wee Hive' or 'Young Beehive'. Notoriety, however, came at a price. During the winter of 1933–4, the Beehive Boys were targeted in the most concerted police campaign to be launched against any of the Glasgow gangs during the 1930s, singled out because of their collective record of property crime as well as violence. Between November 1933 and February 1934, ten of the gang's members were taken into custody in connection with a spate of minor break-ins and fights at South Side dance halls. They stood trial together at Glasgow Sheriff Court, where they faced twenty-seven charges – of house-breaking, breach of the peace, assault and assaulting the police – dating back to July 1933. Peter Williamson and Herbert Howie were among those to stand trial.

Housebreaking accounted for nineteen of the twenty-seven charges brought. None of the hauls was spectacular and no mention was made at the trial of the ambitious heists attributed by Sillitoe to Herbert Howie's careful planning. In many cases, the gang's members were caught following raids on South Side pubs. Working in *ad hoc* groups of two and three, they had in some instances cleared pubs' entire stocks of whisky and ciga-rettes. In September 1933, forty-six bottles of whisky, three of brandy and seven of gin were stolen from a pub in the Gorbals, along with 4,600 cigarettes and 17 shillings and sixpence in cash. There were plenty of willing buyers, including unscrupu-lous shopkeepers as well as impoverished friends and neigh-bours, but even with stolen whisky fetching 9 shillings a bottle, there were no fortunes to be made this way.

The court proceedings, which lasted four days, were the culmination of a determined effort on the part of the police to break up the Beehive gang. The trial attracted extensive coverage in the local press, as the 'gang-busting' chief constable, Percy Sillitoe, no doubt anticipated.

Courtroom exchanges during the trial provided glimpses of the strategies deployed by the police in their efforts to track the gang. Motor vans had been routinely used to monitor the movements of the Beehive Boys within the Gorbals. In August 1933, William Rae was stopped and searched by the members of a motor patrol after he was spotted carrying a wooden box through the streets – the box was found to contain bottles of whisky, stolen from a pub in Crown Street. Sillitoe was equally determined to exploit fingerprint techniques (he had appointed specialist officers upon his arrival in Glasgow). At the trial of the Beehive Boys in February 1934, fingerprints were successfully used in evidence against three of those charged with housebreaking. Additional information was gleaned from Sillitoe's network of paid informers. In October 1933, Peter Williamson and William Shannon were arrested after the police were tipped off ahead of a break-in at a private house in the Gorbals.

The remaining eight charges, of breach of the peace, assault and assaulting the police, arose out of a series of incidents that took place in the Gorbals between September and December 1933. Civilian witnesses were reluctant to identify individual Beehive Boys as the perpetrators of assaults, despite repeated prompting by the procurator fiscal, so the prosecution rested heavily on police evidence. Officers from the Southern and Central Divisions described scenes of frenzied violence during two fights at local dance halls. The first saw the Beehive Boys clash with the South Side Stickers; the second saw the Beehives turn on two constables who had the misfortune to arrive while the fight was in progress. Dan Cronin struck one of them on the face with a knuckle-duster, before kicking him on the face, legs and body. He then fled the scene. He was apprehended by two detectives in Cumberland Street a week later, but did not surrender willingly: he head-butted both of the officers and kicked one of them 'on the private parts' before he was subdued.

At the opening of the trial on 19 February, two of the gang pleaded guilty. Edward Doran pleaded guilty to two charges of housebreaking, three breaches of the peace, one assault and assaulting a police officer. Herbert Howie pleaded guilty to two housebreaking charges. The remaining prisoners pleaded not guilty. Police witnesses sought to depict the Beehive gang, both collectively and individually, as a profound menace to property and public order: Peter Williamson and James Crearie were singled out as particularly vicious and dangerous. Detective Sergeant Kenneth McNab of the Southern Division told the court that the prisoners were 'members of a gang whose head-quarters were at the corner of Thistle Street and Cumberland Street'. When Williamson challenged this characterisation, McNab retorted: 'You are the worst character in the gang; in fact, you are the one sent by the Beehive Gang to settle disputes with other gangs.'

As the trial progressed, Williamson displayed the courtroom skills which were to earn the respect of Percy Sillitoe – not only quizzing detectives, but even cross-examining civilian witnesses who described events in which he was not personally implicated. In keeping with their image as hard men, the Beehive Boys displayed the customary bravado in the dock: William Shannon interrupted a detective's evidence, shouting: 'Tell us the one about the three bears,' while Herbert Howie refused to name his accomplice in a case of attempted housebreaking to which he had confessed. Repeatedly instructed by the procurator fiscal and Sheriff Haldane to name the man involved, Howie refused, stating: 'I do not think it is a fair question.' Told that he would be further charged with contempt of court, Howie grinned at the other prisoners in the dock.

In addition to Edward Doran and Herbert Howie, who had already pleaded guilty, the jury found a further six of the pris-oners guilty of the majority of the charges levelled against them. Pressing for exemplary sentences, Procurator Fiscal J. D. Strathern described the Beehive Boys' exploits as 'a veritable debauchery of crime'. The police, he added, viewed the case as 'one of great gravity'. Sheriff Haldane jailed Peter Williamson for twelve months on three counts of housebreaking. Dan Cronin was sentenced to five months with hard labour for breach of the peace and assaulting the police. The remaining prisoners received sentences ranging from two to nine months.

The Beehive Boys were far from deterred, however. On the night of Wednesday, 28 November 1934, they severely assaulted Police Constable Frank Mulvey in Cumberland Street, close to the gang's adopted corner. Mulvey claimed that he was head-butted by Peter Williamson, and then struck with a weapon from behind by James Crearie. The constable fought back and managed to strike Williamson on the head with his truncheon before he was rescued by a young woman, who dashed into the crowd that had surrounded him. PC Mulvey required seven stitches to a wound above his right eye, while Williamson – who was arrested after a 'ceaseless comb-out of the city' – appeared at the Central Police Court the following week with his head swathed in bandages (which would suggest that he had suffered a severe beating in the cells). During his trial at Glasgow Sheriff Court, Williamson insisted that he had 'never used a weapon to anybody in his life' and protested that he had been on his way to visit friends when the constable accosted and then assaulted him. Deriding another police officer's claim that the Beehive Boys 'terrorised' the South Side, Williamson remarked that while he did not belong to the gang himself, he knew its members to be merely 'a nice lot of fellows who ran about the corner'. He was jailed for thirty days.

Subsequent court appearances by members of the Beehive Boys revealed glimpses of more handsome rewards from their thieving expeditions, some of which were carried out far away from Glasgow. On Christmas Eve, 1934, Dan Cronin and Tommy Boyle broke into a pub in Lawmoor Street in the Gorbals by cutting through the floor of the house above. They were appre-hended by two detective constables, one of whom was badly injured in the fight that followed. Cronin, who had nine previous convictions, was jailed for eighteen months with hard labour. Boyle got twelve months. At the time of their arrest, Boyle had just completed a ten-month stretch in Strangeways Prison in Manchester, where he had been convicted of stealing 53,000 cigarettes in raids on three tobacconists' shops.

The size of Boyle's haul suggests that some of the gang's schemes, at least, might have been highly profitable. Peter Williamson was periodically flush from his successful scams, although constant attention from the police meant that he was rarely able to enjoy his riches for long. In August 1935, he was jailed for thirty days after he was convicted of 'being a known thief and having in [his] possession £39 without being able to give a satisfactory account of how it came into his possession.' This was equivalent to three months' wages for a manual worker during the 1930s.

Motor Bandits

The spread of the motor car posed new problems for the police from the 1920s onwards. In Glasgow, car ownership was largely the preserve of the higher echelons of the middle class – a marker of the social standing of the city's professional and business elites. By 1930, however, joy-riding was increasingly widespread. This new form of crime was difficult to contain, not least since intent to steal was frequently impossible to prove: most joy-ridden cars were abandoned, leaving the police with the frustrating task of repeatedly returning the vehicles to their owners. By the mid-1930s, the youthful joy-rider had become a 'perfect pest', according to the *Sunday Mail*. In February 1936, the *Mail* reported that the police had received nightly complaints from irate car owners on the city's South Side since the New Year. The offenders were choosy and crafty in equal measure: 'Invariably the cars taken were of the latest type and the most expensive. Later the cars were found in other streets, but before abandoning them the youths were in the habit of removing the starting key, precluding the possibility of any immediate chase.'

Joy-riders were a growing nuisance, but they paled in comparison to another new breed of criminal: the 'motor bandit'. In August 1929, crowds of pedestrians were startled by a sudden smash-and-grab raid at a jeweller's shop in Duke Street, on the eastern edge of Glasgow city centre. The thieves struck at seven o'clock on a Friday evening, snatching a display pad containing forty-eight diamond rings before speeding off in a stolen car. The vehicle was later found abandoned in the Queen's Park district on the South Side. The rings were valued at £700.

The unpredictability of smash-and-grabs made them difficult to prevent, and spates of raids were reported in the local press throughout the early 1930s. In November and December 1931, raiders targeted city centre furriers as well as jewellers. Fur coats worth £50 to £60 apiece were snatched in early morning raids in Sauchiehall Street and Great Western Road, while two Argyle Street jeweller's shops were raided on consecutive nights in November under cover of heavy fog: rings and watches worth £180 were snatched.

Stolen cars were also used by city youths to carry out robberies and thefts in the towns and countryside surrounding Glasgow. Shops, post offices and public houses were commonly targeted. In a memoir published in the *People's Journal*, George Anderson, a former detective inspector, recalled an epidemic of thefts in the Glasgow region during the winter of 1931–2. Thieves used stolen cars to carry out break-ins across Lanarkshire, Renfrewshire and Stirlingshire before Anderson traced one of the culprits to a tenement in Glasgow's East End. Three men subsequently appeared at Glasgow Sheriff Court, where they were charged with stealing property worth £1,500. The prisoners had all been in receipt of unemployment allowances, and Sheriff Mercer had been aghast to learn that they had been taught to drive at an instruction centre for the unemployed. He jailed each of them for eighteen months with hard labour.

The Insurance Man's Tale

Larry Johnson of the Beehive Boys was one of the motor bandits – dubbed as such by the press – who routinely used stolen cars to carry out smash-and-grab raids. He was not part of the gang's inner circle around Peter Williamson and Herbert Howie, but he was a prolific housebreaker nonetheless. In interviews with historian and documentary film-maker Steve Humphries conducted during the 1980s and 1990s, he gave a unique inside account of the gang's activities.

Johnson was born in Thistle Street in the Gorbals in 1912. Both of his parents were Protestants, and his father worked as a warehouseman. Larry served an apprenticeship as a boiler-maker, but in common with other members of the Beehive Boys, he was unemployed for much of his twenties. He had joined the Beehive Boys during his teens and remained an active member of the gang once he was married. At the time of his marriage, in June 1936, he was still living with his parents. His only legitimate source of income was his poor relief: 17 shillings a week. Most of his time was spent hanging around the Beehive corner, talking and larking about, gambling and playing football in the streets. He turned to theft to fund nights out at local dance halls, cinemas, pubs and billiard halls, along with occasional bouts of more conspicuous consumption.

Johnson was taught to drive by a Gorbals milkman, for whom he did some work 'on the side'. He became a habitual car thief:

> It was an easy thing for me to pick up cars. In those days all you had to do was get a screwdriver. On the side of the car you only had two screw nails, unfasten them and the handle would turn, and when you turned the handle it was an easy thing to link up the wires and that was you getting away with a car. It would take about three or four minutes and you were away.

Johnson and his friends were quite meticulous in choosing which cars to steal:

> We decided there was no point in stealing a car that wasn't a nice car so we always made sure that we went over to the centre of town. We'd pick up a decent car to go around in because we found that we got more respect that way. If you go about with an old car the police were liable to pull you up, but [if] they saw you with a good car they just nodded their head and helped you on your way.

In an era when working-class car ownership was extremely rare, young men derived enormous kudos from stealing expensive cars for joy-rides when they were courting: Johnson and his wife-to-be toured all over the West of Scotland.

Larry Johnson was an energetic and enterprising criminal. Along with other members of the Beehive Boys he regularly broke into warehouses, shops and pubs, either in the Gorbals and adjacent districts or in Glasgow city centre. Thefts from pubs varied in scale, with alcohol and cigarettes stolen for the gang's own consumption as well as for resale. Raids upon warehouses and city centre shops were more likely to hinge upon contacts made by members of the gang within broader criminal networks – having identified a market for stolen clothing and textiles, the Beehive Boys planned raids upon warehouses in Glasgow's South Side:

> Some of the boys would say, 'We've got a wee job to do, down at South Portland Street. There's a warehouse there, somebody wants a lot of clothing.' So we would go there, break into the place . . . We got the clothes, put them into our car, took it away to where we knew [somebody] who'd buy it, a place in Hamilton. It was never a lot of money involved, but there was enough to keep us going.

Shops were sometimes raided by appointment: Larry Johnson played a pivotal role in staging break-ins with a shopkeeper who was planning to make fraudulent insurance claims:

> They used to call me the 'insurance man'. We would go to this particular shop in Duke Street, we'd break in at the back . . . and he would get the insurance money. He would claim insurance for what we had done. He would tell us, 'You've got about half an hour to pick up what you want, and then I'll do the rest myself.'

According to Johnson, such arrangements 'happened quite a lot'.

Johnson and his friends also used stolen cars to mount thieving expeditions across Glasgow and the surrounding counties. In March 1936, he took a car from Cadogan Street in Glasgow city centre and drove two of his friends to Kilmarnock, eighteen miles south-west of the city:

Three of us, Billy, James and myself, out for a night out. It was a lovely car we had, a smasher. So we head for Kilmarnock. We get a couple of pints each and we look around, nothing to do, but we can't just get a car and do nothing. So we head back through Kilmarnock and we decide, we'll stop here. So we just stopped at this store, smashed the windows in.

The records of Kilmarnock Sheriff Court identify the premises as those of Messrs Nimmo, Gardner, Napier and Son, radio dealers, of 102 Portland Street, Kilmarnock. The raiders loaded three wireless sets into the car, and set off back for the Gorbals at around 10.30 p.m. with James Cullen at the wheel. Neighbouring police forces were alerted and the stolen car was spotted at a road-block at Newton Mearns, six miles south of Glasgow. Cullen doubled back, then headed east with a police car in pursuit. After a short chase the bandits pulled up, ditched the car and tried to flee on foot. Cullen was quickly caught, and Billy Knotts was apprehended nearby at around midnight. Larry Johnson gave the police the slip. He stole another car and made his way home on his own. He was arrested two days later by detectives from Glasgow's Southern division and picked out by a police officer in an identification parade at Kilmarnock. (Johnson still maintained, nearly sixty years later, that the parade was rigged.)

Along with Cullen and Knotts, Larry Johnson was jailed for ten months. Johnson applied for leave to appeal against his conviction, protesting that the sheriff had disregarded his alibi – two of Johnson's neighbours had perjured themselves on his behalf – and alleging that his photograph had been shown to the officer who identified him as Cullen and Knotts's accomplice. The appeal was not granted.

The Beehive Boys saw themselves as a criminal élite, uninterested in sectarian skirmishing. 'They were more for stealing and plundering,' Johnson insisted, and they looked down on those they considered to be mere fighting gangs. Johnson was adamant that the Beehive Boys were different from 'the usual type of gang':

They were a gang which looked after themselves, and they were always in the habit of having more money than a normal gang, so most of the time they were well dressed, they could go dancing and different places and they were looked on by the other gangs as being dapper. We had cars, we could go and get a car when we wanted one and take some of the boys out and the girls out. We had a higher standard of living than the usual gangs. The Beehive Boys were better dressed than a normal gang. We used to go to a tailor's shop in the Gorbals and it cost you five pounds for a real good suit of clothes. We used to go about and we were well dressed, going to the dancing and we could go into restaurants and even the police accepted us as being on a higher standard, whether they liked it or not, they looked on it that way.

Louis Scragowitz – one of the gang's foremost street fighters – worked as a tailor's presser and it is likely that his connections helped to ensure that his fellow Beehive Boys were well turned out. But their stylish appearance was noted by the police as well as by rival gangsters. Detectives targeted young men whose fashionable clothes stood out in poor districts, and Johnson described how he was once arrested in Glasgow city centre:

I've got on a nice blue suit, well geared up, collar and tie, and as I'm walking along somebody [tapped] me on the shoulder and it was a detective. 'Where are you going, laddie?' 'Oh, just . . .' 'You're looking well today,' he says. 'Aye, why not?' 'That's a good suit you've got on, where did you get it? I'd like to get one like that.' That's the way they would talk. 'You get one from the Jewish tailors.' He says, 'That's not where you got that one.' 'So what?' He says, 'You're coming down to the Central (police office), you know where it is.' So he takes you down and says, 'How much money have you got in your pocket?' 'I don't know, maybe two or three pounds.' 'Where did you get the suit and where did you get the money?' (You got your unemployment benefit.) 'I saved it up.' 'No, that won't do. We'll have to charge you with having money that you can't give an account of.'

On this occasion, Johnson was sentenced at Glasgow Sheriff Court to sixty days' imprisonment with hard labour. To prominent Beehive Boys, this was an occupational hazard.

By his own account, Larry Johnson was only apprehended for a small proportion of the crimes he committed, even though he was well known to the police. Nonetheless, he served at least five prison sentences for theft during the 1930s, and he was never far removed from the sanctions of the law. However, when questioned sixty years later about the impact of imprisonment upon his attitudes and behaviour, Johnson replied that in the absence of legitimate employment during the 1930s he had no choice other than to turn to crime. His parents were in no position to support him financially, and he was not prepared to eke out an existence 'on the parish'.

Larry Johnson was reluctant to describe his involvement in gang fights. (His reticence is unsurprising as he was being interviewed on camera for a forthcoming BBC television series, which meant that his identity could not be shielded by the use of a pseudonym.) He insisted that: 'The Beehive Boys weren't so much a razor gang' – by his account, when they did clash with other gangs, it was generally because their rivals had 'interfered with their exploits'. However, he did admit that the Beehive Boys fought with wooden clubs ('What they now call baseball bats'), adding with a hint of pride: 'They mostly won all their fights. They were a powerful gang, well known, and well supported by each other.'

10

The Old Firm

The passion for football appeared to be near universal among men and boys in Glasgow's tenement districts. As social investigator, Charles Cameron, noted during the late 1930s: 'Pass along any street in the working-class areas . . . at any time of day, and where there is a vacant piece of ground you will most probably find a group of young men kicking a ball.' Gang members were no exception: many were first hauled before the magistrates for playing football in the street. Some gangs formed their own teams, challenging each other to matches on Glasgow Green, although these encounters frequently descended into brawls between players and supporters alike. Most young men followed either Rangers or Celtic – allegiances were dictated by religious affiliation: the clubs were firmly identified as Protestant and Catholic respectively, which meant that football rivalry frequently inflamed the city's sectarian antagonisms.

Rangers and Celtic supporters routinely travelled to their team's matches in brakes (motorised charabancs). These were festooned with flags and banners proclaiming allegiance to the rival national causes of Britain and Ireland – religion and nationalism were inseparable in the minds of many supporters. Many Rangers supporters drove through districts with sizeable Irish-Catholic communities en route to Ibrox Park, Rangers' stadium in Govan. Likewise, Celtic followers passed in huge numbers through the vicinity of the Billy Boys' stronghold of Bridgeton Cross on their way to Celtic Park. The conduct of 'brake clubs' was calculated to offend: the waving of flags, singing of party songs, shouts of sectarian abuse and issuing of threats to passing pedestrians frequently met with violent ripostes, and many 'brakists' armed themselves before setting off to matches.

In October 1925, for example, police tracked a brake carrying Celtic supporters from the Garngad on its way to Ibrox. Green and white flags had been draped around the vehicle before it set off, and the occupants were waving banners and Celtic colours, shouting and singing as the charabanc wound its way through the city centre and crossed the River Clyde – their songs included an improvised ditty in which Celtic's leading players formed an alternative royal family, with Paddy Gallagher crowned King of Ireland and Jimmy McGrory Prince of Wales. Police stopped the vehicle in the Gorbals and confiscated the green and white banners, flags, scarves and painted bowler hats, along with a concertina. Twenty-nine young men were arrested; all but two were subsequently fined for disorderly conduct.

Billy Fullerton told the readers of *Thomson's Weekly News* in 1932 that the gang employed its own 'official' poet – nick-named Kipling – who penned poems and songs celebrating the exploits of 'the Billy Boys and the Rangers' alike. Kipling, who dressed smartly but avoided 'gangster' fashions, was known not just to the members of the Billy Boys' committee but also to 'several of the best-known sportsmen in the city'. He was a regular fixture at Rangers home matches at Ibrox Park, where he stood apart from the Billy Boys and used a series of signals to warn them of the approach of the police and the presence and numbers of rival gangs. While games were in progress, a dozen Billy Boys worked their way round the terraces selling printed copies of Kipling's latest verses at twopence per sheet. Fullerton himself sold thirty-six dozen at one match early in 1932; his takings of £3 and 12 shillings went towards the gang's funds.

On the days of 'Old Firm' matches, territorial gang rivalries were momentarily eclipsed. Larry Johnson, fiercely proud of his standing as a Beehive Boy, was also a proud Protestant, and when Rangers played Celtic he would make his way to Bridgeton to join up with the Billy Boys. In his words:

> when it came to the Rangers and Celtic game, I always went over to Bridgeton and became one of the Billy Boys for the day . . .

you were always getting involved . . . it was usually bottles that
they were throwing, and you didn't know who was hit with them
anyway so you didn't care so much . . .

Some of Johnson's fellow Beehive Boys were likely to be among
the crowds of Celtic supporters that he was bombarding. Yet
this form of violence was relatively impersonal, and meant that
his gang loyalty could be reconciled with his allegiance to
Rangers.

Even children could be at risk when banter over the respective
teams' fortunes turned to abuse. In March 1929, an eight-year-
old boy appeared at the Eastern Police Court to testify to an
assault that he had suffered at the hands of three youths aged
in their mid-teens. The boy described how they accosted him
in Tobago Street in the Calton, telling him that Celtic had been
defeated that afternoon. When the boy contradicted them, they
kicked him in the stomach, pulled his hair and grabbed him by
the neck, squeezing his throat until the boy's aunt came to his
rescue. Bailie Stevenson asked the victim if he knew why he had
been assaulted. The boy replied: 'It is because I am a Catholic
and they are not.' The three accused claimed that they had been
acting 'in fun' and had only 'shaken him a little'. Bailie Stevenson
fined them 10 shillings each.

Bigotry and Ballots

Glasgow's sectarian antagonisms worsened during the early
1930s against the backdrop of prolonged mass unemployment
and fierce anti-Catholic agitation by a new figure in Glasgow
politics, Alexander Ratcliffe. The high profile of the Red
Clydesiders in Parliament tended to deflect attention from the
importance of sectarianism in Glasgow's municipal politics.
While socialist candidates won the majority of local seats at
four successive general elections from 1922, the Unionist-
dominated 'Moderate' (Tory) group retained control of Glasgow
Corporation until 1933. Ironically, it was to be the short-lived
growth of Ratcliffe's militant Scottish Protestant League (SPL)
during the early 1930s that paved the way for Labour's eventual

municipal triumph: in the 1933 local elections, the SPL polled a quarter of the vote, fatally undermining the Moderates.

Working-class support for the SPL derived in significant part from unemployment: the decline of the shipbuilding and engineering industries had led to significant downward social mobility among Protestant manual workers. Many of the skilled craftsmen who had previously formed an élite among the industrial workforce now found themselves jobless. If their sons found work at all, it was frequently unskilled, low status and temporary.

Against this backdrop, even matches between junior football teams were played in a climate of simmering hostility. In June 1933, S. Hardie Stewart – news editor of the *Scottish Daily Express* – told how 200 police officers were required to keep the peace during a game played at Barrowfield Park in Dalmarnock. One of the teams was Catholic while their opponents, despite having no religious affiliation, were adopted by local Protestants as honorary 'Orangemen'. The match drew a crowd of 1,500. However, as Stewart noted, 'thousands' of people stood in the adjoining streets watching the spectators. Stewart was repeatedly warned that 'if the Roman Catholics won there would be murder.' A scrimmage broke out at half-time, and police were quick to rush in, making two arrests and retrieving a bayonet, a poker and a hatchet in the process. While the promptness of their action deterred the combatants for the remainder of the match, hostilities were renewed later that night in Salamanca Street in Parkhead, although there, too, police were quick to quell the disturbance.

Local residents told Stewart that their lives would be 'hell' for the next six weeks 'until after the march of the Orangemen in July'. Hostilities were ratcheted up each year on the last Sunday in May, when Catholic children processed to Sacred Heart Chapel in Old Dalmarnock Road for their confirmation into the church. The processions, headed by a pipe band, invariably aroused the ire of the Billy Boys.

Stewart toured Mile End, Bridgeton and Parkhead to gauge the atmosphere for himself. He found streets:

crowded with silent, shuffling mobs . . . every one moves in an electric atmosphere. Even the children stop playing their games. They ask every one when the fight is to start and where.

His appraisal of the gangs of the East End was scathing:

the Norman Conks, the Billy Boys, the Sally Boys – bands of undersized, underfed human beings, spoiling for a fight. These are the 'gangsters.' Boys – even men of thirty and forty – with 3 [foot] long bayonets concealed down their trouser legs, hatchets, pokers, files, iron bars, and stones in their pockets, ready to use them and run whenever they see a policeman with a drawn baton. They fight only when they are in safe numbers.

Stewart paid tribute to Assistant Chief Constable Donald McPherson, who supervised the night's operations from the Eastern Police Office. Order had been maintained, Stewart concluded, due to McPherson's 'organising ability, and the effect of his continual display of police power.'

The Trial of John Traquair

The mutual antipathy between followers of Rangers and Celtic was starkly illustrated following the arrest of a Billy Boy named John Traquair in 1934. Traquair was born in Bridgeton in 1896. He served with the Cameron Highlanders during the Great War and, once the war was over, returned to his former occupation as a rivet-heater. His mother died in 1919 and for the next fifteen years, Traquair lived with his father in Reid Street in Bridgeton. By 1934, he had amassed eleven criminal convictions: eight for assault and three for breaching the peace; however, he had only been jailed twice. His longest sentence – three months' hard labour – followed a stand-up fight between the Billies and the Shanley Boys during an Orange procession in August 1933. On that occasion, Traquair fractured a man's skull with a hatchet.

Some seven months later, on Saturday, 3 March 1934, a crowd of around 500 Rangers supporters gathered at Bridgeton Cross station to wait for the 2.10 p.m. train to Ibrox. Many were wearing blue rosettes and scarves; some were carrying weapons.

At around 1.50 p.m. a train carrying Celtic supporters to a game against St Mirren in Paisley pulled into the station. As the train came to a halt, the rival supporters hurled insults at each other. Celtic supporters claimed that they were met with shouts of 'You Papish bastards' and 'Irish bastards', whilst the train's guard heard cries of 'To hell with the Celtic', 'Papists', and 'A lot of Papish buggers'. A station porter heard shouts of 'Good old Celtic' from those on the train, interspersed with foul-mouthed cries 'running down' Rangers.

A group of Rangers supporters led by Traquair burst into one of the carriages. Traquair struck at John McVey, a twenty-one-year old carter from Saracen Street, Glasgow, who raised his arm to ward off the blow. Traquair then punched McVey's companion, Ranzo Buonaccorsi, in the face. The train's guard ran into the carriage, grabbed Traquair and wrestled him off the train. The guard then promptly signalled for the train to depart, ahead of schedule, as he was afraid that the Celtic supporters would spill out of the carriages to confront their adversaries. Traquair disappeared into the crowd on the platform. Following the disturbance, station porters saw a group of between twelve and twenty men, some carrying weapons, run up the stairs from the platform and out of the station. As the train pulled out, McVey's fellow passengers noticed that he was bleeding from a cut on his left forearm. He got off the train at the next station, and was taken to the Royal Infirmary where his wound was stitched.

Traquair was identified by one of McVey's fellow passengers, and was taken into custody at 10.30 p.m. that night after a pair of constables found him leaning against a wall in Main Street, Bridgeton, surrounded by a crowd of onlookers. He was drunk, bleeding from several injuries and surrounded by broken glass. Traquair told the officers that he had fallen, but they were convinced that he had been fighting. Traquair was initially charged with being drunk and incapable but on Monday 5 March, he was charged along with the notorious Bridgeton fighting man, Johnny Phillips, in connection with the incident at Bridgeton Cross station on the Saturday afternoon. Traquair was subsequently tried at Glasgow High Court on 30 April. He was charged with mobbing and rioting, assaulting John McVey with a knife or razor and his fists, and assaulting Ranzo Buonaccorsi with his fist. His membership of the Billy Boys was cited in the indictment. Traquair pleaded not guilty, although he admitted to assaulting John McVey with his fist.

The story that unfurled at the trial was that of an organised ambush on a train carrying Celtic supporters, carried out by a gang of Billy Boys, who exploited the cover provided by the larger group of Rangers supporters gathered at the station. There was no agreement as to the weapons wielded by the gang: knives, razors, hammers, 'tools', hatchets, bayonets, wooden batons, sticks and stones were all mentioned by different witnesses. Accounts of the threats and insults exchanged by the rival supporters left no doubt that the violence was sectarian: 'Papish' and 'Irish' were used interchangeably as terms of abuse by the Rangers supporters, starkly capturing the fusion of national and religious conflicts embedded in the Old Firm rivalry.

At the trial, McVey, Buonaccorsi and a series of fellow passengers testified to Traquair's part in the fight in the carriage. Traquair's blow against McVey was described as a downward, sweeping motion, suggesting the use of a sharp instrument such as a knife or razor, rather than a punch with a fist. A resident house surgeon from the Glasgow Royal Infirmary testified that the wound on McVey's forearm, which had penetrated to the muscle, was consistent with injuries inflicted by a knife or razor.

Police testimonies in court emphasised Traquair's involvement with the Billy Boys. Lieutenant William Paterson of the Eastern Division told the court that Traquair was frequently to be seen in the ranks of the gang at Bridgeton Cross, the Billy Boys' recognised headquarters. Asked by the Advocate Depute to describe the nature of the Billy Boys, Paterson responded:

> They are a so-called Orange organisation. There is a crowd sometimes of them of about 100 strong. They are known as Rangers' supporters and follow the Rangers everywhere and one of their

songs is 'We are the Billy Boys'. They hang about Bridgeton Cross and cause great trouble. When there are matches at Parkhead and Celtic [supporters] going there and anyone wearing a Celtic scarf, there is a disturbance. We have instructed special policemen to be there on Saturday afternoons to keep down disorder.

In effect, the latter stages of the trial focused on the Billy Boys as a gang, with Traquair liable to guilt by association. Pressed further by the Advocate Depute, Paterson was adamant that the Billy Boys formed 'a definite body'. Their members were easily distinguished at football matches since they were 'usually dressed with orange colours and blue Rangers' colours'.

In cross-examination, Traquair's counsel asked Paterson: 'Don't you know that the chief reason for [the existence of the Billy Boys] is to protect the band at the Orange Walk?' Paterson responded that he '[did] not think the Orange Lodge would admit that' and, in any case, the Orangemen were well protected by the police.

Following a strong steer from the judge, Lord Moncrieff, the jury took just half an hour to find Traquair guilty on all three counts. Before sentence was pronounced, the Advocate Depute highlighted Traquair's string of previous convictions for crimes of violence, while Traquair's counsel portrayed him as a First World War veteran who had fallen on hard times. Lord Moncrieff sentenced Traquair to four years' penal servitude, commenting that in the light of the prisoner's criminal record, exemplary punishment was now required.

Traquair appealed against both conviction and sentence on the grounds of insufficient evidence and that, in any event, the sentence was excessive. Lord Moncrieff submitted a confidential report to the appeal judges in which he confirmed his own belief that Traquair was guilty on all three of the counts against him. Moncrieff explained that the severity of the sentence reflected the evidence that Traquair had aimed a blow with a knife at McVey's face and thus might have struck his neck, adding that he had been influenced by Traquair's list of previous convictions and in particular the 'startling' sentence of a mere three months' imprisonment imposed in September 1933. He pointed out that, 'I have subsequently been told that the case was tried summarily on that occasion because there was reason to distrust the courage of a jury, and because conviction was regarded as of more moment than sentence.' In Lord Moncrieff's view, justice had been eroded by the fear that juries were intimidated in gang cases.

Traquair's appeal was heard at the Scottish Court of Criminal Appeal in Edinburgh on 17 July, when Lord Anderson pronounced that Traquair's conviction was 'well warranted' on the basis of the evidence presented. Commenting on the sentence of four years' penal servitude, Anderson declared that, given both Traquair's previous convictions and the nature of the present offence, 'it was not a day too long'. Lord Hunter and Lord Murray concurred.

In addition to Traquair's own appeal, two petitions were launched on his behalf in the fortnight following his trial. The first, addressed to the Home Secretary, was highly libellous in the accusations it levelled at Lord Moncrieff. Alexander Ratcliffe, leader of the Scottish Protestant League (SPL) and councillor for the East End ward of Dennistoun, quickly launched a more judiciously worded alternative addressed to the Secretary of State for Scotland, Sir Godfrey Collins. Ratcliffe's petition pleaded for a reduction in Traquair's sentence and highlighted the disparity between the sentence of four years' penal servitude imposed on Traquair and those of twelve months' imprisonment passed on five Catholics at the same sitting of the High Court. The Catholics, who included three prominent members of the Kent Star, were convicted of mobbing and rioting following a fight in a Gorbals dance hall, in which a man was fatally stabbed in the neck. Ratcliffe's petition alleged that 'so-called religious differences' had been the cause of both disturbances and added that the disparity in the sentences, especially in relation to the injuries inflicted, had caused grave disquiet among sections of Glasgow's Protestant community. According to Ratcliffe, the sentences had exacerbated the bitterness between rival factions in the East End.

Ratcliffe clearly viewed the Traquair case as an opportunity to rally popular support for the SPL. Protestant youths arrested during sectarian street fights might well have resented punishment for standing up for – as they saw it – church, King and constitution. One of the Billy Boys' songs played on this sense of grievance:

> *Oh, why be so hard on the Brigton Billy Boys*
> *Give honour where honour is due*
> *Do you remember in days gone by*
> *When you were as Orange and Blue*
> *And if there's a fight at the corner of the street*
> *We hope all the boys will be there*
> *So give three cheers for the Brigton Billy Boys*
> *And a kick to the one who interferes*

From their point of view, the Billies were being persecuted for their patriotic loyalty.

Perceptions of judicial bias in the Traquair case fed upon this prior sense of grievance. In any case, Ratcliffe no doubt felt a more tangible obligation to the Bridgeton Billy Boys, whose members had acted as stewards for SPL election meetings.

The extent of Ratcliffe's links with the Billy Boys is difficult to discern. However, he expressed sympathy for another 'gang' founded by Billy Fullerton during the early 1930s, which styled itself the 'KKK'. As Fullerton revealed in an interview with the *Evening Citizen* in 1955, this short-lived body held its meetings in the Foundry Boys' Hall in London Road in Bridgeton. Its aims, according to Fullerton, were identical to those of the 'senior' Billy Boys: loyalty to King, constitution and fellow Protestants. Most of its 200 members already belonged to the Billies; now they wore black and white ties and small brass 'K' badges on their lapels. In an article published in the SPL's paper, the *Vanguard*, in November 1933, Ratcliffe pointed out with some pride that: 'Glasgow is the only place in Britain where there is a Ku Klux Klan.' (Strictly speaking, he pointed out, in Glasgow 'KKK' stood for 'Knights of Kaledonia Klan'.)

Under the auspices of the SPL, Ratcliffe organised meetings across Glasgow in support of Traquair over a period of three weeks. The petition was submitted to the Secretary of State for Scotland in June, with 40,000 signatures gathered throughout Scotland and Northern Ireland, and a promise of support from James Maxton, Independent Labour MP for Bridgeton. The sheer scale of popular support for Traquair indicated that he was no pariah among militant Protestants, whatever his previous record of violence. However, the petition received short shrift from the Secretary of State, who saw no grounds to commute Traquair's sentence.

Despite the failure of the criminal appeal and petition alike, for a brief period in the summer of 1934, John Traquair was championed as a martyr among militant Protestants both in Scotland and in Northern Ireland.

The Killing of Jimmy Dalziel

The Calton gang members whose lighter sentences so infuriated Alexander Ratcliffe had been charged with the murder of Jimmy Dalziel, a thirty-three-year-old bookmaker's clerk from the Gorbals. Their motive, however, was not sectarian – like his assailants, Dalziel was a Catholic. He had lived with his wife and four children in Surrey Street. His friends knew him as 'Razzle' – they had seen the spectacular revue, *Razzle-Dazzle*, during its run in Glasgow and Dalziel, who was a good singer, had memorised the tunes and had sung them to his friends so often that they christened him Razzle.

Along with his brother, Hugh, Dalziel frequented the nearby Bedford Parlour dance hall. They did not need to pay for admission: they knew the hall's owner, and two of their friends – Patrick and John McKenzie – acted as doorman and MC respectively. The hall's regulars called themselves the Parlour Boys. The police viewed them as a gang, and they identified Jimmy Dalziel as one of the leaders. By their account, he was 'popular in the district and had a large following. He always seemed to be flush with money.' He had three convictions: for wife assault, breach of the peace and assault. He had married Violet Kinghorn in 1925, and although she had once prosecuted him for assault, Violet insisted that Jimmy was a family man:

> He was a very good husband, and was very fond of his children. We were married eight years ago, and our life together was very happy. He was a hard worker. We hadn't a great deal of money ever, but managed to maintain ourselves fairly well.

Detectives' portraits of Razzle as a spendthrift were utterly at odds with Violet's account of the family's modest standard of living, and while Jimmy Dalziel might have been an affectionate husband and father, even Violet admitted that he 'was inclined to be quarrelsome' when he had been drinking.

On the night of Friday 2 March, Jimmy went out at nine o'clock, telling Violet that he was going to the pictures. By ten o'clock, however, he had joined his brother at the Bedford Parlour dance hall. An hour later, the brothers left the club to go for a drink. They downed whisky and beer before returning to the dance hall at around a quarter to midnight. Bizarrely, Razzle proceeded to dance with Robert Carlton from Coburg Street. As Carlton, aged twenty-three, later explained: 'Dalziel did not dance with women' – Percy Sillitoe surmised that Dalziel 'would dance only with other burly members of his gang, considering it effeminate to dance with girls.'

Shortly before one o'clock, a group of fifteen to twenty young men entered the hall without paying. Hugh Dalziel's dancing partner, Sadie Queen, recognised them straight away: 'There is a Gallowgate crowd in,' she remarked. 'I think there is going to be trouble. I see the Gancher is with them.' She pointed to John McLaughlan, a twenty-four-year-old porter from the Gallowgate. McLaughlan – 'the Gancher' – was a well-known member of the Kent Star. Jimmy Dalziel had spotted the Calton lads, too. He warned one of the nearby dancers to leave the hall immediately, telling him: '[T]here is going to be murder. These Calton fellows won't get out alive.' Razzle then told one of his companions to: 'Go and get the boys lively.'

The Calton gangsters' initial target was Jimmy Dalziel's

friend, Robert Park, a twenty-four-year-old soldier from Thistle Street in the Gorbals. Park had had a 'misunderstanding' with one of the Parlour's occasional patrons, a ship's steward named Frank Clark from 'the Briggait' (Bridgegate), a dilapidated slum district on the opposite side of the River Clyde, and Clark's brother-in-law had arranged for a group of Calton boys to come to the Bedford Parlour to give Park a 'hammering'. Park was set upon, kicked and butted, sparking a free-for-all in which knives were flashed and the hall echoed to the sound of breaking glass. Park had a stand-up fight with one of the intruders in the middle of the dance floor. As Jimmy Dalziel moved towards them, he was surrounded by four men, one of whom plunged a knife into his neck. Dalziel staggered, holding his hands to his wound. The Parlour's doorman – Dalziel's friend, Patrick McKenzie – helped him out into Eglinton Street. McKenzie hailed a passing milk lorry to take Dalziel to the Victoria Infirmary. By the time they reached the hospital, Jimmy Dalziel was dead.

The Calton gangsters fled the hall leaving devastation in their wake – doctors at the Victorian Infirmary treated four of their victims. Robert Park had been slashed on the neck; Patrick McKenzie and Terence McGhee had both been struck on the head with bottles (McGhee had been stabbed in the left buttock for good measure); and Park's friend, George Temple, had been struck with a broken glass and kicked in the face. Not realising that Razzle was dead, Temple told doctors that: 'It was a grand fight while it lasted. I got a kick in the gob, and that finished me.'

Meanwhile, their assailants returned to the Calton. Some of them stopped off at a social club in Turnbull Street, where Hugh McCormack got a bucket of cold water to wash blood from his face – McCormack had taken on Robert Park in the fight on the dance-floor twenty minutes earlier. They ended the night at Frank Kearney's house in Suffolk Street, off Kent Street, in the Calton. The Gancher was the first to arrive, at around half past two; he had picked up eighteen-year-old Nellie Jones en route. McLaughlan told her that he had 'battered' a man at the Bedford Parlour, adding that 'the fellow had been taken to the Infirmary.' Shortly after they arrived, another nine or ten young men trooped in. They included Vinny Wallace – a prominent member of the San Toy. Wallace washed his hands at the sink before sitting down to play the piano in the kitchen, while the others talked among themselves.

Police launched a 'complete comb-out' of Glasgow's South Side in the early hours of the morning, while detectives swooped on a series of houses in the East End, making seven arrests. By Sunday afternoon, thirteen young men had been taken into custody. They appeared at the Southern Police Court the following morning, where they were jointly charged with the murder of James Dalziel. Police investigations continued: by Monday 12 March no fewer than eighteen suspects had been charged, following what one detective described as a 'wholesale mopping-up campaign'.

Eight of the prisoners were released two days later after a hearing at Glasgow Sheriff Court. Those released included the youngest of the suspects, sixteen-year-old Frank Kiernan, and his brother, Bernard, aged twenty. They were greeted by an ecstatic crowd of several hundred friends and relatives. A photographer from *Thomson's Weekly News* joined the throng and managed to take a picture of five of the liberated gangsters, held aloft by their friends, in return for a donation to the Kent Star's funds.

The police investigation met with a wall of silence. As Robert Colquhoun, then a detective sergeant attached to the Central Division, recalled: 'Gangland stood firm, and for once the informers couldn't find us sufficient witnesses.'

The investigation gradually narrowed to five of the prisoners, all of whom continued to protest their innocence. At their final appearance at Glasgow Sheriff Court, held on 14 April, the solicitor for two of the accused, Francis Clark and William McPhee, named Bernard Kiernan – who had been released from custody on 14 March – as the man who had committed the murder. This was an extraordinary breach of gangland's code of non-cooperation with the police. Clark, however, belonged to the Briggait Boys, as did McPhee – his brother-in-law, and the man said to have arranged for Robert Park to be given a 'hammering', while Kiernan was a member of the Kent Star. In any event, Clark and McPhee withdrew their statements before the trial commenced at the High Court in Glasgow on 24 April.

Clark, McPhee, John McLaughlan, Hugh McCormack and James Collins were charged with mobbing and rioting and five counts of assault, as well as with the murder of James Dalziel. They all pleaded not guilty. Dr John Anderson and Dr Andrew Allison, who jointly conducted the post-mortem examination at the Victoria Infirmary, told the court that they had found just one mark of violence on Dalziel's body – a wound on his neck, nearly two inches deep, which had severed the two main arteries. There were plenty of witnesses to the prisoners' participation in the disturbance, but most were remarkably hazy about who did what to whom.

Only one witness claimed to be able to firmly identify the man who had struck James Dalziel with a knife. Dick McFarlane, a cloakroom attendant at the Bedford Parlour, described how he saw a 'chap' in a blue suit stab Dalziel in the neck with a knife. McFarlane identified the man as eighteen-year-old James Collins.

The Advocate Depute withdrew the charge of murder against the other four prisoners. As the trial drew to a close, he pressed for the capital charge against Collins only, but urged the jurors to convict all five prisoners of mobbing and rioting, plus assault. In his summing up, the judge – Lord Moncrieff – told the jury that it was clear that Collins had been one of the four men to surround Dalziel on the dance-floor at the Bedford Parlour. The judge was less confident, however, that Collins had carried out the stabbing:

> From evidence of how there was an effusion of blood from Dalziel's neck and how it spurted on the wall from about the level of his head, one can hardly understand why all the blood found on Collins' clothing could be covered by a threepenny piece.

The jury found the prisoners guilty of mobbing and rioting only. Lord Moncrieff jailed each of them for twelve months.

The police were furious, as was the local press – the *Glasgow Herald* had 'no hesitation in describing these sentences as ridiculously inadequate'. The city's chief constable, Percy Sillitoe, was still angry when he described the trial in his memoirs published twenty years later:

> The accused men grinned and smirked among themselves, waving from time to time to their friends and admirers who thronged the public galleries. There was no doubt at all that they considered themselves as heroic figures. And they were likely to persist in this delusion as long as they could expect to get only a few months in gaol or a fine (quickly paid on their behalf) for carrying murderous weapons and using them without scruple.

The relative severity of the term of four years' penal servitude imposed on John Traquair had attracted considerable discussion, but most correspondents to Glasgow's evening newspapers agreed that Traquair's sentence was appropriate – their objection was to the leniency shown in the 'dance hall case'.

For Sillitoe, the failure to convict Dalziel's killer was a disaster. Coming less than a fortnight after the highly publicised trial of ten of the Beehive Boys at Glasgow Sheriff Court, the murder at the Bedford Parlour dance hall showed beyond any doubt that Glasgow's 'gang menace' was far from quelled.

'The San Toys will fight anything!'

In the aftermath of the Dalziel case, detectives from the Central Division of the City of Glasgow Police mounted a wider clampdown on the Catholic gangs of the Calton. Their first target was the San Toy, whose regular corner of the Gallowgate at Charlotte Street was closely watched by detectives. On Saturday, 24 March 1934, detectives watched the gang's members gather in a public house on the Gallowgate from eight o'clock in the evening. By half past ten, emboldened by drink, the gang was out on the street. According to Detective Sergeant Bailie, who led the surveillance, they stood on their regular corner bawling: 'The San Toys will fight anything!' Moments later, they attacked a respectably dressed, middle-aged passer-by: Owen Mullen grabbed the man by the coat and punched him in the face; Tommy Mullen – Owen's brother – kicked the man on the legs.

Detective Sergeant Bailie ran across the street and grabbed Owen Mullen, who lunged at the detective with a bottle but missed. Detective Constable Beaton fared less well. Tommy Mullen gave him the slip, striking the constable on the head with a bottle. Before Beaton could respond, he was struck with a second bottle by another member of the crowd. Owen Mullen shouted to his companions to rescue him, yelling: 'Come on, the San Toys.' According to Detective Sergeant Bailie's account, the scene was one of utter pandemonium: 'Pedestrians were running and screaming, tramcar traffic was held up, and drivers and conductors blew whistles to summon the uniformed police.' Along with Owen Mullen, Tommy Mullen and Arthur O'Brien were apprehended, and the detectives dragged their prisoners to the Central Police Office under a hail of bottles and glasses.

The three gangsters appeared before the stipendiary magistrate, George Smith, at the Central Police Court on Friday 30 March. All three prisoners were convicted of breaching the peace, assault and two counts of assaulting the police, but the victim of the original assault in the Gallowgate was unwilling to testify against his assailants. As Detective Sergeant Bailie explained in court: 'the civilian attacked had not come to give evidence because he was terrorised. People in the neighbourhood were always afraid to give evidence in such cases because of threats made to them.' Pressing for heavy punishment, the assistant procurator fiscal described the attack on the detectives as 'an open challenge to the good government of the city'. The stipendiary magistrate agreed, commenting that Glasgow was plagued by such disorder. As a result, he added: 'No decent, self-respecting person is sure of his life or limb.' He jailed each of the prisoners for three months with hard labour.

Alerted by the youths' surnames, Alexander Ratcliffe of the Scottish Protestant League seized on a report of the trial in the *Evening Times*. Reproducing the report in full in his paper, the *Vanguard*, he added his own headline: '**PAPISTS SENT TO PRISON!**' As Ratcliffe saw it, the case demonstrated that:

> the Roman Catholics in Glasgow are the people who keep our gaolers busy. Two Mullens and an O'Brien, probably all from the [Irish] 'Free State,' are sent to gaol for three months, and very likely these Papists regularly attend Mass. Rome is the great Crime-producer . . . The Roman Catholics in Glasgow are only about 20% of the population, yet they are some 65% of our local criminals. The fruits of Popery are crimes of all kinds. *By their fruits shall ye know them.*

This, of course, was sectarian propaganda. Those brought before Glasgow's magistrates were overwhelmingly drawn from the poorer sections of the city's working-class population – the 'other Glasgow'. Catholics were heavily represented but on account of their poverty, not their religion. Ratcliffe failed to acknowledge that the San Toy's principal rivals and scourge of the Eastern Division of the City of Glasgow Police – the Billy Boys – were Protestants to a man. Contrary to Ratcliffe's prediction, the three San Toys were Glasgow-born. All three had multiple previous convictions – mostly for breaches of the peace or assault – but their records were no different from those of long-standing Billies.

The Mullens and Arthur O'Brien were released from Barlinnie in June 1934. Two months later, Tommy Mullen was involved in a drink-fuelled Friday night fracas in the Ritz, a fish and chip restaurant in High Street in Glasgow city centre. The spark was a spontaneous argument over football, meaning that sectarian antagonisms quickly came to the surface. The confrontation involved members of three groups of drinkers, all of whom arrived at the Ritz after the nearby public houses closed. First to arrive were Alec Craig-West, a thirty-year-old unemployed salesman from King's Park on Glasgow's South Side, and his friend Tommy Lyon. Both were heavy drinkers, despite Lyon, too, being out of work. They had set out from Lyon's house in Thistle Street in the Gorbals at half past seven that evening. After calling into two public houses nearby, they headed to the city centre where the pace of their drinking quickened: by twenty past ten both men had downed five pints of beer and two whiskies. They headed to the Ritz, and were sitting at one of the tables eating fish suppers when another group of revellers arrived.

Robert Doris, a motor driver and mechanic, had been drinking in the Mercat Bar at Glasgow Cross with his cousin, John Walsh, and their friend, John Cardle, since half past six. They arrived at the Ritz with an 'acquaintance' of Doris's named Jenny Rice, and Doris ordered sixpence-worth of fish and chips for his friends. As he stood at the counter to wait for the food, he noticed that his friends had struck up a conversation with another group of customers.

Among this third group was Tommy Mullen, who had arrived at the Ritz with John Kerr of the San Toy and Kerr's friend, Edward McGonigle. The three of them had been drinking in Abbott's pub in London Road. Both Mullen and Kerr had set out for the night's drinking with empty pockets: as well-known gangsters, they could try to get drinks 'at the demand' if no one offered to treat them – McGonigle, a twenty-one-year-old who described himself as a 'general dealer', stood drinks for them that night. Before Abbott's closed, McGonigle bought a bottle of wine, which the three of them drank in High Street before they headed to the Ritz.

By the time they arrived, both Mullen and Kerr were fighting drunk. An unemployed miner who entered the restaurant just after them heard one of them tell the other: 'If anybody interferes with us, they are up for it.'

Tommy Mullen and John Kerr sat at one of the tables while Edward McGonigle went to the counter to buy their fish suppers. Mullen took his copy of the Celtic handbook out of his pocket and began to read it. Spotting the handbook, Alec Craig-West asked Mullen: 'Are you going to Parkhead tomorrow?'

(Celtic were due to play a home game against Kilmarnock, while Rangers travelled to Dunfermline.) According to Mullen, West: 'started to talk about Johnnie Crum of the Celts and how it was hard lines on Crum getting his leg broken.' West sat down next to Mullen, and they argued over a photograph in the handbook: Mullen said it was of Jimmy McGrory, the legendary Celtic centre-forward, but West insisted that it was of Alec Thomson.

West, like Mullen, was drunk. Their tempers frayed only too easily and as the conversation between them became more heated, talk quickly turned from football to religion. Mullen and John Kerr took offence at something that West said, and Kerr shouted across to Robert Doris: 'This big fair-headed chap is too damned cheeky.' Mullen and Kerr went out into the street. As they did so, Mullen took a knife out of his pocket and Kerr smashed a bottle against a wall. Holding the neck of the jagged half-bottle in his hand, Kerr muttered something about 'doing this man up.'

When West emerged from the shop, his companion – Tommy Lyon – was told: 'You get off.' Lyon went to look for a police constable. Mullen and West renewed their conversation on the pavement. Robert Doris persuaded the two of them to shake hands, but his peacemaking was in vain. Mullen exclaimed: 'I am a Roman Catholic and you are a Protestant c—.' Someone else made a remark about what would happen 'after the match tomorrow' – a thinly veiled reference to the likelihood of trouble at Bridgeton Cross following Celtic's home matches. Sensing that he was in danger, West told Mullen: 'I am a Protestant; everything is alright, we are pals.' Moments later, John Kerr lunged at West, jabbing him in the neck with the broken bottle. West staggered, and then ran, down High Street with blood gushing from his wound. A witness shouted 'Police!' Most of the crowd bolted, fearing arrest if they remained at the scene.

Kerr ran after Alec West and struck him from behind, knocking him to the ground. Robert Doris, running to flee the scene, tripped over West's body and was promptly apprehended by PC William Cameron. Thinking that Doris had felled West,

Cameron dragged him to the Central Police Office, where Doris was charged with assault and detained in custody.

Doris's friends, John Walsh and John Cardle, went to the police office with Tommy Mullen to protest that PC Cameron had got the wrong man: they were thrown out for 'causing a disturbance'. They refused to leave, and Mullen was arrested for causing a breach of the peace. He appeared at the Central Police Court the following morning, when he was fined 10 shillings with the option of ten days' imprisonment. Having no money to pay the fine, he was taken to Barlinnie.

Alec West spent the night in Glasgow Royal Infirmary. Doctors found that he was bleeding from a deeply lacerated wound at the angle of the neck and jaw on the left side of his face – his jacket was saturated with blood. He was also suffering from shock. He died four days later.

Acting 'on information received', detectives arrested John Walsh and John Cardle, along with John Kerr's friend, Edward McGonigle. Kerr handed himself in a few days later. Tommy Mullen was arrested upon his release from Barlinnie, having served ten days for breaching the peace. Mullen told detectives: 'I have got f— all to do with it.' He subsequently admitted, however, that he had been 'arguing with the man who was killed about football'.

John Kerr, Robert Doris and Thomas Mullen stood trial at Glasgow High Court on 24 October. They were charged with murder. Dr William Reid, a house surgeon at the Royal Infirmary, provided medical testimony at the trial, describing how West had 'seemed on the point of death' when he arrived at the hospital. Detailing West's injuries, the surgeon explained that the deceased man had suffered a shattered jawbone as well as a severed artery. In Dr Reid's view, the wounds were consistent with those inflicted with a bottle rather than a knife. Asked by counsel for Kerr whether he saw many bottle injuries, Dr Reid replied: 'In six months, I have probably treated 100 to 200.'

Doris's friend, John Cardle, was called as a witness for the prosecution. Cardle, however, was noticeably reticent: he had heard no angry words in the Ritz, had seen no weapons brandished and had not seen any blows struck. Cardle admitted that he had met John Kerr in the back room of the Mercat Bar the night after the row at the Ritz. Kerr, who had been accompanied by three other men, had asked: 'Is everything all right?' Cardle understood immediately that Kerr was referring to the assault on Alec West. He gave Kerr a shilling for a drink, and walked out. Under cross-examination, Cardle explained that he had understood Kerr's question to be a warning to hold his tongue. Failure to do so would mean 'A kicking, or something.'

Kerr and Mullen both vehemently denied that the argument about football in the Ritz had led to 'questions about Roman Catholics and Protestants'. Kerr and Mullen tried to shift the blame for the killing onto Doris's friends, John Walsh and John Cardle. In Mullen's words: 'Walsh told me it was him that gied [gave] the man it.' Mullen also described how Cardle had introduced himself to Kerr when their respective parties met at the Ritz:

> We went in and Cardle says to Kerr, 'Hullo, Kerr, do you no' know me? I'm Cardle from the coffee stall . . . And this is a f— Billy Boy,' meaning the man West. Kerr says, 'That's nothing to do with us,' and McGonigle went over the counter and ordered three fish suppers, and me and Kerr sat down.

Mullen insisted that his conversation with West had been amicable: 'me and the man was just arguing about football, just like anybody else, the two of us ourselves.'

Cross-examined by the Advocate Depute, Robert Doris explained that he would have left the Ritz immediately if he had heard a conversation turn to religion.

> Q.– *Why is that?*
> A.– **For the simple reason it is a thing I never discuss.**
> Q.– *Is it not because you would have expected a row to start if you had heard that subject being discussed?*
> A.– **No, but when a man is holding a job down he cannot talk religion with anybody.**
> Q.– *You mean in case he gets into a row. Is that it?*
> A.– **That is correct.**

Quizzed as to why he had run down High Street after Alec Craig-West had been stabbed, Doris told the court: 'Well, any man living in the East End of Glasgow and hearing a shout of "Police" always runs.' Pressed by counsel for Kerr to explain further, Doris replied: 'It is quite a regular thing in that part of town when the police are at hand and there is a struggle to get out of the road. It is always a safe policy. Anybody there knows that.' Asked why he had been arrested, Doris explained that after he fell over: 'I was the easiest man to catch.'

Doris clearly identified John Kerr as the man who struck West on the neck. According to Doris, the blow was quite unexpected – Tommy Mullen, who was standing talking to West, had looked as surprised as everyone else by Kerr's sudden lunge. Doris's testimony was damning: he pointed to Kerr as having struck both the first blow outside the Ritz and the second, when West was felled further down High Street as he attempted to flee.

The charge of murder against Robert Doris was withdrawn on the fourth and final day of the trial. The Advocate Depute pressed the jurors to find both John Kerr and Thomas Mullen guilty of murder. In his summing up, the judge, Lord Blackburn, steered the jury towards a verdict of guilty. He then reflected on the pretext for the assault on Alec West, commenting that: 'For some mysterious reason that [he] could not understand, football and religious prejudice seemed to be very much mixed up in the minds of the particular class of people with whom they were dealing.' As the jury retired to consider their verdict, reporters mingled with the crowd gathered outside the High Court. Many were friends or relatives of the accused. To Robins Millar, a columnist on the *Sunday Mail*, this was a rare opportunity to see the 'other Glasgow' at close quarters:

> I had glimpsed something of that life from the friends who waited outside to know their fate . . . a man with a three-inch scar across his jaw talking to poverty-stricken, prematurely aged women in shawls, every second word a profanity.

After an hour and a half, an electric bell signalled that the jury was ready to give its verdict. When Millar returned to the courtroom he noticed that Kerr had been crying, while Mullen looked 'white and terror-stricken'. The jury returned its verdict against Mullen first: they found him not guilty. They found John Kerr guilty not of murder, but of culpable homicide.

Kerr collapsed in the dock. He leant over the rail of the dock, shaking with sobs, as his counsel pleaded for leniency on account of Kerr's youth – he was twenty-one years old – and his family responsibilities: Kerr was married, and had a two-year-old child. Lord Blackburn commented that the jurors had taken 'a very lenient view of the case' by returning a verdict of culpable homicide rather than murder. He took Kerr's age into account, and his criminal record – the prisoner's previous conviction was for theft rather than violence. He sentenced John Kerr to three years' penal servitude.

Kerr was fortunate that his membership of the San Toy was not mentioned at the trial. If he and Tommy Mullen had stood trial as 'gangsters', they would probably have been much more harshly dealt with.

Robert Doris gave an interview to a reporter from the *Sunday Mail* shortly after his release. He declared that he was 'happy, but not surprised' by the verdict. The reporter accompanied Doris and his wife on a visit to their home in Ross Street in the Calton, and then on to Robert's mother's house in the Gallowgate. His mother had been too frail to attend court; she told the *Mail* that she was 'speechless with joy'. Robert Doris then returned to work 'as if nothing unusual had occurred'.

The *Mail* noted that a lot of people had gathered in Ross Street to congratulate Doris on his acquittal, but 'his relatives kept his whereabouts a close secret' – given that Doris's testimony might easily have sent a member of the San Toy to the gallows, their prudence was understandable. The *Scottish Daily Express* ran another interview with Robert Doris the following day, in which he described the agony he had felt during his ten weeks on remand in Barlinnie: 'They gave me spools of thread to work with. As the thread passed through my fingers it was like life running out . . .'. The *Express*'s feature writer appears to have enjoyed a degree of journalistic licence, but Doris's sentiment was clear enough. Doris then recounted how the prison's inmates had followed his case avidly through newspaper reports: 'One old fellow used to look at me, raise his eyebrows, and turn one thumb up and one down. Things looked so black that most days I had to turn both thumbs down.'

The most sensational account of Robert Doris's ordeal was provided by the *People's Journal*. In a joint interview, Doris and his wife, Elizabeth, revealed that their ordeal had been foretold by a spaewife (fortune-teller) who had predicted that a man close to her – possibly Robert – would find himself caught up in a case of murder. Robert had laughed, but on the day of the fatal stabbing, Elizabeth had had 'a strange feeling'. As her husband had headed out that evening, saying that he would see her later, she had replied: 'Robert, I'll not see you tonight.' The spaewife had been right. The *People's Journal* ran the story – complete with portrait-style photographs of Elizabeth and Robert – on its front page under the headline **WOMAN'S AMAZING WARNING'**. Elizabeth, resplendent in a fur stole, was impossibly glamorous – more like a Hollywood actress than one of the 'prematurely aged women in shawls' spotted outside the High Court by Robins Millar. The *People's Journal* did not question Elizabeth's story – readers were left to judge its veracity for themselves.

The Billy Boys in Belfast

In 1935, Billy Fullerton accepted an invitation to take the Bridgeton Purple and Crown flute band – better known as the Billy Boys' band – to Belfast for the 12 July celebrations. Sectarian tensions in the city had been running high since the spring of that year when a visit by the Duke of Gloucester to mark the Silver Jubilee of George V had irked Nationalist leaders, who protested that there had been nothing in the king's reign 'to inspire satisfaction, let alone rejoicing.' The focal point for resentment was the York Street district, close to the city's docks. Unusually for Belfast, this was a mixed neighbourhood, with both Catholic and Protestant residents. The area was placed under a curfew on 10 May following attacks on houses, and on people passing through hostile streets, while a ten-day city-wide ban on processions was imposed following a shooting in York Street on 17 June, only to be lifted by Northern Ireland's Minister for Home Affairs ten days later after an illegal Orange parade passed off without incident.

Forty thousand people gathered for the Orange rally held on Friday 12 July. As marchers from the North Belfast lodges passed along York Street on their way home that night, a riot broke out at the junction of Lancaster Street. Violence here was much more severe than anything witnessed in Glasgow during the 1930s: the rival factions resorted to firearms as well as stone-throwing. Violence spread to the residential streets adjacent to the docks and by the end of the night, four people – two Protestants and two Catholics – had been killed by gunfire, while nineteen others were wounded.

The two Catholics killed that night were women. A sniper shot Mrs Margaret Broderick outside her house in Marine Street, while eighteen-year-old Teresa Johnston was killed by one of a group of men who knocked at her front door and gunned her down when she opened it.

The following evening, Saturday 13 July, a crowd of 300 to 400 Protestants marched to the adjacent dockland neighbourhood to lay a wreath at the home of Edward Withers, a Protestant youth killed during Friday's carnage. The Billy Boys' band led the procession. They halted outside Withers's parents' house in Nelson Street, where the band played 'Abide with Me', 'Onward Christian Soldiers' and the national anthem. Having delivered the wreath, the crowd headed to a cluster of adjoining streets, home to around 200 Catholic families, shouting 'Redd [clear] them out.' An orgy of violence and destruction followed: fifty-six Catholic houses were torched and two Protestants were shot dead. Fifteen other people suffered gunshot wounds: among them were two Billy Boys. By midnight, the army had been called out to assist the police. Order was finally restored at around four o'clock in the morning.

The Billy Boys were due to return to Glasgow on the night

boat on Monday 15 July. A skeleton band of 'two drums and a few fifes' formed up in Ship Street – close to the scene of the previous night's mayhem – at eight o'clock that evening and set off along York Street escorted by a crowd of supporters, variously estimated to be several hundred or a thousand-strong, who filled the street, dancing and singing 'An Orange Lily, Oh!' They were shadowed by four police vehicles carrying officers armed with rifles.

They met with only shouts and gestures from the inhabitants of the Catholic streets off York Street, but as they reached Castle Place in the city centre, members of the crowd began to shout that they spotted a man with a revolver. The crowd laid siege to a billiard hall in Fountain Street, where the gunman was thought to have taken refuge, but police prevented them from entering the premises.

The devastation that the Billies helped to unleash continued in the weeks that followed. Around 2,500 people were evicted from their homes: 85 per cent were Catholics, many displaced by their own former neighbours in streets that had recently gone 'mixed'. Ten people died in the disturbances in Belfast that summer. The worst outbreak had taken place on the night of 13 July, when the Billy Boys had led a crowd of Protestant mourners into the Catholic dockland district.

The Billy Boys returned to Glasgow without their leader, Billy Fullerton, and his long-standing associate, David Turnbull, as both men had been arrested following the disturbances on 13 July. They were held for two weeks, but then discharged – by Fullerton's own account, he narrowly avoided a wrongful charge of murder. On their return to Glasgow, Fullerton gave an interview to the *Glasgow Eastern Standard*, in which he described how he and Turnbull came to be arrested:

> We were going through a certain street when one of the marshals advised me to give the band the order to double. We refused to run, and walked through the street, stopped in the middle, and played a tune. It was then the bullets began to fly. We were not standing for that, and [we] chased the snipers.

The bandsmen hit by the gunfire were Turnbull – a 'glancing blow' to the stomach – and Robert Burnside, a twenty-year-old flautist, who was shot in the abdomen. Fullerton told the *Standard* that the Purple and Crown flute band had since received fifteen requests from Belfast lodges to take part in the following year's procession.

Twenty-nine of the band's members made the trip to Belfast that year. Fullerton and Turnbull, aged twenty-nine and thirty respectively, were the eldest. Turnbull was one of three marshals. A second marshal, twenty-five-year-old Walter Scott, had more previous convictions that Fullerton and Turnbull combined – including seven counts of theft, two of assault, three of assaulting the police and five breaches of the peace. Most of the flautists and percussionists were younger. They included well-known figures such as William Watson and Samuel Kelly Campbell, both of whom had acquired strings of criminal convictions by their early twenties.

The gunshot wound inflicted during the rioting on 13 July would present Robert Burnside with a money-making opportunity. A series of claims for damages for 'malicious injuries' were submitted by people who had been hurt during the riots, and Burnside made one of the largest claims, requesting £2,000 in compensation. His claim was heard by the Recorder of Belfast on 26 September. Burnside told the recorder that he had arrived in Belfast on the morning of 12 July 'on holiday'. At around half past eight the following night, he 'went out for postcards' and made his way to York Street. He stopped in Ship Street, off York Street, to admire the decorations as he 'never saw anything like it in Glasgow'. Burnside continued: 'I saw a crowd in the street, and there was a bang from it. I fell. I was shot in the side.'

Asked by his solicitor whether he had anticipated trouble, Burnside replied: 'I never heard a gun in my life until I heard that one there.' He confirmed that since the shooting, he had been unable to work. On behalf of Belfast Corporation, a doctor confirmed that only a 'remarkable operation' had saved Burnside's life, that further surgery might yet be required, and that Burnside would be unable to work for another six to nine months. The recorder stated that he regretted the 'bad impression of the city' that Burnside must have formed during his visit and awarded £170 in damages – the equivalent of more than a year's earnings at £3 a week.

Burnside made no mention of his membership of the Billy Boys' band, and none of those reviewing his claim appears to have made the connection.

II

Fighting Men and Family Men

Reputations for fighting prowess spanned the working-class districts of the city. South Side gangs were acutely aware of the activities on their counterparts in the East End and vice versa, with the reputations of individual gangsters – as well as the gangs to which they belonged – adjusted as news of 'rammies' spread. The exploits of the gangs were also widely discussed by the wider population of the tenement districts, many of whom took a keen interest even though they had no intention of taking part themselves.

Gangs marked their territory – and issued challenges and threats – through graffiti on tenement walls. Graffiti bearing a gang's name formed the backdrop for group photographs: one such image was produced in evidence at the Govan Police Court in August 1928 after it was found in possession of a member of the Peril Gang. The prevalence of graffiti was the subject of occasional complaints by irate magistrates, not least on account of the frequent use of obscenities.

Gangs proclaimed their invincibility in song, too. The best-known anthem belonged to the Bridgeton Billy Boys, but gangs with similar verses included the Beehive Boys:

> *Yo ho ho, we are a treat*
> *The Beehive Boys from Thistle Street*
> *When we go into a fight*
> *The Royal Infirmary's busy all night*
> *Yo ho ho, we can't be beat*
> *The Beehive Boys from Thistle Street.*

Such ditties mimicked – and perhaps parodied – the sectarian challenges bellowed by the Billies.

The Allure of the Gangster

Gang members were intensely style-conscious. During the 1930s, they modelled themselves on Hollywood gangsters. Ellen McAllister, who grew up in the Gorbals, remembered them as prominent figures in the local dance halls, where they dressed – and acted – like Jimmy Cagney or George Raft:

> I remember seeing the leader of the Bee Hive in the Gordon ballroom in Paisley Road. His name was Stragovitch, a small dark-haired man who wore his hair sleeked back like George Raft. He had very dark eyes and was reputed to be a very mean and vicious street fighter.

This George Raft of the Gorbals was Louis Scragowitz. One of the Beehive Boys' Jewish members, Scragowitz was thirteen years younger than the gang's more widely recognised leader, Peter Williamson. Like Williamson, Scragowitz made repeated court appearances during the mid- to late-1930s on a range of charges, including housebreaking and reset, as well as breaches of the peace. Youths like Scragowitz exuded menace but, as McAllister acknowledged, they also lent an air of glamour to the halls.

If the risks incurred by gang members – imprisonment and permanent injury – were great, so too were the rewards. These included both peer respect and the promise of sexual favours from those young women who associated with the gangs. As a self-styled 'ex-gangster' boasted to the *Weekly Record* in June 1930:

> we thought it was a great thing to be fighting men who were feared and to have 'gang girls' chewing one another's ear off to go with us. The bigger our fighting reputation, the more fear and girls we got.

Larry Johnson of the Beehive Boys echoed these claims in an interview conducted more than fifty years later. According to Johnson: 'The more deeds that were done by a gang member the more he was chased up by the girls.' He told how he had enjoyed a series of sexual relationships with local young women before he met his wife-to-be. His relationships were consummated in tenement closes late at night – Johnson claimed that young people's love-making, while furtive and hurried, was tolerated by their neighbours: 'The people who lived there just walked past you. I suppose they'd done the same thing in their young days.' Of course, tales of gang members' sexual conquests were prone to exaggeration, but such stories added to the allure of the gangs nonetheless.

Some gangsters were sexual predators. The stigma attached to victims was such that very few rapes or sexual assaults were reported to the police and gang members – with their reputation for assaulting witnesses – were less likely than most to face criminal charges. However, a few did stand trial for sexual offences. In March 1934, a nineteen-year-old Derry Boy named James Wilkie was one of three youths to plead guilty at Glasgow Sheriff Court to committing 'lewd practices' (in one case, allegedly, 'up to full carnal knowledge') towards a girl aged between twelve and sixteen. Sheriff Walsh fined them £4 each. More commonly, gangsters were accused of wanton promiscuity and failing to stand by young women who fell pregnant. A photographer employed by *Thomson's Weekly News*, who visited the clubroom of one of the Catholic gangs of the Calton in 1934, told how those present had boasted of their sexual precocity:

> [One] lad was 21 years of age, and married. He had lived with a woman since he was 17. At 19 he married a different girl, and at the time I write of he was living off the earnings of another girl.

Contrary to the more lurid claims by contemporary journalists, gang members generally raised their children within wedlock. They might have enjoyed sex before marriage, but so did many other young men and women across Britain during the 1930s. Leading members of the Billy Boys and Kent Star who 'had to' get married did so.

Gangsters were widely looked up to by younger boys. Jimmy Boyle, who was born in the Gorbals in 1944, recalled the immense reputation of Dan Cronin of the Beehive Boys:

One feature of the Gorbals subculture was that the men in the district who were put on pedestals by us, and in many ways idolised, were the likes of Dan Cronin. Although he was dead by the time I was six years old he remained very much alive locally being almost a legend in the Gorbals for his fighting abilities.

Cronin had forged his reputation on the streets of the Gorbals during the age of mass, long-term unemployment in the early 1930s. In the East End, as on the South Side, street fighters enjoyed huge kudos among local boys. Matt McGinn, who grew up in the heyday of the Kent Star, recalled how: 'In the Calton culture the fighting men were the heroes. The highest hope of a boy in that culture was to become [one]. The biggest insult you could be given was for someone to say they could fight you.'

Among schoolboys, a refusal to fight when challenged was a source of lasting shame. According to Jack Caplan, who was born in 1915 and grew up in the Gorbals, for a boy to be labelled a coward was simply 'unthinkable'. Aping the local gangsters, schoolboys formed 'gangs' of their own and set out to mimic the territorial and sectarian squabbles of their elders. They also banded together to challenge adult authority. In March 1930, a group of boys from Camden Street School in the Gorbals waylaid their teacher after he gave one of their friends the strap in class – the teacher had persisted with the punishment despite being threatened with a 'knifing'. When he left the school's premises at the end of the day, he was pelted with missiles. He recognised the missile-throwers and reported them to the school's head-master. The culprits were brought before the headmaster the following day. They identified themselves as members of the Rose Street Gang, and named their principal enemies as the Kidston Street Stickers. They described how they used their belts against any members of rival gangs who attacked them, proudly explaining that boys who displayed daring in battle were promoted to their 'senior' section. The Rose Street 'gangsters' were ten and eleven years old.

Fighting Men

In December 1929, four members of the Calton Emmet – James Hume, Peter Donnelly, John Russell and John Doran – were jailed for three months at Glasgow Sheriff Court following a siege at a house in Abercromby Street. The target of their wrath was a young man who had jilted Hume's sister. The prisoners were surprised to be arrested. As eighteen-year-old Doran explained to detectives: 'He thought it was a fighting man they had to deal with and that there would be no court case.'

Doran's phrasing – echoing Matt McGinn's – is significant. Each of Glasgow's tenement districts had its 'fighting men' – those who were renowned locally and sometimes further afield both for their prowess as street fighters and for their ready resort to violence.

Fighting men renounced any claim to respectability, but they enjoyed a different kind of cachet, based on a mixture of admiration and fear. They ruthlessly exploited their notoriety, demanding free drinks in public houses and – as Billy Fullerton admitted – hiring out their services to those unable or unwilling to settle their own grievances with their fists. They also frequently ran the pitch-and-toss (illicit gambling) rings, which operated in clandestine locations across the city. 'Hard' men were required both to maintain order and to ensure that successful gamblers could make their way home without being robbed. Eli Webb – one of Fullerton's predecessors as 'King of the Billy Boys' – performed these duties at a ring in Bridgeton during the 1930s.

Fighting men had their own code. Above all, they were expected to resolve their disputes without involving the police: however badly they were injured, retribution was to be taken on the streets, or in tenement back-courts. They frequently settled their grievances through 'square-goes' – one-to-one fights with fists and boots. As Jack Caplan explained:

> a square-go . . . meant a fight between the two belligerents, without interference from anyone. This was an accepted code of conduct amongst warring factions in Glasgow, a sort of 'gentlemen's

agreement' which was *never* dishonoured . . . They all went into the nearest back-court, a circle was formed, the contestants stripped to the waist, then faced each other. No referee, no rules regarding ethics, no time limits were imposed – certainly Queensbury rules were scoffed at. It was always just two men, bare-fisted in a fight to the finish. One had to win, one to lose.

Kicking an opponent when he was down was permitted in these bouts and Caplan described how his own brother – a respected street fighter then aged in his early twenties – finished off one adversary with a flurry of kicks to the ribs. Some gang leaders were veterans of such bouts. Detective Sergeant McNab of the Southern Division acknowledged Peter Williamson's reputation at Glasgow Sheriff Court in February 1934, when he described him as 'the one sent by the Beehive Gang to settle disputes with other gangs'.

These contests were not the preserve of the fighting man. As Seán Damer has pointed out:

> every street had its own hardmen who were well known. These were ordinary workers who would unhesitatingly go out the back-court, take their jackets off and have a 'square-go' with whoever had offended them.

These 'ordinary' hardmen did not necessarily covet recognition as 'fighting men', but they were unwilling to back down in the face of insults all the same. Fights among men such as these were often drink-fuelled. A drunken Murdoch McLennan picked a fight with a stranger in a Govan ice-cream parlour in December 1930, telling him that 'he could no' put his fist through a wet paper' and challenging him to 'come outside'. The stranger, twenty-two-year old Andrew McBride, followed McLennan into the street, knocked him down and – according to one witness – kicked him. 'Both men,' the witness added, 'were very much the worse of drink.' McLennan died from his injuries the following day. McBride stood trial at the High Court in Glasgow, where he pleaded not guilty to culpable homicide but admitted to having 'struck out to defend himself'. He was convicted of assault. The judge, Lord Sands, showed remarkable leniency: he jailed McBride for four months, commenting that the prisoner would not have shown such malice 'had he been in his sober senses'.

Fights between men tended to be highly public events. Pre-arranged square-goes drew sizeable crowds, some of whom were supporters of the respective fighters, while others were attracted by the spectacle of violence. Clashes between seasoned brawlers became, in effect, a form of spectator sport. Hugh Savage, who grew up in Bridgeton, described a fight that took place around 1930:

> one of the most brutal things I ever remember seeing was a bare-knuckle fight at Emery's farm on the banks of the Clyde. It was between two men, both stripped to the waist. One was quite tall, about 19 or 20 years of age. The other was a small man, heavily built and older, probably in his late twenties or hitting thirty. Within a few minutes the body of the shorter man was covered in blood as the tall man had burst his nose with the first torrent of punches. It seemed so one-sided. But despite being put on the ground repeatedly, the wee man kept getting up and rushing the younger man. This must have went on for at least twenty minutes or half an hour and the crowd were calling for it to stop. But whenever somebody stepped in to try to end it the wee man punched him away and again kept rushing at his opponent.
>
> Eventually he was back down on the ground once again and the tall young man stepped forward and, after helping him to his feet, he held out his hand and said, 'Alright, you win Johnny.' The wee man wiped the blood from his body with his shirt. The next thing was a bunnet was put round the crowd and the cash proceeds were divided between the two protagonists. They smoked a woodbine together then the crowd left the scene.

The 'wee man' was Johnny Phillips. As Savage recalled, Phillips regularly stood at Bridgeton Cross – gathering place of the Billy Boys – where he was notorious for issuing challenges 'at the drop of a hat'. Savage saw a degree of nobility in this encounter. Although unevenly matched, the two fighters were willing combatants and what Phillips lacked in skill, he made up for in gameness and heart.

Fighting men were not always so honourable. Quite the reverse: they frequently bullied those who were much weaker than themselves, relying on intimidation to prevent their victims from complaining to the police. Some of those terrorised did seek legal redress, however. In August 1933, fifty-year-old John McDonagh of Tylefield Street in Mile End told the Eastern Police Court that he had been repeatedly threatened over the previous two months by a neighbour named Henry Ellis. McDonagh, who was blind in one eye, claimed that he had been getting ready for bed at one o'clock in the morning on Tuesday 25 July when Ellis came to his door and shouted: 'Come out, Blind McDonagh, and fight.' Ellis had since 'boasted throughout the East End' that if he were convicted, McDonagh and his wife would be 'kicked up and down the streets'. McDonagh's wife told the court that Ellis had challenged her, too, in the early hours of 25 July, yelling: 'Come out, Snuffing Mary!' outside their door. 'Ellis is a fighting man,' she proclaimed, 'and everybody is afraid of him.'

The McDonaghs attributed the feud to religious differences. Henry Ellis offered a more complex explanation: the McDonaghs went out hawking and had been 'put off the parish' – denied poor relief – as a result. 'They blamed me for this,' he added, 'and that was the whole cause of the trouble. I am the only Protestant on that stair. McDonagh and his relatives all live there. I have not got a chance.' The magistrate found the McDonaghs' tale more plausible: he found Ellis guilty of committing a breach of the peace and fined him £2.

Youthful gangsters craved the recognition – and the privileges – enjoyed by more established fighting men. Gang membership offered a means of seeking collective kudos, and carrying weapons compensated for their lack of physical stature. Many of the gangs' new recruits during the 1920s and 1930s had barely worked since leaving school, and so they had not built up their strength – or proved their manliness – through industrial labour. They generally eschewed the ritual of the square-go and frequently meted out violence towards rivals who were heavily outnumbered. The fighting man's code of non-cooperation with the police was expected to apply in such instances, although reprisal in kind was to be expected.

Proving their mettle meant staging public confrontations with rival gangs in busy thoroughfares. Passers-by who found themselves caught in a sudden outbreak of fighting were frequently terrorised, but those able to watch from safe distances – or from nearby tenement windows – relished the spectacle. As the *Evening Citizen* conceded:

> People . . . rather enjoy seeing such a fight from their windows. It is good fun for them as well as the youths. As soon as the police appear, the fight is over and the gangsters run. Then the public are entertained to the delightful spectacle of the big men in blue in hot pursuit of the youths and girls. It is a cheap 'movie' from real life.

More determined gangs took steps to thwart the police. Around midnight on Saturday, 25 November 1933, the Cheeky Forty and the Chain Gang staged a pre-arranged fight in front of a 'wildly excited' crowd in Cathedral Street in Glasgow city centre. The wires of a nearby telephone kiosk were cut as the fight was due to start to prevent beat constables summoning reinforcements, and the crowd watched as half a dozen of the combatants were felled by blows from bottles, heavy sticks, bayonets and metal-lined coshes, before two police vans belatedly reached the scene.

Exasperated by the frequency with which Glasgow's fighting men resorted to weapons, members of the judiciary implored them to fight fairly. 'If you must fight,' the Lord Justice Clerk, Lord Alness, demanded of Thomas McGuire at the High Court in November 1930, 'why don't you use your fists?' Forty-one-year-old McGuire had stabbed James Cunningham in the neck after Cunningham attempted to act as peacemaker during a drunken Saturday-night brawl outside a pub in the Cowcaddens. McGuire, who was sentenced to three years' penal servitude, claimed that he and Cunningham had previously 'been on very good terms'. The youthful gangster's resort to weapons was likewise repeatedly condemned in Glasgow's courtrooms as cowardly, unmanly, un-British and 'alien to Scottish sympathy'.

In their own defence, youths claimed that they were forced to carry weapons for self-defence. As a sixteen-year-old protested at the Eastern Juvenile Court in April 1936: 'You have to have something in your possession passing Bridgeton Cross or you get your throat cut.'

This was hyperbole, of course, for although gang members fought with lethal weapons, they seldom inflicted fatalities. In effect, the city's warring factions overwhelmingly abided by a fighting code in which the aim was not to kill, but to disfigure, and while many bore scars as lasting reminders of their pursuit of status and reprisal, constraints on the use of weapons were tacitly acknowledged on all sides – none of the gang-related killings reported in the local press during the 1920s and 1930s arose out of a large-scale battle between rival gangs. In this context, the deaths of Jimmy Tait in 1928 and Jimmy Dalziel in 1934 look like aberrations – breaches of gangland's rules by impulsive youths not yet schooled in the art of combining cruelty and restraint. The contrast between Glasgow's 'gang problem' and Chicago's is never more apparent than when the cities' murder rates are compared.

'John the Baptist' and the Kent Star

While the Billy Boys revelled in their reputation as the largest and most powerful gang in Glasgow, the principal Catholic gangs of the Calton – the Kent Star, the San Toy and the Calton Entry Boys – also enjoyed enduring notoriety. The ranks of the Kent Star included a number of fighting men whose fame was such that they were still recalled during the 1980s. Prominent among these local legends was Thomas Falconer, better known by his street name, 'the Hawk'. In February 1927, at the age of twenty-four, he fought a duel in front of a large crowd in the Gallowgate. Falconer was armed with a knife; his opponent wielded an iron bar. Falconer suffered head injuries and his opponent a cut temple before they were both arrested. They were each jailed for twenty-one days. Two months later, Falconer was jailed for thirty days following a 'battle royal' between the Kent Star and the Lilypops in Glasgow city centre.

Falconer was mentioned again – by nickname only – at the Central Police Court in August 1933, when Edward McQuade was charged with committing a breach of the peace in Claythorn Street in the Calton. A police constable told the court that he arrived at the scene of a gang fight after the skirmish was over. According to the constable, McQuade was roaming the street and shouting that he wanted revenge. McQuade's mother testified that her son had been targeted by a gang: 'They even lay in wait for him when he went to the pictures.' She only knew one of them: a man known as 'the Hawk'. McQuade confirmed that a gang had been 'on his track' for the past three months following a misunderstanding over 'remarks about King Billy'. McQuade claimed that, on the night of his arrest, the Hawk had struck him with a bayonet. 'I will fight the Hawk any time, provided there is fair play,' McQuade told the magistrate. 'He will not agree to this, but is always armed with hatchets and bottles.' McQuade refused to give the real names of his tormentors, stating that: 'He did not want to get them into trouble with the police.' He was jailed for forty-two days.

In March 1935, the *Sunday Dispatch* identified the Kent Star and their allies, the San Toy, as the leading Catholic gangs in Glasgow. 'F' of the Kent Star told the *Dispatch*'s correspondent that weapons were routinely used in sectarian skirmishes in the city's East End:

> Sometimes the Billy Boys and the Derry Boys venture in force into our district or we go into theirs. Then there is a street fight. Razors, knives, files, and bayonets are used. This usually happens on a Saturday night when there has been heavy drinking.

'F' explained that weapons were easily concealed: bayonets were carried in special pockets on the inside of a gangster's trousers, while twelve-inch steel files were carried up a jacket sleeve. They were just as easy to acquire. Bayonets – usually souvenirs from the Great War – could be bought in East End pubs for threepence: the *Dispatch*'s reporter purchased one himself to prove the point. As 'F' pointed out, those who were hurt in these battles did not, as a rule, 'squeal' to the police; any gangster who breached the fighting man's code was likely to face retribution at the end of a broken bottle or a 'chib' (razor).

By the mid-1930s, the leading figures in the Kent Star included Andrew Mulvey and James Tinney O'Neill – known in the Calton as 'Scout' O'Neill – both of whom had acquired fearsome reputations as fighting men. Born in 1913, O'Neill acquired a string of convictions for assault and breaches of the peace in his late teens. In October 1933, he pleaded guilty at the Eastern Police Court to striking Charles Wylie with an iron bar. Wylie told how he had been standing with a girlfriend in a tenement back-court when O'Neill rushed at them. Wylie ran into the street, but O'Neill chased him and dealt him a series of blows on the head. Wylie was taken to the Royal Infirmary with a suspected fractured skull. In court, O'Neill explained that he had been out with a girl himself that night when he was attacked by Billy Boys and struck on the back of the head. After going home to get his wound dressed, he 'went out again and assaulted the first Billy Boy he came across'. The swiftness and severity of his response suggest that he resented being attacked while out 'winching' (courting). The target of his retribution – the first Billy Boy he could find – is equally telling. Vengeance was not so much a personal matter as part of the collective feud between the two gangs. The magistrate was remarkably lenient: he jailed O'Neill for just thirty days.

O'Neill was an aspiring criminal as well as fighting man. He suffered lengthy bouts of unemployment during his teens and twenties and, along with other members of the Kent Star, he turned to crime to eke out his dole. Robbing unwary drunks appears to have been one of their favourite tricks, but they tried their hands as housebreakers, too. In May 1934, O'Neill was convicted following a smash-and-grab raid in which twelve pairs of pyjamas and one shirt were reportedly stolen from a shop in London Road. At Glasgow Sheriff Court, three police officers testified that they had witnessed O'Neill put his hand through the shop's plate-glass window. The effort – and risk – barely seemed warranted by the meagre haul.

O'Neill alleged that the police had fabricated their story. He told the sheriff that he had previously lodged a complaint with the chief constable in regard to the conduct of one of the officers, and that this was the police's attempt at revenge. Sheriff Welsh found O'Neill guilty, but fined him £5 with the option of thirty days' imprisonment. O'Neill's accomplice, James Inglis, got sixty days.

Like John Ross of the Billy Boys, O'Neill was known to carry a razor. In October 1936, he was jailed for nine months after pleading guilty to slashing David Greive during a fight in a close in Tobago Street. O'Neill was described in court as a married man of twenty-two with one child; an unemployed labourer in receipt of public assistance; and a member of the Kent Star gang. His victim, Greive, had been standing with friends when they were approached by O'Neill and two other men. The trio asked Greive 'if he was one of the Billy Boys'. Before Greive could reply, O'Neill drew a razor across his face. Greive was permanently disfigured. No motive for the assault was given in newspaper reports of the trial: with the perpetrator identified as a member of the Kent Star, no further explanation was deemed necessary. O'Neill in turn was slashed with a razor two years later while working at Palacerigg – a labour colony (work camp) for the unemployed, situated at Cumbernauld, thirteen miles outside Glasgow. (Young men were sent to Palacerigg for three months of 'reconditioning'; refusal to attend was punished by withdrawal of their dole.)

Andrew Mulvey, who was two years older than O'Neill, was a more sophisticated housebreaker with ambitions as a safe-blower. Son of a bookmaker and 'general dealer', Mulvey grew up in a milieu where enterprise generally took place on the wrong side of the law. In January 1934, he was jailed for six months at Glasgow Sheriff Court after a jury found him guilty of being in possession of explosives. He was released on 9 June, nine days before James Tinney O'Neill's appearance at the sheriff court on the charge allegedly trumped up by a rogue police officer. O'Neill's trial was attended by a 'very large crowd', which left as soon as the case was concluded: the 'crowd' was the Kent Star gang, who had come en masse to monitor the proceedings.

The feud between the Kent Star and the police erupted the following month. At around midnight on Saturday 14 July – the week after the annual Orange Walk – the Kent Star were out in force in the Gallowgate when the shout went up: 'Here's John.' Everyone in the crowd knew who this referred to. Heading towards them, patrolling alone, was PC Gordon Allison of the Central Division of the City of Glasgow Police, known in the Calton as 'John the Baptist'. The first shout was followed by another: 'Kick him.' PC Allison was quickly surrounded. He recognised Andrew Mulvey at the front of the crowd; Mulvey drew a weapon from his pocket and felled the constable with a blow to the neck, while another member of the crowd kicked him as he lay on the ground. The youths then walked away. PC Allison got to his feet and ran after them. He grabbed hold of Mulvey, and when Mulvey kicked out at him, he floored the gangster with his baton. He pinned Mulvey to the ground. The crowd began to hurl missiles at him, and a bottle thrown by Frank Kearney broke the constable's nose.

Alerted by PC Allison's whistle, two other constables ran to his aid. They arrested Kearney, and the three officers began to drag Mulvey towards the Central Police Office. Struggling under a hail of bottles and stones, they 'could only progress a few yards at a time'. Mulvey continued to resist and urged the crowd to rescue him, prompting PC Allison to baton him again. At the junction of Moir Street, PC Allison, who had lost his helmet, was struck on the face by another missile. By the time a police patrol van reached the scene, the constable was covered in blood.

Kearney was eventually taken into custody alongside Mulvey. With every police officer in the vicinity drawn to the scene, a section of the crowd rampaged through the Gallowgate in an orgy of window-smashing and looting: two dozen plate-glass windows were smashed, and youths made off with armfuls of foodstuffs and clothes.

Andrew Mulvey and Frank Kearney were both charged with assaulting PC Allison by striking him with bottles. During their initial court appearances, both prisoners appeared in the dock with their heads heavily bandaged – a sure sign that they had been beaten in the cells. At their trial, which commenced at Glasgow Sheriff Court on 8 October 1934, they were joined by four of their fellow gang members. PC Allison confirmed that he was known by the nickname 'John the Baptist', but was not asked where the moniker came from. He told the jury that his injuries were so severe that he had been off duty for six weeks. He identified all of the prisoners as members of the Kent Star.

His colleague, PC Phillips, explained to the jury that: 'The Kent Star Gang was a group of young fellows who hung about Ross Street, Gallowgate, and Kent Street.' Phillips described how Kearney led the attempt to rescue Mulvey, shouting: 'Come on, boys,' before hurling a bottle. Asked why he did not arrest Kearney, the constable replied: 'If I had gone into that crowd I would not have come out alive.' Sergeant William McIntosh of the Central Division, who had also run to the aid of PC Allison, estimated that the crowd attempting to rescue Mulvey was 200-strong. Despite the overwhelming odds, the sergeant and three constables kept the mob at bay until the patrol van arrived. This is highly revealing: however hostile they were to the police, few gang members were willing to tackle them at close quarters. Glasgow's beat constables were hard men in their own right – and they were known to hold grudges.

Three of the prisoners pleaded alibis, while one of them – Frank Wallace – told the jury that he knew of a juvenile football club called the Kent Star, but had 'never heard of a gang of that name'. Frank Kearney caused a sensation in court when he alleged that he had been beaten by two constables in a cell at the Central Police Office: 'One of the constables had his hand injured,' Kearney claimed. 'He struck it against the wall while hitting me.' The jury found five of the six prisoners guilty of riot. In addition, they found Andrew Mulvey and George McAulay guilty of the assault on PC Allison. Counsel for Kearney, Mr Matthew Peden, pleaded for leniency on behalf of his client since:

[He] was married six months ago, and this might be regarded as a very unfortunate start to his married life. He sustained a permanent injury to his leg six years ago when he dived into the River Clyde to rescue a drowning child.

Mr Peden neglected to mention that six years earlier, Kearney had been jailed for twelve months for perjury following the trial of the South Side Stickers charged with the murder of Jimmy Tait.

Sheriff Haldane imposed sentences of three to six months' hard labour: the longest terms were meted out to Mulvey and McAulay.

The trial was extensively covered in the local press, but none of the reports asked why 'John the Baptist' had been singled out for such rough treatment. It is tempting to ask whether this was the constable who had been the subject of James Tinney O'Neill's complaint to the chief constable earlier that summer. Certainly, the Kent Star appear to have been determined to teach PC Allison a lesson, whatever the likelihood of prosecution and the prospect of rougher justice administered in the cells.

The person who perhaps most resented the apprehension of PC Allison's assailants was Andrew Mulvey's wife, Mary. She had called at the Central Police Office the following day – a Sunday – to ask whether her husband would be released on bail. When she was told that it was too early for bail to be considered, she 'cursed and swore'. She was escorted out of the office by a constable, but when he turned around she 'kicked him on the lower part of the body, inflicting a very painful injury.' She was promptly arrested and charged with committing a breach of the peace and assaulting a police officer. She was held in custody overnight.

When Mary Mulvey appeared at the Central Police Court the following morning, she claimed that she had been 'pushed about' by the constable and therefore wished to plead 'guilty under great provocation'. She appealed to the stipendiary magistrate: 'Please treat me leniently for the sake of my weans [children]. I don't know what's happening to them since I was taken inside yesterday.' The magistrate ordered that the prisoner be remanded in custody for twenty-four hours pending inquiries into the children's whereabouts. The following morning, the court heard that they were in the care of the prisoner's brother and his wife. Mary Mulvey renewed her plea, asking the magistrate to: 'Give me a chance for my children.' He finally relented, fining her £2 with a week to make the payment.

Andrew Mulvey was released from Barlinnie in March 1935. Within four months, he was back in custody after leading a ferocious assault by members of the Kent Star on a group of five men outside a public house in London Road. Two of the victims suffered razor wounds: one of them – fifty-six-year-old John Kerr – needed sixty stitches after he was slashed on the head, face and hands by Thomas McKeeve. Kerr was taken to Glasgow Royal Infirmary, where doctors stemmed his wounds – without immediate medical treatment, he might have died. The attackers fled the scene, but Mulvey and McKeeve were subsequently arrested by detectives. They stood trial at the High Court, where they appeared before Lord Murray on 15 October. Detective Inspector Dow of the Central Division told the court that Glasgow's gangsters had devised a number of methods by which razor blades might be used as weapons:

> There are several ways in which it is done. A common method is to insert a safety razor blade horizontally into a piece of stick, leaving a thin double edge. This method has the advantage of having a handle which can be gripped by the assailant. Another method is to remove the diamond from a glass cutter and substitute a razor blade. A third method is to fasten the blade into the skip [peak] of a cap.

Lord Murray sentenced Mulvey to four years' penal servitude. McKeeve got three years.

Mary Mulvey had married young – not long past her eighteenth birthday – and already five months' pregnant. Now aged twenty-four, she was left to bring up her three children in a 'single-end' on poor relief of just 26 shillings per week. It was her fifth spell 'on the parish' in four years.

To outsiders, Mulvey and his peers might have been renowned fighting men, but they were abject failures in the more conventional male role of breadwinner. Alert to such accusations, however, gangsters used the press to portray themselves in a very different light; by their own account, these men of violence were committed family men, too.

Gangsters as Family Men

Leading figures in the gangs were fond of telling journalists how they provided for the wives of those members who were jailed. Like refusal to cooperate with the police, this was claimed to be a vital part of the gangs' code of honour. In his account of the Billy Boys published in *Thomson's Weekly News* in 1932, Billy Fullerton told how: 'I have known those whose wives were given a £20 note while their husbands were doing a stretch and they had their rent paid besides' while 'F' of the Kent Star made a similar claim to the *Sunday Dispatch*, detailing how 'subscription lists' were taken round shops, dance halls and pubs to raise funds to keep a man's family while he was in prison. Like Fullerton, 'F' was keen to pose as an honourable fighting man: more than willing to meet the challenges posed by rival gangs, but equally determined that women and children should not suffer on account of their activities.

As the case of Mary Mulvey illustrates, these claims to chivalry masked the enormous difficulties faced by the wives of gang members. Whatever provision was made for the families of those in jail, it was not enough to spare them from the indignities of poor relief, with its household inspections and intrusive questioning. Bereft of their share of their husbands' wages – or dole – the wives of prominent members of even the largest and best-organised gangs, including the Billy Boys and the San Toy, as well as the Kent Star, were forced to make serial applications for poor relief to stave off destitution while their husbands served repeated stretches of imprisonment. Of course, gang members could be loving and affectionate husbands and fathers – poor relief case-files detail their involvement in arranging hospital care for sick wives and children – but some were reluctant providers, keeping any profits from racketeering largely to themselves.

Many gangsters appear to have been prone to violence within the home as well as on the streets. In July 1933, Billy Fullerton's lieutenant, David Turnbull, stood trial at the High Court in Glasgow on a charge of unlawfully wounding his wife, Margaret, by cutting her on the face, neck and hand with a razor. On the night of the alleged assault, he arrived home at their tenement house in Fordneuk Street in Bridgeton at half past one in the morning. Margaret was in bed, and as Turnbull began to undress he 'called her some names' and they fought. Margaret went into a neighbour's house, only for Turnbull to follow her and kick her about the body – a doctor found a cut around an inch long on Margaret's left cheek and multiple scratches on her neck and wrists. Bravely risking her husband's further wrath, Margaret complained to the police.

Turnbull stood trial before Lord Anderson. He pleaded not guilty, and the case collapsed when Margaret insisted – to the fury of the Advocate Depute – that her wounds had been caused accidentally during the struggle. Asked why she had summoned the police, Margaret replied: 'It was the only way I could get out my spite on him.' The charge was withdrawn. The judge told Turnbull that his wife had done him 'a good turn', adding pointedly that she deserved better treatment in the future. By waiting until the trial to change her story, Margaret must have hoped to teach her husband a lesson: had he been convicted, he would have been liable to a long term of penal servitude.

Billy Fullerton's public conversion from fighting man to family man for the sake of his wife and children – made through the pages of *Thomson's Weekly News* in 1932 – did not run smoothly. His marriage to Rose Farmer was punctuated by violence and repeated separations, and while the Billy Boys amassed considerable funds through subscriptions and protection organised by Fullerton, Rose was left for long spells to eke out an existence on poor relief.

Rose made her first application to the parish for relief at the end of October 1926. Three weeks earlier – within a week of their wedding – her husband had been jailed for three months for assault. A relieving officer visited the couple's tenement house in the Calton, and noted: 'No income. No funds. House comfortable.' A terse doctor's note gave a better indication of the urgency of Rose's plight: 'Destitution and pregnancy.'

Their first child was born three months later, but despite Rose's repeated promptings, fatherhood did not impede Billy Fullerton's career as leader of the Billy Boys. Rose's case-file, meanwhile, documented the fate of the gangster's wife. Her husband's repeated bouts of imprisonment were interspersed with the birth of three more children, in 1928, 1930 and 1932. Three years into their marriage, Billy walked out on Rose for the first time. Her case-file recorded: '16 September 1929: William Fullerton's wife, 795 London Road. Destitute. Husband in desertion since 7 Sept. 1929.' Rose was granted 20 shillings per week for four weeks; by 28 October, the couple were reconciled: 'Off roll; husband home.' This pattern continued throughout the 1930s. Billy Fullerton's jail terms grew longer, and by the time he was jailed for four months for assault in October 1930, relieving officers were damning of his conduct: 'Twice in prison; twice in desertion; a bad case.' The following April, he was jailed for twelve months for assaulting the police.

Billy Fullerton was unemployed for three and a half years following the sale of his life story to *Thomson's Weekly News* in April 1932. He and Rose moved to Kenmore Street in Shettleston – fulfilling Fullerton's desire to escape from the East End's gangland – and once the 'reformed' Billy Boys opened their social club in July 1933, he began to supplement his dole money by running dances. The quieter streets of Shettleston did not suit Fullerton, however, and after a couple of years he resolved to move his family back to the Calton. Before he could arrange their return, his marriage to Rose broke down.

In October 1934, Billy Fullerton was jailed for four months for wife-assault. Rose told Glasgow Sheriff Court that the altercation had taken place on the night of Monday 1 October. Her husband had been sleeping in a chair in front of the fire in their tenement whilst she prepared his evening meal. She woke him when the food was ready, only to be met with a furious response:

> He accused her of shouting at him, and called her a 'Papish —' and nagged at her. It ended in him spitting in her face, whereon she told him that he was not going to get off with it. He then punched her on the eye and body and kicked her. She ran out for the police, but on her return her husband had gone.

If Rose's earlier declaration (as recorded by parish officials) that she had converted to Protestantism had been meant to appease Fullerton, it had clearly failed. He was spotted by a police constable at three o'clock in the morning; he was allowed to return home before being cautioned. The officer heard Fullerton tell his wife that if she pressed charges 'she would suffer for it', and so would her brothers.

Questioned by the procurator fiscal about her husband's remarks to her, Rose explained that she was, in fact, a Catholic whereas he was a Protestant. For his part, Fullerton told the court that he and Rose had argued on the morning of the altercation after he discovered that they had fallen behind with the rent. That evening, when his wife was getting a meal ready, she sent one of their children out to buy him a fish supper 'which he did not want, and he told her so'. The row that followed was not solely of his making. 'She has as hot a temper as me,' he explained, 'and when she made for me I shoved her.' In his account, Rose fell on the fender by accident. Fullerton admitted spitting at his wife, but denied punching her. He told the sheriff that Rose was a disobedient wife and neglectful mother – she attended dances, ignoring his pleas that she should stay at home and look after their four young children. He had since returned to his mother's house, as Rose refused to let him into his own home.

Billy and Rose Fullerton lived apart for four years. He gave her a portion of his dole money as housekeeping – just 15 shillings per week, by her account in July 1935. In October that year, Fullerton went to sea, leaving his former Bridgeton fiefdom to the Derry Boys and leaving Rose to bring up their children on poor relief, until they reconciled in the summer of 1938.

Like Billy Fullerton, Peter Williamson of the Beehive Boys
portrayed himself as a family man. As a street fighter, the powerfully built Williamson had few peers on Glasgow's South Side
during the late 1920s and 1930s. As Chief Constable Percy
Sillitoe acknowledged: 'There were only three other criminals
in the Gorbals who were considered capable of holding their
own against him.' In court, however, Williamson was adept at
portraying himself as a family man. At the trial of ten members
of the Beehive Boys at Glasgow Sheriff Court in February 1934,
Williamson told the jury that he did not leave his house on the
date of one of the offences of which he stood accused. 'It was
the anniversary of the burial of one of his children,' Williamson
explained, 'and he always stayed in that night.' Similarly, he
told how, on another of the days in question, he was at his
sister's house in the Gorbals:

> I always remember this occasion . . . because I had a tame white
> rabbit in the house, and the wife was fed up with it. I put the
> white rabbit under my jacket and took it to my sister's house to
> see if she would take it for her little boy, but she did not want it.
> I let the rabbit run about the floor and I played a couple of tunes
> on the piano. When I left my sister's house it was after four o'clock.

In accounting for his movements, Williamson presented himself
as a grieving father, subservient husband and kindly uncle in a
series of domestic vignettes, which provided a marked contrast
with detectives' descriptions of him as a dangerous street fighter.
Williamson's rhetoric failed him on this occasion – he was jailed
for twelve months – but police respected his dexterity in the
courtroom as much as his toughness.

Williamson's testimony must have sounded deeply ironic to
his wife, Isabella. The couple had married in 1925 when she
was aged nineteen; he was two years older. As one of Glasgow's
most notorious gangsters, Peter Williamson was rarely out of
the clutches of the police for long and while he served repeated
stretches in Barlinnie, Isabella was left to bring up their three
children on poor relief. Not surprisingly, their marriage was
deeply troubled.

Williamson was frequently flush from the proceeds of the Beehive Boys' thieving expeditions and rackets. He carried large wads of cash – £39 at the time of his arrest in August 1935 – but Isabella saw little of it as housekeeping. In July 1935, the couple's rows over money erupted into violence, when Williamson assaulted Isabella with a bread-knife. She called for the police and two constables put him out of her lodgings, but – no doubt fearful of retribution – she did not press charges. Four months later, Williamson was under investigation for neglecting to maintain his wife and children: whilst he enjoyed the sporadic spoils of gangsterdom, they were living in abject poverty.

'One of the worst outrages ever known'

In accounting for his determination to 'go straight' in the spring of 1932, Billy Fullerton insisted that his principal concern was with the well-being of his wife and children. However, gang conflicts always brought dangers to the families of those involved: some of Glasgow's gangsters took part in square-goes, but the city's gangs never truly abided by the notion of the fair fight, and attacks on the wives and children of their rivals showed the lengths to which gangs would go to hurt a 'marked' man. Robert Black, founder of the Govan Pals movement, described a horrifying episode involving a local gangster to whom he gave the pseudonym 'Harry'. Like Fullerton, Harry grew tired of the gang racket. He confided to Black:

> His young wife had been attacked in the street with her baby in her arms. He himself was a marked man, and not only could he not venture into the street alone, but he had to have three or four chums taking turns at sitting in his house night and day to protect him.

These precautions were necessary, he explained to Black, as his house had been attacked repeatedly by members of a rival gang.

The feud came to a head in what Black termed 'one of the worst outrages ever known in Glasgow gang history'. Harry was sitting in his kitchen one evening with two of his friends when the panel of his front door was smashed in. They rushed to the door, only to find that the initial attack was a diversion. Moments later, someone smashed the window of the room in which Harry's wife and their two children were sleeping:

> A young man climbed half in the window . . . An arm was raised, [and] a large soup-pan of boiling water was hurled into the room. The pot struck the pram. Another foot higher and the water would have scalded to death a baby six weeks old.

According to Black's account, Harry grabbed an axe and ran outside intent on murder, only to find that the intruder had disappeared.

WITH FOUR PAGE GRATIS SUPPLEMENT

THE RIGHT SPIRIT
FOR SPORTSMEN

'Red Tape'
The Whisky

The Central Station
Is Just Opposite
The CORN EXCHANGE
RESTAURANT
for Comfort, Quality & Economy
84 Gordon St.
SMITH (Glasgow) Ltd., Proprietors

The Evening News

With which is incorporated "The Evening Star" and "Glasgow News"

No. 20,594   GLASGOW, SATURDAY, MARCH 3, 1934   ONE PENNY

NINE ARRESTS AFTER DANCE HALL TRAGEDY

Wounded Men And Girls Huddled In Heaps On The Floor

SAVAGE GANG BATTLE

DYING MAN TAKEN IN MILK CART

POLICE COMB-OUT

EARLY MORNING FRACAS IN GLASGOW

NINE men were apprehended by Glasgow Police in the early hours of this morning following a savage mêlée shortly after midnight in the Bedford Dance Hall, Kelty Street, in which a man was brutally injured and three others were wounded and are now in the Victoria Infirmary.

The detained men will be brought before the Magistrate in the Divisional Police Court on Monday morning.

The dead man is James Dalziel (35), of 75 Surrey Street, a married man with a wife and four children. A milk cart was commissioned to take him to the Victoria Infirmary, it being realised by the manager of the dance hall that Dalziel was in such a serious condition that he would not wait for an ambulance waggon.

THREE MEN IN HOSPITAL

TRAGIC FAMILY.—Matty (4), Rose (8), Phebe (3), and Violet (7), the four children of James Dalziel, the Glasgow man, who was involved in the tragedy at the Bedford Dance Hall, Kelty Street, Glasgow.

The victim of the 'Dance Hall Tragedy' of 1934, thirty-five-year-old Jimmy Dalziel, was married with four children. His friends knew him as 'Razzle'. Detectives knew him as a frequenter of the Bedford Parlour dance hall in the Gorbals.

Five of those charged with Dalziel's murder – Bernard Kiernan, John Kane, John Hill, John Reid and Frank Kiernan – are held aloft by their friends outside Glasgow Sheriff Court after the charges against them had been dropped.

The 'Umbrella' at Bridgeton Cross in the 1930s. An unidentified minister competes with the photographer for the attention of the crowd gathered at the 'headquarters' of the Brigton Billy Boys and symbolic heart of the Protestant East End.

The Purple and Crown flute band, better known as the Billy Boys' band, in Belfast for the 12 July celebrations in 1935. The gang's leader, Billy Fullerton, sits in the middle of the front row.

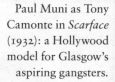

Billy Fullerton in his pomp: 'as powerful a personality in his own sphere as the Al Capones and Spike O'Donnells of the U.S.A.'

Paul Muni as Tony Camonte in *Scarface* (1932): a Hollywood model for Glasgow's aspiring gangsters.

Different from 'the usual type of gang': eight of the Beehive Boys in a Glasgow detective's mugshot album 1934.

Peter Williamson

Herbert Howie

Edward Doran

Daniel Cronin

William Rae

John Boyle

William Shannon

James Crearie

Larry Johnson of the Beehive Boys poses with his mother and sister.

A prolific joy-rider and 'motor bandit', Johnson had been taught to drive by a Gorbals milkman.

Barlinnie: the grim Victorian prison on Glasgow's eastern outskirts where Johnson and his fellow Beehive Boys served repeated 'stretches' during the 1930s.

Men and children flee from the scene of gang fight in Tollcross Road, Parkhead, in May 1933. Local residents told a journalist that their lives would be 'hell' for the next six weeks 'until after the march of the Orangemen in July'.

The glamorous Elizabeth Doris, whose husband Robert – a motor driver and mechanic – was acquitted of murder at the High Court in October 1934 following a drink-fuelled Friday night argument between supporters of Celtic and Rangers.

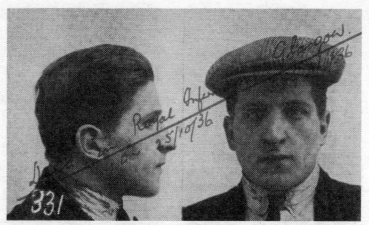

'The Don Quixote of the Gangs': George Stankovitch, or 'Stankie', whose death at the hands of his fellow Savoy Arcadians in October 1936 prompted a flurry of reports in the London-based, British national press comparing Glasgow to Capone-era Chicago.

Stankovitch's sweetheart, Elizabeth Rankin. Her account of their romance made a compelling, human interest story for readers of the popular Scottish papers.

The penalty of gangsterdom: as told to readers of the *Sunday Mail* by Mary Farrell, whose husband, Jim, was one of four men convicted of culpable homicide in the wake of Stankovitch's death.

MEN MUST GIVE UP GANGS

Mrs. Farrell and her three children.

BY MRS. JAMES FARRELL

Wife Of A Man Sentenced Last Week In The Glasgow Gang Case

We Are Paying The Penalty

Self-styled 'gang-buster', Captain Percy Sillitoe: Chief Constable of Glasgow from 1931 to 1943 and widely acclaimed by the local press as 'The Right Man for the Job'.

James 'Killer' McKay of the Derry Boys in 1936. Having been eager to assume the mantle of Billy Fullerton, McKay subsequently complained that he had become a victim of his own publicity.

Glasgow's notoriety cemented: cover illustration for the tenth impression of *No Mean City*, April 1942. The novel had first been published in October 1935.

12

The Big House

Imprisonment was a constant hazard for gang members. Congregating on street corners rendered them liable to arrest for loitering, and while petty offences tended to be punished by fines, those unable to pay served short jail sentences instead. Nor were those convicted of breaching the peace or assault always given the option of a fine. Arrests during clashes between rival gangs were often haphazard: police officers almost invariably claimed in court that they had arrested the ringleaders of disturbances, but identifying the leaders amidst the chaos and confusion of a rammy involving dozens or even hundreds of brawling men and youths was no easy task, and participants claimed that those arrested had often been merely watching the fighting rather than taking an active part.

For Glasgow's gang members, a jail term usually meant time in Barlinnie Prison – the 'Big House' – on the eastern edge of the city. Those sentenced to penal servitude were sent to Peterhead Convict Prison in Aberdeenshire. Penal servitude was only sparingly used, however, and even high-profile figures like Billy Fullerton served successive stretches in Barlinnie without ever being 'sent north' to Peterhead. And while members of rival gangs sometimes clashed within the jail – using tools provided for prison work tasks as makeshift weapons – at moments of heightened tension between inmates and warders, gang affiliations tended to be subsumed within a wider contest for control.

Hard Labour

In 1934, when the eighteen men and youths arrested in connection with the killing of Jimmy Dalziel were admitted to

Barlinnie, the prison's five blocks, known as Halls A to E, could accommodate up to 883 inmates in individual cells. The average daily population that year was 759, or 86 per cent of capacity. All prisoners were required to work from quarter past eight in the morning to quarter past noon and from two o'clock in the afternoon until half past five. Barlinnie contained a stone yard (where those prisoners sentenced to 'hard labour' broke rocks) and two large work sheds, where other inmates worked at mat-making and basket-making, 'teased' hair for the stuffing of furniture and repaired mailbags. The prison's grounds, which lay outside the boundary wall, contained fields where prisoners undertook agricultural labour and a whinstone quarry. Prisoners faced long periods of boredom and isolation – meals were served in the men's cells, and the long evenings spent alone were intensely disliked.

Barlinnie's grounds covered an area of forty-four acres. The absence of a perimeter wall meant that friends of the inmates could easily access the fields or quarry at night to leave parcels of contraband, which could be collected by members of the prison's work parties. The relative ease with which tobacco, in particular, could be smuggled into Barlinnie fuelled a thriving prison sub-culture in which gang members – including prominent members of the Beehive Boys and the Billy Boys – played a leading part.

Relations between Barlinnie's prisoners and their warders were frequently brutal and unforgiving. Officials at the Prisons Department for Scotland were reluctant to discuss outbreaks of disobedience or violence among prisoners, but severe assaults on prison officers led to criminal charges, and the resultant trials exposed incidents in which warders were periodically attacked with hammers, shovels and knives – all of which were routinely issued to prisoners to enable them to carry out their work. In October 1925, a warder suffered a fractured skull during a dispute over working conditions in the stone yard; in January 1929, two officers were stabbed during a fight with prisoners; eight months later, another warder was taken to hospital following an altercation in which he was struck with a shovel by one prisoner and hit over the head with a hammer by another.

By the early 1930s, reports of a breakdown of discipline in Barlinnie began to surface in the Scottish press. The prison was notoriously difficult to handle – more so than Peterhead – on account of what Glasgow's procurator fiscal, J. D. Strathern, termed 'the lawless gang instinct' among Barlinnie's inmates. Strathern alleged that long-term prisoners – those serving six months or longer – exercised 'a more or less dominating influence in the control of the prison'. This was an exaggeration, but Strathern's allegations nonetheless highlighted real difficulties faced by Barlinnie's warders, and these anxieties were ratcheted up in the wake of disturbances in the English prison system during January 1932.

'We will give you Dartmoor'

On the morning of Sunday, 24 January 1932, more than 150 convicts rioted at Dartmoor Prison in Devon. 'The Moor' housed recidivists (repeat offenders), said by *The Times* to include hardened convicts 'of the worst and most desperate type'. Their actions during the riot bore out *The Times*'s worst fears. Trouble began at breakfast, when prisoners began hurling bowls of porridge over the warders. The convicts were subsequently marshalled in the prison yard, where Colonel G. D. Turner, who was visiting Dartmoor in his capacity as Assistant Prison Commissioner for England and Wales, tried to address them. He was greeted with a hail of stones. Three prisoners rushed at the official, but a fourth stepped in to save him from a 'kicking'.

The attack on Colonel Turner unleashed a frenzied revolt. The convicts overpowered their guards and rampaged through the prison, chasing the governor, Stanley Roberts, out of his office – he took refuge in a cell – and setting fire to the central administrative block. For an hour and a half, the convicts effectively seized control of the prison. As fighting raged between prisoners and warders, officers positioned on the perimeter walls fired buckshot to deter would-be escapees.

Order was restored when a squad of fifty police officers

arrived from Plymouth. Led by their chief constable, they charged the convicts with their batons drawn, and after ten minutes of fierce hand-to-hand fighting, the prisoners surrendered. As they did so, the prison clock tower, which had been enveloped by flames, crashed to the ground.

Between sixty and seventy prisoners had been injured during the disturbance – most by blows from police batons. Five warders had also suffered injuries. According to Colonel Turner, the riot had been sparked by grievances over the prison diet. He told the *Daily Mirror* that the mutiny was the direct consequence of the introduction of a new kind of oatmeal in the prisoners' porridge.

Thirty-two prisoners stood trial following the mutiny. Accounting for their actions, the defendants made a series of allegations against the warders, claiming that officers frequently resorted to violence and penalised those who utilised the prison's complaints procedures. They also protested bitterly about the prison diet: according to one defendant, John Jackson, the food served at Dartmoor was 'unfit for human consumption'. Twenty-two of the defendants were convicted of riot. They received sentences totalling ninety-nine years.

The Dartmoor mutiny sent shockwaves through the British penal system, and prison officials in Scotland as well as England and Wales braced themselves for copycat disturbances. Prisoners at Barlinnie devoured reports of the riot, and in the months that followed, whispers of an attempt to emulate – or surpass – the disturbance at Dartmoor circulated throughout the jail.

The prison governor, Robert Walkinshaw – formerly governor of Duke Street Prison – first detected rumblings of discontent on Wednesday, 20 April 1932 when he toured the cells to talk to prisoners. While most appeared satisfied with their conditions, Alf Pellow, a twenty-seven-year-old Glaswegian hairdresser – better known to police as a housebreaker – told the governor that he had heard 'a certain amount of grumbling amongst the prisoners'. According to Pellow, those who had served time in English jails had reported that the food there was better, while others felt that prisoners elsewhere in the Scottish system enjoyed more privileges – including association in the evenings – than were permitted at Barlinnie. Pellow repeated his warning when he next spoke to the governor two days later. Walkinshaw was not impressed: in his view, Pellow was 'stirring up strife'.

The flashpoint came on the morning of Monday 25 April. When Warder John Singers arrived for duty in the mailbag shed at 9. 15 a.m., he was greeted by boos from some of the fifty or so prisoners working at the sewing machines. When a temporary warder entered the shed, the booing grew louder. Singers warned the prisoners that if the noise did not stop, he would 'shift' some of them. John Phillips – the notorious Bridgeton fighting man – jumped to his feet and confronted Singers, shouting: 'What the fucking hell are you narking at, you bastard?' Phillips then pulled a knife from a slot in his machine, his gestures showing exactly what he would do if Singers came any closer. When another warder stepped forward, Phillips warned: 'I will go north [to Peterhead Convict Prison] for some of you. Come on, boys . . . We will give you Dartmoor, you fucking bastards.' Phillips climbed from his work table onto the nearest rafter and shouted to prisoners in the adjacent mat shed: 'Rally round, I am going to be cased. Come on, we are the boys.' Four prisoners from the mat shed ran through.

The warders were wary of Phillips: in 1929, he had been jailed for twelve months for assault after striking a warder with a shovel, and none of them wanted to tackle Phillips when he was armed with a knife. They decided to leave him where he was and sent for assistance.

Order was restored when the prison governor, Robert Walkinshaw, arrived at the mailbag shed. He walked straight up to Phillips, who promptly stood to attention and took off his cap. 'I cannot speak to you here,' Walkinshaw said. 'You must go quietly to your cell.' Phillips assented, and Walkinshaw escorted him back to his cell. There, Phillips told the governor that 'the cause of all the trouble' had been a 'filthy' remark made by Warder Singers. Walkinshaw promised that he would deal with Phillips's complaint. After taking statements from three officers, including Singers, Walkinshaw directed the head warder, Alexander Panton, to return Phillips to the mailbag shed: Walkinshaw feared that if Phillips did not return promptly, the other prisoners would start smashing their machines. 'It was their intention,' Walkinshaw was convinced, 'to try to emulate Dartmoor.'

The governor's actions restored calm to the prison. 'Dartmoor' had been averted, although Walkinshaw remained concerned that a group of agitators among the prisoners was determined to cause trouble. Walkinshaw remained convinced that Pellow was the ringleader. So far as the governor could ascertain, Pellow's co-conspirators included Phillips, and a leading Billy Boy named James Rennie. The following day, Pellow put a number of requests to the governor – 'privileges in the evening, baths once a week, slippers in their cells' – and requested to see the prison's medical officer, Dr George Scott. Pellow told the medical officer that 'he came as the head of a deputation to ask for a change of diet'. When Dr Scott replied that he could only deal with individual prisoners, one hundred prisoners requested to see the medical officer the next morning, Wednesday 27 April.

Dr Scott saw each of the prisoners in turn in their cells. Between thirty and forty of those interviewed confided that 'they had no complaint to make, but that they had been threatened with violence if they did not put their names down along with the others.' Around forty others requested 'the English diet'. When pressed, only one of the forty was able to explain what this meant. The medical officer, like the governor, was adamant that 'the whole trouble was begun by the prisoner Alfred Pellow'. According to Dr Scott, Pellow had fewer than twenty genuine supporters, but these prisoners 'were able to terrorise others into supporting them'.

That afternoon, Walkinshaw arranged for sixteen prisoners to be transferred from Barlinnie to Gateside Prison in Greenock. Among them were Pellow, James Rennie of the Billy Boys and a number of noted fighting men such as Paddy Carraher of the South Side Stickers, and Joe Dinnen, an unemployed labourer with thirty-six convictions for assault and breaching the peace.

The 'troublemakers' were taken to Greenock in two police vans. One of the warders who formed part of their escort reported that the prisoners began to sing and shout obscenities as soon as the vans left Barlinnie, lighting (contraband) cigarettes and passing them round between themselves. Alf Pellow began to shout threats to the two warders in the front of his van, telling them that he had smuggled two letters out of the prison, one to his brother and the other to 'the gang'. Pellow warned that: 'Walkinshaw would be found in his bed with his throat cut before the week was out, and that Bryden and the other [warders] who went to football matches would have to be carted home when the gang found them.'

Governor Walkinshaw made another tour of the cells that evening. Most of the prisoners he spoke to complained about the broth served to them on Tuesdays and Sundays. None raised the 'English diet'. John Phillips remained at Barlinnie to serve punishment for his part in the disturbance: ten days' punishment diet, thirty nights' on a wooden bed and forfeiture of 60 marks of remission – prisoners could earn remission of up to one-sixth of their sentences for good conduct. Phillips was then transferred to HM Prison Edinburgh.

The Secretary of the Prisons Department for Scotland, Colonel Randolph Baird, visited Greenock on 29 April, two days after the arrival of the prisoners from Barlinnie. He noted that they appeared to have settled down well – he found them 'very respectful and industrious' – although he noted that Pellow was capable of fostering discontent 'being possessed of a fluent tongue and . . . a certain power of leadership'.

Baird and his officials in the Prisons Department were aghast, however, when a newly released prisoner began to sell stories of the unrest at Barlinnie to Scotland's national newspapers. The *Scottish Daily Express* ran front-page reports on 29 and 30 April 1932, detailing the confrontation between John Phillips and Warder John Singers, and revealing that the ringleaders of the disturbance had been kept handcuffed in their cells prior to their removal from the jail. The *Express* also disclosed that police officers had been drafted in to patrol the prison on

Tuesday 26 April, while a fire engine stood ready to 'drown' the prisoners should any attempt be made to revolt. While the *Express* applauded the prison authorities for their prompt and firm response, its headlines – including **'LET'S GIVE THEM DARTMOOR'** – were clearly designed to inflate readers' concerns.

The former prisoner appears to have sold his story twice, as the same revelations appeared in the *Sunday Post* on 1 May, along with a detailed account of the horrors of the Barlinnie diet. The *Post* alleged that prisoners frequently refused to touch the food: breakfast consisted of lumpy porridge and dirty bread, while dinner – the main meal of the day, served at 12.30 p.m. – was worse. On four days each week, it consisted of a pint of watery soup and a tiny loaf of bread. Twice a week, the soup and bread were augmented by a ration of four potatoes. The remaining day's fare was worse still: the infamous 'Barlinnie duff' – a boiled pudding, contents unknown, so repugnant as to be 'absolutely uneatable' more often that not. The last meal of the day, served at 5 p.m., consisted of one pint of tea and four slices of bread and margarine. According to the *Post*, 'the whole prison was seething with resentment at the poor quality and monotony of the fare'.

To make matters worse, warders at Gateside Prison in Greenock quickly proved unable to handle the influx of prisoners from Barlinnie. The Glaswegians had seemed pliable enough to Colonel Baird during his visit to Greenock on 29 April, but just three days later, Gateside's governor was forced to arrange for eight of them – Alf Pellow included – to be moved again. They were transferred to HM Prison Perth – the third jail to hold them in a week – as the governor was convinced that the Barlinnie men had been trying to engineer an incident on behalf of one of their number, James O'Hagan, who was shortly due for release. As the governor noted bitterly, the prisoners were determined to provide O'Hagan with 'some sensational news to give to the "Daily Express" or other newspaper willing to buy it'.

The *Scottish Daily Express* took the bait. Under the headline **'JAIL DISCONTENT SPREADS'**, it published a catalogue of complaints from a 'recently released prisoner' on 6 May. Most of the complaints related to the diet at Gateside. According to the *Express*'s unnamed informant – O'Hagan, we must presume – the Barlinnie prisoners had wasted no time in demonstrating the art of defiance to their Greenock counterparts. The day after their arrival, the Glaswegians had breached prison regulations by talking among themselves as they worked. When a warder cautioned one of them, the other fifteen immediately downed tools and surrounded him. 'The men returned to work,' the informant added, 'but they continued to speak.'

The Secretary of State for Scotland, Sir Archibald Sinclair, felt obliged to respond to the allegations surrounding the paucity of the food provided in Barlinnie, and he requested a report on the dietary regime in Scottish prisons. The report, prepared by the medical adviser to the Prisons Department, Robert Fleming, acknowledged that the Scottish diet was monotonous, and notably plainer than English prison fare. However, Fleming insisted that the respective diets had been devised according to national preferences: Scots preferred soup or broth, whereas the English preferred meat dinners. Moreover, statistical returns indicated that the majority of Scottish prisoners gained weight while in jail – in Barlinnie, more than 90 per cent of prisoners put on weight while in prison, something that reveals a great deal about the paucity of diets among the wider population of the 'other Glasgow'. So far as Fleming was concerned, prisoners' recent complaints simply did not ring true, and he could only comprehend them as 'the direct result of the Dartmoor mutiny'.

But the matter did not end there. Allegations of systematic brutality by warders at Barlinnie were made in a letter posted to 'Major Baird, HM Secretary of Prisons' on 19 May. The writer, Patrick Sweeney, claimed to be acting on behalf of a group of current prisoners. Sweeney was an experienced housebreaker, and had recently completed his fifth 'stretch' at Barlinnie. He was full of praise for Robert Walkinshaw – 'a strict and just man' – and for Colonel Baird's own work in improving conditions in Scotland's prisons. However, he claimed that 'dark deeds' on the part of the warders at Barlinnie were routinely concealed from the governor. Sweeney's allegations were three-fold. Firstly, he alleged that some officers were dismissive of prisoners' legitimate complaints regarding the quality of their food. Secondly, according to Sweeney, warders abused the prison's disciplinary procedures, routinely committing perjury with the result that prisoners unjustly forfeited remission. Sweeney's final, and most detailed, allegation was that a group of five officers – including the head warder – routinely 'lift their hands and their boots' to prisoners in their charge.

By Sweeney's account, prisoners suffered humiliation on entering Barlinnie, with officers using physical inspections to taunt new arrivals. Prisoners aged below twenty-one, held separately in E hall, were subjected to particularly rough treatment:

> when a prisoner gets his marks taken in the reception room Mr Warder Hood has a nasty habit of passing remarks about ones' body etc. The boys from E hall, who know so little generally get a punch on the jaw from this man. Mr Singer [sic] kicked a lad one day when I happed to be in the boys hall, and he said, that's the way to make them f--- jump.
>
> Now Sir is that prison reform – I ask you? It is down right cruelty, and what makes it all the more distressing is that both you and the governor do not know about these deeds.

Sweeney stated that he was 'ready to prove my statements to you or the Press at any time'. He also offered to provide a second witness: a former prisoner 'who got his head split open by a warder . . . he is attending a doctor, and the latter has stated that the assault must have been serious.'

Sweeney's letter was passed to Robert Walkinshaw. He interviewed the five warders named in the letter, and replied to Colonel Baird in a confidential memorandum. Walkinshaw 'absolutely refused' to believe that warders Galloway and McInnes used violence: both were 'very level headed' and 'very tactful with prisoners'. He accepted the word of the head warder 'that he has never kicked any prisoner since he came to the prison, and has never used any obscene language.' Warder Hood had admitted to occasionally 'chaffing' – ridiculing – prisoners, but likewise denied using violence. In the case of Warder Singers, whose confrontation with John Phillips had sparked the disturbance on 25 April, Walkinshaw was more equivocal: 'Warder Singers has an aggressive manner but I doubt if he went [to] the length of deliberately kicking a prisoner.'

Of course, Walkinshaw could ill afford to alienate the men under his command, and with the entire British prison system racked with anxiety following the Dartmoor mutiny, this was not the time to expose dark deeds at Barlinnie. However, the vehemence of the governor's defence of Galloway and McInnes is telling in its stark contrast with his comments on the other three warders.

In the wake of the disturbance on 25 April 1932, Barlinnie's governor, Robert Walkinshaw, introduced a system of additional 'privileges' for prisoners serving six months or longer. Subject to satisfactory conduct during the first two months of their sentences, they were permitted to join other prisoners in the jail's recreation room for one and a half hours on two evenings each week to play games such as dominoes and cards, or to box. Provision was also made for two additional periods of exercise at weekends – one hour on Saturdays, and forty-five minutes on Sundays – in which prisoners were allowed to walk in pairs and talk freely. These were significant gains for the long-sentence men, many of whom were veteran housebreakers or gang members, or both.

Not surprisingly, the belief that privileges had been obtained through agitation quickly took hold among the prisoners. In September 1932, Walkinshaw reported to the Prisons Department for Scotland that the new privileges had been well received. His deputy concurred, but pointed out that some prisoners now hoped for further concessions, such as access to newspapers and tobacco. These were not granted, but, unbeknown to officials in the Prisons Department, the additional periods of exercise were extended to all of Barlinnie's inmates.

Walkinshaw made two additional concessions to the jail's long-term prisoners. Firstly, the additional periods of exercise on Sundays were subject to minimal supervision – a single warder stationed on a nearby bridge watched over prisoners in the exercise yard. In effect, this meant that those inmates with supplies of illicit tobacco were able to smoke out of the warder's sight. Secondly, prisoners serving more than six months were now permitted to spend the final month of their sentence working outside the prison in the adjacent fields or the quarry.

This had an unanticipated side-effect: it allowed long-sentence men – many of whom were gang members – to better organise the collection of parcels of tobacco and other illicit goods brought into the quarry and fields adjacent to the prison at night. Tobacco smuggling had always been rife in Barlinnie and now it became more organised, with parcels containing letters, small items of food and, on occasion, razor blades, as well as tobacco deposited at agreed spots under cover of darkness – often by men who had themselves recently been released from the jail. According to warders' wives, interviewed by a journalist on the *Sunday Mail*, parcels were even addressed to individual prisoners. Those who smuggled the parcels into the prison claimed a tariff of 25 per cent of the contents. For men like Dan Cronin of the Beehive Boys, this promised to be good business, although it was not without risk: on one occasion, after being found in possession of a 'large quantity' of tobacco, Cronin was punished by fourteen days' 'gruel' diet.

On 11 January 1934, Robert Walkinshaw died after falling from a train between Glasgow and Ayr. His successor as governor of Barlinnie was Captain James Murray. A military man, Murray had spent twenty years in the Cameron Highlanders prior to entering the prison service in 1926 as deputy governor of Barlinnie. He went on to hold the post of governor at Peterhead Convict Prison and then Edinburgh Prison, before returning to Barlinnie in February 1934.

As Walkinshaw's successor, Murray was faced with a difficult task. The privileges enjoyed by inmates at Barlinnie extended far beyond those recognised by the Prisons Department, but their withdrawal ran the risk of alienating some of the most defiant – and dangerous – prisoners in Britain. In practice, little changed under Murray's leadership for more than eighteen months.

Terry McGhee's Tears

Relations between prisoners and warders were not uniformly hostile, however: while gang members came under considerable peer pressure to resist authority and to show solidarity at moments of collective defiance, under certain circumstances, they – like other inmates – accepted humane gestures by the officers watching over them.

Of the eighteen men arrested following the 'dance hall tragedy' in March 1934, two were themselves victims of the Calton gangsters who fatally injured Jimmy Dalziel. The deceased man's friends, Robert Park and Terry McGhee, found themselves under arrest on suspicion of murder when detectives visited the Victoria Infirmary and apprehended all of those injured in the mêlée, irrespective of which of the two warring factions they belonged to.

Twenty-eight-year-old McGhee lived with his wife, Cathie, and their four children in a single-end house in Eglinton Street in the Gorbals. He was held in Barlinnie from 7 March 1934 under the shadow of the death penalty.

Tragedy struck McGhee's family early the following month when his two-year-old daughter, Marion, was diagnosed first with measles and then with pneumonia. McGhee was permitted to visit her in hospital. Accompanied by a warder, he sat by Marion's bed, his eyes filled with tears as the officer and the ward sister tried to comfort him. Two days later, he was released temporarily for a second time – again escorted by a single warder – to attend Marion's funeral.

McGhee's wife, Cathie, did not attend the funeral at Riddrie cemetery as their youngest child, nine-month-old Annie, was also suffering with measles. Annie's condition quickly deteriorated. This time, Terry McGhee was allowed a home visit: he travelled with a warder by tram from Barlinnie to the Gorbals, arriving in Eglinton Street at around seven o'clock in the evening. For half an hour, he sat with his head in his hands before the warder told him it was time to leave. Annie died a few days later. Both parents attended her funeral. A sympathetic warder allowed them to walk together to Barlinnie before saying their goodbyes at the prison gates.

Cathie McGhee described the family's plight to a journalist on *Thomson's Weekly News*. The story of 'Scotland's Most Tragic Mother' was published on 14 April, with the threat of the gallows still looming over her husband. Terry McGhee was finally liberated – along with Robert Park – on 25 April, the day after the trial of the Calton gangsters charged with Dalziel's murder commenced at the High Court.

Privileges and Punishments

The mood in Barlinnie changed abruptly when, early in December 1934, a bottle of Red Biddy – red wine mixed with methylated spirits – was discovered in a parcel hidden in the quarry attached to the prison. The guard on the quarry at night was doubled, and for a period of two weeks prisoners were unable to get their regular (illegal) 'smokes'. This was grounds for revolt and, as those who had been in Barlinnie during the spring of 1932 pointed out, revolt got results. To makes matters worse, every inmate was aware that prisoners held in Barlinnie while awaiting trial brought cigarettes and tobacco with them, and were permitted to smoke while exercising.

On Friday 21 December, a group of prisoners staged a protest: seven of those working in the stone yard downed tools at 2.45 p.m. and others followed suit, with one prisoner signalling to men in the adjacent work sheds to join them. Between twenty and thirty men then ran to the yard in which the untried prisoners were due to exercise. After overpowering the warder in charge, they helped themselves to the box of cigarettes and tobacco belonging to those awaiting trial. Most of the protestors then headed back to the stone yard while others went into one of the work sheds, chased two warders out and invited the other prisoners to join them in the yard. Paddy Carraher, a veteran of the disturbance at Barlinnie two years earlier, told the warder in charge of the stone yard that if 'sticks' (batons) were used against them, the prisoners would retaliate with hammers. This was no idle threat: the protestors had picked up the heavy hammers used to break stones in the yard. Carraher added that the prisoners 'wanted to see the governor as the parcels had been stopped in the quarry [and] they must have their smoke somewhere.'

The governor was already on alert following a tip-off from a prisoner earlier in the day. Now, Captain Murray headed to the stone yard, where he found a group of around fifty men 'leaning against the wall, lounging about and smoking.' Each prisoner had a hammer at his side. Backed by fewer than a dozen warders, Murray approached the men and ordered them to 'fall in' and lay down their weapons. One of the prisoners asked: 'Is there going to be a shemozzle?' When the governor replied that the men would be taken back into the prison, they laid down their weapons. The prisoners – many of them still smoking – were marched back to their cells.

Murray's courage in facing the mob earned him the lasting respect of the prison's staff; faced by overwhelming odds, he had restored order without a blow being struck. Among the men the governor faced down were a number of prominent gangsters: Clarence Jackson and Walter Scott of the Billy Boys; Hugh McCormack of the Kent Star; Vinny Wallace of the San Toy; and the Savoy Arcadian, Dick McGuinness. Fierce enemies outside the prison, the Billies and the three Catholic gangsters posed a formidable threat when ranged against Murray and his warders.

The protestors were locked in their cells for the remainder of the day and the following morning, they were moved to cells in an unoccupied block – D hall – to isolate them from the rest of the inmates. At around half past one that afternoon – during the warders' dinner-hour – the protestors began to smash up their cells. Having broken their windows, they began shouting to attract the attention of people outside the jail. Archibald

Bates – a veteran warder with little time for the privileges afforded to prisoners at Barlinnie – led a group of thirty officers to D hall to quell the disturbance. Bates told his younger colleagues: 'Don't forget your batons are not ornaments,' then led by example: 'I went into one cell myself first, just to give those young officers a little encouragement.' He hit the occupant so hard that his baton snapped in half. The warders went into every cell that had been damaged and in groups of three or more, they battered each man in turn. Some of the prisoners fought back, but even those who offered no resistance were 'batoned and overcome'.

Forty-five cells in D hall had been wrecked, their windows broken and furniture destroyed. Dr George Scott, the prison's medical officer, treated forty-one prisoners that afternoon. He recorded that none of the men's injuries was serious: most were scalp wounds – 'obviously the result of a stroke with a warder's baton' – although more than half of the men had further injuries to their arms or hands from fending off the blows.

Nothing of this had been witnessed by the governor or the head warder. Captain Murray had been informed by telephone when the protestors had begun smashing their cells, and he had told the officer in charge to telephone the head warder, John Peddie, and ask him to deal with the disturbance.

Murray had left Barlinnie without going to D hall as he had had 'family business' to attend to in Edinburgh. Peddie, too, absented himself: having gone to D hall, he had seen nothing of what transpired as he had promptly left 'to see to the safety of the rest of the prison'.

Both the governor and the head warder were happy to delegate: in effect, they left Archibald Bates to it. As journalist and true-crime writer Robert Jeffrey has pointed out, it is possible that both men were keen to turn a 'blind eye' to the beatings that Bates and his colleagues meted out.

The violence inflicted on the men in D hall left the rest of the inmates seething. The next day, Sunday 23 December, seven more men were moved to D hall after protesting that they had not been granted sufficient exercise. An informer warned that another disturbance was planned for the morning of Monday 24 December, when prisoners were due to be back at work in the quarry and the work sheds – word had reportedly been passed from man to man during the Catholic service held that morning, with prisoners whispering: 'To-morrow forenoon, to-morrow forenoon.'

As a precaution, Captain Murray cancelled the Church of Scotland service due to be held that afternoon, and ordered that all inmates were to be kept in their cells the following day. Prisoners responded with a barrage of noise, 'shouting like madmen' in the cells.

Fighting erupted on Christmas Day after prisoners again alleged that their exercise had been cut short. Two men set about a warder and sparked a scrum in which two officers were injured and a prisoner's arm broken. The atmosphere in the prison appeared to be worsening by the day.

With officials at the Prisons Department refusing to discuss the outbreaks, reporters gathered at the prison gates and pressed those released from custody for news. Ex-prisoners were eager to talk up the turmoil behind the prison's walls: as one man released on 26 December told the *Scotsman*: 'It is like a lunatic asylum.' Paddy Carraher, ringleader of the recent protests, attempted to commit suicide in his cell in D hall that afternoon by smashing his chamber pot and using one of the jagged fragments to cut his own throat. Dr Scott, Barlinnie's beleaguered medical officer, stitched the wound and placed Carraher in the prison hospital under constant guard.

The unrest threatened to extend beyond the prison walls. On 9 January, Captain Murray was informed that gangsters planned to ambush warders who were due to testify in court: Frank Monaghan of the San Toy was due to appear at Glasgow Sheriff Court charged with stabbing a warder during an argument in the basket-making shed at Barlinnie three months earlier. The tip-off came from the prisoner who had warned the governor of the likelihood of disorder on 21 December. The informant also added that tobacco parcels were in future to be thrown over the prison wall by men armed with razors: any warders who obstructed the deliveries would be slashed. The governor took the warnings seriously and passed them on to Chief Constable Percy Sillitoe.

In the event, Monaghan's trial at Glasgow Sheriff Court on 16 January went ahead without disruption. Warder William McQueen alleged that, on Saturday 13 October, Monaghan threw down his materials and refused to work. When McQueen told him to get his jacket and go to his cell – the normal prelude to a disciplinary report – Monaghan stabbed him in the neck with his work knife. Monaghan pleaded self-defence, claiming that McQueen had lost his temper and kicked him. Several prisoners corroborated the prisoner's account, but the jury disregarded their evidence. Monaghan was jailed for nine months for what Sheriff Haldane described as a 'murderous attack'.

In the weeks that followed the unrest, discipline at Barlinnie was noticeably tightened. Some of the privileges introduced by Robert Walkinshaw – such as allowing long-sentence men to work in the prison quarry – were abandoned as part of a continuing clampdown on tobacco smuggling. Murray also re-introduced old practices such as surprise searches of a prisoner's clothing and person in his cell. These measures met with considerable enthusiasm among the longer-serving officers. To Warder George Chessell, discipline was 'twenty times' improved in the aftermath of the disturbances.

Twenty of the prisoners who took part in the 'smash up' in D hall on 22 December were charged with committing a breach of the peace, while five of the twenty faced additional charges of assault. They stood trial at Glasgow Sheriff Court on 25 January. All twenty pleaded guilty. Sheriff Welsh imposed sentences of three to six months' imprisonment, to be served on top of the men's existing jail terms. Twelve of the prisoners were moved to Perth Prison the following day.

Sir Godfrey Collins, Secretary of State for Scotland, commissioned an inquiry into the administration of Barlinnie, to be headed by Sir George Rankin, formerly Chief Justice of Bengal. Rankin interviewed the governor of the prison, Captain James Murray, and his deputy along with seven warders and nine prisoners – seven of whom had taken part in the disturbances on 21–22 December.

The warders were adamant that Barlinnie's inmates were much more difficult to handle than their counterparts elsewhere in the Scottish prison system. George Chessell had twenty-three years' experience as a warder, having previously worked at Peterhead Convict Prison, Dundee Prison and Polmont Borstal. He insisted that the 'gangster type' was the root of the problems in Barlinnie:

> I am speaking my own plain language. These men that you have in Glasgow are an entirely different type of prisoner from what you find in Edinburgh, Dundee, Inverness and these places. This seems to be a class of its own, and there seems to be a kind of a brotherhood between them. You can practically see it through every man in this gaol. There is a kind of striking clannishness between each man. They will stand by one another, and hold by one another.

His colleague, Archibald Bates, agreed. Bates had worked at Perth and Edinburgh Prisons prior to Barlinnie. He told Rankin that:

> The temperament of the Glasgow prisoner – I will put it that way – and the East Coast prisoner is entirely different. The Glasgow man is out to cause trouble at all times. You can get no satisfaction with him, and you can't work him. He always wants to be top dog. He takes everything as a right, not a privilege.

As acting head warder on 22 December 1934, Bates had taken responsibility for dealing with the protestors in D hall on that date. Rankin asked him: 'You think they got a bit of a hammering on that Saturday, and that has done them a lot of good?' Bates replied: 'It has.'

Rankin spoke informally to the prison medical officer and prison chaplain. He also held an off-the-record discussion with the Roman Catholic visiting clergyman, Peter Morrison. On 18 January 1935, Morrison had written to the prison governor alleging that he had witnessed assaults on three prisoners and one Borstal boy by warders in D hall. According to Reverend Morrison, each inmate in turn was punched and kicked by three officers stationed at the entrance to the hall:

> One prisoner was kicked to the ground: another was having his head knocked while both his sides were receiving continuous punchings. When the said prisoners entered their cells, two officers entered and closed the cell doors; again there were screams.

Reverend Morrison reported what he had seen to the warder in charge of the hall – George Chessell – before writing to notify the governor. When questioned by Captain Murray, Chessell denied that any wrongdoing had taken place. Murray strongly defended his officers in a report to the Secretary of the Prisons Department, stating that – contrary to Reverend Morrison's allegations – it was 'most unlikely that any striking of prisoners occurred'. The governor stood firmly behind the warders under his command, just as he had done following the batoning of prisoners on 22 December. However, the clergyman's painfully detailed observations suggest that the warders at Barlinnie had begun to exercise a reign of terror of their own.

No mention of this episode was made in Rankin's report on the administration of the prison, which was issued by the Scottish Office on 1 April 1935. Rankin was mildly critical of Robert Walkinshaw's regime, noting that his relaxed approach to discipline had left Barlinnie – and the 'gangster' element in particular – 'in need of firm handling'. As for the causes of the disorder witnessed on 21 and 22 December, Rankin ascribed the first outbreak to 'the tobacco question', and the second to 'bravado' on the part of prisoners awaiting punishment following the events of the previous day. Their intention in smashing up their cells was 'to create pandemonium partly for its own sake and partly to elicit sympathy from outside'. Rankin commended Warders Bates and Chessell for their part in suppressing the disturbances in D hall on 22 December, noting that Bates had effectively been left to deal with the outbreak without the support of either the governor or the head warder.

Of the former, the report was scathing in its criticism. Rankin concluded that the governor was guilty of a 'a serious breach of duty', noting pithily: 'The presence of the governor is not too much to ask if some forty prisoners are involved in a violent outbreak . . .'

If, as Robert Jeffrey suggests, Murray had wilfully turned a blind eye to the beatings dished out on 22 December, the decision backfired spectacularly. He was transferred from Barlinnie to Greenock Prison – a significant demotion, bringing a reduction in salary as well as status. Barlinnie's warders objected fiercely, protesting to the Secretary of State for Scotland, Sir Godfrey Collins, that Captain Murray was being punished for the failure of a regime established by his predecessor, Robert Walkinshaw. Collins held firm. He appointed Greenock's governor, William Finlayson, as Murray's successor.

Unlike Murray, Finlayson had worked his way up through the ranks of the prison service, and he had thirty years' experience – twenty-six as a warder – to draw upon in dealing with the challenges posed by the 'gangster element' in Barlinnie.

Barlinnie's New Regime

Three months after Finlayson's appointment, Sir Godfrey Collins assured the House of Commons that discipline at Barlinnie had improved under the new governor. The prison, nonetheless, still proved difficult to run: tobacco smuggling proved impossible to eradicate entirely, and allegations of fights between rival prisoners suggest that the inmates were by no means pacified.

As the *Scottish Daily Express* explained, smuggling tended to be organised by gang members prior to their release from the jail. They specified spots in the prison quarry and the surrounding fields where packages were going to be left and, following their release, they either dropped off the parcels themselves or passed on details of the agreed location to someone else with knowledge of the layout of the grounds. This led to some unlikely alliances: in September 1935, the leader of the Beehive Boys, Peter Williamson, was apprehended alongside Walter Scott of the Billy Boys as they deposited a package containing twelve ounces of tobacco, 110 cigarettes, two boxes of matches, a bottle of wine and four letters under a crane in the quarry – officers from the Eastern Division of the City of Glasgow Police had lain in wait nearby following a tip-off.

They appeared at Glasgow's Central Police Court two days later, where they pleaded guilty to attempting to smuggle the goods into the prison. They were each fined £5 with the option of twenty days' imprisonment. Williamson served five days; Scott served nine.

While some rival gangsters joined forces in their attempts to outwit the prison authorities, others pursued their grievances behind Barlinnie's walls. In June 1936, a long-term prisoner – due to be released three days later after serving a two-year sentence – was slashed on the throat by a fellow inmate in the prison's recreation room; the wound required nine stitches. The *Sunday Mail* claimed that this was the third time that the victim had been assaulted by the same prisoner. Again, on Christmas Eve that year, fighting broke out between gangsters from Bridgeton and the Calton, who had been put to work together in the prison's cookhouse. A fellow prisoner described the fight's aftermath to the *Sunday Post* after his release the following week:

> I saw the officers leading four men away. The prisoners were cut and bruised about the face. One of the men tried to get at another, and it took several officers all their time to hold him as he kicked and struggled like a little madman. He managed to wrench one free arm. He picked up a heavy earthenware vessel, and threw it at the other prisoner. I picked up the fragments.

According to the *Post*'s informant, the cookhouse fracas was part of a long-running feud that had begun when an inmate was surrounded by four members of a rival gang in one of the prison's work sheds and stabbed in the head with a pair of scissors.

Prison officials routinely refused to comment on such stories. On this occasion, however, they appear to have been stung by the *Post*'s allegations. When another recently released prisoner sold his story to the *Post*'s rival, the *Sunday Mail*, prison officials took the unusual step of publicly endorsing his comments. The *Mail*'s source had just completed a sentence of eighteen months for fraud, and stated categorically that while outbreaks of violence similar to those described by 'a Glasgow Sunday newspaper' had indeed occurred, none of the instances involved members of rival 'factions'. According to the *Mail*'s informant: 'Under the new governor, all rival gangsters serving sentences are separated, and a clash between them is impossible.' His revelations read like extracts from a report from officials at Barlinnie to the Prisons Department for Scotland: 'the new governor, Mr Finlayson, has effected a great many reforms.' These were said to include 'a complete change in the dinner programme'. It is hard to avoid the suspicion that the prisoner's 'revelations' had been primed by prison officials.

'You had to be one of the boys'

A rare account of Barlinnie from a prisoner's point of view was provided by former Beehive Boy, Larry Johnson, during an interview recorded during the 1990s. Johnson served several stretches at Barlinnie during the 1930s. He described the system of remission, whereby prisoners could reduce their sentences by up to one-sixth by consistently performing more than their allotted work tasks:

> I was thrust into what they called the stone yard . . . and your job was to break huge stones and when the stones were broken you cut them into smaller pieces. You were given, say, six barrow loads of heavy stones to cut and break. If you didn't fulfil that then you wouldn't get your remission, so you were longer in the jail, so you had to do it.

Johnson found the work difficult. 'We were unemployed,' he recalled, 'and my hands were soft.' He persevered, buoyed by the prospect of early release, until he was instructed to down tools by some of his fellow prisoners. The order was given by a group of Billy Boys. Johnson felt that he had no choice but to comply:

> There were quite a number of these boys in the jail at the same time as me, and they decided that they would strike. To me it wasn't a good idea, because I'd only a few days to go, nonetheless it was riskier for me to refuse to do it because I would maybe get my throat cut. So we threw our hammers over the wall . . . The screws [prison warders] immediately seized on us and put us inside, locked us up for as much as three or four days just to quieten us down.

Johnson knew the importance of keeping up appearances in front of his fellow prisoners. He revelled in his status as a Beehive Boy, and any loss of face within Barlinnie would damage his standing on the streets when he returned to the Gorbals:

> I had lost my remission and had to maybe do another three or four days extra but that was the sort of thing you had to accept. It was important to keep your head up. I was more scared of my friends and the other gangs than I was of the prison warders – you could handle them, but it was a different story with the gangs. You had to be one of the boys.

Prisoners sought to control each other's behaviour just as keenly as warders sought to control them: in that enduring battle of wills, there could be no ultimate victor.

Part IV

No Mean City?

13
A Story of the Glasgow Slums

Glasgow's reputation as Britain's gang city was cemented in October 1935. The occasion was not a murder trial, nor a renewal of allegations of American-style racketeering, but the publication of a novel.

To the horror of Glasgow's civic leaders, a fictional tale of a Gorbals gang leader and 'Razor King' brought the city's gangsters to the attention of the British national press as never before, and spread Glasgow's notoriety abroad. The novel was called *No Mean City* and was the result of an unlikely collaboration between Alexander McArthur, a Gorbals baker, and a London-based journalist, Herbert Kingsley Long. As Sean Damer has shown the book startled many of its readers and made the conditions of life in Britain's slums the subject of renewed national debate. The *Daily Record* heralded it as 'probably the most outspoken novel of the century'.

The book's curious gestation helped to account for its remarkable content, while speculation as to who 'really' wrote it – the lifelong slum-dweller or the opportunistic English reporter – helps to explain the extraordinary controversy generated by *No Mean City* even before it had been published.

The Baker and the Wordsmith

The impetus for the novel came from McArthur. Born in the Gorbals in 1901, Alec McArthur – as he was known locally – grew up with his parents and younger brother in a 'single-end' in Waddell Street. After leaving school he found work in a bakery, his wages helping towards the rent of a larger, 'room-and-kitchen' house in the same street. After his father's death in 1930, Alec McArthur remained at home with his mother.

The aspiring novelist was an unprepossessing figure. He was short and bespectacled, but he was quick-tempered, too, and angry at the conditions of life that surrounded him. McArthur submitted the two short novels that together formed the basis for *No Mean City* to the London publishing house, Longmans, in June 1934. Both were set in the Gorbals, with characters based on 'the men and women who shared with himself the tenement houses and the streets'. It is likely that McArthur was inspired by the success of Walter Greenwood's *Love on the Dole*, published the previous year to great critical acclaim. Greenwood's account of the stifling and corrosive effects of poverty and unemployment drew closely on his own experiences and observations of growing up in a Salford slum. *Love on the Dole* was both a powerful social document and a spectacular commercial success.

Neither of McArthur's manuscripts was deemed publishable: the Gorbals baker was no storyteller and neither his plots nor his characters gripped Longmans' professional readers. His revelations of life in Glasgow's slums, on the other hand, were nothing short of 'astonishing'. Spotting a commercial opportunity, Longmans dispatched Herbert Kingsley Long – one of their readers, and a vastly experienced journalist – to Glasgow to verify McArthur's observations. McArthur was in turn invited to Longmans' offices in London, where he attended a series of interviews so that the publishers could satisfy themselves 'as to the essential truth of his account of slum life'.

McArthur initially proved elusive, as A. L. Stanton of Longmans recalled:

> We invited him to come down from Glasgow and see us, and as he had made it clear that he was only a poor baker, we sent him the money for his fare. That was a mistake. He drank it. Next time, we sent him a railway ticket.

After persuading McArthur to agree to what Stanton termed a 'rewrite job', Longmans turned the manuscripts over to Kingsley Long and asked him to put one of them – 'The Idle Years' – into publishable form.

Kingsley Long was no mere hack. Two years earlier, he had ghost-written James Spenser's memoirs for Longmans. *Limey*, an account of Spenser's adventures as an English crook in the American underworld, was drafted in its entirety by Kingsley Long on the basis of conversations between the two men. The result was a racy yarn, laced with violence and sex and enlivened by snappy dialogue, which clearly owed as much to Kingsley Long's prowess as a narrator as to Spenser's own, vivid recollections. The drafting of *No Mean City*, by contrast, was a step-by-step process, with McArthur involved throughout to ensure its authenticity. As A. L. Stanton of Longmans explained, Kingsley Long wrote the book, but 'each chapter was sent to McArthur for his approval'. The 'rewrite' took almost twelve months.

Kingsley Long was adamant that *No Mean City* was primarily his own work. 'Obviously,' he conceded, 'I could not have written this novel without drawing heavily upon McArthur's admirable material and trying to share his vision of the Gorbals scene. But McArthur could not have written this book without a collaborator.' The contract drawn up by Longmans implied as much: 75 per cent of any royalties would go to Kingsley Long, with the remaining 25 per cent going to McArthur.

No Mean City still owed much to McArthur's 'admirable material', which – as Longmans' advertisements pointed out – included a series of notebooks, as well as his unpublished novels. Whereas *Limey* traded on Spenser's first-hand experiences as a racketeer and gunman, Longmans made no attempt to promote McArthur as an 'ex-gangster' – there was no evidence that McArthur ever belonged to a gang, despite growing up in the territory of the South Side Stickers. However, the novel is peppered with vivid descriptions of local customs and makes frequent use of Glaswegian slang.

McArthur was a keen observer of his surroundings, while his notebooks appear to have included a collection of newspaper cuttings, too. Many of the scenes in *No Mean City* bear striking resemblance to specific incidents and wider social trends reported in the local and Scottish national press during the

1920s and early 1930s, and it is tempting to view the novel's intricate portrayal of Glasgow's gangland as a mosaic of personal observation, newspaper articles and hearsay, the latter gleaned by McArthur from workplace conversations and pub talk over many years.

This was a rich seam for Kingsley Long and Longmans to exploit.

The Rise and Fall of 'Johnnie Stark'

No Mean City offered by far the most graphic account of the Glasgow gangs published during the interwar decades. The plot adheres closely to those of the classic Hollywood gangster movies: the rise and fall of the gangster hero, dramatised with spectacular commercial success in *Little Caesar* (1930) and *The Public Enemy* (1931), is vividly reworked in a Glasgow setting through the story of Johnnie Stark, born in a Gorbals slum in 1905. His father – a brutal fighting man – dies in 1923, leaving eighteen-year-old Johnnie as head of the household. Already on the fringes of the local gangs, Johnnie makes his reputation in a dance hall 'rammy' between youths from the Gorbals and the neighbouring Plantation district. Crowned Razor King of the Gorbals, Johnnie becomes a heroic figure among the young men of the district and leader of a formidable division of gangsters.

Johnnie Stark reigns supreme in Glasgow's gangland for four years. His relentless violence is described in harrowing detail. When three 'flash young fellows' foolishly try to belittle him outside a city centre cinema, his retribution is merciless:

> 'Ah'm no mug!' he shouted, as his razor laid open the face of one of his opponents from cheekbone to chin. His movements were incredibly swift. He fought with two hands at once, slashing like lightning at faces, hands and necks . . . Razor King had marked all three of his enemies before the fight lasted two minutes. Their bare fists were no defence against the terrible weapons. They could not even use their feet effectively in their wild efforts to guard their faces. They shouted and cursed and the blood flowed in streams.

Attention lingers on slashings and stompings throughout the novel, with lengthy descriptions of the injuries inflicted. Johnnie leads his division into a series of battles with rival gangs, and when he meets Big McLatchie from Townhead in a square-go on Glasgow Green, a thousand people gather to watch the frenzied exchange of punches and kicks. Johnnie triumphs, but the fight is only a prelude to a huge and bloody battle between his followers and the Townhead mob, in which the Razor King's weapons are wielded to terrible effect.

But, even as he triumphs over his foes, the seeds of the Razor King's decline are being sown. He marries Lizzie Ramsay, a young woman from a respectable Gorbals family, in 1924. However, the marriage is childless and this blow to Johnnie's manhood marks the beginning of his descent. His mind and body ravaged by repeated beatings and alcoholism, and further strained by the demoralising effects of imprisonment and long-term unemployment, by the summer of 1930 the Razor King is a spent force. No longer fit to be champion street fighter of the Gorbals, Johnnie is hunted, beaten and kicked unconscious by a mob of younger hooligans, some of whom had previously fought under his command. He dies the following day.

Two subplots chart the fortunes of Peter Stark, Johnnie's younger brother, and their neighbour and Johnnie's former school friend, Bobbie Hurley. Peter Stark eschews the world of the gangs and finds work in the warehouse of a city centre department store. He marries his sweetheart, Isobel McGilvery, and they realise a shared ambition by moving out of the Gorbals to the more respectable South Side district of Govanhill. Under the influence of his father-in-law, a member of the Labour Party, Peter schools himself in socialist classics. However, he loses his job after reluctantly leading his co-workers' protests at a series of wage cuts. Blacklisted by local employers, Peter turns to drink, and he and his wife eventually settle in a slum district in Anderston.

Like Johnnie Stark, Bobbie Hurley achieves fame throughout Glasgow. Bobbie is a dancing champion, and he is hired by one of the city's leading ballrooms along with his partner, Lily

McKay. They marry and move to the prosperous suburb of Cathcart. However, their marriage is torn apart by the pressure of the 'booking out' system, whereby professional dancers are hired for the evening (and sometimes longer) by the dance hall's wealthier clients. By 1930, Bobbie's career is also in steep decline.

The message of the novel is clear: there are no effective routes out of the Gorbals, while the folly of gangsterdom is mirrored by the futility of attempts to escape from a world of poverty and squalor by legitimate means.

Alexander McArthur's Glasgow

Many of McArthur and Kingsley Long's observations on Glasgow's gangland were familiar to readers of the local press. The gangsters in *No Mean City* are street fighters rather than 'real' criminals – just as senior police officers had insisted in their efforts to downplay allegations of racketeering. They are driven by territorial loyalty, guard their reputations with a desperate ferocity and they abide by the widely espoused code of honour, whereby fighting men shield even their fiercest enemies from the police. Yet *No Mean City* conveys a keener sense of people and place than the myriad court reports and feature articles published by Glasgow's newspapers.

Similarly, the accounts of social trends in *No Mean City* transcend, in terms of their immediacy, much of the reportage in the local press. The dancing craze of the 1920s, for example, is documented through Bobbie Hurley's progress from 'clabber-jiggings' (street dances) to *palais de danse*, and further illuminated by Johnnie Stark's brutal exploitation of dance hall etiquette. In contrast to newspaper reports, which tended to dwell on outbreaks of violence in the public settings of streets, cinemas and dance halls, *No Mean City* locates the brutalities inflicted by the Razor King within a wider culture of everyday violence in the Gorbals, much of it private. The novel is laden with accounts of domestic and sexual violence, and Johnnie is both witness to his father's assaults upon his mother and himself a victim of his father's beatings.

No Mean City deals equally frankly – although less graphically – with sex. Overcrowding dictates that even the young children are 'wide open to all the facts of sex', and Johnnie's first sexual encounter is with his cousin. Young women are drawn to the Razor King as much by his notoriety as his powerful physique. His status as Razor King ensures that there are 'dozens ready to oblige him', yet whilst many local young women yearn to bask in his glory, he remains a violent sexual predator and regularly assaults both his wife and his mistresses. Johnnie embarks upon a series of affairs, both prior to and during his marriage to Lizzie, and although their marriage is childless he fathers two children out of wedlock.

The characterisation of the Razor King as a serial rapist is highly suggestive. No such allegation surfaced in contemporary coverage of the gangs, although it was sometimes asserted that their female followers would do 'anything' for them.

McArthur and Kingsley Long fused economic and psychological explanations for the violence that permeated everyday life in the Gorbals. Poverty, unemployment and cramped tenement 'houses' fractured families and left the rising generation with no legitimate outlets for their energy and ambition. References to the 'complexes' lurking in the subconscious of the slum-dweller recur with sufficient regularity to suggest that one – or both – of the authors had been dabbling with psychology textbooks, as the following extract from the novel illustrates:

> Battles and sex are the only free diversions in slum life. Couple them with drink, which costs money, and you have the three principal outlets for that escape complex which is for ever working in the tenement dweller's subconscious mind. Johnnie Stark would not have realised that the 'hoose' he lived in drove him to the streets or that poverty and sheer monotony drove him in their turn into the pubs and the dance halls or into affairs like the one he was having with Mary Hay. But then, the slums as a whole do not realise that they are living an abnormal life in abnormal conditions. They are fatalistic and the world outside the tenements is scarcely more real to them than the fantastic fairy-tale world of the pictures.

In this grim environment, young men value their reputations above all else and no insult or challenge can go unmet: 'Vanity is an underrated vice. In the Glasgow slums, at all events, it is the very core of ruffianism.'

As a life-long resident of the Gorbals, McArthur was well placed to chart local attitudes towards the gangs. In *No Mean City*, no one is indifferent: 'Fighting is truly one of the amusements of the tenements. Nearly all the young people join in, if not as fighters themselves, at least as spectators and cheering supporters.' Even peaceable older residents of the Gorbals betray a 'queer admiration' for their champion. Many enjoy the spectacle of a gang fight, and tales of mighty battles between the Gorbals division and gangs from rival districts form a welcome diversion in neighbourhood gossip. Alec McArthur – an aloof figure, according to one of his former workmates – clearly shared the wider fascination with the gangs detailed in the book that made his name.

Yet as *No Mean City* made clear, attitudes towards the gangs were double-edged: Johnnie is respectfully addressed by neighbours fearful of causing offence; however, gangsters and their wives forfeit any claim to respectability and even Peter Stark finds it hard to escape his brother's shadow, whether courting Isobel or seeking employment. No one testifies against gang members. Forced to act in isolation against the gangs, the police are reluctant even in large numbers to intervene in full-scale 'rammies', preferring to pounce as the combatants disperse. Stragglers and the wounded are apprehended and paraded as ringleaders in court. This was not a picture that the City of Glasgow Police could afford to accept.

Kingsley Long brings Johnnie Stark's story to a close in 1930. A brief historical sketch in the final chapter of *No Mean City* notes that Glasgow's 'great gang battles' peaked in 1929. Credit is given to the churches for their role in the formation of clubs and recreation rooms in the tenement districts, and the clubs are judged at least a partial success: some of the most powerful gangs are broken up or fall into disarray and, for a while, razors go out of fashion. It appears that the tide of violence has been stemmed.

This was a convenient device. Longmans anticipated a hostile response to *No Mean City* – not least within Glasgow – and situating Johnnie's story during the 1920s enabled McArthur and Kingsley Long to assert the essential truthfulness of their story, while allowing potential critics to respond that conditions had improved significantly since the turn of the decade.

No Mean City ends on a tragic – and cautionary – note. Violence might have diminished due to the efforts of ministers and priests, but new gangs were forming even within the clubs, and when the Razor King emerges from prison for the last time in June 1930, it is the up-and-coming hooligans of the Gorbals who hunt him down.

It is left to his wife, Lizzie, to recognise Johnnie's sole achievement:

> Whit does it matter to the heid yins [top people] what happens in Gorbals or Bridgeton or Garngad or Anderston, or in any ither bliddy slum in Glasgow for that matter, so long as we keep quiet? . . . They need wakin' up once in a while, and it's fellows like Razor King that makes them remember we're alive.

Here, Lizzie speaks for McArthur, whose initial ambition as a writer had been precisely to raise awareness of conditions in Glasgow's slums.

'It grips you by its very grimness'

No Mean City: A Story of the Glasgow Slums by 'Alexander McArthur (of Glasgow)' and H. Kingsley Long was released on 28 October 1935. Publisher R. G. Longman wrote to Edwards Mills at Longmans' New York office on 22 October to alert him to the furore created by the novel, before it had even been published:

> I do not know whether you are aware that a good deal of controversy has arisen about the publication of this book. Glasgow is up in arms about it and several booksellers will not stock the book; a Glasgow paper will not review it and the question of its suppression has been raised in official circles in Scotland. I am

doubtful whether action will be taken, but if it is, we shall defend ourselves with vigour. It is all rather unpleasant but we feel strongly that we are justified in publishing. In our publicity we are being very careful . . . We have the backing of a number of important and dignified people who are disgusted that the book should be called obscene and maintain that the conditions described in the book can to this day be seen in Glasgow.

Longmans had taken a number of steps to fuel the controversy. Advance copies had been circulated to leading politicians, church leaders and other public figures, both in Glasgow and beyond, and carefully selected testimonials were incorporated into advertisements placed in the national press. To deflect criticism, publication had been postponed so that a preface could be inserted stating that the story 'deals only with one seam in the crowded life of the Empire's second city'.

Longmans' other strategy was to promote McArthur as the authentic voice of Glasgow's slums. According to the hastily inserted preface, McArthur had been unemployed for five years by the time that he submitted his manuscripts to Longmans, while advertisements proclaimed: 'This story is based on the unpublished novels and notebooks of Alexander McArthur (of the Gorbals, Glasgow, unemployed) who was born in the slums, and has lived in them all his life.' McArthur's plight seemingly testified to the novel's truthfulness. Meanwhile, for publicity purposes, Kingsley Long remained in the background.

It is possible that McArthur's life story was gilded by Longmans to heighten the novel's veneer of authenticity. McArthur subsequently claimed that he had been dismissed from his job as a baker for smoking during working hours. However, A. L. Stanton, who was working as a sales representative for Longmans in 1935, later claimed that McArthur was still working as a baker when he submitted his manuscripts to the firm's London office in 1934. According to Stanton, it was the success of *No Mean City* that enabled McArthur to give up his job.

No Mean City attracted widespread coverage upon publication.

It was reviewed throughout the Glasgow press, and the opinions of local MPs, councillors, ministers of religion, magistrates and senior police officers were canvassed. An abridged version was serialised in the *Sunday Mail*, Scotland's biggest-selling newspaper, prompting a flood of correspondence from readers as far away as Canada. Reviews also appeared in London-based literary and current-affairs magazines such as the *Times Literary Supplement* and the *Spectator*. These tended to dwell on the authenticity of the novel rather than its literary merit, but there was considerable praise for its vividness. Readers of the *Listener* were urged to read *No Mean City* for themselves: 'It is not only of high documentary value, but also of the utmost moral value. It should be read by everyone.' Some Glasgow-based reviewers were equally effusive. To the *Glasgow Herald*'s reviewer, *No Mean City* was 'a novel of tremendous power, a horrible story that holds one enchained in a shocked fascination.' The *Daily Record* issued the same verdict, albeit more succinctly: 'It grips you by its very grimness.'

To the *Herald*, McArthur's experience of life in a Gorbals slum and his unerring powers of description were the key to the novel's success:

> He is unfalteringly realistic. His characters, vile, pathetic, and contemptible alike, are as real and earthly as a Gorbals tenement. His dialogue would do credit to a veteran dramatist, and his use of Glasgow dialect will convince many Glaswegians that their knowledge of their native city is incomplete . . .

Even the *Evening Citizen*, which deplored *No Mean City*, acknowledged it to be:

> an appalling but undoubtedly faithful picture of life amongst the lowest of the low – the corner boys, the so-called 'gangsters,' the dwellers in the filthiest slums . . . Nor is there any exaggeration. In fact, the authors have evidently felt compelled to exercise some restraint although, we think, they have gone to the utmost limits of what would be tolerable and permissible in print.

A procession of church leaders and social workers, many

claiming first-hand knowledge of the Gorbals and similar districts, likewise testified to the novel's truthfulness.

Other critics argued that the novel's depiction of violence in Glasgow was vastly overdrawn. Councillor Stewart Reid, convener of the Public Health Committee of Glasgow Corporation and an experienced police court magistrate, told the *Daily Record* that the portrayal of the city's gangs was 'grossly exaggerated'. Chief Constable Percy Sillitoe agreed: 'We in Glasgow certainly have our hooligan element, and what city has not? But to compare it with the gangster element in America, [while] good for best-seller purposes . . . has no relation to fact.' Others objected that a story relating only to a tiny part of the Gorbals population could too easily be read as an indictment of the entire district – or even the character of the Glasgow working class as a whole. Bridgeton MP Jimmy Maxton concurred. 'In the main,' Maxton insisted, 'the slum dwellers of Glasgow beat their environment. I have a feeling that Mr McArthur inclines to make the environment beat them.' Glasgow's politicians and senior police officials could hardly endorse *No Mean City*: to do so would have been tantamount to a collective dereliction of duty on their part.

By far the most powerful rebuttal was issued by Reverend J. Cameron Peddie. As minister of Hutchesontown Parish Church in the Gorbals, Peddie had been widely lauded as the man who reformed the South Side Stickers. He, too, could not permit *No Mean City* to go unchallenged, and his response was fierce. In a lengthy article published in the *Scottish Daily Express*, he blasted the novel as 'a scurrilous and revolting lampoon on the poorest class of our Gorbals citizens.' He conceded that the Gorbals had been the scene of repeated clashes between the Stickers and the Liberty Boys during the 1920s, but police and press reports of a 'reign of terror' were grossly exaggerated. Moreover, both groups had long ago renounced gang warfare: since the summer of 1930 they had existed only as clubs, forming part of the city-wide Pals' movement.

Peddie was especially concerned that readers would assume that the character of the Razor King was based on a real 'gangster':

While the Stickers and the Liberty Boys had leaders to direct their activities, none of these leaders was anything like the atrocious character, Johnnie Stark, portrayed in 'No Mean City.' They are today married men, loyal husbands and devoted fathers. I could give their names and addresses. One cannot but resent most intensely the grievous wrong that has been done them if this imaginative novel is to be taken seriously.

Peddie was most offended not by Johnnie Stark's resort to violence, but by his sexual licentiousness. Gang members, the minister insisted, invariably did the honourable thing if they got a girl 'into trouble'. In that regard, Peddie asserted, their moral code was no different from that of people in any other social class.

Peddie was also anxious that *No Mean City* would be viewed as an indictment of the present-day Gorbals; his own reputation hinged on his claim that gang violence had all but disappeared from Glasgow's South Side. He assured the *Express*'s readers that:

> At the present moment there is only one group of lads that may be characterised as a gang in the Gorbals. That group is known as the Bee-Hive, and on several occasions their leaders have asked me to take them off the street and give them a club, as they are tired of the street life.

Peddie had been unable to meet their request – his responsibilities were too heavy already – but he now pleaded for other, more prosperous Glaswegians to assist. Peddie ended his diatribe by lamenting that the authors of *No Mean City* had closed their eyes to the extraordinary generosity displayed by the poor towards those in most urgent need:

> One could tell of neighbours sharing their meagre meals with destitute families, housing homeless unfortunates, nursing lonely and helpless invalids, even opening up the graves of their own dead, that a neighbour's child might have an honourable burial . . .

As Peddie remarked, these untold acts of kindness and self-sacrifice required a different chronicler.

Some critics claimed that *No Mean City* ought never to have been published. To the *Evening Citizen*, the social problems described in the novel were well known in Glasgow, and local politicians, social workers, welfare organisations and the churches were already striving to combat them. No further publicity was needed: quite the reverse, so far as the *Citizen* was concerned, the furore surrounding the publication of *No Mean City* could only serve to confirm Glasgow's unwarranted reputation as violent and lawless, thus exacerbating the damage to the city's economic prospects caused by the myth of the 'Red Clyde'. Most of Glasgow's booksellers refused to stock *No Mean City*. The city's libraries followed suit, despite repeated requests from readers, after Corporation Treasurer Patrick Dollan told the municipal Libraries Committee that the novel 'gave an unfair and inaccurate representation of working-class life in Glasgow'.

By contrast, the majority of reviewers deemed *No Mean City* to be an important social document. To the editor of the *Sunday Mail*, it was potentially 'of more use than a hundred Commission reports or sermons'. Most reviewers agreed that the novel could hardly fail to prick the consciences of its readers and if, as many suggested, the novel inspired pity for those crammed into Britain's slums, then in McArthur's own terms *No Mean City* was an immediate success.

The *Daily Record* gave McArthur a platform to respond to his critics. McArthur claimed that his 'fellow slum-dwellers' had responded positively to the novel, and implied that his critics had no first-hand knowledge upon which to base their objections. By his own account, *No Mean City* was an attempt to expose the horrors of the Glasgow slums, paving the way for a 'real' investigation of the city's social problems and a renewed effort to provide decent housing for the thousands of working-class people trapped in districts such as the Gorbals. As for the charge that it damaged Glasgow, McArthur responded tartly that the harm already done to the city's working-class population by the conditions described in *No Mean City* would take many years to remedy.

No Mean Cities of Britain

The controversy was re-ignited in March 1936 when *No Mean City* was serialised in thirteen instalments in the London edition of the *Daily Express*. With its circulation of more than 2 million, the *Express* made the Gorbals and its fictional Razor King the talk of England. The serial's launch was carefully timed to capitalise on a visit to Glasgow by King Edward VIII. The new monarch visited John Brown's shipyard at Clydebank to inspect the giant liner, the *Queen Mary*, before proceeding to a Glasgow Corporation housing estate at Knightswood. His tour ended with a visit to slum tenements in Anderston, where he was heard to remark, somewhat gracelessly: 'Isn't it terrible? But I've seen worse in Durham.'

The *Express* issued a bold challenge to its readers through its opinion column the following day:

> The King goes down to the Clydebank slums, but have *you* been?
>
> He sees how the second city of Britain keeps its poor in hovels and rags, but have *you* seen?
>
> The King expresses his disgust with these conditions because he KNOWS, but do *you* know?

Readers in London, Manchester, Liverpool, Leeds and Birmingham were urged to read this tale of Glasgow's slums. Their blood would 'run fast,' the *Express* promised, 'if there's any pity and anger and shame left in folk.'

Readers were introduced to Alexander McArthur through a biographical portrait. This 'Citizen of No Mean City', they were told, still lived in a two-roomed house in the Gorbals: 'His mother has one, he has the other.' After six years without employment, his life had assumed a settled pattern: 'Every fortnight he has gone to draw his poor relief – 34s. – and that and his mother's old-age pension have maintained life.' The hundred pounds he had received in royalties had been used to settle debts and purchase clothes. McArthur confirmed that he had seldom set foot outside the Gorbals, and had no plans to leave the district. Only 'a tiny few' managed to escape the slums, he pointed out, and he did not expect to join them. His ambition was merely to avoid the strain of industrial labour: 'I am looking for a light job at £3 a week.'

McArthur claimed to have written 'Idle Years' – the short novel that formed the basis for *No Mean City* – in three weeks. 'At first,' he told the *Express*, 'I began writing it as a joke.' However, as the story took shape it became anything but comic. The *Express* acknowledged that the published version had divided opinion within the Gorbals: 'Having read it, the "respectable" folk regarded it as a slur . . . perhaps true, but better unsaid. Many of the rest just grinned and muttered: "We know worse than that."'

The novel's title, meanwhile, had inspired endless wisecracks: '"No mean . . ." is applied to everything in Glasgow these days. A comedian in a cheap theatre is cheered when he comes out on the stage, looks up at the audience and says: "No mean audience."'

Introducing the first extract from the novel, the *Express* repeated its challenge to its readers: 'It is slum life in Everycity. Is it slum life in YOUR city?' Readers were quick to respond, but bitterly divided. Some praised the newspaper for exposing the 'repugnant truth' about life in Britain, while several readers from the south of England shared what they claimed to be their first-hand experiences of Glasgow's gang terror. W. M. Fleming of Margate wrote:

> Your serial 'No Mean City' is the truest I have ever read . . . In 1932 I was sent to supervise canvassers working the south side of Glasgow for six months. I saw many gang fights with razors, started without apparent provocation, ending in ghastly and bloody sights. Respectable citizens have to take immediate cover.

Other readers remained unconvinced. Mrs B. F. Brown, of Westcliff-on-Sea in Essex, insisted that the story was an insult to the 'respectable' poor of Glasgow, while McKinley Hargreaves of Reading demanded a fulsome apology from the editor for subjecting readers to 'such a depraved picture of Glasgow slum life'. Less hostile critics insisted that 'if it was true, it was only true of Glasgow.'

Objections were so numerous that *Express* editor Arthur Christiansen dispatched veteran journalist Frederic Salusbury to investigate conditions in Britain's slums on the paper's behalf. Salusbury's brief was simple: 'To tell the FACTS as he finds them.'

Salusbury went to Birmingham, Cardiff, Liverpool, Sheffield and Leeds before concluding his tour in the East End of London. His findings were published by the *Express* in a six-part series entitled 'No mean cities of Britain'. His main focus was not on gangs, or violence, but on housing conditions. This reflected, in part, the salience of housing as a political issue: the National Government had launched a campaign against overcrowding in 1934 and, following the 1935 Housing Act, local authorities had been required to survey every working-class household in England, Wales and Scotland to ascertain the extent of the problem. The deadline for the survey was 1 April 1936 – just five days before Salusbury's first article appeared in the *Express*.

Salusbury was careful to acknowledge the energetic slum clearance programmes already undertaken in the cities he visited: Leeds had built 19,000 houses and flats since 1919, accommodating more than 70,000 people; Liverpool had an eight-year plan to rehouse 64,000 slum-dwellers at a cost of nearly £8 million; Birmingham's estates were 'models for the rest of England'. Yet for all this municipal endeavour, foul slums remained: in a dingy court off Birmingham's Summer Lane, a single tap served a dozen households; in Liverpool, conditions were worse – the streets off Scotland Road in the city's docklands contained 'probably the most appalling slum properties in England'. Here, Salusbury met families with as many as seven children crammed into dilapidated, three-roomed houses infested with vermin. In one house, he noted: 'Husband, wife and two babies share one bed, a girl of four has a cot, two boys and a girl of eight share the other bed.' The tenants struggled as best they could to keep the houses clean, but constant scrubbing was not enough to rid them of cockroaches and rats. Salusbury blamed unscrupulous private landlords for allowing the buildings to decay.

Salusbury saw a great deal of squalor during his journeys into Britain's slum lands, but he reported few traces of gangs and little sign of the everyday violence that formed such a vital part of McArthur and Kingsley Long's portrait of the Gorbals. In Birmingham, he met 'Herbert Perks' – a police informer, whose criminal career stretched back to childhood. Perks made his living through various 'dodges', some of which required brass knuckle-dusters, but he was no Johnnie Stark. 'The old Birmingham race gangs are broken up,' Salusbury explained with reference to the Racecourse Wars of the 1920s, leaving petty criminals like Perks to fend for themselves. In Sheffield, too, gangs had been suppressed. The Sheffield 'tyke' was still 'a tough lad', Salusbury conceded, but following Sillitoe's spell as the city's chief constable, 'he is nothing like so tough as he was'.

The *Express*'s vast readership was left with the impression that the Gorbals slums were by no means Britain's worst. Similarly, overcrowding in Glasgow was severe – but by no means uniquely so. What made Glasgow different, it appeared, was the extent and resilience of its gangs. And while McArthur and Kingsley Long had been careful to stress that the city's 'great gang battles' had peaked in 1929, the *Express* carried new reports of fresh outbreaks of gang violence in Glasgow that coincided directly with its serialisation.

A front-page report on 17 March described how James Wilkie, stated by police to be the leader of the Derry Boys, had been jailed for two years for his part in a concerted attack which left a man 'lying in the gutter, his skull practically smashed.' Under the headline '"NO MEAN CITY" GANGSTER JAILED', the report directed readers to that day's instalment from the novel. *No Mean City* was thus presented as an up-to-date as well as unerringly accurate account of Glasgow's gangland.

Longmans published an American edition of *No Mean City*

in September 1936. To reviewers familiar with the profits accrued by the likes of Al Capone, the exploits of Johnnie Stark seemed tame. 'His story is small-time – amateurish and aimless,' declared *New York Times* critic, Peter Monro Jack. The spectacle of a 'razor king' fighting for adventure, with no prospect of making 'real money', seemed pathetic: 'There is in this story not so much the modern feeling of gangster terrorism as a sort of primitive cock-fighting sporting element.' *No Mean City* was 'a tenth-rate gangster story', Monro Jack concluded. For him, its interest lay in its factual content – so much so that *No Mean City* 'hardly belongs with fiction at all'.

Other readers outside Britain were horrified. One Canadian reporter claimed to have been so shocked by what he read that he visited Glasgow to see the Gorbals for himself. His findings were as grim as the novel. He confirmed that most Glasgow people were 'fine and upright' – despite the conditions in which they were forced to live – but the Gorbals was 'one of the worst slums in the western world'. In the first tenement he visited, the reporter met a family of eight living in a single-end: their cavity beds were dirty and verminous 'sleeping cupboards'. His most sensational 'findings', however, were based not on personal observation, but on the fictional account by McArthur and Kingsley Long: 'Men and women, girls and boys, live together in their one or two small rooms. Incest and foul brutality are common. Brutalised from youth, boys become gangsters.' Wandering along Crown Street, the reporter saw no need to speak to local youths. Having read *No Mean City*, he was confident he could read their minds: 'I wandered into the dives and bars on this street. I saw several short, but tough and powerfully built, young men whose one ambition in life is to become "razor king" of Glasgow.'

14
Sillitoe and the Derry Boys

The furore that surrounded *No Mean City* was an embarrassment to Captain Percy Sillitoe, Glasgow's ambitious chief constable. More embarrassing by far, however, were widespread reports of a resurgence of gang fighting in the city the following year. The spring and summer of 1936 saw an intensification of 'faction' fighting amidst renewed allegations of witness intimidation and racketeering. Glasgow's reign of terror, it appeared, had been resumed. Attention now switched from the Gorbals – kingdom of Johnnie Stark – on Glasgow's South Side, to the city's East End, and especially to Bridgeton.

The escalation of gang warfare was widely explained with reference to a factor that had been largely absent from *No Mean City*: religious sectarianism. Bridgeton Cross, long notorious as the gathering place of the Billy Boys, now served as the headquarters of a younger generation of Protestant gangsters styling themselves as the Derry Boys. Previously known as the Billy Boys' junior section, the Derries now emerged as a gang in their own right and, in the frequency of their exploits, they began to eclipse the senior Billy Boys. In the process, they acquired the mantle of the most powerful – and dangerous – gang in Glasgow. Their rise posed an unwelcome challenge to Sillitoe's status as Britain's chief 'gang-buster'.

Gangs were by no means the only threat to Sillitoe's authority. As a journalist on the *Evening Times* pointed out, chronic drunkenness and illegal gambling continued to flourish in the city's poorer districts, providing less glamorous yet still alluring prospects of release from the monotony of unemployment or the demands of industrial toil. The *Evening Times* reporter set out to explore the 'backlands' of Glasgow for himself. Within a mile radius of Central Station, and largely hidden from the main thoroughfares, he found a world far removed from the opulent pleasure-spots of the city centre. In districts such as Bridgeton and the Calton, the back streets – and the back-courts between the rows of tenements – took on a life of their own. Much of the activity that took place here was in breach of local by-laws. A host of illicit entertainments was organised by local entrepreneurs, who – along with much of the local population – were embroiled in a never-ending battle of wits with the police.

Despite a decline in convictions for drunkenness during the 1920s and early 1930s, Glasgow remained a hard-drinking city. Many working men considered 'pocket money' for beer, whisky and betting to be their hard-earned right. As Andrew Coleman from the Gorbals insisted at the Southern Police Court: 'After a man had worked hard all week he was entitled to six pints of beer on a Friday, if he wanted them.' Shebeens flourished throughout the East End and South Side during the 1920s and 1930s. Much of their stock was supplied by illicit distillers, whose operations had boomed following the heavy increase in the duty on whisky during the Great War. According to the police, many of the producers were in league with local publicans as well as shebeeners. With duty of 8 shillings payable on a bottle of branded liquor that retailed for 12 shillings and sixpence, there were vast profits to be made by those who dodged the tax.

Red Biddy caused more concern than illicit distilling and shebeening combined. This potent mix of red wine and methylated spirits catered for those seeking oblivion at a fraction of the price of whisky. A 'special investigator' hired by the *Sunday Mail* found the public houses of the Calton doing a roaring trade on a Saturday night. As closing-time approached, fourpenny quarter-pint bottles of red wine flew off the shelves – shortly to be mixed, the investigator feared, with meths. 'Red Biddy,' he warned, 'gives a bantam power to do battle with a bobby.'

'It happens every day in Brigton'

On the evening of Sunday, 12 January 1936, Denis and Ellen McGuire were disturbed by loud knocking at the door of their tenement home in Nuneaton Street in Dalmarnock. The caller was one of their former neighbours, a lad named John Henderson. He brought grim news of the McGuires' fifteen-year-old son, John. 'I saw John being carried into a house in Patna Street,' Henderson whispered. 'I think he is dead.' Henderson accompanied Mrs McGuire as she dashed the short distance to Patna Street, where a crowd had gathered around an ambulance. John McGuire was alive, but unconscious. He was taken to Glasgow's Royal Infirmary, where doctors discovered that his skull had been fractured. They operated on him that night. Nurses told Denis McGuire that the operation was essential to save his son's life.

A reporter from the *People's Journal* called at the McGuires' house shortly after midnight. Mrs McGuire told how John had been 'bright and cheery' when he went out to meet one of his friends at six o'clock that evening. The two boys had gone for a walk. Shortly afterwards, they had been attacked by a gang of youths and John had been struck on the head with a weapon, thought to be either a chisel or a bottle. Mr McGuire, a veteran of both the South African War and the Great War, was no stranger to violence himself. He explained to the reporter that John was unemployed, having been laid off from his job in a wire factory due to poor trade. His son played for a juvenile football team based in Anderston, Mr McGuire added, and was tall for his age. (John's height might well have made him more of a target.)

More journalists arrived at the McGuires' door in the days that followed, all eager to convey the family's distress at the savage and apparently motiveless assault on their son. Mrs McGuire expressed her sheer incomprehension to a journalist from *Thomson's Weekly News*: 'I cannot understand why anyone should have struck him,' she declared. 'He was always so quiet and unassuming. He interfered with no one. He spent most of his time at home, and did all he could do help his father and I.'

Detectives had little difficulty in identifying McGuire's assailants; within a week, they had taken into custody seven members of the Derry Boys. The first of the prisoners to stand trial was James Wilkie, aged twenty-one, and twenty-year-old James Brown. They appeared at Glasgow Sheriff Court on 16 March. Both prisoners pleaded guilty to charges of riot and assaulting John McGuire 'to the danger of his life'. Wilkie pleaded guilty to an additional charge of assaulting McGuire's companion, Archibald McLean.

Procurator Fiscal J. D. Strathern identified the prisoners as 'members of a gang known as the Derry Boys, which was the junior section of a bigger gang . . . supposed to be a Protestant association.' According to Strathern, the Derry Boys roamed Bridgeton and surrounding districts in groups twenty- to thirty-strong, armed with swords, bayonets, bottles, hatchets and stones, seeking fights with gangs 'of a different religious persuasion'. On 12 January, police had observed them 'running from point to point in the Bridgeton district'. In Patna Street in Dalmarnock, they spotted McGuire, who they knew to be a Catholic, in the company of McLean, who was not only a Protestant but was himself a former Derry Boy. McGuire and McLean tried to flee, but McGuire tripped and fell. He was instantly surrounded. Strathern's account of the assault that followed was unflinching: John McGuire 'was battered until his skull was fractured, and he was then left unconscious and bleeding on the street, surrounded by bottles which had been smashed over his head and body.' In his 'last glimmer of consciousness', Strathern continued, McGuire saw Wilkie standing over him 'pointing a sword or bayonet in his face'. As for Brown, he had struck McGuire on the head with a chisel.

Strathern acknowledged that McGuire had made a 'fair' recovery, but insisted nonetheless that the severity of the assault should not be underestimated: McGuire was 'still far from well, and it was probable that he would never be himself again. As the result of the assault his intelligence and memory had been impaired, he was dull, and was entirely different in manner to what he formerly was.' Turning to the difficulties faced by the judicial authorities, Strathern pointed out that:

> Many gangsters had been sentenced to terms of penal servitude for assaults, but it seemed impossible to curb or restrict their activities. Although the police knew perfectly well who [the] gangsters were, and what they were about to do, they could not interfere until something was done. Immediately after gangsters committed their brutal assaults they simply vanished.

Sheriff McDonald jailed Wilkie for two years with hard labour. Brown got eighteen months. The *Daily Express* labelled Wilkie a gangster of 'No Mean City'.

Wilkie and Brown returned to the sheriff court the following month to give evidence at the trial of the five remaining Derry Boys arrested following the assault on John McGuire. On this occasion, the prisoners denied the charges of riot and assault to the danger of life. The first witness for the prosecution was McGuire's companion, Archibald McLean, who identified the prisoners as Derry Boys. Under cross-examination by the procurator fiscal, McLean explained that he left the gang in August the previous year after he was 'lifted' (arrested) at Rutherglen during an Orange procession known as the 'Black Walk'. Asked to explain the purpose of the Derry Boys, McLean replied: 'They go about looking for fights with Catholics.' Their enemies, he added, included a gang of youths from Nuneaton Street known as the Nunney Boys, most of whom were Catholics. Members of the opposing gangs tended to be easy to identify: Derry Boys wore blue handkerchiefs, whereas Nunney Boys generally favoured green. McLean confirmed that the Derry Boys were aggrieved by his conduct since leaving the gang. 'I was seen talking to one of the Nunney Boys,' he explained. Press reports on the trial did not draw out the obvious implication: John McGuire was not a random victim.

James Wilkie and James Brown, both of whom were recalled from Barlinnie to testify, did their utmost to thwart the prosecution. In reply to the procurator fiscal, Wilkie told the court that the Derry Boys were 500-strong. One of their objects, he confirmed, was 'to follow the Orange bands'. Asked to recall the events of 12 January, Wilkie claimed that a group of Derry Boys had gathered at Bridgeton Cross that night with the intention of 'getting' John McGuire. According to Wilkie, McGuire had consistently provoked them – both by hurling abuse and by flaunting Celtic colours:

> McGuire was always shouting at us, and we objected to the colour of his scarf, which was green and white. We made it clear that if he did not stop wearing the scarf we would be after him ... I hit him over the head with a bottle, which broke, and Brown stuck a chisel into his head three or four times. When we left he was 'out'.

Having already been jailed for their parts in the assault, Wilkie and Brown had nothing to lose by insisting that they alone were responsible for inflicting McGuire's injuries. Questioned as to the identity of those who fled the scene alongside him, Brown replied: 'I am not giving anybody's name.' Despite repeated prompting by the procurator fiscal, Brown refused to budge. Sheriff McDonald found him guilty of contempt of court and added a month to his existing sentence.

Despite Brown's defiance, the gangster's code of honour was soon breached. John McGuire told the jury that one of the prisoners – William Greig – had hit him over the head with a bottle. Greig, in turn, claimed that he had been thirty yards away when the assault took place: he was close enough, however, to witness one of his fellow prisoners, Richard Clark, take part. Clark insisted that Greig's testimony was false. Relations between the prisoners were so fraught that police officers were stationed between them in the dock to keep the peace.

Detective Lieutenant Paterson of the Eastern Division told the court that Bridgeton and Dalmarnock were 'terrorised' by gangs. Paterson named the Baltic Fleet, the Shanghai Boys and the Chanty Boys along with the Derry Boys and the Nunney Boys. 'They prowled about the streets,' the detective complained, 'looking for isolated members of other gangs. When they found them it meant a kicking.'

In his summing up, Sheriff McDonald acknowledged that the jurors must have been shocked by what they had heard:

> Most of the jury would well remember the days of the Great War, and would have played a part in it. Even in those days, when many times they might have had cause, they never allowed their feelings to run riot so as to deal out such cowardly and terrible treatment as had been stated in the case before them.

The jury found four of the prisoners guilty. The case against the fifth, Robert Gardiner, they found not proven. Richard Clark and William Greig, whose counter-accusations had led to a furious mutual loathing, were both jailed for fifteen months with hard labour. The remaining prisoners, John Reddie and John Limond, got nine months. The trial prompted an angry editorial in the *Glasgow Herald*. 'It is high time,' the *Herald* asserted, 'that Glasgow as a city looked this depravity in the face.'

John McGuire's difficulties were far from over. At fifteen, he was a marked man. On Saturday 13 June, he suffered further head injuries in a street fight near his home in Nuneaton Street. Violence had flared in Dalmarnock for two nights. Four police officers were injured on the Friday – one was stabbed in the leg with a bayonet. On the Saturday, groups of young men gathered 'in larger numbers than usual' in Baltic Street as well as Nuneaton Street. Police reinforcements flooded the district, but could not prevent a series of running fights.

John McGuire appeared at Glasgow Sheriff Court for the third time in four months on 6 July. On this occasion he was in the dock as one of seven youths charged with riot and assault to severe injury following a fight on Glasgow Green on Sunday 5 April. The victim of the assault, Robert Smith, had been struck on the head and body with weapons that included a bayonet and a sword. Smith told the court that he had been at the Bridgeton Social Club in Kerr Street that afternoon when a group of young men set off for the Green to play football.

He decided to accompany them, as he was due to visit someone over on the South Side. When they reached the Green, a game was in progress between members of the Nunney Boys and 'the Dale Street crowd' (better known as the Shanley Boys). Smith claimed that he left his companions at the Green and headed for the South Side.

As he walked on alone he heard the noise of a fight breaking out: the Nunney Boys and the Dale Street lads had combined forces to attack his companions. Smith tried to run away, but the prisoners caught him: he was cut on the head, knocked down and kicked as he lay on the ground.

Smith presented himself as the chance victim of a brutal and unprovoked assault. He did not mention that the Bridgeton Social Club was run by Billy Fullerton, 'former leader' of the Billy Boys. Under cross-examination, Smith denied that he was a member of the Billies, the Derry Boys or the Orange Order. He did admit, however, that he had formerly 'played in a flute band in Cambuslang'.

The prisoners told a different story. Smith, they claimed, had arrived at the Green brandishing a sword and shouting: 'Get at the Fenian —!' According to Joe Mullen, aged seventeen, the Nunney Boys had only just arrived at the Green when they were attacked: 'We were only punting the ball about for a few moments when a crowd came from James Street. They were shouting: "Come on, the Derry Boys!"' Mullen recognised 'Seaman' Smith and a lad named Muirhead among the crowd. A second prisoner, seventeen-year-old Joe Farrell, corroborated Mullen's account.

Farrell's testimony exposed a trail of assaults stretching back for at least nine months. In November 1935, Samuel Kelly Campbell – a well-known Billy Boy – had been jailed for sixty days following a disturbance in Dalmarnock Road. The key witnesses at his trial included two women with the surname of Farrell, one of whom described how Campbell wielded a sword during the fight. Three days later, Joe Farrell was slashed on the face with a razor by a Derry Boy named Larry Gribben. Farrell identified Gribben as his assailant at the High Court on

4 March 1936. The only reason he could give for the attack, Farrell explained, was that his mother had testified against Campbell and his accomplice. Gribben was jailed for six months.

Farrell now claimed that he had been targeted by the Derry Boys – the Billy Boys' junior section – ever since he testified at the High Court. They had followed him about constantly, he complained, 'especially Smith and Muirhead'. On the afternoon that Smith was assaulted, sixty of them had rushed at him and his friends as they played football. Farrell claimed that he had fled. Asked whether it was 'unusual' to run away from an enemy faction, he replied: 'No, it happens every day in Brigton.' Faced with a bewildering array of counter-accusations, Sheriff McDonald had no easy task. Both sides issued allegations of witness intimidation – police escorted one terrified female witness onto a tram after she gave her evidence. The sheriff eventually found four of the seven prisoners guilty of the assault on Robert Smith. John McGuire and Joe Farrell were among them: McGuire was placed on probation for two years.

The Troubles of 'Killer' McKay

With Billy Fullerton away at sea from October 1935, Jimmy McKay of the Derry Boys assumed his mantle as the most notorious Protestant gangster in Glasgow's East End. On 1 July 1936, McKay was convicted of assaulting James Inglis during a fracas between the Derry Boys and the Kent Star in Orr Street, near to Bridgeton Cross. Inglis told the Eastern Police Court that he had been struck on the back with an iron file; his story was corroborated by a second member of the Kent Star, George McAulay, who claimed that his own 'bunnet' had been slashed with a razor during the fight. In his own defence, McKay testified that he had seen neither Inglis nor McAulay that night and had been nowhere near the scene of the fight. He also denied belonging to the Derry Boys, although he did accept that he was generally known as 'Killer' McKay. Bailie Peter Campbell fined McKay 21 shillings. To the consternation of the acting fiscal,

Superintendent Gordon, McKay was given eight days to pay. He paid it on the spot, even though – according to the police – his only income was poor relief of £1 per fortnight.

As he left the court, McKay was approached by a journalist from *Thomson's Weekly News*. Outside the dock, McKay was frank about his gang affiliation – 'Of course I am a member of a gang,' he admitted, adding for good measure that he was 'the leader of the Derry Boys'.

Like Billy Fullerton before him, McKay claimed to be a reluctant gangster. By his own account, he was trapped by his reputation and especially by his nickname:

> It's dogging me wherever I go. I've had several jobs, but whenever my employers heard me called 'Killer' they sacked me on the spot . . . No matter what part of Glasgow I go to I hear the phrase – 'There's Killer McKay!' I don't get a thrill out of it now. It gets my back up.

If he moved to another part of the city, McKay complained, he would be attacked every time he appeared in the street.

Asked to comment on the allegation that religious divisions were a convenient 'excuse' for fighting, McKay replied: 'That's wrong as far as I am concerned. I'm quite sincere about my religion.' He nonetheless admitted that gang fights had become a habit: they took place 'nearly every night', he explained. To restore the thrill of combat, gangs had resorted to cruising rival districts in motor cars, seeking to catch their enemies unawares: 'On Friday nights,' McKay explained, 'we hire a taxi and prowl round the districts where rival gangs hang out. Or sometimes they hire a taxi and come up to Bridgeton.' The reporter then asked about the prospect of imprisonment. McKay was adamant that short stretches in Barlinnie were no deterrent to gang members. 'Barlinnie doesn't worry us,' he insisted. What did scare McKay and his friends was the thought of penal servitude: Peterhead daunted them. The *Weekly News* seized on this admission for its headline: '**HOW I'D STAMP OUT THE GLASGOW GANGS. By "Killer" McKay of the "Derry Boys".**'

McKay was not alone in alleging that Glasgow's gangsters

had begun to use motor cars in their raids. Two weeks earlier, the *People's Journal* had reported how a 'large, dark coloured' vehicle had toured Bridgeton and Dalmarnock in the early hours of the morning of Sunday, 14 June 1936. The car's occupants – thought to be members of a gang – had attacked two young men in separate incidents. According to the *Journal*, this method of attack – while 'common in American gangster circles' – was new to Glasgow. The first victim, John Johnstone, was returning home after visiting a friend in Fordneuk Street when six or seven men got out of the car and attacked him. Johnstone was wearing a blue pullover at the time. 'It is possible,' he explained ruefully, 'that the men mistook me for someone else.' The intended target was probably David Turnbull, a prominent Billy Boy and a resident of Fordneuk Street. The second victim, twenty-year-old Robert Drew, was attacked after the same car pulled up in Swanston Street in Dalmarnock. Four men got out, and two of them approached him and requested directions to Boden Street, before asking: 'Is that where the Billy Boys hang out?' When Drew replied that he did not know, the men drew weapons from their pockets and struck him on the head. Boden Street in Dalmarnock was home to Eli Webb, former 'King' of the Billy Boys.

'Midsummer Madness'

Killer McKay was not the only frequenter of Bridgeton Cross brought before the Eastern Police Court on 1 July 1936. Two Billy Boys were convicted of breaching the peace following a clash between the Derry Boys and the Shanley Boys in Main Street, Bridgeton, at 11.30 p.m. the previous Saturday night. Plate-glass windows valued at £100 had been smashed during the fight. Superintendent Gordon, leading the prosecution, explained that the police had been expecting trouble that weekend: 'This is the regular midsummer madness which breaks out between the Orange crowd at Bridgeton Cross and a Catholic crowd at Dale Street at this time of the year, before the 12th of July.' Bailie Campbell imposed modest fines after the superintendent pointed out that both prisoners had been out of work for several years: one was on the dole, the other 'on the parish'.

The Orange Walk, held at Airdrie on Saturday 11 July, attracted 100,000 participants and fifty-eight bands from across the west of Scotland and Belfast. As the Glasgow processionists returned to the city, violence flared in Townhead and the Cowcaddens, but Bridgeton was calmer than anticipated. The *Eastern Standard*, happy to report a 'very quiet "Twelfth"', applauded both the preparations made by Superintendent Gordon, who had deployed 200 officers to keep the peace, and the processionists themselves for their orderly conduct. As the *Standard* acknowledged, however, a series of minor disturbances had broken out – in London Road, Gallowgate, the vicinity of Bridgeton Cross, Savoy Street and Old Dalmarnock Road. In Parkhead, James Freer and his daughter were in the middle of their evening meal when a stone came hurtling through the window of their house in Kinloch Street. The daughter ran outside to discover that the stone had been thrown by the follower of a flute band. Her protests met with 'filthy' abuse, and when her father leaned out of the window to see what was happening, more missiles were thrown at him. The Freers had been targeted on account of their green and white curtains. The band's followers had assumed – mistakenly, as it transpired – that the house's occupants were Catholics. In another misunderstanding, a Shettleston woman was struck by several processionists when she stepped out of her house in a green apron to watch an Orange band pass by. Her attackers did not realise that the woman was a Protestant: she had come into the street to cheer on her husband, who was a member of the procession.

The Derry Boys' religious convictions were called into question by Detective Inspector William McDougall at Glasgow Sheriff Court on 13 July. Speaking at the trial of seventeen-year-old Samuel Patrick, McDougall declared angrily: 'They profess to be Protestants but they do not know a thing about religion. It is a cloak for their activities.' Patrick was charged with breach of the peace and assaulting three police constables with a bayonet – one of the officers had been off duty for eleven days after Patrick stabbed him on the arm. The officers claimed that they had saved the prisoner from a hostile crowd in Nuneaton Street. 'He would not be here today if we had not taken him in,' one of them claimed. Patrick was dazed when he was taken into custody: a doctor who examined him found a large swelling on the back of his head, while his left eye and cheek were also badly swollen. Patrick alleged that his injuries had been inflicted by the police. By his own account, he was 'struck on the back of the head with a baton, knocked down and kicked all over the place by [the] policemen.' Sheriff Kermack jailed him for six weeks.

On Friday 17 July – four days after Patrick's trial – two youths took part in a bayonet duel in Nuneaton Street in Dalmarnock in front of a 300-strong crowd. Police managed to arrest one of the combatants, eighteen-year-old John Dey, but his opponent escaped. Dey, who was on licence from Borstal, lived with his parents at 233 Nuneaton Street. He had suffered three wounds to his hands by the time he was taken into custody. A search revealed a bayonet sheath down one of the legs of his trousers and a knife in his jacket pocket. Dey stood trial at the Eastern Police Court three days later. He confirmed that there were frequent fights between the Nunnies and the Baltic Fleet at the corner where he was arrested, but strenuously denied that he belonged to the Nunney Boys himself. Dey's father pleaded for his son to be given another chance: 'He is a good boy at home, and has never been in trouble of this kind before' – his son's previous convictions were for housebreaking. Bailie Armstrong jailed John Dey for sixty days, telling his father: 'I have never known a good boy to brandish a bayonet in the street.'

Taking their cue from police testimony in the city's courtrooms and judicial condemnations of hooliganism and sectarian bigotry, journalists rarely paused to consider the appeal of gang membership to youths in the city's poorer districts, yet occasional accounts of gang life from the inside could be found in weekly newspapers such as *Thomson's Weekly News*, which needed to find a fresh angle on incidents that had already been extensively covered by the daily press. In the midst of Glasgow's 'midsummer madness' in July 1936, the *Weekly News* followed up its profile of Killer McKay with an interview with a second – unnamed – gang member, published the day after John Dey's bayonet duel in Nuneaton Street. The anonymous gangster claimed that he and his friends laughed at the magistrates and ministers who tried to reform them. Giving up the gang, he explained, would mean giving up afternoons spent gambling on card games in their club room, not to mention nights spent hosting jiggings (unlicensed dances), for which they charged sixpence admission. As for the rammies (gang fights), these were something to look forward to – the combination of fear and excitement generated a thrill that nothing could diminish.

Towards the end of July, the Derry Boys were enraged when members of a rival gang disrupted a funeral at Sandymount cemetery. This sparked an intensification of street fighting in Bridgeton, with a spate of clashes between rival gangs reported during the first week of August. An irate local resident wrote to the Lord Provost of Glasgow, John Stewart, complaining that the trouble was being aggravated by inflammatory speeches 'of a so-called religious description' and demanding that steps be taken to deal with the problem. The Lord Provost forwarded the letter to Chief Constable Sillitoe, who responded by drafting extra officers into Bridgeton and promising that 'extra precautions' would be taken.

Ambushes were often mounted outside labour exchanges and public assistance (poor relief) offices. Gang members were frequently obliged to leave the relative safety of their own territory to join the queues at a 'buroo' (labour exchange) or attend interviews with parish officials. This immediately put them at risk, since their adversaries knew these schedules only too well. On the afternoon of 4 August, police dispersed a group of Derry Boys who had gathered outside the public assistance office in Broad Street, Bridgeton, to wait for members of a rival gang to emerge. Once the street had been cleared, the beleaguered claimants gathered their forces and marched forty-strong to confront the Derry Boys at Bridgeton Cross, where they challenged the Derry Boys with: 'Come on, you Orange —, if you have any guts!' Bricks and bottles rained back and forth between the opposing factions until two police patrol cars arrived. Two arrests were made. When the prisoners appeared at the Eastern Police Court the following morning, Bailie Matthew Armstrong fined them both 63 shillings, pledging to make Bridgeton Cross as safe for 'decent people' as middle-class suburbs like Pollokshields.

Armstrong was setting himself a hefty task. That night, Wednesday 5 August, the Derry Boys paraded through the East End with a flute band in protest at the disruption of the funeral the previous week. The demonstration provoked a series of confrontations with Catholic gangs, and a second parade was planned for the Friday night.

'Sillitoe's Cossacks'

On Friday, 7 August 1936, the Derry Boys paraded again. Led by the Star of the East flute band, they set out from Bridgeton Cross at 7.40 p.m. and headed east along London Road towards Parkhead singing party songs. The procession was 500-strong. Most of its members were displaying orange or blue colours, signalling their support for the Orange Order and Rangers Football Club.

Anticipating a renewal of the disturbances that had blighted the district throughout the week, the police had drafted officers from other divisions into the East End: patrol vans and motor cars were stationed in side streets off London Road and four mounted officers were positioned in Davaar Street in the shadow of Celtic Park, while three patrol vans, containing forty officers, drove along London Road past the procession and drew up at the junction of Davaar Street. They forced the band to halt, and Lieutenant James White asked its leaders where they were heading. When he received no reply, he told them that they were to go no further.

The crowd's mood changed in an instant. One of the band's followers lunged at a police officer with a spear, and stones were hurled at the police lines. White ordered his men to draw their batons and disperse the procession. As they waded in, the four mounted police charged the crowd from a side street – the Billy Boys' junior section was effectively ambushed.

Chief Constable Percy Sillitoe, who claimed to have authorised the police tactics, described the scene with some relish:

> Using their long riot batons, the police scattered the Billy Boys' parade from flute band to tail. The road was littered with casualties and the entire band, together with many of its followers, was arrested and charged with creating a disturbance and assaulting the police. There was, of course, a tremendous outcry against police brutality, and the mounted police were called 'Sillitoe's Cossacks,' but I was proud to stand by . . . White in what he did.

In fact, police made twenty-five arrests – fewer than Sillitoe implied, but more than enough to cause a stir in Bridgeton.

The police maintained a heavy presence in the district into the early hours of the morning. Members of local gangs had also expected trouble that night and they, too, took to the streets. At around 9 p.m., an off-duty detective constable was badly beaten in Shettleston Road. At 11 p.m. police dispersed a 300-strong crowd that had gathered at Bridgeton Cross. The crowd retaliated by attacking property, smashing the plate-glass window of a nearby shop. At midnight, with gangs still gathered at street corners, police patrolled the district in vans. Bottles were thrown at press reporters' cars as they, too, drove around the neighbourhood.

Twenty-four of those arrested during the Derry Boys' parade appeared at the Eastern Police Court on the morning of Saturday 8 August. Six of the prisoners stood in the dock with their heads heavily bandaged. Bailie Matthew Armstrong remanded them in custody.

Despite additional police being drafted into Bridgeton for the remainder of the weekend, a series of disturbances were reported around Bridgeton Cross: members of the Derry Boys took part in at least four of these incidents on the Saturday alone. Killer

McKay was arrested at 10.20 p.m. following a fight at the Cross involving around thirty men.

The following day's *Sunday Mail* featured an article by Bailie Armstrong denouncing the gangsters of Glasgow's East End as 'religious illiterates'. Armstrong called for mandatory prison sentences for gang members – since fines would be levied from local shopkeepers – and for police patrols to be trebled in the afflicted areas. Armstrong concluded with a plea for religious tolerance: 'Let us be done once and for all with this degrading conduct.' His plea was ignored. That afternoon saw a series of parades around Bridgeton and Dalmarnock by flute bands and their followers. The processions were monitored closely by the police, but were still punctuated by minor outbreaks of disorder: in Baltic Street, rival gangs fought with sticks, batons and iron bars, while a police constable was struck by a bottle flung from the window of a tenement as he escorted a band along Arcadia Street.

War on the Gangsters

Extra police were placed on duty both inside and outside the Eastern Police Court in Tobago Street on Monday 10 August. Hundreds of people gathered to seek admission to the public gallery, and when the door to the courtroom was opened shortly before nine o'clock, the court officer was swept off his feet as members of the crowd swarmed inside. Most of those clamouring for admission were denied entry; they gathered in groups outside the court and waited for two and a half hours until the proceedings were over.

Inside the court, Bailie John Young dealt with more than fifty people arrested during the weekend's disturbances. Lieutenant White led the prosecutions. Among those jailed were ten Derry Boys, including Killer McKay. Lieutenant White gave McKay a dramatic introduction, citing the gangster's recent interview in *Thomson's Weekly News*. 'This is the famous "Killer" McKay, as he is known in the district [of Bridgeton Cross]. He has everyone afraid of him.' McKay was jailed for thirty days.

More gangsters appeared at the court over the course of the week. Faced with a succession of Shanley Boys, Chanty Boys, Fanny Boys and Tiger Boys, Bailie Young began to issue sentences of sixty days' hard labour – the maximum penalty at his disposal – for even minor breaches of the peace. The Star of the East bandsmen and their followers apprehended following the rout by 'Sillitoe's Cossacks' were admitted to bail of £10 each on 17 August – within two days, the combined bail costs of £240 had been paid by 'four persons who wish to remain anonymous'. This testifies either to the Derry Boys' prowess as racketeers or more likely, given the amount raised at such short notice, to surreptitious support for the Billy Boys' junior section among wealthier sections of the Protestant community in Glasgow.

At the instigation of the Lord Provost, John Stewart, a special subcommittee of Glasgow's magistrates was established on 11 August 1936 to address the problems posed by youths carrying lethal weapons 'for criminal purposes', along with 'the question of gangs in the city'. The subcommittee consisted of the senior magistrate, Bailie Joseph McClounie, and four of his colleagues – including Bailie John Young, who had presided at the Eastern Police Court the previous day. This declaration of war on the city's gangsters was greeted with considerable acclaim by the local press.

The Lord Provost re-ignited concerns with racketeering, telling the *Evening Citizen* that the magistrates should stop imposing fines in gang cases. The *Scottish Daily Express* launched its own investigation. Its reporter, having been 'admitted into the inner councils of a leading gang', disclosed that: 'One gang even retains the services of a law agent, who receives a weekly sum of about £2 for his services. His job is to defend the gangsters when they come up to court.' After detailing how weekly payments were extorted from shopkeepers, cinema managers and publicans, the *Express*'s investigator claimed that:

In one area of the East End there are about one hundred shops, two cinemas, and a dozen public houses which pay for the 'protection' of the gangsters. The fund of the gang is not allowed to fall below a weekly total of £30. The police have continually tried to stamp out this form of racketeering. But no shopkeeper will come forward to give evidence. He might as well give up business in the area for ever.

The reporter did not name the gang in question, but another of his 'revelations' – that gang funds were used to support the wives of those who were jailed – had been made more than once by Billy Fullerton.

Following discussions between the magistrates' subcommittee and Chief Constable Sillitoe, Glasgow's magistrates issued a resolution on 31 August declaring their intention to jail all of those convicted of charges involving the carrying or use of lethal weapons. Any person convicted of offences with a 'gang element' would likewise be jailed without the option of a fine. Support for the abolition of fines was unanimous: those magistrates who had initially expressed unease at the loss of judicial discretion fell in line, mindful no doubt of the widespread clamour in the press for a 'real clean-up'. The magistrates now appealed to the press to avoid giving undue publicity to gang cases and, in particular, to refrain from publishing the names and addresses of those convicted.

The only magistrates to voice their disapproval at the resolution were those who believed it did not go far enough. Sensing an opportunity to embarrass the Corporation's ruling Labour group, Bailie John Murdoch, Moderate (Tory) councillor for suburban Langside, told the *Evening Times* that the magistrates ought to have petitioned for the powers to impose flogging in 'serious' cases:

We have no desire to have Glasgow ranked on the same level as Chicago. While our gangsters stop short of the use of revolvers and 'Tommy' guns, they adopted weapons that make one 'grue' at the injuries involved. Any man who is prepared to ram a bayonet through another man's stomach or who snaps off the end of a bottle and jams the broken part into his opponent's face has only a brute mind and should be treated as a brute.

The demand for the 'cat' (flogging) met with a mixed response. The *Glasgow Herald*, in particular, was not convinced of its utility as a deterrent.

Press responses to the magistrates' resolution were largely favourable. The *Scottish Daily Express*, which had urged support for the measure, noted approvingly: 'It is going to be a harder world for Glasgow gangsters.'

The magistrates' new policy was informed by a report on the gang problem and the measures that might be taken to address it prepared by Chief Constable Sillitoe. The terms of Sillitoe's report were discussed at a meeting of the magistrates held on 25 August, but its contents were never made public. Sillitoe was generally hungry for publicity, and might have been expected to drum up approval for his plan to suppress the gangs of Bridgeton, but perhaps he was embarrassed by the reported escalation of gang warfare four years into his term of office. Alternatively, Sillitoe's methods might not have borne public scrutiny.

Sillitoe's strategy for dealing with Glasgow's gangs had combined intelligence-gathering with the increased use of motor vehicles and radios and an unflinching resort to force. Police violence was overshadowed, according to Sillitoe's biographer, Art Cockerill, by more dubious methods:

[He] was known to have had some gangsters committed for observation to a mental institution where they were confined for a period beyond their sentence. They were then released on the threat of being permanently certified should they for any reason be returned to jail.

By Cockerill's account the threat was sufficient to cause some gangsters to leave Glasgow permanently. These stories – divulged more than a decade after Sillitoe's death – suggest that his methods for dealing with Glasgow's gangsters went far beyond the bounds of legality. Suffice to say, no hint of such unorthodox tactics was forthcoming in reports of Sillitoe's meetings with the city's magistrates in August 1936.

Heightened concern with the gang menace led to renewed

interest in the role of young women within the conflicts. The *Sunday Mail* published the 'amazing confessions' of a self-styled girl gangster, who told how she had joined an East End gang the previous year after she began courting one of its members. The gang's ten female members apparently performed a set of distinctly feminine duties: they helped to maintain the gang's meeting places, each of which held a store of weapons; they acted as spies, allowing themselves to be 'picked up' by members of opposing gangs in order to learn their plans; they delivered challenges to rival mobs; and accompanied the male members of their own gang when they went to dance halls in search of more spontaneous confrontations. The interviewee, who gave her age as eighteen, described how she served as 'mother' to the gang, and regularly bandaged their wounds after battle. She also looked after the wives of the gang's members during their pregnancies, helping with household chores and child-minding. While she did not take part in their fights, the *Mail* implied that the gang could barely function without this 'Pretty Gang "Mother" Who Dresses Wounds, Tends Babies And Guards An Arsenal.'

The *Mail's* interviewee spoke on condition of anonymity, but some young women earned considerable local notoriety in the wake of the upsurge in sectarian skirmishing. The Derry Boys' most prominent female follower, Isabella Scott, was arrested on the night of Friday 3 July when fighting broke out after an Orange flute band passed through Main Street in Bridgeton. Scott claimed that she 'had been set upon because she had been wearing an orange-coloured scarf.' Her companion, Jane Watson, was arrested alongside her after 'shouting remarks about the Pope' and lunging into the fight. Both women were fined 10 shillings at the Eastern Police Court.

The Derry Boys were not without their defenders on Glasgow Corporation, even if support for the Protestant gangsters had to be voiced obliquely. The week before the trial of the Star of the East bandsmen and their followers commenced, Bailie Muir Simpson – Moderate (Tory) councillor for the Sandyford ward on the western fringe of Glasgow city centre – gave a remarkable speech to members of the city's Progressive Synagogue. Simpson went out of his way to praise the Derry Boys' founders, the Brigton Billy Boys:

These Billy Boys are a most remarkable lot. When King George and Queen Mary were here they took charge of the East End of Glasgow. If anyone had dared even to suggest that the King and Queen were not the most desirable persons to visit Glasgow they would have been slashed. These men are intensely loyal. They do not wreck buildings, although they may break windows in the excitement.

Simpson told his audience that, as a member of the Corporation, he 'appreciated' the fact that the city's Jewish community did not have their 'pocket[s] tampered with'. This extraordinary comment obscured the persistent targeting of Jewish traders in the vicinity of Bridgeton Cross. So far as the shopkeepers were concerned, the Billy Boys might have been patriots, but they were anti-Semites, too. Simpson's declaration shows that some of Glasgow's Tories still valued the Bridgeton gangsters' fervent loyalty to church and constitution, even if the Billies could no longer openly act as stewards at the party's election meetings.

The bandsmen and their followers stood trial at Glasgow Sheriff Court on 14 September, more than a month after the ambush by 'Sillitoe's Cossacks'. Twenty-three men faced charges of committing a breach of the peace. One young woman appeared beside them on the same charge: Isabella Scott. None of the male prisoners was a prominent gangster – only four of them had previous convictions.

Breaches of the peace were seldom tried before a sheriff, but this was no ordinary case: more than 100 witnesses were due to testify, and the proceedings were expected to last over a week. In a highly theatrical display, weapons alleged to have been brandished by the crowd had been fixed to one of the walls of the courtroom: spears, wooden batons, iron bars and pieces of lead were displayed, alongside instruments and uniforms belonging to members of the band.

Police evidence was led by Lieutenant White, who insisted that his men only drew their batons after they were attacked. Several other officers corroborated White's account. Defence witnesses, however, told an entirely different story. Four women made startling allegations of police brutality, telling how the band had stopped playing and their leader was in the process of turning them around when the police charged. The women claimed that they had witnessed the mêlée as passers-by, but had themselves been assaulted as the police ran amok. Mrs Mary Rennie insisted that the disturbance had been caused by the police: 'They were hitting everybody, and people were shouting from their windows, "The poor bandsmen, the poor bandsmen!"' Mrs Watson of Marquis Street alleged that she had been holding her child in her arms when a policeman struck her with a baton. Sixty-year-old Mrs Margaret Usher alleged that she had been standing at the corner of the street when the police charged. Two officers had grabbed her and pinned her arms behind her back. She was then bundled into a police van and told to lie on the floor. At the police station, she had protested that she had nothing to do with the band and was told to 'Get out.' Asked whether it had been a brutal attack, she replied: 'It wasn't half. I have never seen such a brutal attack in my life. It was worse than the General Strike.'

Sheriff Kermack paid little heed to the women's testimonies. Describing the prisoners' conduct as a deliberate challenge to the forces of law and order, he found nineteen of the male prisoners guilty and jailed each of them for one month. He found the case against the remaining four men not proven. He convicted Isabella Scott, but deferred her sentence of fourteen days' imprisonment for six months, declaring that he was unwilling to send a 'foolish girl' to prison. Evidently perturbed by the appearance of a young woman in the dock, Kermack commented that Scott 'had somehow or other got mixed up in the disturbance'. He appeared to be unaware of Scott's history of getting 'mixed up' in sectarian skirmishes.

Kermack appeared untroubled when faced with two conflicting accounts of what had taken place on the night of 7 August, saying that he considered the discrepancies in police evidence to be only 'as one expected from honest witnesses in such circumstances'. The evidence for the defence, by contrast, 'did not impress him as genuine'. Turning to the allegation that the police had used unwarranted violence, Kermack declared that: 'The use of force by the police is a necessary matter, and when used, has to be used in a determined manner. How far it is to be used must be, to a large extent, left to the discretion of the officers in charge at the time.' If the sheriff was aware of Sillitoe's determination to beat the gangs at their own game, he clearly approved.

All Quiet on the Eastern Front?

The day after the trial ended, Sheriff McDonald addressed a dinner at Glasgow's Trades Hall. McDonald had tried several batches of Derry Boys earlier in the year, and he now proclaimed that he 'knew for a fact that the police had got the matter of the gangs well in hand, and would deal early and effectively with it.' So far as he was concerned, the 'gang menace' was over.

The sheriff's speech was widely reported in the local press; his 'timely tribute' to the police was echoed by the *Scottish Daily Express*, which offered its own endorsement of Sillitoe's regime. The *Express* insisted that: 'Glasgow citizens should ignore the mud that is slung at the police from time to time. There is NO finer force in Britain. None is better administered. The leaders trust their men, the men trust their leaders.' To the publicity-conscious chief constable, the *Express*'s paean provided ample vindication of the decision to meet force with force in Bridgeton. Finally, it appeared, the stigma of *No Mean City* was beginning to fade.

Just three days later, the *Sunday Mail* seized on an admission by a police superintendent that his officers only dared to enter some districts at night in pairs, such was the danger posed by local gangs of youths. To the *Mail*, this was still further evidence that McArthur and Kingsley Long had been right all along. The superintendent's caution was vindicated as the *Mail* went to press: a lone policeman was bitten on the hand and kicked on the head when he remonstrated with a disorderly youth in the Garngad in the early hours of the morning.

The following month saw a renewal of the long-running feud between the Derry Boys and Catholic gangs in Bridgeton and Dalmarnock. On Saturday 3 October, two police constables watched from the safety of a darkened signal-box as a fight erupted in Baltic Street, close to Bridgeton Cross. The officers subsequently described how they watched a crowd of between fifty and sixty men march along the road at around 11.10 p.m. shouting 'Up the Shanley Boys!' and 'Up the Nunnies!' The crowd halted at the corner of Albany Street and shouted for the Derry Boys to 'Come out and fight!' The challenge was soon answered, leading to a running fight amidst a hail of bricks, bottles and stones.

Faced by the combined forces of local Catholic gangs as well as heightened police attention, the Derry Boys remained undaunted: members of the gang were jailed at the Eastern Police Court over the course of the month following a series of clashes – in Glasgow Green, outside the League of the Cross hall in Muslin Street and at Bridgeton Cross. Percy Sillitoe, it appeared, still had some way to go before he repeated his triumph as a gang-buster in Sheffield.

15

The 'Don Quixote of the Gangs'

Jurgis Stankawicus was born into a family of Lithuanian migrants in Hamilton, twelve miles south-east of Glasgow, in 1912. His father, a coalminer, returned to Lithuania in 1917 – war had tested his loyalties, and his home nation triumphed over his ties to his family. Jurgis and his two siblings were left with their mother, Vera, who was forced to apply to the parish authorities for poor relief. In 1919, Vera set up home with another miner, Franciskas Sedekis, to whom she bore her fourth child the following year. In October 1925, Franciskas left her. Vera moved to Glasgow, settling with her children in Savoy Street in Bridgeton, and applying once more to the parish for subsistence.

Jurgis, now aged thirteen, briefly attended Sacred Heart School in Savoy Street, where he quickly became known as 'George Stankovitch', or 'Stankie'. Vera, who spoke little English, struggled to control him, and George grew into a daring and persistent housebreaker. As clumsy as he was bold, he served repeated terms of penal confinement: spells in reformatory school and Borstal were followed by six months in Barlinnie, in 1933. In January 1935, he was jailed for two years after pleading guilty to four counts of housebreaking and one of assaulting two police officers. His hauls were modest, mainly comprising small items of jewellery such as bracelets, brooches and rings, but they were spread across the Glasgow conurbation: two of the houses burgled were in Cambuslang, six miles outside the city. His friend and accomplice in the Cambuslang expedition, Archie McLellan, got six months.

Stankie and the Billy Boys

During his short spells at liberty, Stankie hung round with the Savoy Arcadians. The Arcadians, who took their name from the row of shops outside which they congregated, were Catholics. They were too few in number to take on the Billy Boys en masse, but they fought frequent, small skirmishes in Main Street, the thoroughfare running south from Bridgeton Cross. As a game fighter, and a Catholic, Stankie was a welcome recruit into the Arcadians' ranks.

Stankie, however, was no respecter of the sectarian divide. His partner-in-crime, Archie McLellan, was a Protestant. More damagingly in the eyes of his associates, Stankie was spotted drinking with members of the Billy Boys in public houses around Bridgeton. His liaisons did not go unnoticed.

On the night of Friday, 23 October 1936, Stankie was seen accompanying two Billy Boys to Bridgeton Cross. The following night, he met a group of Arcadians in a billiard hall in Main Street. An argument erupted when 'Big Dick' McGuinness challenged Stankie over his association with the Protestant gangsters. Stankie explained himself – what he said to appease McGuinness is unclear – peace was temporarily restored, and by eleven o'clock that night, the party had moved on to Jim Farrell's tenement house in nearby Reid Street. Stankie joined in the carousing for an hour before suddenly leaving, returning ten minutes later armed with a baton and challenging Dick McGuinness to fight with the cry, 'Who's a Billy Boy now?'

The baton was wrestled out of Stankie's hands and he was quickly ushered out onto the stairway. The door was slammed behind him. He had brought two friends – including Archie McLellan – with him, and they stood by as he began to kick at it. Suddenly, the door flew open, the occupants of the house rushed out and Stankie and his companions tore down the staircase under a hail of bottles. As they ran out into the street, Stankie again challenged Dick McGuinness to fight, only to be confronted by half a dozen opponents. In the frenzied assault that followed, Stankie was punched, kicked and struck repeatedly on the head with a poker. His cheek was ripped open by a knife before the blade was plunged into his chest, narrowly missing his heart.

Passers-by carried Stankie into a nearby flat, where an elderly neighbour tried to stem his wounds before Stankie was taken by ambulance to Glasgow's Royal Infirmary. Detectives interviewed him shortly after he arrived at the hospital: Stankovitch named Dick McGuinness, Dan McGuinness, Jim Farrell and Robert Longmuir as his assailants. He told the detectives how 'Dick McGuinness stabbed me with a knife about the heart.' Asked what had caused the assault, Stankovitch replied: 'The McGuinnesses thought I was too friendly with some of the Billy Boys.' Six hours later, George Stankovitch was dead.

Eastern Division detectives arrested the four men named by Stankovitch in the early hours of Sunday morning. Interestingly, Longmuir was a Protestant. He had grown up in Savoy Street, and the Arcadians – less doctrinaire than the Billy Boys – had accepted him into their ranks. William 'Chin' Brannigan was also taken into custody; Stankovitch had identified him as a member of the crowd that had rushed out of the Farrells' flat. Farrell, aged twenty-six, was married with three children. He had just been released from Barlinnie after serving sixty days for his part in an ambush on members of the Billy Boys' junior section.

On the Monday morning, all five prisoners appeared at the Eastern Police Court, where they were charged with murder. They were remanded in custody and made a series of court appearances as Crown officials in Edinburgh prepared the case against them. The hearings drew large crowds, with members of the Savoy Arcadians occupying prominent positions in the public galleries. The prisoners' demeanour outraged court reporters. They exchanged waves with their friends and affected boredom with the legal proceedings, yawning and smiling as the charge against them was read out.

Dan McGuinness, the eldest of the prisoners, was a steel erector by trade. He 'had to' get married at the age of twenty-six in

November 1929: the first of his two daughters was born five months later. In July 1934, he was arrested – along with his brother, Dick – for breaching the peace. His wife was forced to apply for parish relief. She reported that her husband had been unemployed for four years and stated that the family's sole source of income was his unemployment allowance of 32 shillings a week. This was half the average wage of a manual worker in Britain during the mid-1930s. She applied again for parish relief when her husband was arrested for murder in October 1936. By this time, she reported, Dan McGuinness had been continuously unemployed for seven years – the duration of their marriage.

Jim Farrell, in whose house the fatal row between Stankovitch and the McGuinness brothers had erupted, was born in 1909. He got married in 1928, just two weeks before the birth of his first child. When his daughter fell ill with pneumonia in June 1930 he applied for her to be admitted to Glasgow's Eastern District Hospital. The family home in Reid Street was visited by an inspector from the Public Assistance Committee, whose terse case-notes recorded: 'He has been idle since 1928. In receipt of 28 [shillings] weekly, UAB [unemployment allowance]. Last employed with Glasgow Cotton Spinning Co[mpany], Bridgeton, for four years. No other income.' In 1931, Farrell worked for three months at the Palacerigg labour colony, where his pay was 37 shillings a week. By November that year, he was once more in receipt of an unemployment allowance: 29 shillings a week to provide for his wife and their three children. By 1936, his allowance had increased to 35 shillings a week.

As the five Savoy Arcadians languished on remand, journalists on the best-selling Scottish weekly papers quickly got to work on the human-interest story behind the latest 'Scottish Stabbing Tragedy'. The *People's Journal* and *Thomson's Weekly News* traced Stankovitch's 'sweetheart', Elizabeth Rankin, to her tenement house in Finnart Street in Bridgeton. Both papers carried Elizabeth's account of her ill-fated courtship on Saturday 31 October – the *People's Journal* splashed the tragic love story across its front page, complete with photographs of Elizabeth, George and his friend, Archie McLellan.

Their 'strange' romance – as the *Weekly News* termed it – had begun when Elizabeth was introduced to George in December 1934. She had found him to be 'a wild fellow, but very likeable', and he had promised to 'turn over a new leaf' for her. Four weeks later, he had been jailed for two years for offences committed before the couple had met. They had already discussed marriage, and he wrote to her from prison asking her to wait for him. She had agreed, and their relationship had blossomed through the exchange of love letters. A month before his release, he had written to propose marriage, promising to 'settle down and go straight'.

After George returned to Bridgeton on 15 September 1936, he and Elizabeth had seen each other every other night. They were due to marry at New Year and their plan – at his instigation – was to make a fresh start away from Glasgow. 'Now all my dreams have been smashed,' Elizabeth declared, her anguish compounded by the fact that George had asked to meet her on the night he was fatally injured – she had declined, as she had already promised to visit her brother in Polmont Borstal, near Falkirk. 'How I wish now I had seen him,' she told the *People's Journal*. 'He would be with us today.'

The trial of Stankovitch's assailants at the High Court in Glasgow commenced on 14 December. Lord Justice Clerk Aitchison, Scotland's second most senior judge, presided. The four men initially named by Stankovitch – Dick and Dan McGuinness, Jim Farrell and Robert Longmuir – were charged with murder. Five of those present at the party at Farrell's flat on the night of 24 October appeared as witnesses for the prosecution. Two of them, William McSwiggan and John O'Neill, admitted under cross-examination that they were themselves members of the Savoy Arcadians, and both gave graphic accounts of the violence inflicted upon Stankovitch. Their willingness to testify is significant, given the gangs' code of honour: for McSwiggan and O'Neill to testify against their fellow Arcadians suggested that the killing of George Stankovitch had been too much even for gangland to stomach.

In a widely reported exchange, Lord Aitchison questioned

McSwiggan about the enmity between the Arcadians and the Billy Boys. McSwiggan admitted that fights between members of the two gangs were a regular occurrence. The judge asked, 'What are the fights about?' McSwiggan gave a one-word answer: 'Religion.' Lord Aitchison was appalled. He demanded: 'Is that your idea of religion?' McSwiggan replied, 'Yes.'

The medical evidence presented in court was gruesome. Professor Burton of Glasgow University, consultant to the Royal Infirmary, stated that the knife with which Stankovitch had been stabbed 'must have been driven home with absolute savagery' – it was the wound to the chest that had proved fatal. Burton added that Stankovitch's skull was unusually hard; it was heavily scarred, but numerous old wounds had effectively healed. During the fatal assault, Stankovitch had been clubbed repeatedly 'with a degree of violence that would have broken many a head'.

No witnesses were called for the defence. Counsel for the McGuinness brothers questioned the reliability of the eye-witness evidence before making a desperate appeal to the jury's social conscience:

> The jury had to keep in view the unfortunate social circumstances in which these sad events occurred. Given better conditions and better opportunities, these sorts of happenings in Glasgow streets might never occur at all.

Jim Farrell's counsel told the jury that Stankovitch had returned to his client's flat to provoke a fight. Lord Aitchison agreed. Describing Stankovitch's behaviour on the night of 24 October as 'outrageous', the judge concluded that: 'Stankovitch in one sense was the author of his own death.' He steered the jury towards a verdict of culpable homicide – the equivalent of manslaughter in the Scottish legal code – on grounds of provocation.

As the packed courtroom waited for the jury's decision, Catherine McGuinness – whose sons Dick and Dan would face the gallows if the jury went against the judge's advice – paced back and forth along the street outside in a ritual that she had followed for the past four days. A reporter from the *Scottish*

Daily Express observed: 'She could never pluck up the courage to go inside. From 9.45 until 5 each day she walked up and down the pavement. Pale, trembling, moist-eyed.' Elizabeth Rankin, similarly unable to face the ordeal of the courtroom, stayed at home to wait for the verdict. As the trial drew to a close, the *Express* sent a journalist to her tenement house in Bridgeton, where the 'auburn-haired girl' of twenty-seven, as the *Express* described her, was busying herself with housework and sewing.

Taking their cue from the judge, the jury found the prisoners guilty of culpable homicide. Before pronouncing sentence on the defendants, Lord Aitchison warned them that: 'But for the fact of provocation, you would this moment be under sentence of death.' Their ages offered no grounds for leniency: the youngest, Robert Longmuir, was twenty-four – a year older than Stankovitch – while the eldest, Dan McGuinness, was thirty-two. Their records, too, counted against them. Dick McGuinness, who had inflicted the fatal blow with a knife, had been jailed in 1932 after stabbing two men in a street fight. On that occasion, the judge observed, his punishment had been a mere three months' imprisonment.

Lord Aitchison sentenced Dick McGuinness to ten years' penal servitude; his brother, who had pinned Stankovitch down as the fatal blow was struck, would join him for seven years. Longmuir got four years for wielding a hatchet in the affray. Jim Farrell, who had struck Stankovitch on the head with a poker, got three. Catherine McGuinness learned her sons' fate from one of her friends, who dashed outside the moment their sentences had been pronounced. Reporters watched as she broke down in 'a storm of weeping' before relatives led her away. Elizabeth Rankin heard the news from a posse of boys who ran straight from the High Court, their shrill voices piping through the streets of Bridgeton: 'Ten years for McGuinness!'

Lord Aitchison was all too aware of the damage being done to Glasgow's reputation by sensational reports on the trial of the Savoy Arcadians in the English press. 'It is a lamentable thing,' he declared, 'that this great city of Glasgow, whose people are known the world over for their character and worth, should have its good name besmirched by these nefarious and infamous gangs.' At the close of the court, Lord Aitchison claimed that the gangs were a stain on an otherwise law-abiding city: 'I have been looking into the figures and I find that if you take out the gang crime from this city, the amount of serious crime in Glasgow, in relation to its size and population, is probably less than any other city I know.' This was a purely rhetorical exercise: there was no distinction in judicial statistics between gang crimes and 'ordinary' offences. Nonetheless, it enabled the Lord Justice Clerk to rail against Glasgow's gangs while simultaneously defending the integrity of the city.

'All his pals got a share of the spoil'

For readers of the Scottish national press, the death of George Stankovitch was a compelling, human drama. The *Scottish Daily Express* cast Stankie as a remarkable romantic hero: the 'Don Quixote of the Gangs'. This scene-setting owed much to *No Mean City*, but the *Express* added a few fictions of its own, christening Stankovitch the 'most feared gangster in the East End' – a title to which it is doubtful Stankie himself had ever aspired – and describing his killers (one of whom was nine years older) as his former school 'playmates'. The newspaper hyperbole did not end there. In between his frequent spells of imprisonment, the *Express* told its readers, Stankie had 'lived gaily, [and] fought gaily on behalf of anyone who sought his aid.' In a lengthy front-page report published the day after the trial at the High Court ended, the *Express* noted that few people had died in Glasgow's gang conflicts: 'Hundreds of scarred faces in the East End . . . tell of the ferocity with which the razor and broken-bottle war has been waged in recent years. But, strangely, few have died. The razor kings are skilled in the art of mutilation without killing.'

To the *Express*, Stankovitch was an intriguing product of his environment. He had grown up 'among the criminal and desperate class inside Borstal institutions, prisons, and (between times) in the dark alleys, corner dives, and lower haunts of the East End tough guys' and had spent almost eight years behind bars between the ages of eleven and twenty-three. Yet despite the poverty of his upbringing, his physique was remarkable. He stood a little over five feet tall, but he was broad shouldered and powerfully built – on one occasion, he had thrown off a pair of six-foot policemen when they attempted to arrest him. The doctors who examined his body declared that they had never seen 'a body more perfectly developed, or a frame naturally sturdier.'

The *Express* painted Stankovitch as a chivalrous figure who lived by a strong moral code. One of his associates told an *Express* reporter how Stankie had kowtowed to no one and had always fought fairly, without weapons, confident that he could smash any opponent in a square-go. (The *Express* chose not to remind its readers that Stankovitch had been armed with a baton on the night he was killed.) The associate also testified to Stankovitch's generosity: 'Whenever Stankie had pulled a job, all his pals got a share of the spoil.' An Eastern Division detective told the reporter that Stankovitch 'wasn't what we would call a "clever" criminal' – he was easily apprehended because he never covered his tracks. But the police respected him on account of his physical strength and his eschewal of weapons: 'He was a strong wee lad, and by his own lights, clean.'

'The Right Man For The Job'

In an accompanying editorial, the *Express* called on Glasgow's police and magistrates to join the 'war' on the gangs. The call was loudly echoed by Glasgow's evening papers.

The police were quick to respond. The following day, the *Express* carried a photograph of Chief Constable Percy Sillitoe on its front page, alongside the headline '**SECRET PLAN TO WIPE OUT GANGS**', while readers were assured that the city's gangsters feared the 'tall, burly, rugged-jawed' police chief. Sillitoe's 'plan', which was already in operation – and far from secret – was to meet force with force. Paid informants ensured that the police were tipped off ahead of impending gang fights and a flying column of officers in patrol cars was dispatched to break up the disturbance and make arrests at the scene. (In reality, of course, these tactics were nothing new.) Following the intense spate of gang fighting in the East End that summer, it was Sillitoe who had requested that every gang member convicted in the city's police courts should be sent to prison without the option of a fine. The magistrates had agreed. They had also endorsed Sillitoe's request that gang cases should be afforded no publicity. The killing of George Stankovitch had generated unwelcome headlines, but the magistrates were adamant nonetheless that the campaign against the gangs was working. Sillitoe's officials insisted that it had already 'cut down East End gangsterdom by half.'

Taking its cue from Lord Aitchison, the *Sunday Post* railed against the 'Slur on Glasgow's Good Name' cast by the city's gangsters and had no doubt that Chief Constable Sillitoe was 'The Right Man For The Job'. He had rid Sheffield of its gangs before moving to Glasgow, and the police were doing sterling work under his command, only to find their efforts undermined by undue leniency on the part of some of the city's magistrates. Judicial leniency was misplaced, warned the *Post*, since: 'The Glasgow gangster is a creature of undeveloped mind. His body has grown to manhood, but his thoughts and ideas have remained those of a child. One thing he does fear is severe punishment.'

Eager for a fresh human-interest angle, the *Sunday Mail* interviewed Mary Farrell, whose husband, Jim, had been sentenced to three years' penal servitude for his part in Stankovitch's death. 'Jim is not a gangster at heart,' Mary insisted. In her account, he was a family man, who took a great interest in their three children. She insisted that Jim had only been in trouble once before, and when he had returned from prison, he had told her that they needed to move away from Bridgeton – three weeks later, he was facing a murder charge.

Her dreams of a new house and fresh start on hold, Mary Farrell faced the bleak prospect of raising her children for three years on her own. She still fervently hoped for a better future for her family. The *Mail* issued an appeal to the people of Bridgeton in her name: 'If every wife and sweetheart made up their minds . . . I believe we could get the men to give up the gangs. To those who think gang fighting is great, that cadging round shopkeepers to pay fines is fun, that it's smart to be a big man before the "Molls," I say think of my home now.'

Chicago in Scotland

Sensational coverage of the Stankovitch case in English newspapers caused yet more dismay in Glasgow. The London edition of the *Daily Express* repeatedly invoked the fictional portrayal of the city's gangs by McArthur and Kingsley Long: this was a 'Midnight Drama in No Mean City'. The conviction of the four Savoy Arcadians – or 'gang kings', as the *Express* styled them – was presented as incontrovertible proof of the veracity of the novel. The *Daily Mirror*, by contrast, once again raised the spectre of Chicago in Scotland, claiming that the gangs 'prey on shopkeepers and stall holders for protection money in the method of Chicago gangsters, and fights take place when one gang accuses another of trespassing on its territory.' The *Mirror* again pointed out that the police were hampered by the fact that offenders were hard to trace, as their victims were generally too scared to go to the police.

The conclusion of the trial prompted a flurry of articles in the mass-circulation Sunday newspapers on 20 December. The *Sunday Graphic* dispatched a female correspondent to Glasgow. She talked to police officers and Corporation officials before visiting Bridgeton to interview George Stankovitch's sweetheart, Elizabeth Rankin. Her report on **'GLASGOW'S WEAKLING GANGS'** made grim reading. She found a city leading a 'double life'. Venturing east from the city centre, she found, 'Great tracts of the city are infested with gangs, and you have only to walk down the closely packed, evil-looking slum areas to sense very strongly the presence of something utterly at war with the ordered life of a community.'

Her characterisation of the city's gangsters was based on a

mixture of police information and her own observations of the East End. She was shocked by the physical condition of the youths she saw on the street corners: 'They are mostly under-sized, pale and under-nourished, with the peculiar bow-legged jaunty walk which follows rickets during childhood.' A police officer told her that most gang members were aged between fifteen and twenty-five. He added: 'Their mentality is low, almost to the point of deficiency. They are unemployed, and 60 per cent are unemployable.'

Within Bridgeton, however, she heard a different story: people insisted they were desperate for work, but none was to be had. When asked George Stankovitch's occupation, Elizabeth Rankin had laughed bitterly: 'He had no work.' The *Graphic*'s correspondent found conditions there 'indescribably tragic'. She declared: 'It is a vicious circle of environment creating evil, which in its turn crushes the will or the power to escape from the environment.'

Forced to live 'like rats', she concluded, the youth of the slums had banded together to 'get their own back at life'. Strength in numbers gave them 'truculence, arrogance and bravado'. Their Chicago-style rackets were on a small scale since 'there are not sufficient brains among them to organise in the grand manner'. Although gang membership enabled unemployed youths to overcome their deep 'self-pity', their outlooks remained 'warped'. The *Graphic*'s report made no mention of the religious affiliations among the East End gangs, merely noting: 'They delude themselves as to their motives both for their internal unity and their enmity with other gangs.' Prompted by the police, the *Graphic* demanded firmer action on the part of Glasgow's magistrates: the 'decent' people of the East End, cowed into a 'dour, sullen reticence', had suffered too long already.

The socialist-leaning *Reynolds News* confirmed that Glasgow's gangs were some of 'the best-organised, most powerful and most dangerous' in Britain. *Reynolds*'s correspondent identified the East End and South Side of the city as the headquarters of five major 'terror organisations' and scores of minor ones. The police were well aware of the scale of the problem; on Chief Constable Sillitoe's instruction, they had compiled a dossier on 'every person known to associate with gangs' in the city. Sillitoe was determined to crush the gangs, and *Reynolds*'s headline – '**TERROR GANGS TO BE WIPED OUT**' – was echoed in the *News of the World*. In explaining Glasgow's gang menace, *Reynolds* told a very different story from the *Sunday Graphic*'s – in which sectarianism was entwined with party politics. Noting that Stankovitch had been a member of a sectarian gang, *Reynolds* observed that 'most of these roughs claim to be adherents of religious faiths . . . and police are afraid that a big sectarian battle is brewing'.

Meanwhile, Patrick Dollan, the treasurer of Glasgow Corporation, told *Reynolds* that the furore over the city's gangs was being used to discredit the Labour Party, which had won control of the Corporation for the first time in 1933. Dollan had no doubt been stung by Unionist (Tory) claims that the city magistrates – most of whom were elected councillors – ought to have pressed for the reintroduction of flogging for those gang members convicted of crimes of violence. (No such step had been taken during the long years of Unionist rule.) Dollan was further aggrieved that Independent Labour Party councillors had opposed a proposal to curb parades by sectarian marching bands. He complained to *Reynolds*'s correspondent: 'It is suggested that Labour is not doing its best to deal with this trouble. It is an attempt to introduce politics into the treatment of social offenders and drag the law into party politics.'

An unnamed magistrate hinted that there were darker forces at play, too. In what appeared to be a thinly veiled reference to the Unionist-dominated opposition group on Glasgow Corporation, he declared: 'I really suspect that there are some agents provocateurs – subagents of a certain political party – who could tell a good story.' Links between the Billy Boys and the Unionist Party in Glasgow had surfaced in the press during the 1931 general election campaign; now, it was alleged, the city's gangs were being used to undermine the fabric of local democracy. As Dollan put it: 'We will not tolerate Chicago law, whether in the East End or the West End.'

The commotion over the Stankovitch case was not confined to the popular press. The weekly political magazine, the *Spectator*, commented that the revelations at the High Court provided ample vindication of *No Mean City*. As the *Spectator* saw it, 'Glasgow's good name is at stake. That great city cannot afford the reputation of the Scottish Chicago.'

The prominent Scottish journalist and novelist, George Blake, was moved to respond. Blake conceded that Glasgow had already been twinned with Chicago in the British imagination, albeit in his view on the basis of 'only a few very lurid facts'. Blake claimed that in Glasgow's population of over 1 million, there were no more than 500 gangsters – this was one-tenth of the figure an anonymous detective had supplied to the *Daily Mirror*.

Blake saw Glasgow's gangs as a product of industrialisation. More precisely, they were its casualties, herded together in a small, dark corner of the city. 'There are always bugs in slums,' he observed tartly. 'Glasgow's gangsters are bugs fed up with sticking to the wall.' Blake doubted the sincerity of the gangs' professed religious affiliations; nor were their conflicts racial ones: their members were of Lowland and Highland Scots, Southern and Northern Irish, Italian, Polish and even English descent – 'a pretty bunch of society's castaways'. Rather, he concluded, gangs were 'a simple social phenomenon, a matter of health and housing.' Their members had an 'environmental need to express themselves'. Gangster movies 'did the rest'.

Blake also noted how much gangsters enjoyed their notoriety. They were fashionably dressed 'on the thirty-shilling scale', their 'lingo' was highly topical, and they preened themselves in front of their molls: 'They love the publicity their clumsy exploits earn them. They are playboys in the shabby melodrama of their own creation.' And while their 'clan warfare' was funded by the petty terrorism of small traders:

> Glasgow is not Chicago for the plain reason that its gangsters are dull creatures and lack an economic motive for their acts. Capone after all had a certain air of spaciousness about him. A Latin, he could do things on the grand and gilded scale. His

exploits in Big Business had a certain grace and grandiose artistry. The Glasgow gangster is much more like the prototype bug – a dull and repulsive fellow.

Capone at least qualified as a romantic outlaw; his Glasgow counterpart, in Blake's view, failed even that test.

Like the *Sunday Graphic*'s correspondent, Blake was adamant that the gangster was a distinctive physical type: 'He is, like "Stankie," almost invariably undersized, but with great breadth of shoulder as a rule: the typical anthropoid development.' Stankovitch was a perfect example: 'He was undersized, but he had the physique of a gorilla.'

Blake's mixing of animal and insect metaphors belied wider ambivalences in commentaries on the gangs. Their members – simultaneously bug-like, rat-like and ape-like – were both underdeveloped in terms of height, yet overdeveloped in their fearsome brute strength. Deeper ambivalences were at play here, too: gangsters were casualties of the social system, yet in the more apocalyptic commentaries, threatened to devour it.

Glasgow's Fury

As interest in the London press subsided in the week following the trial of Stankovitchs killers, Glaswegians were left to assess the damage to the city's reputation. The controlling Labour group on Glasgow Corporation bitterly resented what it saw as unwarranted attacks in English newspapers. Particular ire was aroused by a 'slanderous' report in the *News of the World* which claimed that a constant procession of men 'with broken heads and slashed faces' at Glasgow's Royal Infirmary bore witness to the city's 'razor kings'. The spectre of *No Mean City* – already invoked by the *Daily Express* and the *Spectator* – loomed large here, too. Councillors hinted at a libel action against the *News of the World* ahead of a meeting of the Labour group on 23 December.

In the event, the treasurer, Patrick Dollan, emerged from the meeting with a statistical riposte. He told the *Scottish Daily Express*: 'Glasgow is as well behaved as any other community in the country. There is an average of only eight convictions a day in respect of crimes committed in this city, which has a population of 1,200,000.' Dollan was adamant that, following stern action by the police and magistrates, the city was 'more free from gangs than it had ever been in its history', while the remaining sporadic outbursts of disorder were 'far removed from the typical everyday life of the Glasgow working class'. Recognising the damage caused by the furore over the Stankovitch case, the city's magistrates had resolved to meet early in the New Year to consider the initiation of 'propaganda' to counter the belief held in England that Glasgow was a 'gangster-ridden city'.

Dollan's comments were widely reported in Glasgow's newspapers and in the Scottish national press. However, the Corporation still did not escape criticism. The pro-Tory *Evening Citizen* declared that responsibility for Glasgow's 'evil, though unmerited, reputation' lay squarely with the bailies, especially with those elected to serve as magistrates. According to the *Citizen*: 'Town councillors need not blame the English newspapers, and they need not seek for a remedy outside the walls of their own council chamber and their own courts.'

The debate on the causes of gangsterdom was brought to a head by George Buchanan, Independent Labour Party MP for the Gorbals. Opening a House of Commons debate on housing conditions in Glasgow on 18 December (the day after the four Savoy Arcadians were convicted at the High Court), Buchanan declared:

> I read today with considerable pain, as I am sure all honourable Members did, of the trial in the City of Glasgow. I am not going into the question of whether the sentences are heavy or light, but it is a terrible thing. I would, however, ask those who criticise Glasgow, whether these things happen in the West End of the city or even in the more comfortably off districts where the well-to-do artisan and the [Corporation] workers live. Gang fights like that are unknown in the better-off quarters. They never take place in Pollokshields or the West End; they take place in places where the conditions are shocking and squalid.

If slums bred gangs, as Buchanan asserted, it was no surprise that Glasgow was Britain's 'gang' city. A nationwide government survey had recently revealed that 200,000 Glaswegians were living three or more to a room – the benchmark for overcrowding laid down by the 1935 Housing Act.

The Commons debate generated further adverse publicity both for Glasgow as a city and for the ruling Labour group on the Corporation. *The Times* observed: 'Glasgow has achieved an unenviable pre-eminence in housing failure.' The newspaper was quick to blame the city's socialist administration, pointing out that the rate of municipal house-building had slowed since Labour took control of the Corporation three years earlier. Within Glasgow, a fierce debate erupted once again on the causes of the gang problem – and the possible solutions.

Buchanan's claim that gangs were a product of the city's slums was fiercely attacked in sermons preached on 20 December. Reverend John Macmillan, Church of Scotland minister of St James's at Glasgow Cross, firmly rejected Buchanan's diagnosis, insisting that: 'Bad housing never made a gangster.' Reverend Macmillan claimed that he had found 'some of the best people in the worst houses'. For him, the roots of the problem lay in a lack of parental discipline, exacerbated by drunkenness and the corrosive influence of American gangster films. Macmillan's prescription was corporal punishment for the young, reinforced by religious indoctrination among the poor:

> Bad public-housing and bad picture-housing, combined with care-less parenthood, make the gangster. If I were a Town Councillor I would order a big supply of good, thick straps and send them to every home. Parents could make early and practical use of them. There should also be compulsory Sunday schools or Bible classes in the poorer districts.

To Macmillan, religion offered a solution to the gang problem. To the Savoy Arcadians – like the Billy Boys – it was grounds for enduring hostility.

16
Britain's 'Gangster City'

In the wake of the trial of the Savoy Arcadians in December 1936, the Lord Provost of Glasgow, John Stewart, led the campaign to repair the damage to the city's reputation. In a series of widely reported speeches delivered during the spring and summer of 1937, Stewart insisted that firm action by the civic authorities had effectively curbed the gang problem. In March, he told the annual meeting of the local branch of the Discharged Prisoners' Aid Society that: 'Gang warfare in Glasgow seemed to have passed its worst stages.' Three months later, he proclaimed that cooperation between the magistrates and the police had 'pretty well killed the gang warfare that was so prevalent in the East End of the city'.

Stewart was assisted by the editors of some of the city's newspapers. The *Evening Citizen*, for example, acceded to the request by the magistrates for the press to refrain from publishing the names of those convicted following disturbances involving gangs. The *Citizen*'s readers learned only that 'young men' had been jailed. Police officers, too, adjusted their courtroom rhetoric: those dragged before the magistrates were still labelled 'hardened' gangsters, but they were increasingly depicted as the ringleaders of isolated disturbances.

There are grounds for treating the Lord Provost's claims with caution, as the streets of the East End were by no means pacified. Feuds between sectarian gangs persisted in Bridgeton and the Calton, and spilled over into Mile End, Whitevale and Parkhead. Nor were these reported incidents isolated ones. As a young man told the Eastern Police Court in March 1937: 'There has been fighting in Calton for weeks.' And while the East End remained the epicentre of gang strife, further outbreaks were reported across the city's poorer districts, from the Gorbals to the Garngad, and from Anderston to Mile End.

'Everyone ran when they saw a gang coming along the street'

The latest phase in the war on the gangs failed to bring peace to the streets of the East End. The principal target of police operations in the Eastern Division – the Derry Boys – remained the most active and, by all accounts, the most dangerous of the city's gangs. One of their regular forays into the Calton from their base at Bridgeton Cross, on the night of 25 April 1937, led to the appearance of two Derry Boys at Glasgow Sheriff Court. The scene was vividly described by a passer-by: 'A crowd of young men [came] rushing along Stevenson Street down to London Road, shouting "Get the Fenian." Some had bayonets, and others had iron bars and pieces of wood.' Another witness told how the Derry Boys cleared the street: 'Everyone ran when they saw a gang coming along the street, the children knowing to run upstairs.'

A police constable told the court that just as the Derry Boys had once formed the junior branch of the Billy Boys, they now had their own junior section – known as the Mickey Boys. (The provenance of this name was not explained.) In any event, the constable added: 'The junior gang was now more or less merged into the Derry Boys.' John Sweeney, known as 'the Bull', and James Reddie, were jailed for three months for their part in the disturbance.

Again following in the footsteps of the Billy Boys, some of the Derries served repeated stretches in Barlinnie with only brief spells at liberty in between. Richard Clark, jailed for fifteen months in April 1936, was sentenced to another sixty days' labour in December 1937. On the latter occasion, he had been 'shouting party epithets' and 'We are the Derry Boys!'

The Derry Boys inevitably spawned imitators across the East End. The previously little-known Fanny Boys from the Whitevale district to the north of Bridgeton gained considerable notoriety in 1937 when they took to marching through the streets on Friday and Saturday nights armed with wooden batons and iron bars, singing 'The Sash My Father Wore' and hurling threats and abuse at 'the Papes'.

While the Billy Boys featured less prominently in reports of gang fighting by the late 1930s, the gang's leading members continued to take part in sectarian skirmishes in the East End. In June 1937, David Turnbull was jailed for twelve months after a man was slashed on the neck with a razor during a fight between the Billy Boys and the Shanley Boys outside the Premierland boxing stadium in Bridgeton. The victim, a man named John Brady, required five stitches. The Shanley Boys got their revenge on 27 August, when they ambushed the Billy Boys in Bridgeton's Main Street. Billy Fullerton was among those injured when their adversaries pounced with bottles, hammers and batons. Three Shanley Boys were jailed for their part in the attack: among them was John Brady.

By the late 1930s, Samuel Kelly Campbell of the Billy Boys had become a marked man – much as Fullerton had been at the beginning of the decade. Campbell – who formed part of the Billy Boys band that travelled to Belfast in July 1935 – was jailed for twelve months the following year for assault by cutting. By June 1938, he had provoked such enmity that twenty men turned up at his house in Bonnar Street in Bridgeton determined to 'get' him. One of the would-be assailants was arrested at the scene. Thomas Wylie, aged twenty-six, admitted to breaching the peace when he appeared at the Eastern Police Court on 12 July. He justified his actions by stating that Campbell had previously threatened him with a bayonet. Campbell was himself arrested three days later: he got thirty days for assault. In November that year, he was jailed for five months following yet another conviction for assault. He was now aged twenty-four, and married with three daughters. It was his tenth stretch in Barlinnie.

Despite the enduring sectarian tensions in Bridgeton and surrounding districts, by no means all of the gang violence in Glasgow's East End was shaped by 'religious' affiliations. During the autumn of 1936, two of the leading Catholic gangs of the East End – the Shanley Boys and the Norman Conks – fell out after an argument in a Bridgeton billiard hall. The Shanley Boys ran down Main Street shouting '— the Conks!' They then felled two of their opponents, one of whom was taken to hospital by ambulance after being struck on the head with a bottle. This sparked a bitter feud between the two gangs, which spanned the following two years. Two men were arrested during one Thursday night clash at the corner of Norman Street and Poplin Street in August 1938. More than a hundred people took part in the fight. A local resident told the Eastern Police Court that 'it was a usual occurrence for a crowd from Dale Street [the Shanley Boys] to invade Norman Street.'

In the Gorbals, the Beehive Boys fought a series of pitched battles at their adopted corner of Thistle Street and Cumberland Street, some involving as many as 300 combatants. The gang's members – like their counterparts in the East End – continued to trade on their notoriety, not least to run protection rackets. Peter Williamson and Dan Cronin, in particular, added to their already fearsome reputations towards the end of the decade. Now approaching his mid-thirties, Williamson was jailed for twelve months in August 1937 for an assault with a broken bottle, while Cronin got twelve months for an assault in a Gorbals public house in November that year. Five months after his release, he was involved in an altercation in a local dance hall, when members of the Beehive Boys objected to a 'coloured' man named Alfred Wheeler dancing with one of their sisters. Wheeler was struck with a bottle and kicked. When two bystanders tried to intervene, they too were attacked: one lost an eye when he was stabbed with a broken bottle. Cronin, whose 'deplorable record' was detailed in court, got another twelve months for his part in the affray.

It was now more than ten years since the emergence of the Billy Boys signalled a new degree of organisation and menace among Glasgow's 'gangsters', yet there was still no consensus among the police and judiciary on the causes of gang formation and conflict. Superintendent Thomas Crawford, who retired in

March 1937 after more than thirty years' service in the City of Glasgow Police, was asked for his views on the gangs of the East End. He told the *Eastern Standard* that while he deplored the bands of hooligans in the Calton and Bridgeton, their existence was a 'reflex' of the lives of their members: 'They are unemployed and have nothing to do but hang about the corners – and then one crowd fights with another. That is about the problem.'

Unemployment and poor housing conditions were still also widely cited as the causes of gangsterdom, but some members of the judiciary still saw neither as grounds for diminished responsibility. Three months after Superintendent Crawford gave his interview to the *Eastern Standard*, Sheriff Robertson reacted angrily when the agent for two Derry Boys, both of whom were unemployed, pleaded for leniency on the grounds that 'their environment had been against them and the poor housing conditions led to their mode of life.' The sheriff replied bluntly: 'It was not the housing conditions that made the gangster, nor was it poverty that made the thief.'

Nor, still, was there any consensus on the vexed issue of how to deal with the city's gangs. As J. D. Strathern, procurator fiscal for Glasgow since 1918, told a parliamentary inquiry into corporal punishment in 1937:

> In Glasgow many cases occur in which extreme and brutal violence is used. It is a common experience that gangs [associate] together for the definite purpose of committing acts of wanton personal violence. They are armed with razors, bayonets, knives and similar weapons.

Strathern was adamant that lengthy sentences of imprisonment and penal servitude had done little to deter the city's gangs and insisted that flogging was the only solution. The former Lord Justice Clerk, Lord Alness, agreed. In a speech delivered in London in December 1937 he declared: 'A gangster, whether in Chicago or Glasgow, was always a bully, and a bully was always a coward. He could understand one language, however – the language of pain.'

Alness admitted that a reign of terror had prevailed during his term of office:

> The most disquieting feature of the situation was the difficulty of getting witnesses to give evidence regarding these affrays. They were afraid to speak. I was told by a responsible official in Glasgow that 100 cases of razor-slashing were reported in a year, and that only in four [cases] was evidence available which warranted a prosecution.

These hawkish views, however, were out of line with mainstream opinion, both within Glasgow and further afield. In the wake of the Stankovitch case, the editors of the city's three evening newspapers had all pressed for stiffer prison sentences rather than the 'cat', while both the *Evening Citizen* and the *Evening Times* identified economic conditions – especially unemployment – as a principal cause of Glasgow's gang problem.

The parliamentary inquiry concluded with the unanimous recommendation that birching and flogging ought to be abolished as judicial punishments.

'Where people are afraid to walk alone'

Despite the Lord Provost's best efforts, the combined impact of *No Mean City* and the Stankovitch case was to make even relatively minor disturbances in Glasgow national news. As Charles Oakley – then a consultant to the Scottish Development Council – pointed out, sensational reports of street fights in Bridgeton and the Gorbals became so common in the London press in the years 1937 to 1938 that a private inquiry was begun in Glasgow into the source of the stories.

A survey of the *Daily Mirror* suggests that Oakley's concern was well founded: the 'Glasgow gangster' was by now a stock figure in British crime reporting, his weapon of choice the razor. In January 1937, the *Mirror* reported on a Metropolitan Police operation to clear London of 'crooks and undesirables' ahead of the coronation of George VI. The featured pair of villains included 'ex-Glasgow gangster' Peter Brewer – 'only twenty-two, but known already as a dangerous and vicious criminal.' He had served two terms of imprisonment and now faced three years' incarceration following 'an armed hold-up in Chicago-gangster style' in which a South London businessman was robbed of £50. Detectives had traced Brewer without difficulty after the victim described the scimitar-shaped scar stretching from his assailant's temple to his neck. Brewer, the *Mirror* noted by way of explanation, 'came from the Glasgow slums'.

Even Brewer's exploits paled in comparison with those of the man the *Mirror* termed an 'ex-bookmaker and Glasgow razor-slasher', Alf Pellow. In 1932, Pellow had been identified as the ringleader of the serious disturbances in Barlinnie. Now based in London, Pellow headed a nine-strong team of safe-crackers known to detectives at Scotland Yard as 'the Gelignite People'. Five of the nine were from Glasgow. According to the *Mirror*: 'They were the first . . . men in this country to imitate the methods of American safe-crackers – gelignite, detonator and fuses.' Pellow was sentenced to five years' penal servitude at the Old Bailey in June 1937.

In the national press, no feature article on Glasgow was complete, it seemed, without a gangster. In February 1938, the *Mirror* set out to uncover the human stories behind the exodus of young people from Glasgow in search of work. Their determination and courage drew keen praise, but so did the resourcefulness of a shopkeeper from Bridgeton – 'the district where people are afraid to walk alone for fear of razor gangs'. The shopkeeper's only son had joined a gang and took to 'prowling the streets ready to fight and smash his enemies'. She had managed to save £30 from her meagre profits and paid for him to make a new start on condition that he moved south. 'He's doing alright now,' reported the *Mirror*. Safely removed from the 'evils' of Bridgeton, he was working in a Birmingham steel works and soon to be married. The *Mirror* concluded that Glasgow should be ashamed of its gangs. 'The police must know who the ringleaders are,' it helpfully pointed out. 'They ought to round them up and the judges should give them really severe sentences. That would soon put a stop to their filthy way of living.' The Lord Provost, John Stewart, must have been furious, and Chief Constable Percy Sillitoe equally so.

The *Mirror*'s labelling of Glasgow reached a high point in March 1938 when it carried a brief report on the appearance of thirty gangsters – members of the Derry Boys, the Nunney Boys and the Baltic Fleet – at the city's Eastern Police Court. The *Mirror*'s report was less remarkable than the accompanying headline: '**GANGSTER CITY'S WEEK-END TERROR**'.

City of Empire

An historian Irene Maver has pointed out, it was partly in response to the negative stereotypes engendered by *No Mean City* that vigorous attempts were made to promote economic regeneration in Glasgow during the late 1930s. The key event was the Empire Exhibition, mounted in Bellahouston Park, which ran from May to October 1938. The focal point of the 175-acre site was a spectacular modernist tower, which, as Scottish Development Council consultant Charles Oakley noted, 'rose like a gleaming silver pencil, 300 feet above Bellahouston Hill.' With Palaces of Industry and Engineering, as well as Art, a new concert hall and the biggest amusement park in Europe, the exhibition was designed to bring new business to Glasgow and the rest of Scotland, and to bring visitors in their millions: more than 12 million people visited. (The organisers had anticipated still greater numbers, but their hopes were doused by the worst summer in West Scotland for more than a hundred years.) Asked to reflect on what the exhibition had done for Glasgow, Councillor Patrick Dollan replied on behalf of the Corporation that the city was now 'better understood and appreciated not only in the British Commonwealth, but in every country in the world.'

As visitors flocked to admire the displays at Bellahouston Park, the former South Side Sticker Paddy Carraher generated precisely the type of headlines that the exhibition's organisers were striving to supersede. At around one o'clock in the morning on Sunday 14 August, Carraher stabbed a soldier named James

Shaw in the neck following a drunken 'needle' at Gorbals Cross. He stood trial for murder at Glasgow High Court on 12 September. Following a clear steer from the judge, Lord Pitman, the jury convicted Carraher not of murder, but of culpable homicide – as the journalist George Blake observed, the judge 'had much in mind the factor of drink'. Carraher was sentenced to three years' penal servitude.

The Troubles of Bernard Kiernan

In the records that survive from the late 1930s, only glimpses of the suffering endured by the parents of youthful gangsters are seen. For Bernard and Julia Kiernan of the Calton, their anguish was two-fold as both their sons – Bernard Jr and Francis – joined the Kent Star.

For Bernard Jr, gang membership had disastrous consequences: his notoriety was such that he was unable to find work and he remained dependent on his parents well into his twenties. He was jailed for two months in the summer of 1931 following a confrontation with the Billy Boys, but worse followed in the spring of 1934, when both sons were arrested following the death of Jimmy Dalziel in the 'Dance Hall Tragedy' at the Bedford Parlour in the Gorbals. They were released within a week, but Bernard Jr was subsequently named as Dalziel's killer by two of their co-accused. The statement was subsequently withdrawn, but only after it had been reported in the *Scottish Daily Express*.

In September 1938, Bernard Sr applied to poor law officials for his son's 'removal'. The relieving officer's' case-file recorded:

> The father said he [Bernard junior, aged twenty-five] was dangerous to stranger[s]. Dr McGregor visited and certified the boy as a 'dangerous lunatic'. The father and mother on looking at the certificate and seeing the word asylum refused to allow him to go. After several unsuccessful attempts in persuading them to let him go I asked the father to sign a declaration relieving the Dept of all Responsibility.

Bernard Jr remained in the care of his family. His parents were not wealthy – Bernard Sr earned £3 a week at Sir William Arrol's engineering works – but they were able to provide for their son's day-to-day needs. However, they could not ensure his safety on the streets.

Bernard Jr was a marked man. On Saturday 5 November, he was taken to hospital after he was badly injured in a street fight – his father told a relief officer that his son had been 'assaulted by a gang'. He remained in hospital for two weeks. By February 1939, he was in hospital again – the case-file does not record why, but notes that his father was to be charged 5 shillings per week for his care.

Finally, Bernard Kiernan Jr was admitted to Stobhill Hospital for 'mental observation' in January 1940. Two months later, he was certified insane and admitted to Woodilee Asylum.

Since being named as the man who murdered Jimmy Dalziel in 1934, Bernard Kiernan Jr had barely worked. His association with the Kent Star had initially provided comradeship and adventure, but it brought danger and repeated injury, too. His parents' concern is only fleetingly captured in the records of his father's dealings with poor-law officials. The family's pain can only be imagined.

The Killing of Felix Valaitis

Felix Valaitis, alias Smith, was born in 1910. His parents were Lithuanian migrants and they settled in Savoy Street in Bridgeton, close to the parents of George Stankovitch. Their son was well known on the streets of the East End by his nickname 'Felix the Pole'. Tall, fair and powerfully built, he worked as a coalminer and was renowned for his exceptional strength as well as his gameness as a fighter. He married Elizabeth Miller at Sacred Heart in Bridgeton in June 1934, but lost his job the following year. In September 1936, he and Elizabeth moved to a room-and-kitchen house in the quieter East End district of Shettleston. This might have heralded a fresh start, but Felix spent much of his time back in Bridgeton, leaving his wife and two daughters at home while he hung around his old haunts.

At around midnight on Saturday, 1 May 1937, Valaitis was slashed on the face when a group of thirty to forty Derry Boys made a raid on the corner of Dalmarnock Road and Pirn Street. A doctor at the Royal Infirmary stitched the wound, which left a scar from Valaitis's ear to his mouth. Valaitis, who was a Catholic, named his assailant as William Bradley, a notorious Derry Boy. However, when the case came before Glasgow Sheriff Court, it was found to be not proven.

The following year, Valaitis was charged with breaching the peace, malicious damage and assaulting the police following a disturbance at a Bridgeton public house. The publican claimed that Valaitis had come to his premises after closing-time 'at the demand' – he wanted four bottles of beer. The publican had refused and barricaded the door, sparking a fracas in which Valaitis was arrested, only to be rescued by his friends. It was subsequently alleged in court that 'Valaitis was trying to terrorise a new licence-holder so that he would give the accused drink whenever he wanted it.' Valaitis was jailed for thirty days.

On Saturday, 17 December 1938, Valaitis left home at midday and made his way to Bridgeton. He stayed out for the remainder of the day, having a meal with his parents at five o'clock before touring local public houses and billiard halls. By ten o'clock, he was 'winding up' everyone he came across. Shortly after ten, he headed for the Hampden billiard saloon in Dalmarnock Road with three companions. At the corner of Nuneaton Street, Valaitis stopped to confront an accordionist who was playing 'Afton Water' outside a public house as he 'disliked the tune'. Around twenty Nunney Boys were standing nearby. Four of them stepped forward and Valaitis had a 'needle' with twenty-one-year-old John Dey – a prominent Nunney Boy, despite his denial under oath two years previously. They traded punches and Dey knocked Valaitis down.

Valaitis went to fetch a cleaver from a house in nearby Pirn Street and returned to challenge the Nunney Boys, aiming a blow at Dey's friend, nineteen-year-old William Turner. Turner dodged the blow and lashed out twice with a butcher's boning knife, slashing Valaitis's throat and then puncturing his lung. Valaitis died on the spot and Turner and Dey fled. As they started to run, Turner thrust the knife into the hands of a startled sixteen-year-old passer-by named Helen Kay.

A reporter from the *Scottish Daily Express* called at Valaitis's house in Pettigrew Street in Shettleston the following day. His wife, Elizabeth, told the journalist that her husband had been a kind-hearted family man and loving father. The reporter also called on Valaitis's mother. She, too, had only glowing words for a devoted son. Felix the Pole might have been a well-known fighting man and a minor racketeer, but he was an affectionate husband, father and son, too.

Turner and Dey stood trial for murder at the High Court in Glasgow. Lord Aitchison, who had tried the killers of George Stankovitch at the same court in December 1936, once again presided. Turner admitted a reduced charge of culpable homicide, pleading self-defence. Lord Aitchison accepted the plea: he was swayed by the police investigation, which confirmed that Valaitis had wielded a cleaver during the fight. He sentenced Turner to five years' penal servitude. Dey, who admitted a charge of assault, was jailed for twelve months.

No mention was made in court of the gang affiliations of any of those involved, and the local press did not report the killing as a 'gang' case. Perhaps as a result, the London-based national newspapers barely covered it at all. Despite the obvious resonances with the Stankovitch case two years earlier, the killing of Felix Valaitis was effectively downplayed as a news story. Here, perhaps, was some small vindication of the efforts by Glasgow's civic leaders to lessen the magnifying effect of *No Mean City*.

Jim Farrell's Revenge

Jim Farrell was twenty-seven years old when he was jailed for three years in December 1936 for his part in the killing of George Stankovitch. While he served his time in the convict prison at

Peterhead, his wife Mary moved to Springburn, a tenement district known for its locomotive works rather than its gangs, where she brought her children up 'on the parish'.

Jim Farrell returned to Glasgow following his release from Peterhead in March 1939 and found work for the first time since 1928, albeit on wages of just £2 and 13 shillings per week. His desire to rebuild his family life was, however, overshadowed by his determination to exact revenge on one of his former friends, William McSwiggan, whose testimony at the High Court had helped to convict Stankovitch's assailants.

His opportunity came on the night of Friday 7 July. McSwiggan had spent the evening drinking in a public house in Main Street in Bridgeton and, as he made his way home, Jim Farrell stepped out of a crowd of men gathered at the corner of Baltic Street and Nuneaton Street and struck him on the head with a bottle. McSwiggan fell to the ground. Farrell's younger brother, Joe, joined in the assault, and the two of them dished out a terrible kicking. By the time they had finished, McSwiggan was unconscious. The Farrell brothers were soon taken into custody. Mary Farrell renewed her application for outdoor relief for herself and her children the following day.

On 9 August, Jim Farrell stood trial at the High Court in Glasgow for the second time. On this occasion, his brother appeared in the dock alongside him to face the charge of assaulting William McSwiggan 'to his severe injury'. They denied the assault, and protested furiously that the prosecution witnesses were 'all liars'. The jury was more swayed by the testimony of a doctor from the Glasgow Royal Infirmary, who told the court that McSwiggan had almost died from his injuries, and they took little time to find the two brothers guilty.

The defence counsel described Jim Farrell's lust for revenge as 'very wrong, but very understandable'. The judge, Lord Russell, urged Jim Farrell to learn 'the folly and weakness of giving way to uncontrollable impulses'. He then jailed Jim Farrell for four years, which meant 'going north' to Peterhead

– again. Joe Farrell would go to Barlinnie for eighteen months. Reporters noted that 'a woman in court' burst into tears on hearing the sentences. If it was Mary Farrell, her anguish was only too understandable.

17
From Gangsters to Heroes?

It was to be the Second World War that did more than the combined efforts of churchmen, police officers, magistrates and judges to disrupt the gang conflicts that had spiralled in Glasgow from the late 1920s onwards. In Bridgeton, it was said that no fewer than half of the Derry Boys presented themselves en masse to enlist at the drill hall in Main Street on 4 September 1939, the day after war was declared.

Around 150,000 Glaswegians served in the armed forces during the course of the conflict. Members of the Billy Boys and Derry Boys served alongside their former adversaries from Catholic gangs such as the San Toy and the Cheeky Forty. To the local press, this was a striking manifestation of the wartime spirit of national unity. Throughout Britain, social commentators such as George Orwell and J. B. Priestley proclaimed, class divisions had been subsumed by a patriotic determination to 'pull together'. In Glasgow, hostility between Protestant and Catholic street gangs likewise appeared to have been set aside.

War cast the city's fighting men in a new light – as brave patriots rather than vicious gangsters. Their combative spirit was thought to bode well for their contribution to Britain's struggle against the forces of Hitler and Mussolini, while even the gangster's dexterity with the razor became the subject of humour rather than disdain. As R. E. Porter observed in the *Glasgow Eastern Standard* in July 1940:

> Most of the gangsters who terrorised the district and earned Glasgow the name of 'The Chicago of Scotland' are in the army. By all accounts many of them have turned out to be excellent soldiers. Some are earning promotion.

There's a story that one of these has become a sergeant. During a scuffle he lost his rifle. In a hand-to-hand fight his men noticed that he was using a razor. A German attacked him. Panted a corporal, 'Thought you were hot stuff, sarge? You haven't put a mark on that Boche.'

'Hiv ah no?' came the reply. 'Jist you watch when that fella tries to shake his heid.'

Porter returned to the gangsters' war service later that year:

East End gangsters, those men who carried on a 'civil war' around Bridgeton in the days of peace, are now engaged in a crusade – Britain's crusade against Nazi opposition . . . The gangsters were one of the tragedies of the post-war slump. Unemployment and other social evils drew young men into fights. It was the only manner in which they knew how to express themselves. Now in the Army, many have found their natural bent. Two of the most notorious have already attained sergeant's rank. Look out, Jerry!

A year into the conflict, the reputations of the Billy Boys and their former enemies had been transformed: gangsters had become heroes.

Former gang members took part in some of the most dangerous operations mounted by British forces. Many lost their lives. As the journalist and novelist George Blake noted, by 1942 an officer from the Eastern Division of the City of Glasgow police 'could show from his careful records that most of his notoriously bad boys were by then serving, if they had not already fallen, in North Africa or in the various Commando raids on the European coasts.'

On the flip side, however, some of the city's best-known gangsters – perhaps unsurprisingly – found military discipline unbearable. Andrew Mulvey of the Kent Star was discharged from the army as an 'undesirable' in 1941; in November that year, he was also charged with failing to maintain his wife and his four children. An exasperated poor-relief official recorded that: 'He earns his living through attending dog race meetings and clubs . . . He refuses to sign at the Labour Exchange for employment and is a man who lives by his wits.'

James Wilkie, formerly a leading figure in the Derry Boys, was similarly ill-suited to soldiering. He was arrested for desertion in January 1941, and sent back to his regiment by order of Glasgow's procurator fiscal. Within a month he was back in Barlinnie having been jailed for three months for attempted housebreaking. His war record showed little improvement: in 1944, he served another three-month sentence for housebreaking and theft.

Other prominent gangsters had less distinguished war records than was generally supposed. In local lore, Gorbals legend, Peter Williamson – the leader of the Beehive Boys – proved as capable a soldier as he was a street fighter, rapidly earning promotion to the rank of sergeant. In reality, he deserted in 1943.

Nor did wartime work always appeal. Andrew Mulvey's long-standing associate, James Tinney O'Neill, served a stretch in Barlinnie in 1943 after he was jailed for eighteen months that summer for assault and robbery. O'Neill had previously been earning £5 per week in a munitions factory.

Some of Glasgow's fighting men even managed to maintain their private vendettas during the war and beyond. Matt McGinn, who grew up in the Calton, vividly recalled the enmity between James Tinney O'Neill and 'Tam the Hawk' (Thomas Falconer):

> they fought and fought and fought and ran between them a thirty-year feud. With razors and bayonets they had fought in youth and then had kept the fight going into old age and were over the fifty mark when Tam the Hawk was shot in the buttock through the door of his house in the Gallowgate.
>
> For years Tam drank in a pub in Kent Street, always with his back to the wall and with a wary eye open in case his rival would appear. The Scout [O'Neill] for his part had always to keep his eyes peeled for the Hawk.

The shooting described by McGinn took place in October 1945. Police made four arrests: three men subsequently stood trial at the High Court in Glasgow for attempted murder, while a fourth – 'Scout' O'Neill – was charged with assaulting Falconer's sister. Falconer was then aged forty-two; O'Neill thirty-one, while the three men charged with the shooting were in their early twenties. The charge of attempted murder was found not proven, while O'Neill was found not guilty of assault. All four prisoners were convicted of committing a breach of the peace. O'Neill, who had twelve previous convictions, was jailed for three months with hard labour.

Matt McGinn characterised the shooting – hitherto a rare event in Glasgow's gangland – as yet another round in a seemingly endless private feud. McGinn did not speculate on the origins of the quarrel, but it was not borne out of gang rivalry: both men had been long-standing members of the Kent Star. The fighting culture of districts like the Calton had destroyed men like these. As McGinn put it: 'What a culture, what a drag down of human dignity.'

The Shadow of No Mean City

More than ten years after its publication, eminent Glaswegians were still irked by the success of McArthur and Kingsley Long's novel. Charles Oakley, former consultant to the Scottish Development Council and now acting as Scottish Regional Controller for the Board of Trade, was convinced that the success of *No Mean City* was hindering Glasgow's prospects of economic renewal. In his history of *The Second City*, published in 1946, Oakley wrote:

> No one . . . can be pleased that Glasgow is now thought of as the 'tough' city of Great Britain . . . associated in many minds abroad with Chicago, Marseilles and Barcelona . . . Glasgow certainly has her unsavoury quarters – as, unfortunately, most other large ports have – and she has her share of criminals. But the Buenos Aires businessman, found some years ago at Euston Station, trembling because his directors had instructed him to go to Glasgow, was alarming himself unduly. No one was lurking near the Central Station waiting to . . . attack with him a cut-throat razor.

The terrified commercial traveller had evidently heard either of *No Mean City* or the ballet it had recently inspired, *Miracle in the Gorbals*.

First performed by the Sadler's Wells Ballet Company in London in 1944, *Miracle in the Gorbals* featured a Christ-like figure who arrives in the notorious district, resurrects a young woman who has just committed suicide and then redeems a prostitute before he is set upon and slashed by members of what the *Manchester Guardian*'s critic described as 'a still unregenerate razor-gang'. To Charles Oakley, the ballet served only to bolster the misrepresentations of Glasgow that civic leaders had hoped were gradually dying out.

No Mean City's co-author, Alec McArthur, was himself tormented by the book's success. Desperate for further acclaim, he wrote prodigiously in the years that followed, but found it difficult to get his sole-authored work published – Longmans and H. Kingsley Long had clearly been right in their initial assessment of McArthur's manuscripts in 1934. McArthur had few friends, and he spent most of his evenings in the Stag, a public house in Waddell Street in the Gorbals, where he still lived with his mother. The Stag's landlord, Charles Canning, remembered McArthur as an increasingly desperate figure: 'He would suddenly beat the bar with his fist and shout "Clods! Clods! They're all clods!" or "They'll talk about me after I'm dead!"'

McArthur's bitterness stemmed in part from a belief that Glasgow's literary élite was persecuting him. He was also convinced that he had been the victim of plagiarism, alleging that Robert McLeish's play, *The Gorbals Story*, first staged in Glasgow in 1946, was derived from a script that he had himself submitted to two local theatres without success the previous year.

McArthur's mother died in March 1947. He planned his own death a few months later. In his diary, he wrote:

Unless I let them see what authentic Glasgow is I am through. To-day I bought a blotting pad twopence-ha'penny; nib twopence; nails for boots; cigarettes. I have a ha'penny left. I could feed myself till Monday next. After that, starvation.

In his final diary entry, he noted that he had sold his house and all of its contents – bar his manuscripts – for £50, before concluding: 'Not much time to the end.' McArthur spent the proceeds from the sale of the house on a lavish meal for himself and a group of acquaintances on 4 September 1947. He was discovered later that afternoon, unconscious, on Rutherglen Bridge and died five hours later in Glasgow Royal Infirmary, where the cause of death was found to be Lysol poisoning (Lysol was a common disinfectant). He was identified by the ration book in his pocket.

The shadow cast by McArthur's collaboration with Kingsley Long continued to linger over Glasgow, and especially over the Gorbals – by now more emblematic of Britain's slums even than Whitechapel, once the haunt of 'Jack the Ripper'. In January 1948, *Picture Post* published a lengthy essay on conditions in the Gorbals by A. L. Lloyd. His text was illustrated by a series of photographs by Bert Hardy, which captured the cramped decay of what Lloyd termed Britain's 'most loathsome slum', alongside a couple of its bright spots – a pub and a dance hall. In a passage closely reminiscent of *No Mean City*, Lloyd dwelled on the overcrowding endured by the Gorbals' 40,000 inhabitants:

> They live in apartments that are mostly small, dark and dirty. They live five and six in a single room that is part of some great slattern of a tenement, with seven or eight people in the room next door, and maybe eight or ten in the rooms above and below. The windows are often patched with cardboard. The stairs are narrow, dark at all times and befouled not only with mud and rain. Commonly there is one lavatory for thirty people, and that with the door off.

Hardy's photograph of two boys perched on a crumbling stairwell provides a stark illustration.

Like McArthur and Kingsley Long before him, Lloyd was concerned that overcrowding led to a precocious awareness of sex. As he put it, for youngsters who slept huddled close to adults, there were 'few mysteries among the facts of life'. Lloyd, however, sought to allay the fear – stoked by *No Mean City* – that proximity led inevitably to vice. Illegitimacy rates in the district were 'not remarkably high', he pointed out, and one young woman that he spoke to described the care that was taken to preserve the modesty of siblings aged in their teens and early twenties. 'We're eight in the one room,' she explained. 'We go to bed in relays. My elder brothers walk round the court while we girls undress. Then they come back and kip down on their mattresses on the floor beside us.'

Lloyd was equally determined to dispel the notion that the Gorbals was blighted by violence. The district had had its share of criminals, he asserted, but no more: razor-slashings were uncommon and 'organised crime, in the sense of "gangs" hardly exists.' A desk sergeant in the police station on Lawmoor Street conceded that the Gorbals was 'a pretty rough area', but insisted that there were plenty of places 'just as rough' elsewhere.

The district's younger residents felt the stigma of *No Mean City* more keenly than their elders. As another young woman told Lloyd: 'I hate it in the Gorbals. If I meet anyone new I have to give a false address.' In the postwar years, most local adults were able to find work – a crucial contrast to the era of the 'Razor King' – but the tenements were beyond saving. Lloyd was adamant that wholesale clearance of the district was essential. A 'new' Gorbals, he insisted, was a priority not just for Glasgow, but for Britain.

The Gorbals was by no means the most 'loathsome' district in Britain, as local readers angrily pointed out to *Picture Post*, but it was certainly the most notorious. In July 1948, the *Daily Mirror* claimed that the district was still plagued by violence and racketeering. Under the headline '**RAZOR GANGS IN RENT WAR ON WIVES**', the *Mirror* cited James Phillips of the Gorbals Housing Association, who claimed that local gangsters were exploiting the post-war housing shortage by buying up tenements houses and forcing the existing inhabitants to pay excessive rents for single-end apartments. Since women generally managed their family's budgets, they were especially vulnerable. According to Phillips, those who complained faced terrible retribution: a woman in Warwick Street was beaten up when her husband was out at work, while a man whose rent had been reduced by a tribunal was slashed with a razor.

Tragedy struck the district in October that year after a married couple discovered that their fifteen-year-old daughter was pregnant. They attempted to kill themselves and their five children by leaving the gas on overnight in their room-and-kitchen house in Eglinton Street – both parents were sentenced to hang after three of their daughters died. Prior to their reprieve, the *Mirror*'s columnist, 'Cassandra', wrote movingly of the family's plight, noting that neighbours had described them as 'respectable':

> People laugh at that word. But in the Gorbals where disease and crime and filth and dishonesty go hand in hand, it is something of a triumph. Where poverty and corruption abound it is not a bad thing to be *respectable*. It is the hardest fight against the toughest thing in the world.

Cassandra's sympathy for the condemned parents was framed squarely by *No Mean City*: the fictional account had become the inevitable backdrop to factual reports on conditions in 'this grim and terrible district', while in the British national press, the district's name had become a byword: three weeks after the tragedy in Eglinton Street, the *Daily Express* dispatched journalist James Cameron to Jamaica to report on the repercussions of the collapse of the banana trade. In Kingston, Cameron found 'a squalid infestation of mean streets, haunt of the homeless and the hungry, the beggar and the sneak-thief, a sort of Caribbean Gorbals.'

Gangsters and Cops

The Second World War had seen a decisive shift in perceptions of Glasgow's gangsters, with former 'thugs' lauded as war heroes. A second phase in the refashioning of the collective reputation of the gangs of the 1920s and 1930s began in 1955, prompted by the publication of the memoirs of Sir Percy Sillitoe, the city's former chief constable. Sillitoe had been knighted in 1942 and had left Glasgow the following year to take command of Kent County Police – an important strategic post in the build-up to the Allied invasion of the French coast. In 1946, he became director general of MI5, retiring in 1953, at which point he planned to begin compiling his memoirs immediately. Writing was delayed after he accepted an invitation to head the International Diamond Security Organisation, but his book – *Cloak Without Dagger* – appeared in April 1955.

Publication was keenly anticipated in Glasgow. The *Evening Citizen* attempted to steal its thunder by running a series of articles by Reverend J. Cameron Peddie – introduced as 'The man who *really* broke the Glasgow gangs' – followed by a three-part interview with 'William' Fullerton. Peddie's work with the South Side Stickers had been widely praised during the 1930s, and he spoke warmly of his former charges, explaining that they had never merited the label gangster in the 'American' sense. 'They were just high-spirited young men with nothing to do, and so they often banded themselves together for fun which often ended in crime.' Peddie also revealed that he had been deeply impressed by 'their amazing loyalty to their class': their refusal to cooperate with judicial authorities – widely bemoaned by police and prison officers alike during the 1930s – was interpreted by Peddie as proof of the lads' determination to look after each other. Looking back as he was from the vantage point of the mid-1950s – an age of near-full employment – the gangs of the interwar decades looked like an inevitable by-product of the shortage of work.

The *Citizen*'s interview with Billy Fullerton was conducted by a veteran journalist named David Stewart. A testimonial received by Fullerton following his wartime service in the Merchant Navy was used to illustrate one of the articles, and Stewart stressed the sacrifice made by former gangsters during the conflict: 'The Billy Boys and their contemporaries were scattered to the four corners of the globe . . . Many of them never came back.' Those fortunate enough to return to Glasgow,

Stewart insisted, 'were absorbed into industry and became steady and reliable workers'. In this light, Stewart – like Peddie – was able to characterise the gangsters of the 1920s and 1930s as victims of economic circumstances:

> Industrial depression was hitting Clydeside hard. There was not a great deal of employment to go round and the youth of the city was hit harder than any. The gangs and their exploits were a counter to the boredom of idleness. The craving for excitement was satisfied.

This, of course, was a story that the *Citizen* and its readers could be comfortable with – and there was much truth in it. However, it contrasted sharply with the coverage of gangs in the local press during the 1920s and 1930s. Before the war, recognition of the damage wrought by mass unemployment had been set alongside depictions of gang members as mindless brutes, and calls for 'the lash'.

Fullerton used the interview to restate claims that he had made during the 1930s. By his account, the Billy Boys were loyal patriots who had assisted the authorities during the General Strike and used the gang's funds to look after the dependants of those married members who were jailed. Stewart accepted Fullerton's claim that his followers had never resorted to theft. The journalist commented:

> In that respect, the ordinary individual in Bridgeton was as safe then as he is today. He could walk the streets freely, always provided he was discreet enough not to display party colours, but he would never be robbed.

The *Citizen*'s own files told a much more complex story in which allegations of 'gang terrorism' loomed large, but this newly sanitised account – in which the gangs fought only among themselves and posed no danger to 'ordinary' people – quickly became the orthodox view.

Fullerton made one new admission to the *Citizen* in January 1955, revealing that he had joined the 'Fascist Party', acting as a 'section captain' with 200 men and women under his command.

Fullerton was vague as to the details of his involvement, but it is likely that he joined the British Fascists, founded in 1923, whose members – like the Billy Boys – were notorious for confronting Communist demonstrators on the streets. The British Fascists – again like the Billy Boys – were also known to supply stewards for Tory election meetings. In August 1925, the *Evening Citizen* had itself reported that the British Fascists drew a crowd of more than 1,000 people to a meeting at Bridgeton Cross – a supporter wrote to the paper to confirm that the meeting had been widely advertised in an attempt to rally the district's 'loyalists'. The writer claimed that the meeting had lasted ninety minutes, culminating in the singing of 'Rule Britannia' and 'God Save the King'. By this account, the meeting had been a resounding success: 'Many new members have since been recruited.'

Another glimpse of the British Fascists in the Billy Boys' Bridgeton heartland came later that year, when the *Citizen* reported that a Communist meeting at the Cross had been the scene of 'considerable friction' after a 'rival party' approached and began to sing 'loyal' songs – once again, these included 'Rule Britannia' and the national anthem. On this occasion, three men were arrested: a Communist steward was subsequently fined 42 shillings for assault; two others who appeared at the Eastern Police Court were found not guilty.

Fullerton told David Stewart: 'I couldn't give you the definition of Fascist to this very day. It just seemed like a good thing to belong to at the time.' However, the former 'boss' of the Billy Boys was not as naïve as this comment suggests. Fullerton's commitment to the causes of 'King, Country and Constitution' was as devout and every bit as visible as his disdain for Catholic gangsters and Communists.

Sir Percy Sillitoe devoted an entire chapter of *Cloak Without Dagger* to an account of how he suppressed Glasgow's gangs. He began with a brief historical sketch in which he traced the rise of the gangs back to the aftermath of the First World War, before providing a detailed profile of the Beehive Boys and a racy, action-packed account of the feud between the Billy Boys and the Norman Conks. His portrait of Fullerton was highly ambivalent:

> Fullerton, I must say, was never a criminal in the accepted sense of the word. He was a fighting man, who undoubtedly derived considerable pleasure and excitement from pitting his gangsters against the Norman Conks, and his generalship was both ingenious and reckless. He left the thieving to others, and his only conviction was for assault.

Sillitoe proceeded to tell how he brought about Fullerton's downfall, describing with some relish the ambush of the Orange procession in Parkhead by 'Sillitoe's Cossacks' and Fullerton's arrest by Sergeant Tommy Morrison. According to Sillitoe, Fullerton emerged from Barlinnie 'a broken man': his days as a gang leader were over, and his demise marked 'the end of the Billy Boys, and without them the Norman Conks seemed to pine away.'

Sillitoe concluded his account with the sentencing of John McNamee at the High Court in Glasgow in April 1935. McNamee was convicted of culpable homicide following a street fight in Anderston. Lord Aitchison sentenced McNamee to fifteen years' penal servitude – according to Sillitoe, the severity of the sentence was prompted by an appeal that he had himself made to the judge. With the Billy Boys already vanquished, this exemplary sentence was all it took to cleanse Glasgow of the evil of the gangs.

This was a vivid and compelling account, but it was a self-serving one, too. It was also highly misleading – not least since Sillitoe had purposefully altered the sequence of the events that he described. Sillitoe featured the murder of Jimmy Dalziel at the Bedford Parlour dance hall in his potted history of the gangs, but claimed that it took place in 1924, 'which was, of course, before I went to Glasgow.' In fact, Dalziel's death took place in 1934, more than two years after Sillitoe's arrival. He then swapped the sequence of two police actions against the Billy Boys, placing the ambush by his 'Cossacks' – which took place in August 1936 – before the arrest of Billy Fullerton by Sergeant

Morrison in April 1931. Significantly, Fullerton's arrest *did* take place before Sillitoe reached Glasgow.

Concluding his chapter with the jailing of John McNamee in 1935 made for a satisfying ending, not least since it enabled Sillitoe to omit the killing of George Stankovitch in September 1936 and the resultant flurry of articles in the London press labelling Glasgow the 'Scottish Chicago'.

Sillitoe's version of events would quickly become the definitive account of the gangs of the 1920s and 1930s. His tales of the Billy Boys and the Norman Conks – and how he curbed their exploits – have informed journalists' sketches of Glasgow's gangland ever since. The veracity of Sillitoe's account has not been challenged, and few have questioned the extent of his 'triumph' over the gangs. His resort to violence – 'giving them a taste of their own medicine' – has been widely praised, but there has been much less recognition for the alternative approaches pioneered by Reverend Sydney Warnes in Bridgeton and his counterpart, J. Cameron Peddie, in the Gorbals. Moreover, the relentless focus on the violence meted out by the City of Glasgow Police during the 1930s has all too frequently obscured Sillitoe's other vital observation: that the city's gangs were in large part the products of poverty and unemployment.

Farewell to King Billy

Billy Fullerton died in July 1962 at the age of fifty-six. His funeral confirmed his standing as an emblematic figure in Glasgow's East End as his former followers turned out en masse to pay their respects to 'King Billy': more than 2,000 people crammed into the street outside Fullerton's single-roomed flat in Brook Street. *The Times*' Scottish correspondent described the scene:

> A flute band played 'Come to the Saviour' as the plain coffin was carried from the common entry of the tenement. Foremost on the banks of wreaths on the coffin was a huge cushion of marigolds, roses and other flowers, across which the metal letters proclaimed: 'To our one-time leader.'

The band led the cortège through the streets of Bridgeton to the strains of 'Onward Christian Soldiers', stopping the traffic at the Billy Boys' former gathering place at Bridgeton Cross. Local residents, noted *The Times*, 'spared neither time, tears, nor tokens of regret in celebrating his passing'. Around 600 people marched behind the funeral car to Riddrie Park cemetery.

Reports on the funeral were prefaced with references to the legendary battles between the Brigton Billy Boys and the Norman Conks. Once again, these episodes were widely explained as a by-product of the enforced idleness and squalid housing of the 1920s and 1930s. Describing the youthful Fullerton as 'the self-appointed leader of hundreds of young men like himself, restless and bored through lack of work and money,' the *Daily Record* retrospectively endorsed the view which Fullerton himself had forcibly expressed to the *Sunday Dispatch* in 1935.

It was universally agreed that Fullerton had been a reformed character in his later years, living alone but at peace in his former 'kingdom'. The reputations of the Billy Boys and their opponents continued to mellow, too – notably in the claim that ordinary people had had nothing to fear from the gangs of the 1920s and 1930s. In a lengthy portrait of 'the quiet man who led the Billy Boys' for the Glasgow *Evening Times*, penned in the wake of the funeral, Jack Skilling insisted:

> I do not want to glorify Fullerton, who had a tremendous list of convictions for breach of the peace and assault, or the gangs of the East End, but, by and large, they were not a danger to the ordinary public.

Adamant that the Billy Boys had only fought against rival gangs, Skilling was able to mourn Fullerton's passing: 'The Bridgeton of the depression and the slums is no more, and the gangs have gone. For that I am glad, but I grieve at the death of Billy Fullerton.'

The British national press meanwhile, raised the spectre of Johnnie Stark. The headline in *The Times* – 'Former Razor King Buried With Pomp' – located Fullerton squarely in the milieu of *No Mean City* (no matter that Fullerton's 'kingdom' was not the Gorbals, but Bridgeton, or that Fullerton, for all his pugnacity, had never been renowned for fighting with a razor).

The death five years later of Eli Webb – one of Fullerton's predecessors as 'King' of the Billy Boys – attracted much less attention. At the age of sixty-two, Webb had been working as the caretaker of a betting shop in Dalmarnock Road in Bridgeton. On 16 June 1967, Webb 'had words' with James Rankin, a labourer eleven years his junior, and asked the younger man to go into the back-court behind the shop for a square-go. The veteran fighting man was no match for his younger opponent, who felled him with a flurry of blows to the face, head and body. Webb died the following day. Rankin, who had six previous convictions, was initially accused of murder, but the charge was downgraded to culpable homicide by the time he appeared at Glasgow Sheriff Court on 19 September. Acknowledging that Rankin had been provoked, Sheriff Bayne jailed him for nine months. The leniency of the sentence seemed almost to signal a degree of resignation among the judiciary, as though they expected no different from the denizens of the city's slums when drink had been taken.

Johnnie Stark's Ghost

The first edition of *No Mean City*, published by Longmans in October 1935, sold 30,000 copies before the sensation surrounding the novel died down and it was allowed to go out of print. Transworld Publishers bought the paperback rights to the novel in 1957, and Johnnie Stark appeared on the cover of their edition later that year in a leather jacket, sporting a Teddy boy's quiff. It sold 250,000 copies in two years – eclipsing the sales of John Steinbeck and Sir Winston Churchill, as the *New Yorker* pointed out. In Glasgow, 45,000 copies were sold in four months.

The *Daily Mail* sent its book critic, Kenneth Allsop, to Glasgow to research a profile of its co-author, Alec McArthur. Readers were duly introduced to 'the slummie who read Dostoyevsky' and had lived in 'a grey rat-run . . . a bug-crawling room where he warmed up turnip soup and wrote and wrote.' Allsop's feature was entitled 'A Ghost Rises From the Gorbals'.

No Mean City's renewed success during the late 1950s was all the more poignant since the Gorbals had recently been earmarked for comprehensive redevelopment. In February 1959, John Maclay, Secretary of State for Scotland in the Conservative government headed by Harold Macmillan, approved a plan devised by Glasgow City Council planners to flatten a site of 111 acres; the tenements that once housed the families of the South Side Stickers, Liberty Boys and Beehive Boys were bull-dozed. In their place rose a series of tower blocks – symbols of 'the new Glasgow and, indeed, of the new Scotland' as the *New York Times* noted approvingly in 1964. Basil Spence, celebrated architect of Coventry's new cathedral, was commissioned to design some of the Gorbals blocks. Both the planners' eagerness to demolish the district wholesale and the attention of the world's press testified to the legacy of *No Mean City*.

'Glasgow's Miles Better'

In June 1983, Glasgow City Council launched an ambitious and highly enterprising publicity campaign. Brainchild of advertising guru, John Struthers, and energetically promoted by the city's Labour Lord Provost, Michael Kelly, its aim was 'to inform and educate people that Glasgow was no longer the proverbial "No Mean City".' Fifty years on, the legacy of McArthur and Kingsley Long's novel was still painfully apparent, not least in the negative perceptions of Glasgow held elsewhere in Britain and overseas. As the council's own website explains, the campaign's target audience was the 'ABC1 market' – defined as 'those people who make or influence decisions, particularly of a commercial nature.' The campaign utilised a well-known cartoon character – 'Mr Happy' – whose smiley face 'illustrated the double meaning of the slogan "Miles Better / Smiles Better".' The corrective was much needed: the previous year, a survey of London-based civil servants revealed that their primary impressions of Glasgow were of 'The Gorbals, tenement slums, violence and industrial corrosion.' Struthers' strategy was to acknowledge this image – and ostentatiously defy it.

In its own terms, 'Glasgow's Miles Better' was an extraordinary success, helping to pave the way for the Garden Festival of 1988 and the designation of Glasgow as 'European City of Culture' for 1990. Critics pointed out, however – with ample justification – that this process of civic rebranding tended to mask the staggering poverty and widespread unemployment that still blighted the lives of too many of Glasgow's citizens – 40 per cent of the city's population depended on supplementary benefit in 1987: in that all-too-real sense, the economic inequalities highlighted by McArthur and Kingsley Long still remained to be tackled.

Perhaps the most profound legacy of 'Glasgow's Miles Better' was the recognition by outsiders that there are at least two Glasgows (something the city's *Eastern Standard* newspaper had pointed out in 1926). It was no mean achievement to bring the city's spectacular architecture and rich cultural life out from the shadow of Johnnie Stark.

Against this backdrop, a proposal in 1991 that Alec McArthur should be commemorated in Glasgow by a plaque, or perhaps even a statue, was quickly rejected. Patrick Lally, a Gorbals-born Labour councillor, dismissed *No Mean City* as 'a distorted work of fiction'. Lally subsequently rounded on its co-author: 'This man McArthur did neither Glasgow nor the Gorbals any favour by writing his book, and we will certainly not be doing anything to remember him.'

The Myth of the Honourable Fighting Man

The gangsters of the 1920s and 1930s are today for the most part remembered as honourable fighting men. Billy Fullerton contributed to his own legend, notably in his interview with the *Evening Citizen* in 1955, but others aided and abetted his re-invention as a 'hard man with "a heart of gold"'. Journalist Jack House, whose long-running 'Ask Jack' column in the *Evening Times* gave him a privileged vantage point as the custodian of the city's popular memory, insisted in 1980 that: 'The big difference between the old gangs and the present mobs is that [the old gangs] only fought each other and never attacked anyone else.' That the gangs of the 1920s and 1930 posed no danger to ordinary people is a claim that has been widely articulated, ever since the *Evening Citizen* applied its gloss to the Billy Boys' former leader in the mid-1950s.

Fullerton's own image was carefully crafted. His revelation that the Billy Boys' funds were used to support the wives and children of those members who were jailed was intended to portray him as a chivalrous figure. It worked, not least in diverting attention from the convictions for wife-beating shared by Fullerton and some of his fiercest opponents. Equally, recognition of the heroism and sacrifice displayed by many former gang members during the Second World War obscures the chequered war records of some of the city's most notorious gangsters. Former Beehive Boy, Peter Williamson, is remembered not for his desertion in 1943 but for his legendary prowess in 'square-goes'. In 1980, he featured in a letter published in the 'Ask Jack' column of the *Evening Times* in which reader Douglas Kerr made the claim that Mathieson Street in the Gorbals had produced 'more champions than any other street in Glasgow'. Kerr's list included one runner, four boxers – among them world flyweight champion, Benny Lynch – and, lastly, 'Peter Williamson, a champion street fighter, who fought some great fighters on the banks of the Clyde.' Williamson's friend and fellow Beehive Boy, Dan Cronin, likewise features in Gorbals lore as a legendary street fighter. According to George Forbes and Paddy Meehan, writing in 1982, Cronin's funeral in 1948 was 'attended by more mourners than any lord provost's.'

Their reputations softened by the passage of time, such men can appear as Robin Hoods – stand-out figures in once-teeming tenement streets full of 'characters', who stood up for the poor and needy like cloth-capped crusaders. In a post on the Gorbals Live website in 2003, David Kerr remembered Dan Cronin as a hero of the community:

My true Gorbals icon, Dan Cronin, the Gorbals gangster with a heart. He would come up the street if somebody's furniture was out in the street to be evicted, and he would pay the debt and that was a man with a heart.

Another poster, writing the following year, remembered the same former Beehive Boy very differently. He recalled: 'Dan Cronin and his mob trying to beat our family up in 320 Lawmoor Street, the chain and hatchet marks [were still] on the door even when we left there in the 50s!' At a distance of more than sixty years, even terrifying incidents in which families were besieged in their own homes become colourful – even humorous – anecdotes.

As criminologist Geoffrey Pearson has pointed out, every generation romanticises the past – not least as a means of making sense of its own, pressing anxieties. To be reminded that crime and violence 'have always been with us' risks undermining the very real fears felt in the present, while ignoring these unpalatable aspects of our history brings its own risks – not least in fostering shallow explanations of gang conflict and knife-crime, whose historical roots run much deeper than we readily admit.

Crime and the City

The history of Glasgow's gangs during the 1920s and 1930s reminds us that crime does not exist on the margins of urban life: quite the reverse, as crime is central to both the experience of living in cities and to people's understandings of city life. Similarly, investigating the composition of the gangs, and delving – as far as the historical sources allow – into the family lives of 'hooligans' and 'gangsters' reminds us that gangs and their members were, above all, ordinary, sometimes almost painfully so. Whatever their grievances, and however strong their mutual loathing, Glasgow's gangsters had much in common: young people from different parts of the city and on both sides of the sectarian divide led lives blighted by poverty, slum housing and unemployment, leavened by a grim determination to have their share of the pleasures of the modern city.

It is, of course, no coincidence that gangs were embedded in districts characterised by high levels of economic and social deprivation. It is no coincidence, either, that gangs formed deeper roots in Glasgow than in other British cities during the 1920s and 1930s. Deindustrialisation was more acute, and more sudden, in Glasgow than elsewhere, while the city's enduring sectarian antagonisms provided recurrent incendiary sparks. Similar stories have been told of New York in the 1950s. Here too, 'gang culture' was rooted in industrial decline and ethnic discord, producing startling parallels with Glasgow during the 1920s and 1930s.

It is also no coincidence that the most optimistic stories to emerge from Glasgow in the decades after the Great War stemmed from attempts to work with – rather than against – young people in the city's poorest districts. The handful of Church of Scotland ministers who took it upon themselves to meet their local 'gangsters' found these notorious men and youths to be surprisingly affable. Given the opportunity to re-establish themselves as social clubs, some of the city's most incorrigible gangs proved surprisingly willing. The ministers did not attempt to tackle the wider inequalities that lay behind Glasgow's 'gang menace' but, even so, their endeavours showed more glimpses of success than the repeated 'wars' waged on the gangs by the police and the courts. So long as these wider inequalities persisted, gangs and gangsters were bound to remain part of Glasgow's story.

Acknowledgements

This book was long in the making, but many people helped me along the way. It is a pleasure to thank them for their advice, encouragement and support.

The first phase of my research, in 1995–6, was funded by the Economic and Social Research Council as part of a research programme on 'Crime and Social Order', award no. L210252006. The late Geoff Pearson was a source of inspiration from the start, as was the late Ian Taylor. Subsequent phases of research and writing were made possible by the support of the School of History (now part of the School of Histories, Languages and Cultures) at the University of Liverpool.

Most of the sources were located at the Mitchell Library in Glasgow, the National Records of Scotland, Edinburgh, or the British Library Newspaper Library in London. I benefitted enormously from the expertise and enthusiasm of the librarians and archivists who dealt with my endless requests for material. Special thanks go to the staff of the Glasgow Room at the Mitchell, and to Dr Irene O'Brien, Elaine MacGillvray and Lyn Crawford of Glasgow City Archives for their enthusiasm and interest in my work as well as for helping me to navigate through the thickets of the D-HEW series. I also wish to thank John Bruce and Ruth Jones at the National Records of Scotland for supplying me with photocopies, and Keith Cumming, Justiciary Office Manager at the High Court of Justiciary in Edinburgh, for arranging access to trial papers from the late 1930s. The late Tony Hepburn generously provided me with copies of notes he had taken in the Public Record Office of Northern Ireland. Further thanks are due to Steve Humphries of Testimony Films, for permission to use his interview with the 'Larry Johnson'; Will McArthur, of glescapals.com, for permission to use the photograph of the Billy Boys' band in 1935; and Alice Stewart, Records Manager at Strathclyde Police.

When I first arrived in Glasgow in the autumn of 1995, Callum Brown, Anne Crowther, Seán Damer and Arthur McIvor all took time out from their own work to help with mine. I remain grateful for their generosity, and for their continued interest in the project. In subsequent years, I have benefitted greatly from the advice, encouragement and critical engagement of the city's historians, sociologists, curators and journalists, many of whom I now consider friends as well as colleagues. I wish to thank Lynn Abrams, Jon Bannister, Angela Bartie, Susan Batchelor, Moira Burgess, Michele Burman, William Duff, Linda Fleming, Alistair Fraser; Mark Freeman, Eleanor Gordon, Annmarie Hughes, Mo Hume, David Leask, Anthony Lewis, Elaine McFarland, Jim McKenna, Alex Shepard and John Stewart.

I have benefitted, too, from extensive discussions with historians, sociologists and criminologists elsewhere in Britain and further afield. Particular thanks are due to Judith Allen, Peter Bailey, John Baxendale, Amy Bell, Alyson Brown, Carl Chinn, Art Cockerill, Carolyn Conley, Pam Cox, Clive Emsley, Steve Fielding, John Flint, Vic Gatrell, Barry Godfrey, the late Jill Greenfield, Trevor Griffiths, John Hagedorn, Matthew Hilton, Jim Hinks, Dick Hobbs, Matt Houlbrook, Helen Johnston, Joanne Klein, Paul Knepper, Claire Langhamer, Jon Lawrence, Linda Mahood, Peter Mandler, Tim Newburn, Sian Nicholas, Robert Ralphs, Alastair Reid, Helen Rogers, Eric Schneider, Heather Shore, Craig Stafford, Betsy Stanko, Julie-Marie Strange, Pat Thane, Penny Tinkler, Chris Waters, Klaus Weinhauer, Lucy Williams and Andy Wood. John Carter Wood deserves special thanks: without his tip-off, I'd still be searching for Billy Fullerton's life story. John Archer, Louise Jackson, Sean O'Connell and Pamela Walker all helped me to sustain momentum at crucial stages in the project.

I am grateful to Suzanne Yee, Sandra Mather and Ian Qualtrough of the University of Liverpool for their work on the maps and photographs.

Graeme Hamilton put me up in Glasgow in 1995–6, and

helped me to find my way around: I remain grateful for his hospitality. Andy Marsh made sure I never took my eye off the ball since (even when we were at the match).

I am grateful to my agent, Gordon Wise, for his enthusiasm for this project and his guidance on how my findings might best be presented. I am grateful to Peter Walsh in this regard, too, having learned a lot from working with him on my previous book, *The Gangs of Manchester*. Rupert Lancaster and Kate Miles at Hodder and Stoughton provided invaluable editorial support. I am grateful for their encouragement as well as their insight. Thanks are also due to Juliet Brightmore for her assistance in finding illustrations, and to Belinda Jones for her work as copy-editor.

My biggest debt by far is to Selina Todd. This book is in better shape than it could ever have been without her love and support – and so am I.

Picture Acknowledgements

Notes on Sources

The following abbreviations are used: BLSA (British Library Sound Archive); ECL (Edinburgh Central Library); GCA (Glasgow City Archives); MLG (Mitchell Library, Glasgow); NRS (National Records of Scotland); PRONI (Public Record Office of Northern Ireland). Books and articles in journals are cited by the author's surname and year of publication: for full details, see the bibliography.

INTRODUCTION

'City of gangs': *Evening Citizen*, 4 August 1930. Police estimate: *Daily Mirror*, 18 December 1936. Racecourse wars: *Daily Express*, 24 August 1925; Chinn (1991); Shore (2011). Sheffield gang wars: Bean (1981). Sectarian violence in Liverpool: Ayers (1988), pp. 58–60. Economic decline and unemployment in Glasgow: Ministry of Labour (1931); Fogarty (1945), pp. 154–6; Cunnison and Gilfillan (1958), p. 841; compared to Birmingham: Stevenson (1984), pp. 272–3. Discrimination against Catholics: McGuckin (1992), p. 204; Savage (2006), pp. 91, 125–6; counter-claim: Bruce *et al* (2004), pp. 11–12. Gangster's swagger: Mackie (1972), p. 34. Cinema as a 'propaganda-agent': *Evening Citizen*, 16 September 1926. Gang-related homicides in Chicago: *Sunday Post*, 14 December 1930. Readership of the *Glasgow Herald*: Damer (1990a), pp. 98–9. 'Brigton' Billy Boys and their adversaries: *Sunday Dispatch*, 10 March 1935. Gangs run by committees, with secretaries and treasurers: *Thomson's Weekly News*, 16 April 1932; 12 September 1936. Senior / junior sections: *Weekly Record*, 17 May 1930. Billy Boys / Derry Boys: *Glasgow Herald*, 17 March 1936; *People's Journal for the West of Scotland*, 18 July 1936.

1: 'THE TERRORISTS OF GLASGOW'

Gangs of the 1880s: *People's Journal*, 18 November 1916; *Evening Citizen*, 9 May 1930; *Evening Times*, 14 August, 15 September 1936.

Party Bands and Fighting Mobs. Penny Mob: *People's Journal*, 18 November 1916. Daniel Harvey: *Weekly Record*, 11–25 January 1930. Orange Order in Glasgow: McFarland (1990), pp. 63, 73–4, 96, 142. Hostility to Home Rule: *Glasgow Herald*, 19 August 1880. St Patrick's Day celebrations: Gallagher (1987), p. 63. Disturbances in 1879: GCA, E2/4, pp. 1–4, 7–8; *Evening News*, 10, 11, 14, 18 November 1879; *Evening Times*, 10, 11, 14, 18 November 1879; *Glasgow Herald*, 25 March 1879; 15 January 1880; McFarland (1990), p. 142. Assault on William Kerr: *Glasgow Herald*, 2 October, 9 December 1880. 'The Havannah': *Weekly Record*, 25 October 1930. Children's challenges: Glasser (1987), pp. 2–3; Sinfield (2011).

Glasgow's Hooligans. 'Waves' of gang conflict: *Glasgow Eastern Standard*, 20 February 1926. Hooliganism in London: Pearson (1983), p. 74. Glasgow scare: *Glasgow News*, 3, 5, 12 March 1906. Hi Hi: *Glasgow News*, 23, 26, 27 March 1906. Meetings of Glasgow Corporation / magistrates' response: *Glasgow Herald*, 23, 27 March 1906; *Glasgow News*, 10 April 1906. Size of major gangs: *Glasgow Herald*, 8 June 1906. San Toy: *Glasgow Herald*, 11 April 1907; *Glasgow Eastern Standard*, 20 February 1926; *Evening Citizen*, 9 May 1930. Tim Malloys: *Glasgow News*, 12 July 1906; *Evening Citizen*, 9 May 1930. Village Boys: *Manchester Guardian*, 16 July, 25 August 1906. John Johnstone: *Glasgow News*, 19 February, 26 March 1906. Debate on corporal punishment: *Glasgow Herald*, 3–29 August 1906. Chief constable's report on 'hooliganism': *Glasgow Herald*, 26 September 1906.

Hooligans in Wartime. Reign of terror: *Bulletin*, 23 March, 22 April, 16, 18 May 1916; *Glasgow News*, 15 May 1916; *Glasgow Herald*, 16 May 1916; *Scotsman*, 15 June 1916; Smith (1991), p. 120. Redskins: *Bulletin*, 23 March 1916. Dance hall rackets: *Glasgow Eastern Standard*, 20 February 1926. Hooligan scare downplayed by police: *Bulletin*, 16 May 1916. Defence of the police: *Bulletin*, 18 May 1916. 'Terrorists' of Glasgow: *Sunday Chronicle*,

21 May 1916. Causes of hooliganism: *Glasgow News*, 27 May 1916. Police clampdown: *Southern Press*, 26 May, 9, 16 June 1916. Arthur Green: *Glasgow Herald*, 22 July 1916; *Evening Times*, 12 September 1916. John Evans: GCA, D-HEW 16/13/2888, no. 43168. Discussion at Glasgow Corporation: *Scotsman*, 8 September 1916. Night patrols: *Manchester Guardian*, 10 September 1916. Police response: *Southern Press*, 15 September 1916. Pronouncement by Sheriff Lyell: *Glasgow Herald*, 7 October 1916. Annie Rennie: *Scotsman*, 8 November 1916. Apaches of Paris: *Scotsman*, 22 January 1910; *People's Journal*, 18 November 1916.

2: FROM HOOLIGANS TO GANGSTERS

The Eclipse of the Gangs. Red Clydeside: Oakley (1946), pp. 314–16; Damer (1990a), pp. 116–36. General Strike of January 1919: *Daily Express*, 31 January, 1 February 1919; *Daily Mirror*, 31 January, 1 February 1919. Hooliganism 'practically ceased': *Evening Times*, 19 January 1920. 'Terrorist' gangs: *Sunday Mail*, 10 October 1920. Brutalising effects of the Great War: Lawrence (2003), pp. 562–6. William Lamont: *Glasgow Herald*, 12 May 1920. Shooting of DI Johnstone: *Scotsman*, 6, 9 May, 23 July, 9–22 August 1921; *The Times*, 9 May 1921; O'Hagan (1995), pp. 24–8. Communal assaults on the police: *Glasgow Herald*, 9, 15, 21, 22, 23 August 1922; *Evening Times*, 22 August 1922. Alleged volatility of Irish population: *Glasgow Herald*, 23 August 1922. Razor-slashing: *Evening Times*, 19 July, 11 August, 5 October 1922; *Evening Citizen*, 1 January 1924; *Glasgow Herald*, 4 January, 4 March 1924. On American racial stereotypes: Dormon (1988).

The Killing of Noor Mohammed. *Scotsman*, 18 May, 1, 2, 3, 4, 18 September 1925; *Evening Citizen*, 18 May 1925; *Evening News*, 31 August, 1, 2 September 1925; Maan (1992), p. 113; Fraser (2009), pp. 58–9. Brilliant Chang: *Daily Express*, 11 April 1924; Kohn (1992), pp. 161–70. Petition on behalf of John Keen: *Evening News*, 7 September 1925. Keen's execution: *Daily Express*, 24 September 1925; *Scotsman*, 24 September 1925; *Evening News*, 24 September 1925. 'Hooligan Problem in Glasgow': *Evening Citizen*, 20 May 1925.

The Rise of the Gangster. Orange Walk disturbances: *Scotsman*, 13, 24 July 1925; *Evening Citizen*, 13, 23 July 1925; *Glasgow Eastern Standard*, 18 July 1925. Resurgence of sectarian gang fighting: *Glasgow Eastern Standard*, 20 February 1926. Clarence Jackson: *Evening Citizen*, 24 March 1926; *Scotsman*, 25 March 1926. John Brogan and William Murray: *Evening Citizen*, 13 July 1926. Blame attached to Orange Order / Ancient Order of Hibernians: *Glasgow Eastern Standard*, 17 July 1926. General Strike: *Emergency Express*, 7 May 1926; *Scotsman*, 11, 21, 22 May 1926; *Evening Citizen*, 18 May 1926; Smyth (2000), pp. 107–8. Billy Boys' pledge: *Evening Citizen*, 17 January 1955. Norman Conks: *Scotsman*, 11 May 1926; Grant (1973), p. 91. 'Two Glasgows': *Glasgow Eastern Standard*, 14 August 1926. Sauchiehall Street / city of extremes: Morton (1929), p. 249. 'C3': Stevenson (1984), p. 62. Proliferation of gang warfare: *Evening Citizen*, 20 August 1926. Pronouncement by Sheriff Robertson: *Scotsman*, 23 August 1926. James Foley: *Glasgow Eastern Standard*, 28 August 1926. How razors are used: *Scotsman*, 23 August 1926. Call for flogging: *Evening Citizen*, 20 August 1926. James McIntosh and Eli Webb: *Evening Citizen*, 2, 3, 8 September 1926. 'METHODS OF GLASGOW GANGSTERS': *Evening Citizen*, 3 September 1926. William Carr and Samuel Marshall: *Evening Citizen*, 21 September 1926; *Scotsman*, 22 September 1926; *Glasgow Eastern Standard*, 25 September 1926. Billy Fullerton: *Evening Citizen*, 5 October 1926. David Turnbull: *Evening Citizen*, 9 November 1926. Kent Star: *Glasgow Eastern Standard*, 21 August 1926, 29 April 1927. Dirty Dozen: *Evening Citizen*, 14 October 1927. Tripe Supper Boys: *Evening Citizen*, 4 February, 21 May 1927. Lollipops versus Romeo Boys: *Evening Citizen*, 17 August, 16 November 1926; versus Kent Star: *Glasgow Eastern Standard*, 21 August 1926, *Evening Citizen*, 29 April 1927. 'Gang spirit is universal': *Evening Citizen*, 18 May 1927.

3: THE SAD TALE OF JIMMY TAIT

Young Calton Entry and South Side Stickers: NRS, AD15/28/77/1, p. 11 (Hugh Martin); pp. 44–5 (James Cunningham); pp. 50–51

(Jessie Crawford). Paragon: Peter (1996), pp. 57–8; *Evening Citizen*, 28 June 1928.

'I've put that in one of them'. Events of 6 May 1928: NRS, AD15/28/77/1, pp. 1–5 (Joseph Adams); p. 10 (Hugh Martin); p. 15a (Andrew McCarthy); pp. 32–7 (DL John Montgomery); pp. 43–8 (James Cunningham), pp. 51–4 (Jessie Crawford), p. 56 (Catherine Scanlan); p. 64 (Prof. J Glaister). 'Dixon's Blazes': http://www.theglasgowstory.com, accessed 19 October 2012. Coverage of Tait's death: *Evening Citizen*, 9, 12 May 1928; *Thomson's Weekly News*, 12 May 1928; *Weekly Record*, 12 May 1928.

The Trial of the Sticker Boys. Proceedings at High Court: *Evening Citizen*, 28, 29 June 1928; *Evening Times*, 28, 29 June 1928; *Glasgow Herald*, 30 June 1928. 'GIRLS BEHIND GANG MENACE': *Sunday Mail*, 1 July 1928. Witness statements: NRS, AD15/28/77/1, p. 15a (Andrew McCarthy); p. 19 (deposition by James Tait); AD15/28/77/3, p. 7 (Frank Kearney).

Ordinary Lives. Background reports: NRS, JC26/1928/80; HH16/192. Anti-Semitism in Britain: Orwell (1945).

'You want to say something like that'. Trial of Frank Kearney: *Glasgow Herald*, 28 August 1928. 'Honour amongst thieves': *Pictorial Weekly*, 11 June 1927.

4: THE DRYGATE TRAGEDY

March to Anderston: *Scotsman*, 3 June 1929; *Evening Citizen*, 3 June 1929. Deputation to Home Secretary: *Evening Citizen*, 19 July 1928. St Valentine's Day Massacre: Bergreen (1996), pp. 304–14. Edward Glancey and John McGrory: *Evening Citizen*, 2 April 1929. 'The Gangster': *Glasgow Herald*, 3 April 1929. Manchester lads' clubs: Davies (2008). 'Bid to rival Chicago' / transfer system: *Evening News*, 10 May 1929. Gang fights on Sunday evenings: *Evening Citizen*, 2 April 1929.

Picture Houses and *Palais de Danse*. Glasgow's cinemas: Maver (2000), p. 296. Importance of cinema-going: Cameron *et al* (1943), pp. 104–5. Plaza: *Evening Times*, 28 December 1922. Glaswegian passion for dancing: Nott (2002), p. 158; Cameron *et al* (1943), pp. 102, 105. Unlicensed dances: *Weekly Record*,

22 March 1930. Billy Smith / Romeo Boys: *Evening Citizen*, 7, 14, 24 December 1926. Jimmy Kane: *Evening Citizen*, 17 October 1929. Tower Palais: recollections of George Chisholm: Sinfield (2011); *Evening Citizen*, 20 February 1928; McAllister (1986), p. 27. Partick Picture House / Bailie McLellan: *Evening Citizen*, 12, 18 February 1929. Superintendent McPherson: *Glasgow Eastern Standard*, 2 March 1929. Gang fights at cinemas: *Evening Citizen*, 1 August 1928; 19 November 1928; 12 April 1929; 21 January 1930. Lieutenant McDade: *Glasgow Eastern Standard*, 17 August 1929. Govan Picturedrome / meeting of magistrates / Bailie Doherty: *Evening Citizen*, 26, 28 August 1929. Oatlands Picturedrome / Superintendent Cameron: *Evening Citizen*, 7 October 1929; 17 December 1929. Govan Picturedrome: *Evening Citizen*, 26 February 1930. George Stokes and Abraham Zemmil: *Evening Times*, 2 December 1929; *Scotsman*, 3 December 1929; *Weekly Record*, 7 December 1929.

'I gave one of your crowd it solid'. Feud between boys from Drygate and Sydney Street: NRS, AD15/30/70, p. 7 (John McCraw); pp. 35–7 (John Malley); p. 45 (Mary Mackin); pp. 46–8 (Catherine McMahon); pp. 128–9 (Robert McFadyen); pp. 161–2 (Anthony McVey). Events of 11 March 1930: NRS, AD15/30/70, p. 9 (John McCraw); pp. 162–9 (Anthony McVey); *Evening Citizen*, 12 March 1930; *Evening News*, 6 May 1930; *Evening Times*, 6, 8 May 1930. Interview with Mrs McLellan: *Thomson's Weekly News*, 15 March 1930. Search for John Booth / Booth gives himself up: NRS, AD15/30/70, 'Statements for defence re case of John Booth' (Jane Smith McCraw or Booth); *Scottish Daily Express*, 9 May 1930. Police round-up suspects: *Weekly Record*, 15 March 1930; *Scottish Daily Express*, 9 May 1930. Murder charge: *Evening Citizen*, 12 March 1930. Liberation of Jimmy Bole: NRS, AD15/30/70, pp. 110–12 (DL Montgomery). Funeral of Alec McLellan: *Sunday Mail*, 16 March 1930; *Sunday Post*, 16 March 1930.

'No wonder people is frightened to come forward'. Anonymous letters: NRS, AD15/30/70 (unpaginated); McFadyens' denials: NRS, AD15/30/70, p. 116 (DL Montgomery). Discovery of dagger: *Sunday Mail*, 30 March 1930; *Evening Times*, 8 May 1930.

Barbarism on Trial. Solicitor's statement / Strathern's response: NRS, AD15/30/70 (letters from William P. Toner and J. Drummond Strathern). McVey's evidence: NRS, AD15/30/70, pp. 161–8. Trial at High Court: *Evening News*, 6 May 1930; *Evening Times*, 6–8 May 1930; *Scottish Daily Express*, 7–9 May 1930; *Glasgow Herald*, 8 May 1930; *Thomson's Weekly News*, 10 May 1930; *Sunday Post*, 18 May 1930. 'State of barbarism': *Evening Citizen*, 9 May 1930.

Unlikely Gangsters. Background reports on prisoners: NRS, AD15/30/70. John Booth's educational record: *Scottish Daily Express*, 9 May 1930; employer's character reference: NRS, AD15/30/70 (statement for defence by James Grayson); mother's testimony (statement for defence by Jane Smith McCraw or Booth); *Evening News*, 8 May 1930. Borrowed money for tickets to dance: NRS, AD15/30/70, p. 47 (Catherine McMahon). Alexander Ratcliffe: NRS, AD15/30/70; *Glasgow Observer*, 9 May 1930. Berty McFadyen, *Glasgow Herald*, 21 June 1930; *Glasgow Eastern Standard*, 28 June 1930; NRS, 15/30/70, p. 161 (Anthony McVey). 'MYSELF AND THE DRYGATE DRAMA': *Sunday Mail*, 11 May 1930.

5: RAZOR THUGS AND GIRL GANGSTERS

All-female gangs/'most rigorous punishment': *Weekly Record*, 31 May 1930.

'War on the Razor Thugs'. Trials of George Clark and Angus Hunter: *Evening Citizen*, 9 May 1930; *Evening Times*, 9 May 1930; *Glasgow Herald*, 10 May 1930. 'WAR ON RAZOR THUGS': *Scottish Daily Express*, 10 May 1930. Pronouncement by Lord Alness: *Scottish Daily Express*, 13 May 1930. Legal restriction on use of the 'lash': *Glasgow Herald*, 3 June 1930. Interviews with Bailies Hunter, Holmes and Kennedy: *Evening Citizen*, 13 May 1930. Victims 'afraid to come forward': *Evening News*, 13 May 1930. Interview with Bailie Reid / gangs' armouries: *Scottish Daily Express*, 14, 15 May 1930. Calls for flogging: *Glasgow Herald*, 13 May 1930; *Evening Citizen*, 13

May 1930. Disquiet in legal circles: *Sunday Post*, 18 May 1930.
Girl Gangsters. Nature and origins of the Glasgow gangs / role
of girls and young women: *Weekly Record*, 17, 31 May 1930.
Female followers incite fights: *Evening News*, 10 May 1929.
'Molls' and their caprices: *Sunday Mail*, 3 February 1935. Paddy
Cousins: *Weekly Record*, 7, 21 March 1931. Eve-like figures /
drift into prostitution: *Weekly Record*, 9 February 1929. Fears
of independent young women: Graves and Hodge (1941), pp.
44–5; Todd (2005), pp. 214–17; Savage (2007), p. 240. Auxiliary
roles: *Evening Citizen*, 24 December 1926; *Weekly Record*, 31
May 1930; *Evening Citizen*, 7 August 1930. Elizabeth Millar
and Patricia McCormack: *Glasgow Eastern Standard*, 12
October 1929. Margaret Dawson: *Glasgow Eastern Standard*,
29 October 1932. Elizabeth McLeod *et al*: *Evening Citizen*, 6
November 1929. Billy Boys' female followers: *Sunday Mail*, 8
July 1928. Mary Pritchard, Isabella McMillan and Bridget
Cartwright: *Evening Citizen*, 9 May 1927. 'BATTLE OF
ARMED GIRLS': *Weekly Record*, 1 June 1929; *Glasgow Eastern
Standard*, 1 June 1929.
The Queen of the Nudies. Gang 'Queens': *Weekly Record*, 17
May 1930. Mary Mooney: *Evening Citizen*, 22, 29 April 1929;
Weekly Record, 27 April 1929; *Evening Times*, 29 April 1929;
Evening Citizen, 7 August 1930. Nudie Boys: *Evening Citizen*,
28 August 1929.
The Queen of the Redskins. Agnes Reid: Cockerill (1975), p. 142;
Grant (1973), pp. 52–3; *Evening Citizen*, 20 May 1925; prison
sentences: NRS, HH21/32/83-5 (fifty-ninth spell in Duke Street
Prison: HH21/32/85, no. 1385). Jailed by Sheriff Lyell: *Evening
Citizen*, 5 February 1925. Margaret Robinson: *Glasgow Eastern
Standard*, 28 February 1931.
'How I Would Deal With the Glasgow Gangsters'. Report by
chief constable: *Scotsman*, 4 June 1930; *Glasgow Herald*, 5 June
1930. Professor of psychology: *Sunday Post*, 15 June 1930.
Wild Rumours. 'TRUTH ABOUT GLASGOW'S GANGS':
Evening Citizen, 4–8 August 1930.

6: **SAVING HOOLIGANS FROM HELL**

Meikle: *Scottish Daily Express,* 16 May 1930. Existing organisations: *Glasgow Eastern Standard,* 24 May 1930; Cameron *et al* (1943), p. 118. MacLean Watt: *Scottish Daily Express,* 17 May 1930. Whitelaw: *Scottish Daily Express,* 26, 27 May 1930.

From Gangsters to Pals. Murray and Warnes: *Glasgow Herald,* 11 June 1930; *Scotsman,* 10, 11 June 1930; *Scottish Daily Express,* 10, 11 June 1930; *Manchester Guardian,* 10 June 1930. Formation of Bridgeton Pals' Association: *Evening Citizen,* 17 September 1930. 'Street-corner' football league: *Glasgow Herald,* 13 September 1930. Bridgeton Pals' inaugural public meeting: *Evening Citizen,* 31 December 1930. Black's work in Govan: *Glasgow Herald,* 16 September 1930; *Scotsman,* 16 September 1930; *Sunday Post,* 28 September 1930; *Sunday Mail,* 19 October 1930; *Thomson's Weekly News,* 13 October 1934.

Good Citizenship in the Gorbals. Assault on Robert Cotton / trial of Arthur Boyle *et al*: *Evening Citizen,* 17 April 1930; *Evening Citizen,* 11 July 1930; *Glasgow Herald,* 12 July 1930. Peddie's intervention: *Weekly Record,* 7 March 1931; *Scotsman,* 8 November 1932; *Evening Citizen,* 10 January 1955. (There are notable discrepancies between Peddie's own accounts of his initial approach.) Concert evening: *Evening Citizen,* 9 August 1930. Plans modelled on those of Warnes and Murray: *The Times,* 25 August 1930. Support from Superintendent Cameron: *Evening Citizen,* 15 August 1930. Membership figures / appointment of officers: *Evening Citizen,* 16 August 1930. Heralded by *The Times*: 25 August 1930. Praised by Superintendent Cameron: *Evening Citizen,* 24 November 1930, 5 November 1931. Praised by Bailie Kate Beaton: *Scottish Daily Express,* 26 December 1930.

The Official History of the South Side Stickers. Paddy Cousins' history: *Weekly Record,* 7–21 March 1931. Peddie's observations: *Evening Citizen,* 10–13 January 1955. Peddie as character witness: *Evening Citizen,* 9 April 1931; *Evening Citizen,* 12 January 1955.

The Rehabilitation of James McCluskey. McCluskey's prison record / release on licence: NRS, HH13/6. Feud with Andrew

McCarthy: *Evening Citizen*, 12 January 1955. (McCluskey and McCarthy were thinly disguised in Peddie's account.) Biographical information from www.scotlandspeople.gov.uk.

The Unfortunate Gardener of the Garngad. *Thomson's Weekly News*, 22 November 1930; *Scottish Daily Express*, 22 July 1932.

A City's Youth Saved? Donald Brown: ECL (undated press cutting) Holdings of Edinburgh and District Juvenile Organisations Committee, qHV756: C73360. Warnes's estimate (sixty clubs): *Scotsman*, 16 April 1932. Speeches by Warnes: *Scotsman*, 22 January, 19 February 1932. Peddie's speech to Speakers' Club: *Scotsman*, 8 November 1932. Police support cited: *Weekly Record*, 21 March 1931; *Scotsman*, 8 November 1932. Police circumspection: *Evening Citizen*, 5 November 1931. John Boyle: *People's Journal for the West of Scotland*, 17 January 1931.

7: BILLY BOYS AND THE SAN TOY

Trial of Dan Hands and Joe Willis: *Evening Citizen*, 29 July 1926; *Scotsman*, 30 July 1926; *Glasgow Eastern Standard*, 7 August 1926. Billy Boys, 'Fenians' and Norman Conks: *Evening Citizen*, 24 March, 13 July 1926. Billy Boys' anthem / 'Boyne Water': Hanley (1958), p. 23; Murray (1984), p. 145; McFarland (1990), p. 142.

Orange Walks. Disturbances in 1927–8: *Sunday Mail*, 10 July 1927; *Evening Citizen*, 11, 22 June 1928; *Glasgow Eastern Standard*, 16 June, 14 July 1928. Recollections of Larry Johnson: BLSA, C590/02/177-180, pp. 20–21. Ross Prete: NRS, HH21/70/62, nos 2844, 5485; *Evening Citizen*, 22 June 1928.

The King of the Billy Boys. Assault on William McIlhinney: *Evening Citizen*, 11 April 1927. Proceedings against Eli Webb *et al*: *Bulletin and Scots Pictorial*, 16 June 1927; *Evening Citizen*, 21 July 1927. Appeal rejected: *Evening Citizen*, 19 July 1927; *Glasgow Eastern Standard*, 23 July 1927. Trial of John Ross: *Evening Citizen*, 21 July 1927; *Glasgow Eastern Standard*, 30 July 1927. Eli Webb injured during fight with Norman Conks: *Evening Citizen*, 2, 3, 8 September 1926. Biographical information on Eli Webb / his standing as 'King of the Billy Boys':

GCA, D-HEW 16/13/568, no. 85190. John McKernan: *Evening Citizen*, 3 September, 29 October 1928; *Glasgow Herald*, 4 September 1928. James McKernan: *Evening Citizen*, 19 November 1928.

The Razor King. NRS, AD15/30/103, 'Statement of Facts as to Case of John Ross', pp. 2–3. Assault on girl named Hyndman: *Glasgow Eastern Standard*, 9 August 1930. Assault on William Rankin / trial of John Ross: *Evening Citizen*, 11, 16 December 1930; *Daily Express*, 17 December 1930; *Daily Record*, 17 December 1930; *Scotsman*, 17 December 1930; *Empire News*, 21 December 1930. Discipline among Billy Boys: *Weekly Record*, 20 December 1930. Persecution of Isabella McLaughlan: *Glasgow Weekly Herald*, 3 January 1931; *People's Journal for the West of Scotland*, 3 January 1931. Biographical information on John Ross: NRS, AD15/30/103 'Report by The Governor, H.M. Prison, Duke Street, Glasgow, I.C. John Ross', pp. 1–2.

The Trials of Billy Fullerton. Convicted in May 1926: *Evening Citizen*, 29 May 1926; GCA, D-HEW 16/14/67/10039. Convicted in October 1926: *Evening Citizen*, 5 October 1926; *Scotsman*, 6 October 1926. Assault on John Evans: *Glasgow Eastern Standard*, 1 November 1930. Incident on 4 February 1931 / trial of Billy Fullerton: *Evening Citizen*, 7, 8 April 1931; *Glasgow Herald*, 8, 9 April 1931; Sillitoe (1955), pp. 131–3. Pitched battle between Billy Boys and Norman Conks: *Evening Citizen*, 18 May 1931.

Catholic Gangs of the Calton. Calton Entry: *Evening Citizen*, 4, 6 August 1930. Fullerton on the Kent Star and San Toy: *Sunday Dispatch*, 10 March 1935. Incident in June 1931 / trial at sheriff court: *Evening Times*, 19 June 1931; *Scotsman*, 8 July 1931; *Glasgow Eastern Standard*, 11 July 1931. Incident on 5 July 1931/ members of rival gangs knew each other: NRS, AD15/31/48, pp. 1–2 (John Riddell), pp. 3–4 (William Watson), p. 6 (William Nisbet), p. 11 (William Smillie), p. 16 (George Jordan).

'"Gangsters" as Tory Stewards'. Billy Boys' pledges: *Evening Citizen*, 18 January 1955. Support for Tories: McAllister (1935), pp. 94–5. Disruption of speech by Arthur Cook: *Evening Times*, 20, 25 February 1929. Disruption of Communist Party meeting in Bridgeton: *Evening Citizen*, 8 September 1930; McShane and

Smith (1978), p. 205. National Unemployed Workers' Movement: Damer (1990a), pp. 146–7. Meeting on Glasgow Green: *Evening Citizen*, 2, 7 October 1931. Disturbances in the Calton: *Evening Citizen*, 3, 27 October 1931. Damage to Glasgow's economic prospects: *Evening Citizen*, 9 October 1931. Catherine Gavin's election meetings: *Evening Times*, 14 October 1931. Billy Boys as stewards: *Bulletin*, 17 October 1931; *Evening Citizen*, 17 October 1931; *Evening Times*, 17 October 1931; *Daily Mirror*, 21 October 1931. Students as stewards: *Evening Citizen*, 22 October 1931. Charlie Forrester's election meetings: *Bulletin*, 31 October 1931; *Evening Citizen*, 30, 31 October 1931, 26 January 1932; *Evening Times*, 26 January 1932. Susan Cameron's election meetings: *Evening Citizen*, 29 October 1931; *Bulletin*, 3 November 1931; *Daily Record*, 3 November 1931; *Evening Citizen*, 3 November 1931. Disturbance in Muslin Street: *Glasgow Eastern Standard*, 7 November 1931. Thomas Davidson: MacDougall (1991), p. 252. Assault on Tommy Hastings: *Evening Citizen*, 26 October 1932. Thomas Davidson: MacDougall (1991), p. 252.

8: THE ABDICATION OF BILLY FULLERTON

Petition to Sillitoe: *Scottish Daily Express*, 19 February 1932; *Sunday Mail*, 21 February 1932; *Sunday Post*, 21 February 1932. Sillitoe's appointment as Chief Constable of Glasgow / introduction of new technology: Sillitoe (1955), pp. 107, 109–11; *Evening News*, 27 December 1932. Informants and 'special irregulars': Cockerill (1975), pp. 103, 133–4. 'Deaf Burke': *Scotsman*, 25 November 1925. Police response to petition: *Scottish Daily Express*, 23 February 1932.

Billy Fullerton's Life Story. Peterhead Convict Prison: *Annual Report of the Prisons Department for Scotland for the Year 1932* (Edinburgh: HMSO, 1933), pp. 17, 31, 39; *Thomson's Weekly News*, 24 October 1936; Forbes and Meehan (1982), pp. 135–7. Fullerton's life story: *Thomson's Weekly News*, 16 April 1932. Family background / marriage / employment history / wife and mother state their religion as 'Protestant': GCA, D-HEW 16/4/67/10039, D-HEW 16/13/517/77552, D-HEW

18/1/58478, D-HEW 18/2/7288. Billy Boys' role in the General Strike: *Evening Citizen*, 17 January 1955. Marriage of Billy Fullerton and Rose Farmer: www.scotlandspeople.gov.uk. Fullerton's conviction at Glasgow Sheriff Court: *Evening Citizen*, 5 October 1926.

The Gangster and the Major. Profiles of Speir / his thrashing of Fullerton: *Weekly Record*, 7 February 1931; *Glasgow Herald*, 26 December 1940; *Evening Citizen*, 19, 20 January 1955.

Fullerton's New Life. Appearance as prosecution witness: *Glasgow Eastern Standard*, 7 May 1932. Opening of Billy Boys' club: *Glasgow Eastern Standard*, 15 July 1933.

Defenders of John Knox. Attack on Catholic children's procession in Muslin Street / raid on Bridgeton Cross: *Glasgow Eastern Standard*, 3, 24 June 1933. Complaints to chief constable: *Glasgow Eastern Standard*, 1 July 1933. James McKay: *Glasgow Eastern Standard*, 1 July 1933; NRS, HH21/70/66, no. 3833. 'Twelfth of July' disturbances: *Glasgow Eastern Standard*, 15, 29 July 1933. Scottish Covenanters' Defenders in Clydebank: *Glasgow Eastern Standard*, 1 July 1933. William Watson: *Glasgow Eastern Standard*, 8, 29 July, 16 September, 28 October 1933. James Leadingham: *Glasgow Eastern Standard*, 11 November 1933. Robert Bowes: *Glasgow Eastern Standard*, 11 November 1933.

9: GANGS, RACKETS AND CRIME

Fears of crime wave: *People's Journal for the West of Scotland*, 20 February 1932; *Sunday Mail*, 21 February 1932. Sillitoe's report: MLG, *Report on the State of Crime and the Police Establishment with Tabulated Returns for the Year Ended 31st December 1932*, Corporation of the City of Glasgow (1933), p. 9. Sillitoe's relationship with the press: Maver (2000), p. 255. 'Wars' on crime: *Evening Citizen*, 23 December 1931; *Scottish Daily Express*, 23 February 1932; *Sunday Post*, 6 March 1932.

Scots and the American Underworld. Al Capone's Scottish bodyguard: *Weekly Record*, 13 April 1929. James Gilzean: *Weekly Record*, 22 March 1930. Resort to firearms: *Glasgow Weekly Herald*, 8 October 1932.

Glasgow's 'Reign of Terror'. Chicago-style 'rackets': *Sunday Mail*, 10 July 1932. Superintendent McClure / allegation of 'terrorism': *Glasgow Weekly Herald*, 18 June 1932; *Sunday Mail*, 19 June 1932; *John Bull*, 25 June 1932; Goldsmith (1993), p. 181; New form of blackmail: *Sunday Mail*, 10 July 1932. Police rebuttal: *Evening Times*, 13 July 1932. Calling 'at the demand': *Evening Times*, 13 May 1930; *Weekly Record*, 20 December 1930; *Sunday Mail*, 10 July 1932; *Sunday Mail*, 16 August 1936. 'F' of the Kent Star: *Sunday Dispatch*, 10 March 1935. Confessions of an 'ex-gangster': *Weekly Record*, 12 July 1930. Billy Fullerton: *Thomson's Weekly News*, 16 April 1932. Local resentment: *Evening Citizen*, 26 August 1926; *Evening Citizen*, 8 June 1927; *Evening Times*, 29 June 1934. Walter Scott: *Glasgow Eastern Standard*, 3 August 1929. Gang members help themselves to goods and services: *Weekly Record*, 21 March 1931; Grant (1973), p. 52; Pieri (2001), pp. 33, 126–8. South Side Stickers: *Weekly Record*, 17 May 1930. Bookmakers and 'protection': *Weekly Record*, 12 July 1930; *Sunday Dispatch*, 10 March 1935; *Sunday Mail*, 16 August 1936. Peter Williamson: GCA, D-HEW 18/3/20/2904. James Crearie: *Thomson's Weekly News*, 24 April 1934. Prendergast (1992), pp. 36–40, 55, 92: bookmaker stands up to gangs. Dan Cronin: Burrowes (1992), pp. 104–5. Burniston defies the Cheeky Forty: *Belfast Telegraph*, 5 June 1935. Bookmakers and the police: Davies (1992).

'Never a criminal in the accepted sense of the word'. Billy Boys did not resort to theft: *Evening Citizen*, 17 January 1955. Distinction between Fullerton and his followers: Sillitoe (1955), p. 128. Criminal records of the gang's members: PRONI, CAB.9B/236/1, 'Disturbances in Belfast, 1935.' Fullerton charged with housebreaking: NRS, HH21/70/65, no. 3331. David and Robert Turnbull: *Thomson's Weekly News*, 31 May 1930; GCA, D-HEW 16/4/187/B27908. Edward Livingstone and James Rennie: GCA, SR22/63/19. John Louden: *Scotsman*, 27 February 1934. DL Paterson: NRS, JC34/1/179, 'Application for Leave to Appeal against Conviction and Sentence by John Traquair'; 'Notes of Evidence', pp. 56–8. 'GANG TERRORISM IN GLASGOW': *The Times*, 1 May 1934.

The Trial of the Beehive Boys. Gang's key figures: Sillitoe (1955), pp. 124–6. Network / group profile: GCA, SR22/63/19. Louis Scragowitz: McAllister (1986), p. 28; NRS, HH21/70/69, no. 6504. Queen Bees / 'Wee Hive': McAllister (1986), p. 28; *Evening Times*, 11 August 1936. Police operation / trial at Glasgow Sheriff Court: NRS, SC36/56/164, 'Record of Criminal Trials, 4 January 1934–28 June 1934', pp. 133–50; SC36/60/11, 'Indictment against William Shannon *et al*, 8 and 19 February 1934'; *Bulletin*, 21 February 1934; *Daily Record*, 21, 23 February 1934; *Glasgow Herald*, 21 February 1934; *Evening Times*, 22 February 1934. Price of stolen whisky: *Glasgow Eastern Standard*, 10 January 1931. Police use of motor patrols: *Bulletin*, 21 February 1934. Use of informers: Cockerill (1975), pp. 133–4, 143. Peter Williamson and William Shannon arrested following tip-off: *Bulletin*, 22 February 1934. Witnesses' reluctance to testify: *Glasgow Herald*, 21 February 1934. Beehive Boys' resort to violence: *Glasgow Herald*, 21, 22 February 1934. Police evidence at trial: *Daily Record*, 21 February 1934; *Glasgow Herald*, 21 February 1934. Peter Williamson quizzes witnesses: *Daily Record*, 21 February 1934. Prisoners' bravado: *Bulletin*, 21 February 1934; *Daily Record*, 23 February 1934. Strathern's rhetoric: *Evening Times*, 22 February 1934; *Daily Record*, 23 February 1934. Assault on PC Mulvey: *Sunday Mail*, 2 December 1934; *Glasgow Herald*, 4 December 1934; *Thomson's Weekly News*, 16 March 1935. Dan Cronin and Tommy Boyle: *Glasgow Herald*, 11 January 1935. Boyle's conviction in Manchester: NRS, SC36/60/12. Peter Williamson: GCA, D-HEW 18/3/20, no. 2904. Wage levels during the 1930s: Stevenson and Cook (2010) p. 25.

Motor Bandits. Joy-riding: *Evening Citizen*, 28 October 1931; *Sunday Mail*, 9 February 1936; O'Connell (1998). 'Smash and grab' raids: *Glasgow Eastern Standard*, 3 August 1929; *Evening Citizen*, 10, 11 November, 1 December 1931. Epidemic of thefts in 1931–2: *People's Journal for the West of Scotland*, 10 October 1936.

The Insurance Man's Tale. Two interviews with 'Larry Johnson' (pseudonym) were conducted by historian and documentary film-maker, Steve Humphries. Excerpts were published in

Humphries (1988) and Humphries and Gordon (1994). The second interview is held at BLSA, C590/02/177-180. Additional biographical information: GCA, D-HEW 18/3/194, no. 29097. Kilmarnock expedition: NRS, SC7/33/14; JC34/1/235; *Glasgow Herald*, 9 June 1936.

10: **THE OLD FIRM**

Passion for football: Cameron *et al* (1943), p. 106. Matches between rival gangs: *Evening Citizen*, 25 August 1927. On football, religion and national identity in Glasgow, see Murray (1984), p. 1; Gallagher (1987), p. 1. Brake clubs: Murray (1984), p. 175. Celtic brake club from the Garngad: *Evening Citizen*, 19, 21, 22 October 1925. Billy Fullerton / 'Kipling': *Thomson's Weekly News*, 16 April 1932. Larry Johnson: BLSA, C590/02/177-180. Assault on eight-year-old boy: *Glasgow Eastern Standard*, 30 March 1929.

Bigotry and Ballots. Control of Glasgow Corporation by 'Moderates': Maver (2000): pp. 234–6. Impact of Scottish Protestant League: Bruce *et al* (2004), pp. 48–50. Downward social mobility: Cameron *et al* (1943), pp. 24–5. (Cameron and his co-authors did not distinguish between Protestants and Catholics.) Junior football match at Barrowfield Park / S. Hardie Stewart on East End gangs: *Scottish Daily Express*, 1, 2, June 1933.

The Trial of John Traquair. Biographical details: www.scotlands people.gov.uk. Traquair's conviction in 1933: *Glasgow Eastern Standard*, 16 September 1933. Incident on 3 March 1934 / trial at Glasgow High Court / Traquair's appeal: NRS, JC34/1/179, 'Application for leave to appeal against conviction and sentence by John Traquair': Notes of evidence, 30 April 1934; 'Lord Moncrieff's charge to jury', 30 April 1934; 'Confidential report by Lord Moncrieff', 19 May 1934; 'Note of application under S.1 (b) for leave to appeal against a conviction and sentence, Criminal Appeal (Scotland) Act, 1926', 28 June 1934; Davies (2006). Appeal rejected: *Glasgow Herald*, 18 July 1934. Petitions on behalf of Traquair: *Vanguard*, 16 May 1934. Conviction of Kent Stars: *Glasgow Herald*, 28 April 1934. Resentment among Protestant youths: Walker (1992), pp. 204–5. 'Oh why be so hard on the Brigton Billy Boys': BLSA, C590/02/177-180, p. 22. 'Knights of Kaledonia Klan': *Vanguard*, 8 November 1933; *Evening Citizen*, 18 January 1955. Meetings in support of Traquair: *Vanguard*, 23 May, 13 June 1934. Petition submitted with 40,000 signatures: *Vanguard*, 27 June 1934; rejected by Secretary of State: *Glasgow Herald*, 20 August 1934.

The Killing of Jimmy Dalziel. Biographical details / origins of nickname: *Thomson's Weekly News*, 10 March, 28 April 1934. Parlour Boys: *Evening Times*, 24–6 April 1934. Police view of Dalziel: *Glasgow Herald*, 25 April 1934; *Evening Times*, 26 June 1934. Violet Dalziel: *Sunday Mail*, 4 March 1934; *Scottish Daily Express*, 25 April 1934. Incident on 2 March 1934 / trial at High Court: *Evening Times*, 24–6 April 1934; *Glasgow Herald*, 25 April 1934; *Scottish Daily Express*, 25–8 April 1934; *Thomson's Weekly News*, 28 April 1934; Sillitoe (1955), p. 126. Arrest of suspects: *Evening News*, 3, 5, 12 March 1934; 'wholesale mopping-up campaign' / 'Gangland stood firm': Colquhoun (1962), p. 37. Release of eight prisoners: *Glasgow Herald*, 15 March 1934; *Thomson's Weekly News*, 17 March 1934, *Scottish Daily Express*, 24 April 1934; *Thomson's Weekly News*, 12 September 1936. Bernard Kiernan named as Dalziel's killer: *Sunday Mail*, 15 April 1934; NRS, JC26/1934/18. 'Special defence' withdrawn: *Glasgow Herald*, 25 April 1934. Sentences condemned: *Glasgow Herald*, 28 April 1934; Sillitoe (1955), p. 127; letters to press: *Evening Times*, 30 April, 2, 8 May 1934.

'The San Toys will fight anything!' Incident on 24 March 1934: *Evening Times*, 30 March 1934. 'PAPISTS SENT TO PRISON!' *Vanguard*, 11 April 1934. Fatal assault on Alec Craig-West: NRS, JC26/1934/26 (Robert Doris); JC36/83, pp. 21–50 (Thomas Lyon), pp. 51–98 (John Walsh), pp. 100–130 (John Cardle), pp. 138–86 (Janet Rice), pp. 189–90 (Edward McGonigle), pp. 246–50 (William Bryson), pp. 257–68 (PC William Cameron), pp. 297–9 (Inspector John Samuel), pp. 310–14 (DI James Tait), pp. 319–28 (William Reid), pp. 399–423 (John Kerr), pp. 427–41 (Thomas Mullen), pp. 459–62 (Mrs Elizabeth Doris), pp. 463–506 (Robert Doris). Thomas Mullen jailed for breach of the peace: NRS, HH21/70/67, no. 5176. Trial at High Court /

interviews with Robert and Elizabeth Doris: *Scottish Daily Express*, 27, 29 October 1934; *Sunday Mail*, 28 October 1934; *Glasgow Herald*, 29 October 1934; *People's Journal*, 3 November 1934. Previous conviction against John Kerr: NRS, HH21/70/67, no. 3166.

The Billy Boys in Belfast. Invitation: *Glasgow Eastern Standard*, 20 July 1935. Sectarian tensions in Belfast: Hepburn (1990), pp. 77–9. Disturbances of 12–13 July 1935: Hepburn (1990), pp. 79–80, 90; *Belfast Newsletter*, 15 July 1935; *Irish News*, 15 July 1935; *Glasgow Eastern Standard*, 3 August 1935. Billy Boys' departure: *Irish News*, 16 July 1935; *Irish Times*, 16 July 1935; *Scottish Daily Express*, 16 July 1935. Further violence in Belfast: Hepburn (1990), pp. 82–5. Billy Fullerton and David Turnbull: *Glasgow Eastern Standard*, 3 August 1935; GCA, D-HEW 18/2/7288; *Evening Citizen*, 14 January 1955. Membership of Billy Boys' band / previous convictions: PRONI, CAB.9B/236/1, 'Disturbances in Belfast, 1935'. Robert Burnside: *Scotsman*, 27 September, 1 October 1935; reports of shooting: *Belfast Newsletter*, 15 July 1935; *Irish News*, 15 July 1935.

11: FIGHTING MEN AND FAMILY MEN

Interest in gangs among wider population: *Evening Citizen*, 6 August 1930. Graffiti / photographs: *Evening Citizen*, 24 August, 3 September, 2 October 1928. 'The Beehive Boys from Thistle Street': verse featured in 'Peaky Blinders and Scuttlers', written and presented by Steve Humphries, BBC Radio 4, broadcast 25 August 1987.

The Allure of the Gangster. Louis Scragowitz: NRS, HH21/70/67, nos 4924, 7713; HH21/70/68, nos 2016, 4326; HH21/70/69, nos 287, 6504; McAllister (1986), p. 28. 'Ex-gangster': *Weekly Record*, 28 June 1930. Larry Johnson: Humphries (1988), pp. 115, 141, 144–5, 148, 160. James Wilkie *et al*: NRS, SC36/57/17, case no. 827; 'up to full carnal knowledge': HH21/70/67, no. 1339. Photographer's visit to clubroom of the Kent Star: *Thomson's Weekly News*, 12 September 1936. Gang members got married when they 'had to': GCA, D-HEW 16/14/67/10039 (Billy Fullerton), D-HEW 23/62/1/19049 (Andrew Mulvey).

Broader social trends: McKibbin (1998), pp. 296–7. Dan Cronin: Boyle (1977), p. 23. 'Fighting men were the heroes': McGinn (1987), p. 32. Cowardice 'unthinkable': Caplan (1991), p. 35. Gangs formed by schoolboys: *Glasgow Eastern Standard*, 16, 30 November 1935. Rose Street gang: *Scotsman*, 21 March 1930. **Fighting Men.** Calton Emmet: *Evening Times*, 26 December 1929. Demanding free drinks: *Glasgow Eastern Standard*, 18 July 1936 (John Phillips). Gangs as hired muscle: *Thomson's Weekly News*, 16 April 1932 (Billy Fullerton). Eli Webb: Savage (2006), p. 99. 'Square go': Caplan (1991), pp. 15–17; Damer (1990a), p. 150. Peter Williamson: *Daily Record*, 21 February 1934. Murdoch McLennan: *Glasgow Herald*, 18 February 1931. Fight on banks of Clyde: Savage (2006), p. 118. Henry Ellis: *Glasgow Eastern Standard*, 19 August 1933. Gang fights as spectacle: *Evening Citizen*, 6 August 1930. Cheeky Forty versus Chain Gang: *Sunday Mail*, 26 November 1933. Thomas McGuire: *Scotsman*, 22 November 1930. 'Cowardly' resort to weapons: *Sunday Mail*, 11 August 1935; *Glasgow Herald*, 17 October 1935. 'You have to have something in your possession passing Bridgeton Cross': *Glasgow Herald*, 15 April 1935.
'John the Baptist' and the Kent Star. Thomas Falconer: *Evening Citizen*, 14 February 1927, 29 April 1927; McGinn (1987), p. 32. Edward McQuade: *Glasgow Eastern Standard*, 12 August 1933. 'F' of the Kent Star: *Sunday Dispatch*, 10 March 1935. James Tinney O'Neill: GCA, D-HEW 23/63/1/67068; NRS, SC36/60/14; *Glasgow Eastern Standard*, 23 July 1932; assault on Charles Wylie: *Glasgow Eastern Standard*, 21 October 1933; convicted of theft: NRS, HH21/70/64, no. 247; HH21/70/69, no. 2292; *Glasgow Eastern Standard*, 25 April 1936; assault on David Grieve with razor: *Glasgow Herald*, 27 October 1936; *Glasgow Eastern Standard*, 31 October 1936; slashed at Palacerigg: GCA, D-HEW 23/63/1/67068. Andrew Mulvey: family background: GCA, D-HEW 23/62/1/19049; D-HEW 23/62/2/9929; jailed for possession of explosives: NRS, HH21/70/66, no. 8065. Trial of James Tinney O'Neill at sheriff court: *Glasgow Eastern Standard*, 23 June 1934. Assault on PC Gordon Allison / trial at sheriff court: *Sunday Mail*, 15 July 1934; *Vanguard*, 1 August

1934; *Evening Times*, 8–11 October 1934. Mary Mulvey: *Glasgow Eastern Standard*, 21 July 1934. Assault on John Kerr / trial of Andrew Mulvey and Thomas McKeeve: *Glasgow Herald*, 13, 15 July, 16, 17 October 1935; *Scottish Daily Express*, 17 October 1935. Mary and Andrew Mulvey: GCA, D-HEW 23/62/1/19049; D-HEW 23/62/2/9929; D-HEW 33/24/1/1/19049. **Gangsters as Family Men.** Billy Fullerton: *Thomson's Weekly News*, 16 April 1932. 'F' of the Kent Star: *Sunday Dispatch*, 10 March 1935. Gang members apply for hospital treatment for wives and children: GCA, D-HEW 23/55/2/35972 (Samuel Kelly Campbell), D-HEW 23/63/1/67068 (James Tinney O'Neill). David and Margaret Turnbull: NRS, JC26/1933/19; *Evening Times*, 5 July 1933; *Glasgow Herald*, 6 July 1933. Billy and Rose Fullerton: GCA, D-HEW 16/14/67/10039, D-HEW18/2/7288; *Glasgow Eastern Standard*, 3 November 1934. Peter Williamson: *Evening Times*, 22 February 1934; GCA, D-HEW, 18/3/20, no. 2904; Sillitoe (1955), p. 124.

'One of the worst outrages ever known'. Govan episode as recounted to Robert Black: *Thomson's Weekly News*, 13 October 1934.

12: **THE BIG HOUSE**
Arrest of a 'spectator': *Evening Citizen*, 4 July 1929.
Hard Labour. Barlinnie prison population in 1934: *Annual Report of the Prisons Department for Scotland for the Year 1934*, p. 17. Lay-out of prison / daily regime: Scottish Office (1935), pp. 4–5; *Sunday Post*, 30 March 1930; *Evening Citizen*, 11 January 1955. Contraband: Scottish Office (1935), p. 18. Assaults on warders: *Evening Citizen*, 23 December 1925; *Evening Times*, 10 January 1929; *Manchester Guardian*, 22 September 1929. Strathern on 'lawless gang instinct': NRS, HH57/655, 'Disturbance at Barlinnie Prison: Summary of points contained in the Procurator Fiscal's Report', p. 1.
'We will give you Dartmoor'. Dartmoor 'mutiny': Brown (2007); *Daily Express*, 25, 26 January 1932; *Daily Mirror*, 25, 26 January 1932. Reports of 'mutiny' devoured in Barlinnie: *Sunday Post*, 1 May 1932; *Perthshire Constitutional*, 22 June 1932. Alf Pellow:

NRS, HH21/70/64, no. 5187. Events on 25 April 1932 / responses by prison staff: NRS, HH57/661; statements by John R. Singers and D. Fyfe, 26 April 1932; report by R. Walkinshaw, 29 April 1932; letter from Dr G. M. Scott to Secretary, Scottish Prisons Department, 29 April 1932; letter from Colonel R.E.W. Baird to Under Secretary of State, Scottish Office, 6 May 1932; excerpt from Prison Visiting Committee Inspection Book. Joe Dinnen: *Evening Citizen*, 31 March 1932. System of remission: *Sunday Post*, 14 December 1930. Threats issued by Alf Pellow: NRS, HH57/661, letter from Warder Dowall to governor of Barlinnie, 29 April 1932. Colonel Baird visits Greenock: NRS, HH57/661; letter from Colonel R.E.W. Baird to Under Secretary of State, Scottish Office, 30 April 1932. 'LET'S GIVE THEM DARTMOOR': *Scottish Daily Express*, 29, 30 April 1932. Revelations by ex-prisoner: *Sunday Post*, 1 May 1932. Eight prisoners transferred from Greenock to Perth / resentment at prisoners selling their stories to press: NRS, HH57/661, letter from governor, H.M. Prison Greenock, to Colonel R.E.W. Baird. 'JAIL DISCONTENT SPREADS': *Scottish Daily Express*, 6 May 1932. Scottish prison diet: NRS, HH57/661; Robert W. Fleming, 'Report on the question of Dietaries in Scottish Prisons as requested by the Secretary of State for Scotland', 19 May 1932. Letter to 'Major Baird' from Patrick Sweeney: NRS, HH57/661; Sweeney's criminal record: SC36/56/158; response by governor: HH57/661, Confidential memo from Robert Walkinshaw, Governor, to the Secretary, Scottish Prisons Department, 26 May 1932. New system of privileges / tobacco smuggling / Dan Cronin: Scottish Office (1935), pp. 21–5; *Perthshire Constitutional*, 22 June 1932; *Sunday Mail*, 23, 30 December 1934; NRS, HH57/655, 'Minutes of Evidence' (Archibald Bates). Death of Robert Walkinshaw: *Scotsman*, 13 January 1934. Appointment of Captain James Murray: *Scotsman*, 10 February 1934. Murray's regime: Scottish Office (1935), pp. 21–3.

Terry McGhee's Tears. *Thomson's Weekly News*, 14 April 1934. **Privileges and Punishments.** The account of the disturbances of December 1934 draws on the report of the inquiry conducted by Sir George Rankin: Scottish Office (1935) and the associated papers held in NRS, HH57/655: 'Minutes of Evidence' (testimonies of Warder Arthur Bates and Warder George Chessell); letter from Captain J. Murray to the Secretary, Prisons Department for Scotland, 23 December 1934; memo from medical officer to procurator fiscal, 3 January 1935; letter from visiting clergyman, Peter Morrison, to Governor of Barlinnie, 18 January 1935; responses by Captain James Murray and Warder George Chessell, 21 January 1935; 'Disturbances at Barlinnie Prison: Summary of points contained in the Procurator-Fiscal's Report'; HH57/662: report by prison medical officer, Dr Geoffrey Scott. Press reports: *Sunday Mail*, 23 December 1934; *Scotsman*, 27 December 1934. 'Blind eye' turned by governor and head warder on 22 December 1934: Jeffrey (2009), p. 134. Trial of Francis Monaghan: HH57/662, letter from governor of Barlinnie to chief constable, 9 January 1935; *The Times*, 17 January 1935. Trial of Barlinnie prisoners at sheriff court: *Glasgow Herald*, 26 January 1935. Twelve men moved to Perth: *Sunday Mail*, 10 February 1935; NRS, HH57/655, 'Minutes of Evidence' (Warder Archibald Bates). Sir George Rankin's findings: Scottish Office (1935) pp. 22–3 (need for 'firm handling'); pp. 17–20 (causes of disturbances); pp. 12–13 (praise for Warders Bates and Chessell; criticism of governor). Murray transferred to Greenock / appointment of Finlayson: *Scotsman*, 5 April 1935; *Evening Citizen*, 8 April 1935.

Barlinnie's New Regime. Sir Godfrey Collins: *Scottish Daily Express*, 5 July 1935. Smuggling: *Scottish Daily Express*, 12 August 1936. Peter Williamson and Walter Scott: *Glasgow Herald*, 7 September 1935; NRS, HH21/70/68, nos 5817, 5818. Prisoner slashed: *Sunday Mail*, 7 June 1936. Gang fight in cookhouse: *Sunday Post*, 3 January 1937. Prison officials refuse to comment: *Sunday Post*, 11 October 1936. Members of rival gangs segregated within prison: *Sunday Mail*, 23 May 1937.

'You had to be one of the boys'. Interview with Larry Johnson: BLSA, C590/02/177-180, pp. 2–5.

13: **A STORY OF THE GLASGOW SLUMS**
Daily Record, 28 October 1935.

The Baker and the Wordsmith. On McArthur's biography, the genesis of *No Mean City* and the novel's reception in 1935, see Damer (1990b); Burgess (1998). McArthur's appearance and temperament: Watts (1959), p. 160. *Love on the Dole*: Croft (1990), pp. 108–9. Role of Kingsley Long / McArthur's visit to London: McArthur and Kingsley Long (1935), v–vi; *Daily Express*, 9 March 1936. Stanton on McArthur's elusiveness: Watts (1959), p. 160. Profile of Kingsley Long: Damer (1990b), pp. 27–8. Drafting of *Limey*: Spenser and Kingsley Long (1958), pp. 9–10. Drafting of *No Mean City*: Watts (1959), p. 160; *Daily Express*, 10 March 1936; *Sunday Times*, 13 December 1959 (letter to editor from Kingsley Long). Division of royalties / McArthur's 'facility for social observation' / incorporation of pub talk: Damer (1990b), pp. 27–8, 39.

The Rise and Fall of 'Johnnie Stark'. Passages from McArthur and Kingsley Long (1935): 'Ah'm no mug!', p. 97; fight on Glasgow Green, pp. 148–51; demise of the 'Razor King', pp. 312, 317.

Alexander McArthur's Glasgow. I owe this phrase to Burgess (1998), p. 14. Passages from McArthur and Kingsley Long (1935): gangsters as street fighters: p. 138; ferocity and adherence to code of honour: pp. 133, 157, 309; dancing craze of the 1920s, pp. 13–14, 131–2, 159, 166–8; domestic violence, p. 24; children's awareness of sex, pp. 20–21; sexual relationships, pp. 254, 295–6; 'Battles and sex', p. 39; 'Vanity is an underrated vice', p. 47; fighting as an amusement, p. 39; 'queer admiration', p. 120; neighbourhood gossip, pp. 278–80; double-edged attitudes towards gangs, p. 133; police strategies, p. 153; gang battles peak in 1929, p. 311; role of churches / decline of gangs, pp. 311–12; 'It is left to his wife', p. 311. Female followers do 'anything' for gang members: *Weekly Record*, 9 February 1929. 'Amateur psychology' in *No Mean City*: Burgess (1986), p. 44.

'It grips you by its very grimness'. Letter from R. G. Longman: MLG, ms accession no. 891704. Advertisements in national press: *Observer*, 27 October 1935. Insertion of preface: *Evening*

Times, 28 October 1935. McArthur's experience of unemployment: *Daily Express*, 6 March 1936; Watts (1959), p. 160; Damer (1990b), p. 27. Responses to *No Mean City*: Damer (1990b); *Sunday Mail*, 27 October, 3, 10 November, 1, 8 December 1935; *Daily Record*, 28 October 1935; *Glasgow Herald*, 28 October 1935; *Evening Citizen*, 28 October 1935; *Evening Times*, 28 October 1935; *Scottish Daily Express*, 29, 30 October 1935; *Scotsman*, 31 October 1935; *Times Literary Supplement*, 2 November 1935; *Observer*, 3 November 1935; *Listener*, 20 November 1935; *Spectator*, 8 December 1935. Serialisation by the *Sunday Mail*: 3 November–8 December 1935. Peddie on *No Mean City*: *Scottish Daily Express*, 30 October 1935. Dollan on *No Mean City*: *Glasgow Herald*, 19 November 1935. McArthur on *No Mean City*: *Daily Record*, 1 November 1935.

No Mean Cities of Britain. Serialisation by the *Daily Express*: from 10 March 1936; readers' letters: 13, 17, 20, 24 March, 6 April 1936; 'No Mean Cities of Britain': 6–14 April 1936. Housing survey: White (1977), pp. 86–8. James Wilkie: *Daily Express*, 17 March 1936. Review of *No Mean City*: *New York Times*, 13 September 1936. Canadian reporter's visit to the Gorbals: *Sunday Mail*, 8 March 1936.

14: SILLITOE AND THE DERRY BOYS

Derry Boys: *People's Journal*, 18 April 1936. Tour of the 'backlands': *Evening Times*, 8 August 1936. Drinking patterns: Hughes (2010), pp. 143–4. Andrew Coleman: *Sunday Mail*, 11 April 1937. Illicit distilling: *Evening Times*, 8 May, 20 December 1922; *Evening Citizen*, 31 January 1928; *Sunday Post*, 13 April 1930. 'Red Biddy': *Sunday Mail*, 12 October 1930.

'It happens every day in Brigton'. Assault on John McGuire: *People's Journal*, 18 January 1936; *Thomson's Weekly News*, 18 January 1936. Trial of James Wilkie and James Brown: *Daily Express*, 17 March 1936; *Glasgow Herald*, 17 March 1936; *Scotsman*, 17 March 1936; *People's Journal*, 21 March 1936; *Thomson's Weekly News*, 21 March 1936. Trial of Richard Clark *et al*: NRS, SC36/60/14; *Glasgow Herald*, 15, 16 April 1936; *Scotsman*, 16 April 1936; *Glasgow Eastern Standard*, 18 April

1936; *People's Journal*, 18 April 1936. *Glasgow Herald* editorial: 16 April 1936. Assault on John McGuire / violence in Dalmarnock: *Glasgow Herald*, 13 June 1936; *Sunday Mail*, 14 June 1936. Trial of John McGuire *et al*: *Glasgow Herald*, 7, 16, 17, 22 July 1936; *Glasgow Eastern Standard*, 11, 25 July 1936. Trial of Samuel Kelly Campbell: *Glasgow Herald*, 29 November 1935. Assault on Joe Farrell / trial of Larry Gribben: *Glasgow Herald*, 5 March 1936.

The Troubles of 'Killer' McKay. Conviction for assault on James Inglis: *Glasgow Eastern Standard*, 4 July 1936; NRS, HH21/70/69 no. 4347. Interview in *Thomson's Weekly News*: 11 July 1936. Assaults on John Johnstone and Robert Drew: *People's Journal*, 20 June 1936.

'Midsummer Madness'. Statement by Superintendent Gordon: *Glasgow Eastern Standard*, 4 July 1936. Orange Walk / subsequent disturbances: *Sunday Mail*, 12 July 1936; *Glasgow Eastern Standard*, 18 July 1936. Trial of Samuel Patrick: *Scotsman*, 14 July 1936; *Glasgow Eastern Standard*, 18 July 1936; *People's Journal*, 18 July 1936. Bayonet duel: *Glasgow Eastern Standard*, 25 July 1936; *Thomson's Weekly News*, 25 July 1936. Interview with anonymous 'gangster': *Thomson's Weekly News*, 18 July 1936. Disruption of funeral: *Sunday Mail*, 9 August 1936. Sillitoe promises 'extra precautions': *Evening Times*, 12 August 1936. Incident on 4 August / pronouncement by Bailie Matthew Armstrong: *Scottish Daily Express*, 5 August 1936; *Evening Citizen*, 5 August 1936; *Glasgow Eastern Standard*, 8 August 1936. Parades by Derry Boys: *Sunday Mail*, 9 August 1936.

'Sillitoe's Cossacks'. Disturbances on 7 August: *Daily Record*, 8 August 1936; *Glasgow Herald*, 8 August 1936; *Evening Citizen*, 8 August 1936; Sillitoe (1955), p. 131. Renewed disturbances / arrest of 'Killer' McKay: *Evening Citizen*, 8 August 1936; *Daily Record*, 11 August 1936. Bailie Armstrong denounces 'religious illiterates': *Sunday Mail*, 9 August 1936. Renewal of parades: *Daily Record*, 10 August 1936.

War on the Gangsters. Proceedings at Eastern Police Court: *Evening Citizen*, 10 August 1936; *Daily Record*, 11 August 1936. Bailie Young's sentences: *Evening Citizen*, 12, 14 August 1936.

Bandsmen admitted to bail / anonymous benefactor: *Glasgow Herald*, 18, 20 August 1936. Sub-committee of magistrates: *Glasgow Herald*, 12 August 1936. Interview with Lord Provost: *Evening Citizen*, 12 August 1936. Investigation by *Scottish Daily Express*: 12 August 1936. Magistrates' resolution: *Evening Times*, 1 September 1936; *Glasgow Herald*, 2 September 1936. Clamour for 'real clean-up': *Scottish Daily Express*, 26 August 1936; *Sunday Post*, 30 August 1936. Magistrates appeal for restraint by press: *Evening Times*, 1 September 1936; *Glasgow Herald*, 2 September 1936. Bailie John Murdoch: *Evening Times*, 1 September 1936. *Glasgow Herald* questions the utility of the 'cat': 2 September 1936. Resolution praised by *Scottish Daily Express*: 2 September 1936. Sillitoe issues report to magistrates: *Glasgow Herald*, 22, 26 August, 2 September 1936. Sillitoe's methods: Cockerill (1975), pp. 147–8. 'Confessions' of a 'girl gangster': *Sunday Mail*, 23 August 1936. Isabella Scott and Jane Watson: *Glasgow Eastern Standard*, 11 July 1936; *Thomson's Weekly News*, 11 July 1936. Bailie Muir Simpson: *Scottish Daily Express*, 7 September 1936. Trial at Glasgow Sheriff Court from 14 September: NRS, SC36/57/19, Glasgow Sheriff Court, Roll Book of Criminal and Quasi-Criminal Cases, no. 5553; *Evening Times*, 14–22 September 1936; *Glasgow Herald*, 15–23 September 1936. Speech by Sheriff McDonald: *Evening Citizen*, 23 September 1936. Sillitoe praised by *Scottish Daily Express*: 24 September 1936.

All Quiet on the Eastern Front? Police patrol in pairs: *Sunday Mail*, 27 September 1936. Assault on police officer in the Garngad: *Scottish Daily Express*, 29, 30 September 1936. Fight in Baltic Street: *Evening Times*, 7 October 1936; *Glasgow Eastern Standard*, 10 October 1936. Derry Boys: *Glasgow Eastern Standard*, 24 October 1936; *Evening Times*, 26 October 1936.

15: **THE 'DON QUIXOTE OF THE GANGS'**
Biographical information on George Stankovitch: GCA, D-HEW 16/14/21/B/3084; D-HEW18/2/3/15352; *Scottish Daily Express*, 18 December 1936. Stankovitch's criminal 'career': NRS, SC36/60/12.

Stankie and the Billy Boys. Assault on Stankovitch / trial at Glasgow High Court: *Glasgow Herald*, 26 October 1936; *Evening Times*, 14–16 December 1936; *Scottish Daily Express*, 18 December 1936. Previous conviction against Jim Farrell: *Evening Citizen*, 13 August 1936. Demeanour of assailants in court: *Evening Times*, 28 October 1936. Employment histories: GCA, D-HEW 23/59/1/78911; 23/59/2/28973 (Dan McGuinness); D-HEW 23/58/2/2265 (Jim Farrell). Interviews with Elizabeth Rankin: *People's Journal*, 31 October 1936; *Thomson's Weekly News*, 31 October 1936.

'All his pals got a share of the spoil'. Portrait of George Stankovitch: *Scottish Daily Express*, 18 December 1936.

'The Right Man For The Job'. 'War on the Gang' / 'Secret Plan to Wipe Out Gangs': *Scottish Daily Express*, 18, 19 December 1936; 'Slur on Glasgow's Good Name', *Sunday Post*, 20 December 1936. Interview with Mary Farrell: *Sunday Mail*, 20 December 1936.

Chicago in Scotland. *Daily Express*, 16–18 December 1936; *Daily Mirror*, 18 December 1936; *Sunday Graphic*, *Reynolds News* (interview with Patrick Dollan), *News of the World*, 20 December 1936. Unionist criticism of magistrates: *Evening Times*, 1 September 1936. Dollan's criticism of Independent Labour Party / refutation of 'Chicago Law': *Scottish Daily Express*, 4 September 1936. *Spectator*'s assessment / response by George Blake: 18, 25 December 1936.

Glasgow's Fury. Response to *News of the World*: *Evening Citizen*, 23 December 1936; *Glasgow Herald*, 24 December 1936; *Scottish Daily Express*, 24 December 1936. Speech by Buchanan: *Hansard*, 18 December 1936. Overcrowding in Glasgow: Stevenson (1984), p. 227. Criticism of Glasgow Corporation: *The Times*, 22 December 1936. Macmillan's sermon: *Glasgow Eastern Standard*, 26 December 1936.

16: BRITAIN'S 'GANGSTER CITY'

Speeches by John Stewart: *Scotsman*, 23 March 1937, 12 June 1937. 'Young men' jailed: *Evening Citizen*, 4, 16 January 1937. 'Isolated' disturbances: *Scotsman*, 27 August 1937; *Evening*

Times, 17 February 1938. Persistence of sectarian feuds: *Sunday Mail*, 28 March 1937; 3 July, 6 November 1938. Fighting in the Calton 'for weeks': *Sunday Mail*, 28 March 1937. Spread across Glasgow: *Sunday Mail*, 25 April 1937, 2, 9, 16 May 1937, 13 May 1938; *Glasgow Herald*, 24 August 1937.

'Everyone ran when they saw a gang coming along the street'. Derry Boys: *Evening Citizen*, 8 April 1937; *Evening Times*, 17 February 1938. Raid on 25 April 1937 / Mickey Boys: *Glasgow Eastern Standard*, 19 June 1937. Richard Clark: *Belfast Telegraph*, 4 December 1937. Fanny Boys: *Sunday Mail*, 3 January 1937; *Evening Citizen*, 4 January 1937; *Glasgow Eastern Standard*, 14 August 1937. David Turnbull: *Glasgow Eastern Standard*, 5 June 1937. Assault on Billy Fullerton by the Shanley Boys: *Glasgow Eastern Standard*, 30 October 1937. Samuel Kelly Campbell: GCA, D-HEW 23/55/2/35972; NRS, HH21/70/69, no. 3692. Thomas Wylie: *Glasgow Eastern Standard*, 16 July 1938. Clashes between the Shanley Boys and the Norman Conks: *Glasgow Eastern Standard*, 29 January, 3 December 1938; *Scotsman*, 13 August 1938. Beehive Boys: *Sunday Mail*, 13 February 1938; 23 October 1938; 21 May 1939. Peter Williamson: *Glasgow Herald*, 24 August 1937. Dan Cronin: *Glasgow Herald*, 23 November 1937, *Glasgow Herald*, 27–29 June 1939. Superintendent Thomas Crawford: *Glasgow Eastern Standard*, 6 March 1937. Pronouncement by Sheriff Robertson: *Glasgow Eastern Standard*, 19 June 1937. Strathern: written memorandum submitted to the Departmental Committee on Corporal Punishment (1937). (I am grateful to Linda Mahood for sharing her notes on Strathern's submission with me.) Speech by Lord Alness: *Scotsman*, 11 December 1937; *Daily Mirror*, 11 December 1937. Parliamentary inquiry: *The Times*, 18 March 1938.

'Where people are afraid to walk alone'. Oakley (1946), pp. 313–14. Peter Brewer: *Daily Mirror*, 20 January 1937. Alf Pellow: *Daily Mirror*, 28 September 1937. Exodus of young people from Glasgow: *Daily Mirror*, 23 February 1938. 'GANGSTER CITY'S WEEK-END TERROR': *Daily Mirror*, 1 March 1938.

City of Empire. Economic regeneration: Maver (2000), pp. 255–6. Empire Exhibition: Oakley (1946), pp. 270–71; Maver (2000),

pp. 257–8. Patrick Dollan: *Scotsman*, 31 October 1938. Patrick
Carraher: Blake (1951), pp. 4–9; *Glasgow Herald*, 16 August, 3,
13, 14 September 1938.
The Troubles of Bernard Kiernan. Named as killer of Jimmy
Dalziel: *Scottish Daily Express*, 24 April 1934. Case-file / admission to Woodilee Asylum: GCA, D-HEW 23/61/2/23157.
The Killing of Felix Valaitis. Biographical information: GCA,
D-HEW 23/65/1/8985, D-HEW 23/65/2/41978; *Sunday Mail*, 18
December 1938; *Scotsman*, 3 March 1939. Assaulted by Derry
Boys: *Glasgow Eastern Standard*, 26 June 1937. Attempt to
terrorise publican: *Glasgow Herald*, 22 April 1938. Incident on
17 December 1938 / trial of William Turner and John Dey: NRS,
JC36/110; *Scotsman*, 3, 4 March 1939; *Scottish Daily Express*,
4 March 1939. Interview with Valaitis's wife and mother:
Scottish Daily Express, 19 December 1939. Coverage in local
press: *Glasgow Herald*, 20, 22, 27 December 1938.
Jim Farrell's Revenge. Wages in 1939: GCA, D-HEW 23/58/1/73589.
Assault on William McSwiggan: *Evening Times*, 9 August 1939;
Scotsman, 10 August 1939. Trial at High Court: *Evening Times*,
9 August 1939; *Scotsman*, 10 August 1939.

17: FROM GANGSTERS TO HEROES?
Derry Boys: *Evening Times*, 26 July 1962. Glaswegian contribution to war effort: Oakley (1946), p. 329. War service of members
of rival gangs: Samuel Kelly Campbell (Billy Boy): GCA,
D-HEW 23/55/2/35972; Owen Mullen (San Toy): GCA, D-HEW
23/62/1/22555; Gavin Mair (Cheeky Forty): GCA, D-HEW
23/62/1/44886. Orwell and Priestley: Clarke (1996), pp. 207–11.
R. E. Porter: *Glasgow Eastern Standard*, 13 July, 21 Dec. 1940.
Blake (1951), pp. 23–4. Andrew Mulvey: GCA, D-HEW
23/62/1/19049, D-HEW 33/24/1/1/19049. James Wilkie: NRS,
HH21/70/74, no. 254, no. 887; HH21/70/77, no. 1635. Peter
Williamson: GCA, D-HEW 18/3/20/2904; Forbes and Meehan
(1982), p. 67. James Tinney O'Neill: GCA, D-HEW: 23/63/1/67068,
33/24/1/7/U. 1797. James Tinney O'Neill and Thomas Falconer
/ 'drag down of human dignity': McGinn (1987), pp. 31–2;
Glasgow Herald, 12-14 December 1945.

The Shadow of *No Mean City*. Here I have adapted Moira Burgess's phrase 'The Shadow of the Gorbals' (1998), p. 162. Oakley (1946), p. 313. *Miracle in the Gorbals*: *Manchester Guardian*, 20 Sept 1945; Haskell (1946); Oakley (1946), p. 314. My précis of the storyline is drawn from Watts (1959), p. 160. Plight of Alexander McArthur / his suicide: Damer (1990b), pp. 34–8. Recollections of Charles Canning / extracts from McArthur's diary: Watts (1959), pp. 160–63. A. L. Lloyd on conditions in the Gorbals: *Picture Post*, 31 January 1948, pp. 11–16; readers' responses: 14 February 1948. 'RAZOR GANGS IN RENT WAR ON WIVES': *Daily Mirror*, 12 July 1948. Eglinton Street tragedy: *Daily Mirror*, 30 December 1948. 'Caribbean Gorbals': *Daily Express*, 22 October 1948.

Gangsters and Cops. Sillitoe's knighthood / appointments: Sillitoe (1955), pp. 149, 158, 196. Publication of *Cloak Without Dagger*: *Times Literary Supplement*, 29 April 1955. Articles by Peddie / interviews with Fullerton: *Evening Citizen*, 7–21 January 1955; Murray (1984), pp. 159–60. Peddie on the South Side Stickers: *Evening Citizen*, 10, 11 January 1955. David Stewart: Jeffrey (2002a), p. 61. Stewart on Billy Fullerton: *Evening Citizen*, 17, 18 January 1955. Fullerton as 'section captain' in 'Fascist Party': *Evening Citizen*, 19 January 1955. This does not appear to refer to the British Union of Fascists: Cullen (2008), p. 323. British Fascists: *Evening Citizen*, 20, 26 August, 9 November 1925. Fullerton's ideological stance: Murray (1984), p. 157. Sillitoe (1955): on how he 'broke' the Glasgow gangs: pp. 123–31; on Fullerton: p. 128; on Fullerton's downfall: pp. 130–33; on the sentencing of John McNamee: pp. 133–35. Sillitoe's account taken as definitive: *Sunday Mail*, 17 February 1963. 'Giving them a taste of their own medicine': Forbes (1997), p. 11. Sillitoe (1955) on gangs as products of poverty and unemployment: p. 122.

Farewell to King Billy. Funeral of Billy Fullerton: *Evening Times*, 25, 26 July 1962; *Daily Record*, 26 July 1962; *Glasgow Herald*, 26 July 1962; *The Times*, 26 July 1962. Fullerton's claim: *Sunday Dispatch*, 10 March 1935. Jack Skilling: *Evening Times*, 26 July 1962. Spectre of Johnnie Stark: *The Times*, 26 July 1962. Death of Eli Webb: *Glasgow Herald*, 20 September 1962.

Johnnie Stark's Ghost. Sales figures for *No Mean City* / Kenneth Allsop: Watts (1959), pp. 161–4; Damer (1990b), pp. 34, 41. Comprehensive redevelopment: Watts (1957), p. 137. Symbols of 'new Glasgow': *New York Times*, 5 July 1964. Basil Spence: *New York Times*, 23 July 1960; Maver (2000), pp. 265–6.

'Glasgow's Miles Better'. Publicity campaign: Maver (2000), pp. 220, 281–3; http://www.glasgow.gov.uk/en/YourCouncil/PublicRelations/Campaigns/glasgowsmilesbetter.htm, accessed 21 August 2012 (last updated 8 May 2009). Persistence of poverty and unemployment: Damer (1990a): pp. 13–14. Patrick Lally: *Glasgow Herald*, 6 August 1991; 16 November 1995.

The Myth of the Honourable Fighting Man. 'Heart of gold': *Sunday Post*, 17 February 1963. Jack House: *Evening Times*, 30 July 1980. No danger to 'ordinary' people: *Guardian*, 20 December 1994. Douglas Kerr: *Evening Times*, 13 February 1980. Dan Cronin: Forbes and Meehan (1982), p. 179; Gorbals Live: http://www.gorbalslive.org.uk, 27 April 2003, accessed 18 August 2003; 8 February 2004, accessed 9 August 2004. Perils of romanticising the past: Pearson (1983).

Bibliography

Ayers, P. (1988), *The Liverpool Docklands: Life and Work in Athol Street*. Liverpool: Docklands History Project.

Bean, J. [pseud.] (1981), *The Sheffield Gang Wars*. Sheffield: D & D Publications.

Behr, E. (1996), *Prohibition: Thirteen Years That Changed America*. New York: Arcade.

Bergreen, L. (1996), *Capone: The Man and the Era*. New York: Touchstone.

Bingham, A. (2004), *Gender, Modernity, and the Popular Press in Inter-War Britain*. Oxford: Clarendon Press.

Blake, G., ed. (1951), *The Trials of Patrick Carraher*. London: William Hodge & Co.

Boyle, J. (1977), *A Sense of Freedom*. London: Pan Books.

Brown, A. (2007), 'The amazing mutiny at the Dartmoor Convict Prison'. *British Journal of Criminology*, 47/2.

Brown, C. (1997), *Religion and Society in Scotland since 1707*. Edinburgh: Edinburgh University Press.

Bruce, S. (1995), *No Pope of Rome: Anti-Catholicism in Modern Scotland*. Edinburgh: Edinburgh University Press.

Bruce, S., Glendinning, T., Paterson, I. and Rosie, M. (2004), *Sectarianism in Scotland*. Edinburgh: Edinburgh University Press.

Burgess, M. (1986), *The Glasgow Novel*, 2nd edition. Glasgow: Scottish Library Association and Glasgow District Libraries.

Burgess, M. (1998), *Imagine a City: Glasgow in Fiction*. Glendaruel: Argyll.

Burrowes, J. (1984), *Jamesie's People: A Gorbals Story*. Edinburgh: Mainstream.

Burrowes, J. (1992), *Benny: The Life and Times of a Fighting Legend*. Edinburgh: Mainstream.

433

Cameron, C., Lush, A. and Meara, G. (1943), *Disinherited Youth: A Report on the 18+ Age Group Enquiry Prepared for the Trustees of the Carnegie United Kingdom Trust*. Edinburgh: Constable.

Caplan, J. (1991), *Memories of the Gorbals*. Witton le Wear: Pentland.

Casciani, E. (1994), *Oh, How We Danced! The History of Ballroom Dancing in Scotland*. Edinburgh: Mercat.

Chinn, C.(1991), *Better Betting with a Decent Feller: Bookmaking, Betting and the British Working Class 1750–1990*. London: Harvester Wheatsheaf.

Clarke, P. (1996), *Hope and Glory: Britain, 1900–1990*. London: Allen Lane.

Cockerill, A. (1975), *Sir Percy Sillitoe*. London: W. H. Allen.

Colquhoun, R. (1962), *Life Begins at Midnight*. London: John Long.

Cowan, E. (1974), *Spring Remembered: A Scottish Jewish Childhood*. Edinburgh: Southside.

Croft, A. (1990), *Red Letter Days: British Fiction in the 1930s*. London: Lawrence & Wishart.

Cullen, S. (2008), 'The Fasces and the Saltire: The Failure of the British Union of Fascists in Scotland 1932–1940'. *Scottish Historical Review*, 87/2.

Cunnison, J. and Gilfillan, J., eds (1958), *The Third Statistical Account of Scotland. Glasgow*. Glasgow: Collins.

Damer, S. (1990a), *Glasgow: Going for a Song*. London: Lawrence & Wishart.

Damer, S. (1990b), 'No mean writer? The curious case of Alexander McArthur' in McCarra, K. and Whyte, H, eds, *A Glasgow Collection: Essays in Honour of Joe Fisher*. Glasgow: Glasgow City Libraries.

Davies, A. (1992), *Leisure, Gender and Poverty: Working-Class Culture in Salford and Manchester 1900–1939*. Buckingham: Open University Press.

Davies, A. (1998), 'Street gangs, crime and policing in Glasgow during the 1930s: the case of the Beehive Boys'. *Social History*, 23/3.

Davies, A. (2000), 'Sectarian violence and police violence in Glasgow during the 1930s' in Bessel, R. and Emsley, C., eds, *Patterns of Provocation: Police and Public Disorder*. Oxford: Berghahn Books.

Davies, A. (2006), 'Football and sectarianism in Glasgow during the 1920s and 1930s'. *Irish Historical Studies*, 35/138.

Davies, A. (2007a), 'The Scottish Chicago? From "hooligans" to "gangsters" in inter-war Glasgow'. *Cultural and Social History*, 4/4.

Davies, A. (2007b), 'Glasgow's "reign of terror": street gangs, racketeering and intimidation in the 1920s and 1930s'. *Contemporary British History*, 21/4.

Davies, A. (2008), *The Gangs of Manchester: The Story of the Scuttlers, Britain's First Youth Cult*. Preston: Milo Books.

Devine, T. (1999), *The Scottish Nation, 1700–2000*. London: Penguin.

Dewar Gibb, A. (1930), *Scotland in Eclipse*. London: Humphrey Toulmin.

Dormon, J. (1988), 'Shaping the popular image of post-Reconstruction American blacks: the "coon song" phenomenon of the Gilded Age'. *American Quarterly*, 40/4.

Emsley, C. (2011), *Crime and Society in Twentieth-Century England*. Harlow: Longman.

Faley, J. (1990), *Up Oor Close: Memories of Domestic Life in Glasgow Tenements, 1910–1945*. Oxford: White Cockade.

Field, J. (2009), *Able Bodies: Work Camps and the Training of the Unemployed in Britain before 1939*. Stirling: Stirling Institute of Education.

Fielding, S. (1993), *Crime and Ethnicity: Irish Catholics in England, 1880–1939*. Buckingham: Open University Press.

Finlay, R. (1994), 'National identity in crisis: politicians, intellectuals and the "end of Scotland" 1920–1939'. *History*, 79/256.

Fogarty, M. (1945), *Prospects of the Industrial Areas of Great Britain*. London: Methuen.

Forbes, G. and Meehan, P. (1982), *Such Bad Company: The Story of Glasgow Criminality*. Edinburgh: Paul Harris.

Forbes, G. (1997), 'King Billy'. *Scottish Memories,* November.

Fraser, D. (2009), *The Book of Glasgow Murders*. Glasgow: Neil Wilson.

Gallagher, T. (1987), *Glasgow: The Uneasy Peace. Religious Tensions in Modern Scotland*. Manchester: Manchester University Press.

Glasser, R. (1987), *Growing up in the Gorbals*. London: Pan Books.

Goldsmith, A. (1993), 'The Sillitoe years 1931–1939'. *The Criminologist,* 17/3.

Goodman, J. and Will, I. (1985), *Underworld*. London: Harrap.

Grant, D. (1973), *The Thin Blue Line: The Story of the City of Glasgow Police*. London: John Donald.

Graves, R. and Hodge, A. (1941), *The Long Week-End: A Social History of Great Britain, 1918–1939*. London: Faber and Faber.

Hanley, C. (1958), *Dancing in the Streets*. London: Hutchinson.

Haskell, A. (1946), *Miracle in the Gorbals*. Edinburgh: Albyn Press.

Henderson, M. (1994), *Finding Peggy: A Glasgow Childhood*. London: Corgi Books.

Hepburn, A. (1990), 'The Belfast riots of 1935'. *Social History,* 15/1.

Hughes, A. (2010), *Gender and Political Identities in Scotland, 1919–1939*. Edinburgh: Edinburgh University Press.

Humphries, S. (1981), *Hooligans or Rebels? An Oral History of Working-Class Childhood and Youth 1889–1939*. Oxford: Basil Blackwell.

Humphries, S. (1988), *A Secret World of Sex: Forbidden Fruit. The British Experience*. London: Sidgwick & Jackson.

Humphries, S. and Gordon, P. (1994), *Forbidden Britain: Our Secret Past, 1900–1960*. London: BBC Books.

Jeffrey, R. (2002a), *Gangland Glasgow: True Crime from the Streets*. Edinburgh: Black & White.

Jeffrey, R. (2002b), *Glasgow's Hard Men: True Crime from the Files of the Herald, Evening Times and Sunday Herald*. Edinburgh: Black & White.

Jeffrey, R. (2009), *The Barlinnie Story: Riots, Death, Retribution and Redemption in Scotland's Infamous Prison*. Edinburgh: Black & White.

Kohn, M. (1992), *Dope Girls: The Birth of the British Drug Underground*. London: Lawrence & Wishart.

Lawrence, J. (2003), 'Forging a peaceable kingdom: war, violence, and fear of brutalization in post-First World War Britain'. *Journal of Modern History*, 75.

Lucas, N. (1969), *Britain's Gangland*. London: W. H. Allen.

Maan, B. (1992), *The New Scots: The Story of Asians in Scotland*. Edinburgh: John Donald.

MacCallum, R. (1994), *Tongs Ya Bas*. Glasgow: New Glasgow Library.

MacDougall, I. (1990), *Voices from the Hunger Marches: Personal Recollections by Scottish Hunger Marchers of the 1920s and 1930s, Volume I*. Edinburgh: Polygon.

MacDougall, I. (1991), *Voices from the Hunger Marches: Personal Recollections by Scottish Hunger Marchers of the 1920s and 1930s, Volume II*. Edinburgh: Polygon.

Mack, J. (1957), 'The scarred page'. *Scotland*, March.

Mackie, A. (1972), 'Mackie on the move'. *Scotland's Magazine*, 68/6.

Marshall, W. (1996), *The Billy Boys: A Concise History of Orangeism in Scotland*. Edinburgh: Mercat.

Maver, I. (2000), *Glasgow*. Edinburgh: Edinburgh University Press.

McAllister, G. (1935), *James Maxton: The Portrait of a Rebel*. London: John Murray.

McAllister, E. (1986), *Shadows on a Gorbals Wall*. Glasgow: Gorbals Fair Society.

McArthur, A. and Kingsley Long, H. (1935), *No Mean City: A Story of the Glasgow Slums*. London: Longmans, Green & Co.

McFarland, E. (1990), *Protestants First: Orangeism in Nineteenth-century Scotland*. Edinburgh: Edinburgh University Press.

McGinn, M. (1987), *McGinn of the Calton: The Life and Works of Matt McGinn 1928–1977*. Glasgow: Glasgow District Libraries.

McGuckin, A. (1992), 'Moving stories: working-class women' in Breitenbach, E. and Gordon, E., eds, *Women in Scottish Society 1800–1945*. Edinburgh: Edinburgh University Press.

McKenna, J. (2006), *Last Exit from Bridgeton: An East End Childhood Remembered*. Glasgow: Grimsay Press.

McKibbin, R. (1998), *Classes and Cultures: England 1918–1951*. Oxford: Oxford University Press.

McShane, H. and Smith, J. (1978), *Harry McShane: No Mean Fighter*. London: Pluto.

Ministry of Labour (1927–39), 'Local Unemployment Index'. London: H. M. Stationery Office.

Morton, H. (1929), *In Search of Scotland*. London: Methuen.

Morton, J. (1995), *Gangland Volume 2: The Underworld in Britain and Ireland*. London: Warner Books.

Mowat, C. (1956), *Britain between the Wars 1918–1940*. London: Methuen.

Muir, E. (1935), *Scottish Journey*. London: Heinemann.

Murphy, R. (1993), *Smash and Grab: Gangsters in the London Underworld 1920–60*. London: Faber and Faber.

Murray, B. (1984), *The Old Firm: Sectarianism, Sport and Society in Scotland*. Edinburgh: John Donald.

Nott, J. (2002), *Music for the People: Popular Music and Dance in Interwar Britain*. Oxford: Oxford University Press.

Oakley, C. (1946), *The Second City*. London: Blackie.

O'Connell, S. (1998), *The Car in British Society: Class, Gender and Motoring, 1896–1939*. Manchester: Manchester University Press.

O'Connell, S. (2009), *Credit and Community: Working-Class Debt in the UK since 1880*. Oxford: Oxford University Press.

O'Hagan, A. (1995), *The Missing*. London: Picador.

Pasley, F. (1930), *Al Capone: The Biography of a Self-Made Man*. Garden City, NY: Star Books.

Patrick, J. [pseud.] (1973), *A Glasgow Gang Observed*. London: Eyre Methuen.

Pearson, G. (1983), *Hooligan: A History of Respectable Fears*. Basingstoke: Macmillan.

Perrett, E. (1990), *The Magic of the Gorbals*. Glasgow: Clydeside Press.

Peter, B. (1996), *100 Years of Glasgow's Amazing Cinemas*. Edinburgh: Polygon.

Pieri, J. (2001), *The Big Men: Personal Memories of Glasgow's Police*. Glasgow: Neil Wilson.

Prendergast, J. (1992), *Edge Up! Memoirs of a Glasgow Street Bookmaker*. Glasgow: Prendergast Publications.

Robertson, G. and Grant, R. (1970), *Gorbals Doctor*. London: Jarrolds.

Rosie, M. (2004), *The Sectarian Myth in Scotland: Of Bitter Memory and Bigotry*. Basingstoke: Palgrave Macmillan.

Rountree, G. (1993), *A Govan Childhood: The Nineteen Thirties*. Edinburgh: John Donald.

Savage, H. (2006), *Born up a Close: Memoirs of a Brigton Boy*. Glendaruel: Argyll.

Savage, J. (2007), *Teenage: The Creation of Youth 1875–1945*. London: Chatto & Windus.

Scottish Office (1935), *Report of Enquiry into the Administration and Discipline of Barlinnie Prison; and into the Existing Arrangements for the Inspection of Scottish Prisons*. London: HMSO.

Shettleston Activity in Retirement Group (1985), *Dolly Tubs and Dabbities*. Glasgow: Workers' Educational Association.

Shore, H. (2011), 'Criminality and Englishness in the Aftermath:

the Racecourse Wars of the 1920s'. *Twentieth Century British History*, 22/4.

Sillitoe, P. (1955), *Cloak Without Dagger*. London: Cassell.

Sinfield, B., 'Gentleman of jazz' (http://georgechisholm.tripod. com, accessed 2011).

Smith, D. (1991), 'Juvenile delinquency in Britain in the First World War'. *Criminal Justice History*, 9.

Smyth, J. (2000), *Labour in Glasgow 1896–1936: Socialism, Suffrage, Sectarianism*. East Linton: Tuckwell Press.

Spenser, J. and Kingsley Long, H. (1958), *Limey: An Englishman Joins the Gangs*. London: Transworld. (First published in 1933.)

Spring, I. (1990), *Phantom Village: The Myth of the New Glasgow*. Edinburgh: Polygon.

Stevenson, J. (1984), *British Society 1914–45*. Harmondsworth: Penguin.

Stevenson, J. and Cook, C. (2010), *The Slump: Britain in the Great Depression*. Harlow: Pearson Education.

Thomas, D. (2004), *An Underworld at War: Spivs, Deserters, Racketeers and Civilians in the Second World War*. London: John Murray.

Thomson, G. (1927), *Caledonia: Or, the Future of the Scots*. London: Kegan Paul, Trench, Trubner & Co.

Thomson, G. (1928), *The Re-discovery of Scotland*. London: Kegan Paul, Trench, Trubner & Co.

Todd, S. (2005), *Young Women, Work, and Family in England 1918–1950*. Oxford: Oxford University Press.

Walker, G. and Gallagher, T., eds (1990), *Sermons and Battle Hymns: Protestant Popular Culture in Modern Scotland*. Edinburgh: Edinburgh University Press.

Walker, G. (1992), 'The Orange Order in Scotland between the wars'. *International Review of Social History*, 37/2.

Watts, S. (1959), 'The metamorphosis of the Gorbals'. *New Yorker*, 24 October.

White, J. (1977), 'When every room was measured: the

overcrowding survey of 1935–1936 and its aftermath'. *History Workshop Journal*, 4/1.

White, J. (1986), *The Worst Street in North London: Campbell Bunk, Islington, between the Wars*. London: Routledge & Kegan Paul.

Wilkinson, R. (1993), *Memories of Maryhill*. Edinburgh: Canongate.

Index

Index